Joseph

Faa

di Bruno

Catholic Beliefs

A Short And Simple Exposition Of Catholic Doctrine 1880

Joseph
Faa
di Bruno

Catholic Beliefs
A Short And Simple Exposition Of Catholic Doctrine 1880

ISBN/EAN: 9783742856654

Manufactured in Europe, USA, Canada, Australia, Japa

Cover: Foto ©Lupo / pixelio.de

Manufactured and distributed by brebook publishing software (www.brebook.com)

Joseph

Faa

di Bruno

Catholic Beliefs

CATHOLIC BELIEF:

OR

A SHORT AND SIMPLE EXPOSITION
OF CATHOLIC DOCTRINE.

BY THE

VERY REV. JOSEPH FAA DI BRUNO, D.D.,

*Rector-General of the Pious Society of Missions;
Church of SS^{mo} Salvatore in Onda, Ponte Sisto, ROME,
and St. Peter's Italian Church, Hatton Wall, London, E.C.*

"And Nathanael said to him Can anything of good come from Nazareth?
Philip saith to him: Come and see."—*St. John* i. 46.

Third Edition. Revised.

BURNS AND OATES,
17 PORTMAN STREET, LONDON, W.
1880.

PRICE SIXPENCE.

NIHIL OBSTAT.

   Pius Melia, S.T.D.

IMPRIMATUR.

   HENRICUS EDUARDUS,
    Card. Archiep. Westmon.

Die 24 Junii, 1880.

ENTERED AT STATIONERS' HALL.
ALL RIGHTS RESERVED.

"GRACE BE TO YOU, AND PEACE FROM GOD THE FATHER, AND FROM OUR LORD JESUS CHRIST" (Galatians i. 3).

PREFACE.

DEAR READER,—During the thirty years passed as a Missionary Priest in England, I have found that nearly all the objections so often repeated against the faith and practice of the Roman Catholic Church come from misunderstanding the true teaching of our Holy Religion, the holy Catholic faith which, in order to be respected and beloved by all well disposed Christian minds, needs only to be known.

A fairer field has now been granted to Catholics in England, their principles have become better known, and many prejudices against the Catholic faith have died away, yet, alas! some more deeply rooted still remain.

Pondering over these things, and lamenting the estrangement from the Church of so many souls, each one so dear to JESUS CHRIST, and longing to do service to my neighbour, I have ventured to take in hand this little work.

My hope is that this short and simple exposition of Catholic doctrine may help many to get rid of some unhappy misconceptions or some prejudices, and may bring a blessing and a comfort to many an earnest soul.

As my purpose is to give, though briefly, a summary of Catholic Belief, the reader will understand why I include in these pages those doctrines in which both Catholics and Protestants happily agree.

Sometimes, in order to be better understood by unlettered persons, I have used familiar, rather than scholastic, expressions, and in some places, (overstepping the short limits of this little work), I have enlarged upon some of those points most liable to be misunderstood by Protestants.

All I have here written I believe to be trustworthy, nevertheless I humbly submit all to the unerring judgment of the Church.

According to the rule of charity, I have carefully endeavoured to avoid using any expression that might give just cause of offence to any one, without, however, compromising or disguising the truth.

I have been kindly encouraged and materially aided by several friends, and by one more especially. I am glad of this opportunity to return them my sincere thanks. May each enjoy a large reward from Him in Whose Name they have assisted me.

The great desire of my heart for you, dear reader,

is, that you may gain some good from this little labour of love. May it help you on your way to our true home, to Heaven! There may we, by the mercy of God, all meet, to be for ever "*filled with the joy of His countenance*". Farewell.

Ever your humble servant in JESUS CHRIST,

JOSEPH FAA DI BRUNO,
Priest of the Pious Society of Missions,
Founded in Rome by Father Vincent Pallotti,
Servant of God.

St. Patrick's College for Foreign Missions,
Masio (Felizzano). Piedmont.
Feast of the Most Holy Redeemer, October 23rd, 1879.

The quotations from Holy Scripture in this little book are taken from the Catholic English Version, translated from the Latin Vulgate Version made by St. Jerome from the Hebrew and Greek about the year 400, after Christ. This Version of St. Jerome is declared by the Council of Trent to be authentic.

The New Testament, speaking of the said English Version, was translated by the English College at Rheims, Marne, France, A.D. 1582, and the Old Testament by the English College at Douay, Nord, France, A.D. 1600, both republished, from time to time, in the United Kingdom with approbation of the Catholic Bishops.

This Catholic English Version is commonly called "The Douay Bible".

NOTICE TO THE THIRD EDITION.

THE second edition of this little book, (15,000 copies), published in October, 1878, having been exhausted, I have the pleasure of putting forth the third duly revised.

The chief *additional* subjects treated of in the second edition were—*the Infallibility of the Church and of the Pope, the Immaculate Conception, Confirmation, Extreme Unction, Holy Orders, Matrimony, Ceremonies of the Catholic Church, Mortal sin, Prayer, Method of Confession, Short Method of hearing Mass, A notice on the Benediction of the Blessed Sacrament, Sign of the Cross, List of Fathers of the Church, St. Peter in Rome, and Transmission of the sin of Adam to his children.*

All these additions revised have been retained in this edition, to which are added in Chapter VIII. *Few Remarks on the text "Search the Scriptures"*; (S. John v. 39.), and in the Appendix the following subjects:—No. 5. *Difficulties of private interpretation by Father G. Bampfield, B.A., Oxon.*

No. 12. *Observations on Faith by Cardinal Newman.* No. 18. *An extract of Religious Statistics by Hübner.* No. 27. *A letter by Mr. Orby Shipley, M.A., on his conversion.* No. 34. *Remarks on Cusa, Copernicus, Galileo, and Kepler.* No. 36. *A few more remarks on St. Peter having been in Rome.* No. 42. *Extract from Lord Macaulay's Essay on Ranke's History of the Popes.* No. 43. *Parting words to a Protestant who feels convinced of the truth of the Roman Catholic Religion, and who does not join the Church.*

With the desire of aiding the wider distribution of this little work the small price remains unaltered.

IN ALL THINGS MAY GOD BE GLORIFIED.

INTRODUCTION.

ALL men readily admit that, to be in a position to judge fairly of any case, one should hear both sides.

As then, the honest mind naturally shrinks from passing a severe judgment on any one before hearing what he has to say for himself, so no lover of truth and charity should hastily condemn, without a hearing, the largest body of Christians existing, the two hundred millions of Catholics who are living in communion with the See of Rome.

The greater number of those who differ from Catholics, draw most of the information they possess about the Catholic Church from Protestant sources, thus hearing only one side.

It may be, then, that many will be glad of the opportunity this little work affords of learning from Catholics themselves something of what they have to say in defence of their holy Religion.

Some persons, owing to the pressing calls of business or other cares, may not have the inclination or time to read long works about religion, while a brief statement of Catholic Doctrine may be read with interest by all who love the truth and long to meet with it.

Well, then, dear reader, deign to accept this *short and simple exposition of what Catholics really do believe,* written by one who feels it his greatest blessing to be a member of the Holy, Catholic and Roman Church, and who cannot help most earnestly wishing that all men possessed the same peace of mind and happiness which he enjoys in her communion.

The first duty of every man who desires to discover truth, is, as Lord Bacon of Verulam observes, to examine if he has *any prejudice lurking in his mind,* by which the admission of truth is obstructed; for, as this philosopher goes on to remark, the kingdom of men, which is founded in knowledge, cannot be entered in any other manner than the Kingdom of God is entered, namely, by being in the condition of *little children.*

Let me beg the honest inquirer, then, before reading this little book, to place himself in a state of impartiality and lay aside that settled feeling of self-confidence which leads him to take it for granted that Roman Catholics must be in the wrong.

May God grant you, dear reader, a spirit of humility, charity, and justice in reading this little work, and, above all, an earnest desire to know the truth. Do not omit also to pray for this gentle and teachable spirit, feeling encouraged in so doing by those words of St. James (i. 5) ; "*If any of you want wisdom, let him ask of God, Who giveth to all men abundantly, and upbraideth not ; and it shall be given him*"; and by what is said in Psalm xxiv. 9, "*He will guide the mild in judgment ; He will teach the meek His ways.*"

CONTENTS.

PART I.

	PAGE
PREFACE,	v
NOTICE TO THE THIRD EDITION,	ix
INTRODUCTION,	xi

PART I.

CHAPTER
I. God and His Perfections,	1
II. The Holy Trinity,	1
III. Original Sin,	2
IV. The Incarnation of the Son of God,	5
V. Jesus our only Mediator of Redemption,	6
VI. The Holy Bible,	7
VII. The Unwritten Word of God,	12
VIII. The Interpretation of Holy Scripture,	21
IX. Infallibility of the Church and of the Pope,	31
X. Justification,	44
XI. How Christ's Redemption is applied to Men,	49
XII. The Holy Sacraments,	50
XIII. Holy Baptism,	51
XIV. On Sin (nature and consequences),	54

CONTENTS.

CHAPTER		PAGE
XV.	The Sacrament of Penance,	60
XVI.	The Holy Eucharist,	63
XVII.	The Holy Sacrifice of the Mass,	66
XVIII.	Holy Mass serves to apply Christ's Redemption to Individual Men,	71
XIX.	Ceremonies and Ritual of the Catholic Church,	74
XX.	Benediction of the Blessed Sacrament,	84
XXI.	Confirmation,	91
XXII.	Extreme Unction,	92
XXIII.	Holy Order,	93
XXIV.	Holy Matrimony,	94
XXV.	Only one true Church,	99
XXVI.	*First Mark* of the true Church: Oneness of Faith, of Worship, and of Sacraments,	100
XXVII.	Supremacy of the Bishop of Rome,	101
XXVIII.	List of General Councils held in the Church of God from the time of the Apostles until the present (1879),	114
XXIX.	*Second Mark:* Holiness,	122
XXX.	List of some Saints arranged in Chronological Order,	130
XXXI.	*Third Mark:* Catholicity,	141
XXXII.	*Fourth Mark:* Apostolicity,	149
XXXIII.	List of the Sovereign Pontiffs, who, in regular unbroken line, have succeeded St. Peter in the See of Rome,	151
XXXIV.	On the sign of the Cross,	159
XXXV.	On prayer—Necessity and Usefulness of it,	162
XXXVI.	Works of Penance.	166

CHAPTER		PAGE
XXXVII.	Indulgences,	169
XXXVIII	On Purgatory,	171
XXXIX.	On the Invocation of the Saints,	178
XL.	The Blessed Virgin Mary justly called "Mother of God,"	181
XLI.	Honour and Devotion to the B. V. Mary,	184
XLII.	The Immaculate Conception of the B. V. Mary,	186
XLIII.	Reverence to Relics and other Religious Objects,	193
XLIV.	Why the Catholic Church in the West uses the Latin Language,	197
XLV.	Some things that Catholics do *not* believe	201
XLVI.	Conclusion and a Prayer for Light,	206

CONTENTS. xvii

PART II.

APPENDIX.

NO.		PAGE
1.	Answers to some Questions on difficulties, that one earnestly seeking to know the true Religion might wish to ask,	209
2.	The Apostles' Creed,	223
3.	Creed of Pope Pius IV. and Pope Pius IX.,	224
4.	Short Form of Profession of Faith,	229
5.	Difficulties of private interpretation,	230
6.	Earnest Appeal to Protestants,	235
7.	Conversion of Victorinus, and list of some of the Converts to Catholicity of late years in Great Britain,	237
8.	Distinguished American Converts,	243
9.	The postal address of some of the Clergy Houses in or near London, and abroad,	244
10.	The Lord's Prayer, and some other Prayers and Psalms,	247
11.	Selected Hymns,	260
12.	Observations on Faith by Cardinal Newman,	269
13.	Acts of Faith, Hope, Charity, and Contrition,	270
14.	A Short Method of hearing Mass,	272
15.	Method of Confession,	278
16.	List of Fathers of the Church and other ancient Ecclesiastical Writers,	289
17.	List of Canonised Founders of Religious Orders, and Congregations in the Church,	294

CONTENTS.

NO.		PAGE
18.	Census of Religions in the World and Hübner's Religious Statistics,	296
19.	Census of Catholics in the World, and of Catholics and Protestants in Europe,	297
20.	Sects battling within one Church,	299
21.	List of 151 Religious Denominations in England and Wales in 1878,	300
22.	Religious Statistics in Ireland,	301
23.	List of Protestant Denominations in the United States of America,	302
24.	Admirable dawn of a Conversion to the Catholic Church in Rome,	304
25.	Conversion of Mr. Alfred Newdigate, M.A.,	305
26.	Conversion of Mr. Gordon Thomson, M.A.,	306
27.	Conversion of Mr. Orby Shipley, M.A.,	307
28.	Converts to Catholicity *not* unhappy: Letters,	310
29.	Letter from His Emin. Cardinal Newman to the Duke of Norfolk, respecting a remark of the Right Hon. W. E. Gladstone, 1875,	312
30.	Converts within the last thirty years,	313
31.	England never of her own accord rejected the Catholic Faith: extracted from a Sermon by His Em. Cardinal Manning, 1875,	313
32.	Position of the Catholic Church in England, by His Em. Cardinal Manning, 1875,	318
33.	Extract from the Introductory Letter to Rev. F. Bridget's Work, "*The Discipline of Drink*," by His Eminence Cardinal Manning, 1876,	319
34.	Cusa, Copernicus, Galileo, and Kepler,	321
35.	Speech of the Duke of Wellington on Catholic Loyalty,	328
36.	St. Peter in Rome,	331

NO.		PAGE
37.	Communion in one Kind, ...	346
38.	Adam's Sin transmitted to his Children, . .	363
39.	Predestination, ...	368
40.	"Justification by Faith alone," considered .	374
41.	Extract from the Poetry of Prof. Longfellow on the intercession of the Blessed Virgin Mary,	395
42.	Lord Macaulay on the Roman Catholic Church,	396
43.	Parting words to a Protestant who feels convinced of the truth of the Roman Catholic Religion, and who does not join the Church,	397
44.	List of some Catholic Books, for the most part useful also for inquirers, ...	400
	Alphabetical Index, ...	405

SIMPLE EXPOSITION

OF

Catholic Doctrine.

CHAPTER I.

GOD AND HIS PERFECTIONS.

THERE is but one God, the Creator of Heaven and earth, the Supreme, incorporeal, uncreated Being, Who exists of Himself, and is infinite in all His attributes and perfections, such as Holiness, Goodness, Power, Wisdom, Justice, Mercy and Truth.

He always was, He is, and He always will be. He is everywhere present, knowing and seeing all things, even our most secret thoughts. From Him all creatures have and hold existence.

CHAPTER II.

THE MOST HOLY TRINITY.

This is a profound mystery, revealed by God. The Catholic Church teaches that in one God there are three *Persons;* the *Father*, the *Son*, and the *Holy*

Ghost; really distinct one from the other, and equal in eternity, power, immensity, and all other perfections; because all the three *Persons* have one and the same Divine nature.

It would be a contradiction to assert that there are *three Gods and one God*, or *three Persons and one Person;* but it is no contradiction to affirm that God is one in nature and three in Persons. Thus the human soul, though one, is threefold in its powers; namely, the understanding, the memory, and the will.

Comparisons, however, are necessarily imperfect upon such a subject as the Blessed Trinity, which is a *great mystery.*

We are not able to understand *how* each of the three Persons can be God, and yet that there is but One God. It should be borne in mind that many things exist also in nature which we cannot explain, or even comprehend, and yet know to be facts. Such is, for example, the amazing velocity of the electric spark.

CHAPTER III.

Original Sin.

Original sin is distinguished from *actual*, or *personal*, sin, because actual or personal sin is the sin which we *personally with our own will* commit, whilst *original* sin is that sin which our human nature has committed *with the will of Adam*, in whom all our human nature was included, and with whom our human nature is united as a branch to a root, as a child to a parent, as men who partake with Adam the same nature which we have derived from him, and as members of the same human family of which Adam was the head.

If our hand strike a fellow-man unjustly, though the hand has itself no will, yet it is considered guilty, not indeed as viewed separately by itself, but inasmuch as it is united to the rest of the body, and to the soul, forming one human being therewith; and thus, not as having a will of its own, but as sharing in the will of the soul with which it is connected.

Again, the sin committed inwardly by the human will, by a bad desire, belongs to the whole human being.

Of the original sin in which we are born we are not personally guilty with our own personal will, but our *nature* is guilty of it by the will of Adam our head, with whom we form one body through the human nature which we derive from him.

It is a point of Catholic faith that original sin does not consist in concupiscence, which is a propensity to evil of the inferior part of the human soul.

Sin of any kind in order to be a sin, in the strict sense of the word, must be within the sphere of morality, that is, it must depend upon free-will; and hence the noted principle in Moral Philosophy and Theology, *that there is no sin where there is no will.*

Concupiscence, therefore, which is not will, but a blind involuntary inclination of our lower nature, and therefore an irresponsible tendency to evil, is not of itself sinful unless it be consented to by the human will.

Concupiscence is indeed sometimes called sin in Holy Scripture (Romans vii. 7, Galatians v. 24), but it is called so, as the holy Council of Trent explains, not in a *strict*, but in a *wide* sense, that is, inasmuch as it is a *consequence* of original sin, and an *incentive* to actual sin.

This concupiscence, in fact, still remains in those

in whom original sin has been entirely washed away by the Sacrament of Holy Baptism. Moreover, no one is regarded, strictly speaking, as a sinner, merely because he feels tempted to sin. This miserable propensity to evil excites the compassion of God rather than His anger. God said to Noah: "*I will no more curse the earth for the sake of man; for the imagination and thought of man's heart are prone to evil from his youth.*" (Genesis viii. 21.)

Catholic faith teaches that Adam by his sin has not only caused harm to himself, but to the whole human race; that by it he lost the supernatural justice and sanctity which he received gratuitously from God, and lost it, not only for himself, but also for all of us; and that he, having stained himself with the sin of disobedience, has transmitted not only death and other bodily pains, to the whole human race, but *also sin, which is the death of the soul.*

The teaching of the Council of Trent (Session V.) is confirmed by these words of St. Paul: "*Wherefore as by one man sin entered into this world, and by sin death; and so death passed upon all men in whom all have sinned.*" (Rom. v. 12.)

Besides the *guilt* of original sin, which is that habitual state of sinfulness in which we are born (because our human nature is justly considered to have consented in Adam to the rejection of original justice), there is also in man the *stain* of original sin, which is the privation in the human soul of that supernatural lustre, which, had we been born in the state of original justice, we all should have had.

As neither Adam nor any of his offspring could repair the evil done by his sin, we should ever have remained in the state of original sin and degradation in which we were born, and we should have been for ever shut out from the Beatific Vision of God, had not God in His infinite Mercy provided for us a Redeemer.

CHAPTER IV.

The Incarnation of the Son of God.

Respecting this great Mystery, Catholics believe that the Holy Trinity, out of infinite mercy, decreed to provide for us a Redeemer Who could suffer, and suffer as an individual of the human race, and yet be in Himself, at the same time, so exalted as to be able to give infinite value to His sufferings; because sin, being an offence against the *infinite* Majesty of God, could only be atoned for by a ransom of infinite value.

To accomplish this end, God the Son, the second Person of the Holy Trinity, the Eternal Word, chose the Blessed Virgin Mary of Nazareth to become His Mother, and on receiving her consent, He, by the supernatural agency of the Holy Spirit, took human flesh from her, and thus became man, and His Holy Name is Jesus Christ.

By becoming man the Eternal Word did not lay aside His Divine Nature, but, remaining what He had ever been from all eternity, assumed, that is, took upon Himself human nature without a human personality, so that from the first moment of His Incarnation there was in Him, and there ever will be, not one only but two natures, the Divine and the human, *united* in His Divine Personality, the Person of God the Son.

The Divine nature of Jesus is one and the same as that of the Eternal Father and of the Holy Ghost, and His human nature is in all things like ours, sin and tendency to sin excepted. He is equal to the Father according to his Godhead, and less than the Father according to His Manhood.

Our Lord Jesus Christ suffered and died in His human nature on Mount Calvary, and thereby effectually interposed His atonement between His Eternal Father and man, and thus made a plentiful expiation and paid a full ransom to the Eternal Justice for the sins of the whole world.

CHAPTER V.

JESUS OUR ONLY MEDIATOR OF REDEMPTION.

Catholics believe that our Lord *Jesus Christ* is alone the great Centre of the Christian Religion, the Fountain of all Grace, Virtue, and Merit; as in the natural world (if the comparison may be allowed), the sun is the centre and enlivening created source of light, heat, and growth.

This grand truth they believe to be the vital, essential part of Christianity, "*For other foundation no man can lay, but that which is laid; which is* CHRIST JESUS." (1 Corinthians iii. 11.)

They believe that union with JESUS CHRIST is the highest and noblest aim of man, and that only the Holy Catholic Church supplies the means for the closest union with JESUS CHRIST; and they are convinced that the yearning to possess this closer communion with Christ has, by Divine attraction, drawn thousands of earnest minds to seek in the Catholic Church this the highest happiness to be enjoyed on earth.

They believe that Jesus Christ is our Redeemer, because He has redeemed us from the bondage of Satan, with the ransom of His most Precious Blood; that He is our Saviour because He saves us from the stain, the guilt, and the curse of sin; that he is our only Mediator of Redemption, because He alone has efficiently interposed between God and man, to obtain the full pardon of our sins through the sacrifice of Himself: *"There is one God, and one Mediator of God and men, the man Christ Jesus; Who gave Himself a Redemption for all."* (1 S. Timothy ii. 5.) *"Nor is there salvation in any other. For there is no other name under heaven given to men, whereby we must be saved."* (Acts iv. 12.)

They believe that Jesus died on the Cross to purchase Mercy, Grace, and Salvation for all men—*"Who will have all men to be saved, and to come to the knowledge of the truth."* (1 S. Timothy ii. 4.) And that since Adam's fall, Mercy, Grace, and Salvation can be obtained by man only through the Passion and Death of Jesus Christ.

Believing that Jesus Christ is truly God, they hold that the homage of supreme adoration is due to Him, the God-man, as well as to God the Father, and to God the Holy Spirit.

CHAPTER VI.

THE HOLY BIBLE.

That part of Divine Revelation which has been committed to writing by persons inspired by the Holy Ghost, is called Holy Scripture, or the Holy *Bible; the Book* of Books.

Holy Scripture is composed not only of all the Books received by Protestants as divinely inspired, but also of some other Books which were written after the Jewish List or *Canon* of Scripture was closed, but which nevertheless are held in great veneration by the Jewish Synagogue, and by many Protestants themselves.

Such are the Books of Tobias, Judith, Esther, Wisdom, Ecclesiasticus (or the Son of Sirach), the Prophecy of Baruch, and the two Books of Machabees. These Books, though not registered in the Jewish Canon, were nevertheless held by many Fathers of the early centuries as canonical and forming a part of the deposit of revealed truths entrusted to the Church.

In the schismatic Greek Church, and in other separated Churches of the East, the Canon of Scripture agrees with that of the Roman Catholic Church. The efforts made by Protestants to induce the Greek Church to reject that inspired portion of Scripture called the Apocrypha, that is, hidden, only served to call forth repeatedly from them assembled in council new synodical declarations that those Books were inspired.

So long as the Church had not testified with her authority to the Divine inspiration of certain Books some of the Fathers may have hesitated about the inspiration of them, and reasonably thought that such Books could not be quoted to establish revealed truth, until the Church had first cleared away all doubt, by inserting them in the Canon, and thus established the inspiration and canonical authority of those Books.

This the Church did in the celebrated Council of Hippo in Africa, in the year 393, attended by all the Bishops of Africa, at which also the great Doctor and Father of the Church, S. Augustine, was present.*

---

* Possidius in the life of S. Augustine, referring to this Council of Hippo, thus writes :—" About the same time Augustine, when yet a priest, argued (*disputavit*) about Faith and the Symbol in the presence of the Bishops of all Africa gathered in

In Statute XXXVI. of that Council it was decreed*:—"*That nothing be read in the Church under the name of Divine Scripture, except the Canonical Scriptures, and the Canonical Scriptures are*—

Genesis.
Exodus.
Leviticus.
Numbers.
Deuteronomy.
Josue.
Judges.
Ruth.
Four books of Kingdoms.
Two books of Paralipomenon.
Job.
The Psalter of David.
Five books of Solomon.
The books of the Twelve (Minor) Prophets.
Isaias.
Jeremias.
Ezechiel.
Daniel.

Tobias.
Judith.
Esther.
Two books of Esdra.
Two books of Machabees.
(AND OF THE NEW TESTAMENT.)
Four books of the Gospel.
One book of the Acts of the Apostles.
Thirteen letters of Paul the Apostle.
One letter of the same to the Hebrews.
Two of Peter the Apostle.
Three of John.
One of the Apostle Jude.
One of James.
One book of the Apocalypse of John.

This list of Canonical Books issued by these two Councils agrees in substance with the list of divinely-inspired Books held by Catholics in the present day. This any one can see by comparing this list with that prefixed to the Roman Catholic English Bible, called

council, being desired by them so to do." And this he did with such praise and admiration of all that all wished him a Bishop; and Valerius, for fear of losing him from his diocese, asked and obtained that he should be installed Bishop of Hippo in his stead, though he was yet alive. This was done in the year 394.

* In the previous edition (second) the substance only of the list of the inspired books laid down by the Council of Hippo was kept. Here also the order and wording are adhered to. (See Labbe, Vol. IV.)

the Douay Bible, and with that of the old Latin Vulgate, or any other Catholic version of Holy Scripture, and likewise with the Canon of Scripture given by the Œcumenical Council of Trent.

The Council of Hippo in 393, and the 3rd of Carthage in 397, was followed by the Sixth Council of Carthage in 419, attended by two hundred and eighteen Bishops, and by two Legates sent by the Roman Pontiff. The list of Books of Scripture decreed in the 29th Decree of this Council agrees with the list given by the two previous ones just mentioned, and ends with these words: "*Quia a Patribus ita accepimus in Ecclesia legendum.*"* "*Because we have received from the Fathers that these are the books to be read in the Church.*"

These words should not be passed unnoticed by those who allow themselves to be led astray by the assertion that "only those books are to be held as divinely inspired of which there was never any doubt in the Church". Let such persons reflect what an assumption it is to suppose that they themselves are, or that their leaders in the sixteenth century were more competent to judge of the Tradition of the Church of the first four centuries than the Council of Hippo and third of Carthage, both held in the fourth century, and the Sixth Council of Carthage held in the beginning of the fifth century; and better judges than all the Bishops of Christendom of that age; for the above list of Canonical Books sanctioned by these three Councils was thenceforward received by the whole of Christendom.

Before the decision of these three Councils was given,

---

* See the *Works* of Leo the Great, Vol. III., p. 643 or 635; see also Labbe, Vol. IV., p. 430, edition of Florence.

some of the Fathers doubted the Divine inspiration of the Epistle to the Hebrews, and of some other Books of the New Testament. Protestants, however, hold them as canonical. For respecting these Books they justly say : " This dissent of some of the Fathers moves us not. This dissent of a few, before the Canon of Scripture was finally settled, should not be taken into account, especially after the adoption of these Books as divinely inspired by all Christendom in the end of the fourth century. The Bishops of that time were in a better position to judge of the Tradition of the Church about these Books."

This observation is just. Protestants, however, should be fair, and apply the same reasoning to certain Books of the Old Testament known under the name of Apocrypha (hidden). Although the inspiration of these books was held to be doubtful by a few of the Fathers before these two Councils, the same Fathers ceased to have any doubt upon it after the decision of those Councils ; so that these Books have the very same sanction and authority that all the Books of the New Testament have, in addition to the long-standing veneration of the Jewish Church for them.

S. Jerome himself, before the said two Councils of Carthage, seemed to doubt the inspiration of the Books of the Old Law called Apocrypha, yet afterwards, when the declaration made by that Council came to his knowledge, he ceased to doubt, and freely quoted from those same Books as inspired books to uphold Catholic doctrine.

About the importance, and, indeed, the necessity of a decision of the Catholic Church to establish the inspiration, canonicity, and authenticity of Holy Scripture, the saying of the great Doctor of the Church, S. Augustine, Bishop of Hippo, is well known : "*For my* part, I should not believe the Gospel (meaning the written Gospel), were I not moved thereto by the authority of the Catholic Church." "*Ego vero evangelio non crederem nisi me Catholicae Ecclesiae commoveret auctoritas.*"—(Against the Epistle of Foundation, chapter lv.)

CHAPTER VII.

THE UNWRITTEN WORD OF GOD, CALLED BY S. PETER "THE WORD OF THE LORD THAT ENDURETH FOR EVER."

Besides the Written Word of God Catholics believe also the Unwritten Word of God, called in Holy Scripture *The Word of God spoken* (Acts iv. 31)—*The Word of Faith preached* (Romans x. 8)—*The Gospel heard and preached* (Colossians i. 23)—*The Word of God received, heard, believed* (1 Thessalonians ii. 13)—*the Word of Christ heard* (Romans x. 17).

Whenever in the New Testament the Word of God revealed by Christ, or through His Apostles before it was committed to writing, is spoken of, it always refers to the Unwritten Word of God.

Even after the Word of God was in part committed to writing, some passages evidently refer to the Word of God *unwritten*; as, for instance, where S Peter says: "*But the word of the Lord endureth for ever, and this is the word which by the Gospel has been preached unto you*" (I. i. 25.) Therefore, whenever the Word of God, without any qualification is mentioned in Holy Scripture, it should not be taken as referring to the Written Word, for it generally refers both to the Written and Unwritten Word of God.

By TRADITION we do not mean a mere report, a

hearsay, wanting sufficient evidence to deserve belief; or a local tradition started by man, and therefore merely human, as were those traditions of the Pharisees condemned by our Lord; but we mean a Tradition first coming from God, continually taught, recorded, and in all desirable ways kept alive by a Body of trustworthy men successively chosen in a divine, or divinely appointed manner, and well instructed, and who are, moreover, protected by God as a Body from teaching what is wrong, or unfaithfully handing down to others the doctrine committed to them.

St. Paul gives us an idea of how this Tradition should proceed when he says: "*For I* DELIVERED *to you first of all, which I also* RECEIVED." (1 Corinth. xv. 3.) And again, when writing to S. Timothy, he says: "*The things which thou hast* HEARD *of me by many witnesses, the same commend to faithful men, who shall be fit to* TEACH *others also.*" (2 S. Timothy ii. 2.)

HOLY SCRIPTURE and the TRADITION just described are BOTH THE WORD of GOD; the first, inspired by God to some chosen one, who wrote it out; the other, taught by His own Divine lips on earth, or inspired by the Holy Spirit in the mind of one man, or Body of men, to be handed down and perpetuated successively under His Divine protection to their legitimate successors; neither therefore of these DIVINE WORDS can be rejected without the guilt of unbelief.

St. Ephrem says: "Be firmly persuaded of this, not as an opinion but as a truth, that whatsoever has been transmitted, whether in writing only or by *word of mouth*, is directed to this end that we may have life and may have it more abundantly" (Vol. iii., Serm. lix.)

St. Basil says: "Of the dogmas and teachings preserved in the Church, we have some from the doctrine committed to writing, and some we have received transmitted to us in a secret manner from the Traditions of the Apostles; *both these have the same force* in forming sound doctrine, and no one who has the least experience of ecclesiastical laws will gainsay either of these. For should we attempt to reject, as not having great authority, those *customs that are unwritten*, we should be betrayed into injuring the Gospel even in primary matters, or rather in circumscribing the Gospel into a mere name." (Vol. iii., De S. Sanct. cxxvii.)

This divine Tradition is not liable to failure either from human fraud or infirmity, because it has the security of *Divine guardianship*, that is to say, because those whose office it is to keep alive this tradition, are *divinely protected* from teaching what is false. This appears from that passage of Isaias, which even Protestants admit refers to the Church, and in which God says: "*This is my covenant with them: My Spirit that is in thee, and my words that I have put in thy mouth, shall not depart out of thy mouth, nor out of the mouth of thy seed, nor out of the mouth of thy seed's seed, from henceforth and for ever*" (lix. 21). This appears also from those passages of St. John, where it is recorded that Christ said: "*And I will ask the Father, and He shall give you another Paraclete, that He may abide with you for ever, the Spirit of Truth . . . but when He, the Spirit of Truth, is come, He will teach you all truth*" (xiv. 16, 17; and xvi. 13).

Hence St. Irenæus says: "For where the Church is, there is the Spirit of God, and where the Spirit of God is, there is the Church and all grace; and the Spirit of Truth." (Against Heresies, vol. iii., c. xxiv.)

The necessity of believing the *unwritten living Word of God* appears also from the fact that the fundamental virtue of Faith, without which no one is a Christian, is an assent to the Word of God preached by men sent by

God, and charged by Him to preach the truths revealed to them by Him Who is Infinite Knowledge, Greatness and Truth, and Who can neither deceive nor be deceived

Hence St. Paul says: "*Faith cometh by hearing;*' (Romans x. 17), and therefore BY the Word of God PREACHED by the Apostles, or by their legitimate successors to the persons who HEAR and BELIEVE it. Hence the same Apostle also says: "*And how shall they hear without a preacher? and how shall they preach unless they be sent?*" (Romans x. 14, 15.). And to be sent by legitimate, divinely established authority is to be sent by God. (See Acts xiii. 4.)

So long as there are nations to be taught, the command of Christ to His Apostles to teach "*all nations,*" indeed, "*every creature,*" will never cease to be in force; and *divinely authorised teaching* will never cease to be the *Word of God*. Whether this Word is preached without being committed to inspired writing, as was the case during the twelve years which elapsed between the Ascension of our Lord and the writing of the first Gospel, the Gospel of St. Matthew,—whether preached by the Apostles and their successors during the progressive formation of the New Testament up to the year of our Lord 99, when the Gospel of St. John, the last inspired book of the New Testament, was written,— whether preached after the death of St. John (101), that is, in the second, third, and fourth centuries, when only very few possessed all the Books of the Old and of the New Testament, and of some of them they were uncertain whether they were divinely inspired or not, (for the Canon or *authorised list* of the inspired Books of the Old and the New Testament was only finally settled in the Council of Carthage in the year 397)— whether preached after the fourth century for the space of a thousand years, during which time no printed

Bible existed, but only Bibles written by hand, which consequently were very voluminous, costly, and rare, —or whether preached after the year 1450, when the art of printing began to come into use, and printed Bibles could more easily be obtained; that Word of Christ, I say, entrusted by Him with His own Divine lips, or by inspiration to the Apostles, and by the Apostles transmitted in a divinely appointed manner to the whole chain of their legitimate successors, is ALWAYS THE WORD OF GOD, firmly to be believed by every Christian.

Hence St. Paul, in his Second Epistle to the Thessalonians ii. 14, could say: "*Brethren,* STAND FAST AND HOLD THE TRADITIONS (that is to say, the entrusted Word of God), *which you have learnt whether by word* (that is, by my preaching) *or by our Epistle*" (that is, by my inspired writings).

When Jesus Christ said to the Apostles: "*He that heareth you, heareth Me*" (S. Luke x. 16), He did not limit this duty of hearing the Apostles *even as Himself* to the time when the inspired writings of the New Testament did not exist, but extended it to all times; and the duty of preaching applies not only to the twelve Apostles, but also to their legitimate successors, for through their successors alone were the Apostles to teach *all* nations, and their Apostolic office was to last until the end of the world. This we see from the following words of Christ to the Apostles: "*Go ye into* THE WHOLE WORLD *and preach the Gospel to* EVERY CREATURE" (S. Mark xvi. 15). "*Go ye therefore and teach* ALL NATIONS . . . *teaching them to observe all things whatsoever I have commanded you; and behold,* I AM WITH YOU ALL DAYS, EVEN TO THE CONSUMMATION OF THE WORLD." (S. Matthew xxviii. 19-20). And NO ONE is exempted from the duty of believing their teaching, for Christ subjoined: "*But he that believeth not, shall be condemned.*" (S. Mark xvi. 16.)

Hence any legitimate Bishop upholding the Tradition of the Church could say what S. John the Evangelist said in his old age, when nearly all the Books of the New Testament were written: "*We are of God. He that knoweth God,* HEARETH US. *He that is not of God,* HEARETH US NOT. *By this we know the spirit of truth, and the spirit of error.*" (1 S. John iv. 6.)

And S. Irenæus could say, concerning the Heretics of his time: "We challenge them to that TRADITION which is from the Apostles, which is preserved in the Churches through the succession of the Presbyters." (Against Heresies, book iii. chap. ii.) And Origen said: "We are not . . . to believe otherwise than as the Churches of God have by succession transmitted to us." (Book iii. Commentary on S. Matthew.)

S. Chrysostom gave out as an axiom: "It is a TRADITION (of the Church), seek nothing further." (Commentary on the passage 2 Thessalonians ii. 14, book xi., Homily 4.)

To suppose that TRADITION has lost its authority from having been (in part) committed to writing, would be as unreasonable as to say that the natural law was made void from the moment that the Ten Commandments were laid down in writing on Mount Sinai.

Some might ask: Which of these two DIVINE WORDS is the more useful to us?

This question may be considered as answered by the Fathers already quoted. I will, therefore, make only one more citation. The holy Bishop of Hierapolis (Papias), the hearer of S. John and friend of S. Polycarp, referring to Tradition, says: "If any one came to me who had accompanied the elders, I questioned him concerning their words, what Andrew and Peter said; for I did not think that what is in the Books would aid me as much as what comes from the LIVING and ABIDING VOICE." (Apud Eusebium, b. iii., p. 39.)

I will here make a supposition which may perhaps enable the inquirer to see better the import of this answer.

Suppose two rivers running side by side, both abounding with precious stones, which persons standing on the banks of either river were most anxious to obtain, and know the name and value of, that knowledge being of vital interest to them. On one of the rivers floats a noble ship, having on board trustworthy men able and willing to impart this knowledge to these people. On the other river, however, we will suppose to be no such vessel, no such guide. The people who stand on the shores of this second river, who refuse to have recourse to the well-informed guides that are on the ship on the other river, and who in the valuation of the precious stones which they may find, only trust themselves, would be liable to make great mistakes in valuing each stone, and would have widely different opinions among themselves about them.

If some of those self-guided men should happen to set a right value on any of the jewels, it would only be by chance; no one of them could feel sure of not being mistaken about it, whilst those who sought the experienced men on board the ship could easily learn with certainty the right value of each of the jewels found in both rivers.

Like two sacred rivers flowing from Paradise, the Bible and Tradition both bear the Word of God, both are full of the precious jewels of revealed truths.

Though these two divine streams are in themselves, on account of their divine origin, of equal sacredness, and are both full of revealed truths, still TRADITION is to us more clear and safe.

1st, Because TRADITION can testify in its own behalf through the many authorised witnesses who carry this TRADITION in themselves, whilst HOLY SCRIPTURE cannot make good its authority without referring to TRADITION to testify to its inspiration and preservation.

2ndly, Because a word may have two or more different meanings, and an expression may be true in one of these meanings and not in another. Again, as an expression may be true, for example, if taken figuratively, and not true if taken literally—true if applied to some particular person, and not true if applied to all— true if taken in its plain sense, and not true if taken in a strained or fanciful sense—true if taken in a sense that does not exclude other things, and not true if taken in an exclusive sense—true if taken to operate through the medium of other things, and not true if taken to operate without a medium—true if taken to mean an advice, and not true if regarded as a precept— true if taken permissively, and not true if regarded as the active cause of a thing; the Bible, which is a mere letter needing an interpreter, cannot by itself set the mistaken interpreter right.

But TRADITION being a LIVING WORD, because carried in the mind and on the lips of divinely appointed living teachers, can say with regard to each of its own expressions, and also as to the expressions in HOLY WRIT itself, in what sense exactly those expressions are true, and in what sense they are not true; and, if wrongly interpreted by any one, TRADITION can set that person right, and explain the true meaning of it; and all this it can do with an authority which, owing to the promised assistance of God, is infallible, and, owing to the unfailing assistance of the Holy Spirit dwelling in the Church, is divine.

The Ark of old, when in the hands of the Sacerdotal and Levitical order, and carried or preserved by them in the midst of the chosen people of God, was a source of blessings. If carried off to another nation, and kept in the hands of unauthorised or self-authorised persons, it was to them a source of scourges. (1 Kings vi.)

So likewise the HOLY SCRIPTURE, when separated from TRADITION, which is its support and lawful expounder, and thrown into the hands of unauthorised interpreters, instead of being a source of blessing, becomes a cause of endless contention and division, an occasion of doubt, fanaticism, and ceaseless wrangling, as sad experience proves.

TRADITION, without Holy Scripture, Old or New, sufficed for many years, and could still suffice. But HOLY SCRIPTURE has never sufficed by itself; it always stood in need of Divine TRADITION: for it is only by this Divine *Tradition* that we learn that *Holy Scripture* is an inspired book. It is only *Tradition* that can give with authority and certainty the right meaning of Holy Scripture. Without *Tradition* the *Holy Scripture* may be made to speak in many discordant ways, thus destroying its authority altogether.

To use an illustration: a Court of a never-interrupted Body of Judges might by the help of a living, well-known, and well-established Tradition of orally enacted laws, suffice for the guidance and welfare of a people; but no code of written laws could suffice without a Court to testify to the genuine nature of them, to their being still in vigour, and to give with authority the right meaning of them in all cases of dispute.

St. Irenæus testifies that in his time many nations had salvation written in their own hearts without paper and ink, and were diligently guarding the ancient TRADITION. (Book iii,. chap. iv.)

After TRADITION had been in full and successful operation for many years, God added the *written Word*, but it was not for the purpose of superseding *Tradition*, a thing which neither our Lord nor His Apostles ever said; but it was rather to strengthen *Tradition* itself; for in this very *Written Word* He left recorded repeatedly and forcibly, as we have already seen, that *Tradition* or the successive oral teaching of the Body of Teachers instituted and empowered by Himself for that purpose, was to have its full authority and vigour whilst there existed a *Nation*, or even one *creature* to be taught the Gospel; that is, until the end of the world.

Hence the ancient and successive Fathers of the Church always recognised the necessity of appealing to TRADITION, THE UNWRITTEN WORD OF GOD, in order to confute heresies, to settle controversies about Religion, and to establish with authority and certainty what, according to the Revelation of God, we ought to believe and to do in order to be saved.

The Fathers of the Church plainly expressed their belief that the WRITTEN WORD OF GOD by itself, without the help of TRADITION, would always leave disputes unsettled, points of belief and morals undetermined, and true Religion a problem unsolved.

CHAPTER VIII.

THE INTERPRETATION OF HOLY SCRIPTURE.

The Holy Scriptures are the Word of God. This I will assume as admitted by Protestants generally. But it is clear that if the Scriptures are wrongly interpreted, they become the word of man. For, as the Protestant Bishop Walton says: "The Word of God does not consist in mere letters, whether written or printed, but in the true sense of it."* This is what S. Jerome had said many ages before: "Let us be persuaded that the Gospel consists not in the words but in the sense. A wrong explanation turns the Word of God into the word of man, and, what is worse, into the word of the devil; for the devil himself could quote the text of Scripture;" † and he did so when he tempted our Lord in the desert. (S. Matth. iv. 6.)

Let Protestants consider well this point, especially those who so confidently and plausibly boast that "*they stand by the Bible alone*," and imagine that to stand by the Bible alone means that they rely not upon human authority, but upon the Word of God.

Certainly nothing can be better than to stand by the Word of God, but whether what they call "standing by the Bible alone" be to "stand by the Word of God," remains to be seen.

Let us observe, 1st, that the Bible, though divinely inspired, is but a *written document*, and a written document often so obscure, that St. Augustine, though so great a scholar, and a Doctor of the Church, confessed that "there were more things in the Bible he did not understand than that he did".

2dly, That the Bible, because a *written document*, would remain always silent unless interpreted, that is, unless some meaning is affixed to the words, by some one. It is clear that the Bible cannot speak and

---

* Prolegomena or Preface of his Polyglot, chap. v.

† In his comments on the Epistle to the Galatians, speaking against the Luciferians.

interpret itself,—you must take the Book in your hand, open it, read it, compare passages, and attach a certain meaning to those words which fall under your eyes.

Therefore, when a Protestant says: "I stand by the Bible alone," he does not mean that he stands by the Bible uninterpreted, for in such case the Bible is mute. He does not mean that he stands by the Bible as interpreted by the Church, for that would not be the Protestant but the Catholic principle. Nor does he mean that he stands by the Bible as interpreted by somebody else; as that would be, according to his notion, to give up his right of private interpretation. But he means that he stands by the Bible alone as interpreted by himself, and that the sense in which he himself understands it *is the Word of God.*

'The Bible,' a Protestant might continue, 'interpreted by the Fathers, may or may not be the Word of God; the Bible interpreted by the Church may or may not be the Word of God; the Bible interpreted by some one else may or may not be the Word of God; but the Bible interpreted by *me*, that is indeed the Word of God, my only teacher, my guide, my infallible authority.'

But a Catholic might say: 'What, my friend, if you were to understand some passage of Scripture in a wrong sense?' 'That would be a pity,' the Protestant probably would reply, 'but still, not acknowledging any authority but my own private judgment, I have a right to look upon that interpretation of *mine* as the Word of God.'

'But surely,' the Catholic might add, 'it is reasonable to suppose that the interpretation of the Bible by the whole body of Bishops of the Catholic Church, though disagreeing with your private interpretation, should be the right one, and therefore more likely the

Word of God.' 'No,' the objector might still answer, 'because that interpretation would not be *mine*.' 'If you argue so,' the Catholic might justly reply, 'I must say that with you, my friend, the *me* and the *mine* make all the difference.'

Let him who has eyes see what spirit is at the root of this vaunted principle, and how shallow is the argument for standing *by the Bible alone*.

The Bible in its original tongue, or when faithfully translated, is indeed *in itself* the *Word of God*, and infallible; but the Bible is not the Word of God, nor infallible, *with regard to us*, unless *rightly* interpreted, that is, interpreted with authority, certainty, and infallibility. For if the interpretation be wrong, the Bible ceases to be, with regard to the reader, the Word of God; and if the interpretation be unauthorised, doubtful, fallible, the Bible becomes, with regard to the reader, unbinding, doubtful, fallible.

In the Gospel, however, we are commanded, under pain of damnation, to believe; that is, to hold without a doubt as true what is taught as revealed, therefore there must be somewhere the rightful interpreter, and the right interpretation.

Again, the Gospels and the Epistles are full of severe censures on the sin of schism and heresy. It is obvious that all schism and all heresy must be essentially in opposition to truth; it is therefore necessary to know with certainty what is true, before we can know what is opposed to the truth. But by private interpretation, an undoubted belief or infallible knowledge of revealed truth is impossible.

The saying of Christ to the Pharisees: "*Search the Scriptures, for you think in them to have life everlasting; and the same are they that give testimony of me.*" (S. John v. 39), cannot be taken as the *sole* means of salvation recommended, much less recommended *to all*, as to those who cannot read, or who cannot possess a Bible; much less still as a necessary *means* of salvation.

Nor can it be taken as though Christ thereby recommended *private* in disregard of *authoritative interpretation* of Scripture; 1st, because that is not stated nor implied in that passage; 2ndly, because He Himself, in that very place, interprets authoritatively the Scriptures, by saying: "*They testify of me*"; 3rdly, because in fact the Pharisees showed that their private interpretation wrongly led them to look upon Christ as a breaker of the Sabbath (S. John v. 18), and consequently to reject Him as the Saviour; 4thly, because from what our Saviour then said, it cannot be gathered that the Pharisees thought that life was to be had from Scripture *privately* interpreted, to the exclusion of *authoritative* interpretation; for a person may be fond of reading and interpreting Scripture *privately* for his own learning and edification, and yet *respect* and *prefer* authoritative interpretation to his own, at least in those points in which it can be had.

Thus S. Peter recommends us to attend to the prophetical word, reminding us at the same time that "*no prophecy of the Scripture is made by private interpretation*". (2 S. Peter i. 20.)

Thus, Catholics do think to have life in Holy Scriptures, but do not thereby exclude authoritative interpretation, but rather take it for their guide.

But let us, for argument's sake, suppose that the Pharisees went by private interpretation of Scripture. Even in this supposition it would not follow that Jesus Christ, by that saying, meant to approve their conduct; for also Catholics do often say to Protestants who go by private interpretation: "Search the Scriptures, for you will find that they bear testimony to the Divinity of Jesus, to the institution of the seven Sacraments, to the unfailing authority of the Catholic Church"; and no one ever dreamt to affirm that by so saying Catholics mean to approve the Protestant principle of private interpretation.

Again, if that passage and the other in praise of the Bereans (Acts xvii. 11) were to be taken in the Protestant sense to establish the principle of private interpretation, two consequences, quite inadmissible, would follow, namely—1st, that if the Pharisees or the Bereans had found by their private interpretation that the Old Testament (which was the only part of the Written Word they could then have) did not bear testimony to Christ, or that it bore testimony against Him, as many did imagine, they would have been justified in disbelieving Jesus Christ; 2ndly, that not believing in Christ until moved by *private* interpretation of Scripture was better than simply believing in Christ, on the word of Christ, or of His Church, without consulting the Scriptures, as the Apostles and thousands of Jewish and Pagan converts did.

To avoid these two inadmissible consequences, it remains that the above cited and similar passages must be understood in the Catholic sense just mentioned.

To the Apostles our Lord gave the charge to "*teach all nations,*" and the faithful were commanded to hear and believe them. (S. Mark xvi. 16.) This commission was accompanied by a promise that He would be with them in this office of teaching to the *end of time.* (S. Matth. xxviii. 19, 20.) From these expressions it is clear that their lawful successors were also included in the commission and promise given to the Apostles. It follows then that the *authoritative* interpretation of Scripture made by the *lawful successors* of the Apostles is the true one, and truly the Word of God; a contradictory interpretation must therefore of necessity be false, and is not the Word of God; because a thing under the same aspect cannot *be true* and *untrue* at the same time, for truth in all things is *one*, and the contradiction of it is error.

Hence, S. Peter condemns private interpretation of Scripture, saying: "*No prophecy* (or explanation) *of Scripture is made by private interpretation.*" (2 S. Peter i. 20.)* Those who refuse to hear and to follow the legitimate interpretation, and the faith of the Church, often, instead of the Word of God, that is, what God really meant in Holy Scripture, have only their own inventions and errors, and these they mistake for the Word of God.

These persons consequently fall into a maze of perplexities, and often change their interpretation. They are, as S. Paul expresses it: "*tossed to and fro, and carried about with every wind of doctrine.*" (Ephesians iv. 14.) S. Peter warns us of this danger, when referring especially to S. Paul's Epistles, he says: "*In which are certain things hard to be understood, which the unlearned and unstable wrest, as they do also the other Scriptures, to their own destruction.*" (2 S. Peter iii. 16.)

Hence it appears how rash and dangerous is the principle of private interpretation, which emboldens every individual to prefer his own private view of any passage of Scripture to the solemn interpretation and decision of the whole body of Catholic Bishops of past and present time united to the See of Peter. Persons actuated by such pride cannot expect to be led by God unto truth.

Objectors say that to submit to the teaching of the

---

* See foot-note in Catholic (Douay) Bible.

Church is to give up our reason. But if it could not be called a surrender of reason for the early Christians to have submitted to the teaching of the Apostles, because it was a submission to the messengers of Christ, to the witnesses and authorised expounders of Revelation as long as the Apostles lived, surely it cannot be considered a surrender of reason, but a most reasonable act, for other Christians to conform themselves to the teaching of the Catholic Church, that is, to the Body of the Catholic Bishops with the Roman Pontiff at their head, who are the lawful messengers of God, the legitimate successors of the Apostles, the witnesses and authorised expounders of Revelation; for they, in an uninterrupted succession, keep up that Apostolic office, which according to Christ's declaration, and through the promised special assistance of the Holy Ghost, was to last to the end of time.

Objectors also say that every one has the assistance of the Holy Ghost to interpret the Bible rightly. But if this were so, people would agree and would not contradict each other in their interpretation of Scripture; for no passage of the inspired Word of God, in its right meaning can really contradict another passage in matters of faith, of morals, and of fact.

But numerous Protestant denominations often differ one from another and often contradict each other in vital points, and each assumes to prove his particular doctrine from Holy Scripture. I say *vital*, for, on account of these very points, they have thought themselves in duty bound to separate from some other community. This plainly shows that they are not inspired by the Holy Ghost, Who being the spirit of unity and truth, cannot *create discord*, cannot *teach error*, cannot *suggest a false meaning*, and cannot *contradict Himself*.

This principle of private interpretation of Holy Scripture, during the three centuries since Luther's time, has given rise to *hundreds* of sects among Protestants, and this *in spite* of the efforts of several of the civil Governments to prevent such subdivisions. Had this principle been adopted in the beginning of Christianity and gone on working throughout the Christian world for eighteen centuries unrestrained by the civil power the sects would probably by this time have enormously increased.*

The Bible without an authorised, that is, divinely given, interpreter could scarcely condemn any heresy, nor could any of the Christian sects adjudge any individual or any other sect as guilty of heresy, without abdicating its own principle of *private interpretation for all*. In all centuries those persons who maintained and taught their own private interpretation *in opposition* to that of the Church, have been regarded by all the Fathers, Saints, and Doctors of the Church as heretics, and condemned as such by the Church. †

Catholics do well to read and study the Holy Scriptures for their greater instruction and edification, but always in a spirit of submission to the Catholic

---

* According to a return of the English Registrar-General on the 1st October, 1878, the number of Protestant sects having places registered for the performance of religious worship in England and Wales exceeds 150, and in Ireland, where Protestants, as compared with Catholics, are few, there are nearly 150. In the United States of America Protestant denominations are also numerous. (See Appendix, Nos. 21, 22, 23.) Cardinal Hosius enumerated 270 different sects of Protestants in the sixteenth century as then existing.

† "They who solicitously seek for truth, ready to own their error as soon as the truth is discovered, are by no means to be numbered among heretics" says S. Augustine (Epistle 43.) This is also the opinion of all Roman Catholic theologians. Such persons are *material*, not *formal*, heretics.

Church, so as never to *prefer* their own *private* view to the *known* interpretation and teaching of "*the Church of the living God, the pillar and ground of the truth.*" (1 S. Timothy iii. 15.)

The approved Catholic version, with notes, of the Holy Scriptures in English or any other tongue, although not indiscriminately circulated, is not withheld from the faithful; and the reverent reading of it is encouraged by the Church. It is well known that new and cheap editions of Holy Scripture are frequently issued, both in the United Kingdom and abroad, by Catholic booksellers with the approval of the Bishops. To most editions is prefixed a letter of Pope Pius VI. in the year 1778, to the Most Rev. Antony Martini of Turin, Archbishop of Florence, in which His Holiness praises him for " publishing the Sacred Writings in the language of his country suitable to every one's capacity," and encourages the pious reading and studying of Holy Scripture by the faithful.

The reading of Holy Scripture will not induce Catholics to become Protestants, but rather lead sincere, dispassionate Protestants to become Catholics, as has been often the case. Listen to what a distinguished convert says of himself on this subject:

"The first remote cause of my conversion I have always considered to be the delight which I have taken from my youth up in the study of Holy Scripture.

"As a boy at school I read and re-read it, and learned much by heart; and as a clergyman of the Church of England, I read aloud in Church, for five years and more, four chapters nearly every day. And as I read, I became more and more convinced that the doctrines of the Catholic Church were also the doctrines of Scripture.

"This will surprise many, and many will not believe

me; for the lesson which every English child learns, about Catholics is that they dread the Scriptures because their Religion is unscriptural.

"Never was lesson more false. I cannot find language strong enough in which to declare my conviction that the Catholic Church alone honours and loves the Scriptures with real honour and love; and that the faith of the Catholic Church, and that alone, agrees in a wondrous harmony with every syllable of the Word of God. I have stood trembling as an Anglican clergyman, when I read aloud passages which clearly condemned the position which I then held, and it is a mystery to me how any one can with a pure heart read the Scriptures and not become a Catholic."*

CHAPTER IX.

INFALLIBILITY OF THE CHURCH AND OF THE POPE.

God has imparted truths to men, some of which they could not possibly have known by their unassisted reason, and some, only few could discover by mere reasoning and know with certainty. These truths imparted to men by God we call Divine Revelation; and God requires that in order to obtain salvation, men should believe these revealed truths on His Divine authority.

Such Revelation having been given, there must be some way in which these truths can be communicated to us in their purity, and in such a manner as to render us certain of possessing them.

To say that God has merely given to men forms of

* Rev. Fr. George Bampfield, B.A., Oxon. *St. Andrew's Magazine* (Barnet), April, 1879, page 65. See "Difficulties of private interpretation," by the same. Appendix No. 5.

words which admit of different and contradictory interpretation, and has left no authority on earth to declare which is the one true interpretation intended, amounts to a denial of Revelation altogether. A law which would admit of several inconsistent explanations would not have the nature of law if there were not a Court of Justice to declare the true sense. The same might be said of a revelation capable of several discordant interpretations.

The Holy Scriptures do in themselves admit of opposite interpretations on a great number of questions. There are many subjects on which a text may be produced with an apparently opposite meaning; and in these cases, it is clear that one or more of the texts must be taken in a sense consistent with the statement of other parts of Scripture.

If there is an authority to declare the right sense of these passages, then all is simple enough; but without such an authority, it cannot be denied that in the case supposed Holy Scripture admits of contradictory interpretations, and consequently on such questions, ceases to be really a revelation. There must, therefore, be some living authority on earth commissioned by God to decide the meaning of the revelation which God has given us.

Such an authority *must* be infallible. Its infallibility is contained in its very commission. We cannot conceive that God has appointed some one to teach us what His Revelation really is, and *commanded us to listen to it and believe it*, and yet that He would at the same time allow this guide to lead us astray. God, Who is the very truth, *could not command us to believe false teaching.*

Roman Catholics believe that such an infallible authority exists in the Church, and that it belongs to the whole Body of the Episcopate united with the Roman Pontiff. They also believe that this unfailing protection from teaching error is assured by God in a special manner to the Holy Pontiff himself when speaking *ex Cathedrâ*; he being the visible head of the Church and the legitimate successor of S. Peter.

INFALLIBILITY OF THE CHURCH.

That infallibility belongs to the whole Body of Bishops united to the Roman Pontiff is plain from those texts which prove the infallible teaching of the Apostles united to S. Peter their chief, and which applies also to their successors.

The teaching Church is called by S. Paul "*the pillar and ground of truth*". (1 S. Timothy iii. 15.) Our Lord promises that "*the gates of hell shall not prevail*" against His Church (S. Matthew xvi. 18):—that He would always be with His Church (S. Matthew xxviii. 20):—that the Holy Spirit would abide with her for ever for the express purpose of guiding her into all truth: "*I will ask the Father and He shall give you another Paraclete, that He may abide with you for ever.*" (S. John xiv. 16.)

Our Divine Lord has substituted the Body of the Apostles *for Himself* in His Mission upon earth, and in the office of teaching. "*As my Father hath sent me, I also send you.*" (S. John xx. 21.) "*He that heareth you, heareth* ME, *and he that despiseth you, despiseth* ME." (S. Luke x. 16.)

Finally, Jesus Christ, immediately after giving to His Apostles the commission to preach the Gospel to every creature, added: "*He that believeth and is baptized shall be saved; but he that believeth not shall be condemned.*" (S. Mark xvi. 16.) All these texts which demand from the faithful their full acceptance of what the Church teaches show the impossibility that the true Church can teach what is false in matters of faith and of morals.

This infallibility does not depend upon the learning which exists in the whole body of the Episcopate united to the Pope when discussing and deciding points of faith or of morals, but on the aid of the Holy Ghost Who enlightens their minds and guides their counsels. Thus the decision of the first Council at Jerusalem was communicated to the faithful in the following Apostolical declaration: "*It hath seemed good to the Holy Ghost and to us, to lay no further burden upon you than these necessary things.*" (Acts. xv. 28.)

By this divine assistance the Bishops in union with the Bishop of Rome do not become the medium of a new Revelation, but are divinely assisted and enlightened, according to the unfailing promise of God, to understand well what has been revealed, and to declare rightly the true meaning of that Revelation.

From this doctrine it does not follow that the Church arrogates to herself to be more than the Scriptures, as she has been accused of doing, but of being more than those private men who expound the Scripture.

INFALLIBILITY OF THE POPE.

Besides this infallibility possessed by the Church, that is by the Body of the Bishops together with the Pope, Catholics believe that the Pope also alone, as chief Pastor and visible head of the Church is divinely prevented from teaching error; but only when he teaches *ex Cathedrâ*, that is, when, not as a private teacher, but in his office of Supreme Pastor and teacher of the whole Church, he defines any doctrine of faith or morals as true, or so condemns any doctrine of faith or of morals as false.

The infallibility of S. Peter and his successors is plainly proved from the following texts of Holy Scripture.

First from S. Luke (xxii. 31), where we read that our Saviour addressed S. Peter in presence of the other Apostles thus: "*Simon, Simon, behold Satan hath desired to have you, that he may sift you as wheat. But I have prayed for* THEE *that* THY *faith fail not: and* THOU *being once converted, confirm thy brethren.*"

Here Jesus Christ provides against the danger to which His Apostles and their successors would always have been exposed of falling from the faith through the frailty and evil passions of men, and through the instigation and fraud of the devil. And in what way does He provide? By praying in a special manner for *one* of them *that his faith should not fail*, and by commanding him *to confirm his brethren;* thus giving all the other Apostles clearly to understand that they all are bound to adhere to that one, and follow his directions, and that thus they would possess the privilege of being themselves infallible guides.

St. Peter is the one for whom Jesus Christ prayed, and in the person of Peter his successors are of necessity included; for Jesus Christ was providing for the good of His Church, which was to last not for the lifetime of S. Peter only, but to the end of time, against the attacks of the enemy, which would be unceasing.

Were it possible that the Pope *in his capacity of supreme Pastor of the Church, speaking ex Cathedrâ*, could teach error, it might be argued, 1st, That the prayer of our Lord for S. Peter was not granted; 2nd, That the special provision which Jesus Christ made for securing His Church from error, instead of preserving it from erring in faith or in morals, would, at least in certain cases, only serve to drag the whole Church into error, and be an advantage for Satan, not a means of defence to the Church against him.

Another proof is gathered from the words addressed to Simon by our Blessed Lord after having changed Simon's name into that of Peter. [*Kephas, Rock.*] "*Thou art Peter; and upon this rock I will build my Church, and the gates of hell shall not prevail against it.*" (S. Matth. xvi. 18.)

As the Church of Christ was to last beyond the lifetime of S. Peter, even to the end of the world, and as the Church is not a lifeless, material building, but a living body of men requiring a living head to rule them and to be like a foundation of that great Society, this promise of Christ of making Peter a Rock, was meant not only for Peter but also for his successors. There must be proportion between the building and its foundation. The building, namely, the visible Church, being a living successive body of men, the *foundation* also, that is, the visible ruling power which sustains the whole superstructure, must be successive. Therefore the successors of S. Peter as the supreme visible rulers of the Church, are each like S. Peter, the Rock or the visible foundation of it.

If *rocks*, they must stand immovable as teachers of truth; if *foundations* of the Church of Christ, against which "*the gates of hell*" can "*never prevail*," it follows, that much less can the gates of hell prevail against the *foundation* itself; for the house receives solidity from the foundation, not the foundation from the house.

If the foundation could be overturned, the house or church built upon it also could. But the gates of hell cannot prevail against the Church, therefore they cannot prevail against the foundation, which is the support of the Church; the foundation which was made by our Saviour as solid as a rock for the very purpose of rendering the Church indestructible.

The official personal infallibility of the Pope is therefore by this text fully established; and the Fathers understood it in this sense. Among these, Origen, in his commentary on this text, says: "It is manifest, though it is not expressed, that the gates of hell will not be able to prevail either against the Church, or against Peter, because if they should prevail against the rock upon which the Church is based, they would also prevail against the Church".

A third argument is drawn from those words of Jesus Christ addressed to S. Peter, "*Feed my lambs . . . feed my lambs . . . feed my sheep.*" (S. John xxi. 15-17.)

Under the name of lambs who follow the mother-sheep and are fed by them, the Fathers of the Church have understood the lay-Christian people, and under the name of sheep which feed the lambs that follow them, and whose mothers they are, they understood the Bishops and other Pastors (or shepherds) of the Church. The Fathers had no doubt that under that very significant and touching similitude, Jesus Christ meant to commit to S. Peter, and in his person to those who should inherit Peter's office, the care of His own flock, both the faithful lay people and Pastors, the lambs and sheep, of which two parts alone the flock of Christ, the whole visible Church on earth, is composed.

From this Divine charge to S. Peter, there arises the corresponding duty on the part of all the other Bishops and of all the faithful throughout the world to submit themselves to the guidance of the Sovereign Pontiff, the successor of S. Peter, and allow themselves to be fed by him with the spiritual food of his wholesome teaching.

Hence it follows that the Sovereign Pontiff must be Divinely protected from teaching what is wrong; that is, he must, in teaching, be *infallible;* for, if he were not protected by God from error when he teaches the whole Church in his capacity of supreme Pastor, the Church would be liable to be led into error, contrary to the promise of Jesus Christ.

That this was the belief of the early Church, the Fathers of the first five centuries are splendid witnesses. I will quote three of them. 1st. *S. Irenaeus*, Bishop of Lyons, who was a Father of the second century, renowned for his learning and sanctity, and for the purity of his faith, which he sealed with his blood, and who lived some years with the Bishop of Smyrna, S. Polycarp, Disciple of S. John the Evangelist.

We can hardly have a better witness of the sentiments and teaching of the Catholic Church East and West during the first two centuries than this great Martyr and Father of the Church, S. Irenaeus.

Now, in his book against heresies, amongst other things, S. Irenaeus lays down this general principle, that to convince heretics of their errors one might indeed consult the doctrine of his particular Church, founded by some one of the Apostles, and preserved by their lawful successors, but that this long process was not necessary, for there was a sufficient, safe, and shorter way, by looking to what was taught by the Roman Church, as all the other Churches were bound to be united in faith with that Church on account of her *greater principality* (in the Latin version extant, "*propter potiorem principalitatem*"), and that therefore to convince heretics of their errors it was enough to show that the Roman Church never taught their heretical doctrines. (Book iii., Against Heresies, chap. iii.)

St. Irenaeus attributes to the Church of Rome the superior headship, and declares the duty of all other churches to agree with her faith, because of her having been founded by the two glorious Apostles St. Peter and S. Paul, whose faith as preached by them was handed down by an uninterrupted line of Bishops who succeeded S. Peter in the see of Rome. These Bishops of Rome, to the number of twelve up to his time, he enumerates, namely, Linus—Anaclétus—Clement—Evaristus—Alexander I.—Sixtus I.—Télésphorus—Hygínus—Pius I.—Anicétus—Soter—and lastly, Eleutherius, under whose Pontificate he himself was living.

This duty of all churches to adhere to the Church of Rome as branches to the trunk, and to conform their faith to the teaching of the Church of Rome, that is of her Bishop, would be inconceivable unless we admit that it was from the first the universal conviction that the Bishop of Rome was endowed by Christ with *infallibility*.

To this universal sentiment of the Church the great Doctor of the fourth century, *S. Jerome*, is also a noble witness. Being disturbed with the disputes among three parties which divided the Church of Antioch, of which Church or Diocese he was then a subject, he writes for directions to Rome to Pope S. Dámasus I., thus: "I who am but a sheep do apply to my Shepherd for succour. I am united in communion with your Holiness, that is to say, with the chair of Peter; I know that the Church is built upon that *rock*. He who eats the paschal lamb out of the house, is profane. Whoever is not in the Ark of Noe will perish by the deluge. I know nothing of Vitális; I reject Meletius;

I am ignorant of Paulínus : *he who gathers not with thee scatters.*" (Letter to Pope S. Damasus.)

The great African Doctor of the Church, *S. Augustine*, Bishop of Hippo, (near the site of ancient Carthage), who lived in the fourth and in the beginning of the fifth century, must also have been impressed with the same principle and conviction ; for commenting on the condemnation of Pelagianism he says : " Already the decision of two Councils have been submitted to the Apostolic See, and from thence rescripts (or Apostolic Letters) have come to us. *The cause is finished.*" This sentence of S. Augustine has been condensed into that famous maxim which has for ages expressed in a few words the Catholic faith on this point : " *Roma locuta est, causa finita est.*"—" *Rome has spoken, the case is settled.*"

The infallibility of the Pope was defined by the Vatican Council in the Fourth Session, chapter iv., on the 18th of July in the year of our Lord 1870,* in these words : " *Itaque Nos traditioni a fidei Christianæ*
" *exordio perceptæ fideliter inhærendo, ad Dei Salvatoris*
" *nostri gloriam, religionis Catholicæ exaltationem et*
" *Christianorum populorum salutem, sacro approbante*
" *Concilio, docemus et divinitus revelatum dogma esse*
" *definimus : Romanum Pontificem, cum ex Cathedrâ*
" *loquitur, id est, cum omnium Christianorum Pastoris*
" *et Doctoris munere fungens, pro suprema sua Apos-*
" *tolica auctoritate doctrinam de fide vel moribus ab*
" *universa Ecclesia tenendam definit, per assistentiam*
" *divinam, ipsi in beato Petro promissam, ea infalli-*
" *bilitate pollere, qua divinus Redemptor Ecclesiam*
" *suam in definienda doctrina de fide vel moribus*

---

* See " The Vatican Decrees in their bearing on Civil Allegiance." By His Eminence The Cardinal Archbishop of Westminster. (Longmans, 1875, price 2/6.)

"*instructam esse voluit ; ideoque ejusmodi Romani Pontificis definitiones ex sese, non autem ex consensu Ecclesiæ irreformabiles esse.*"

The following is the translation of this definition from the original Latin of the Dogmatical Constitution beginning: "*Pastor Æternus*".

"Wherefore faithfully adhering to the tradition received from the beginning of the Christian Faith, for the glory of God our Saviour, the exaltation of the Catholic Religion, and the salvation of the Christian people, We, the Sacred Council approving, teach and define that it is a dogma divinely revealed: that the Roman Pontiff, when speaking *ex Cathedrâ* —that is, when discharging the office of Pastor and Teacher of all Christians, by virtue of his supreme authority, defines a doctrine regarding faith or morals to be held by the universal Church—he, by the Divine assistance promised to him in Blessed Peter, is possessed of that infallibility with which the Divine Redeemer willed that His Church should be endowed in defining doctrine regarding Faith or Morals: and that therefore such definitions of the Roman Pontiff are of themselves irreformable and not from the consent of the Church."

Consequently, Catholics believe that the Pope is infallible when he teaches the faithful *ex Cathedrâ*, that is, "*from the Chair*" of S. Peter, in matters of *faith* or of *morals*.

The word *infallibility*, as applied to the Pope, means that when he teaches the faithful as Head of the Church in the manner described in the definitions just quoted, he in such cases is protected by the special promise and Providence of God, Who is Himself the only source of infallibility, from wrongly interpreting the Word of God, and from teaching error.

By teaching *ex Cathedrâ* is meant, when he is speaking, not as a private theologian, or in some other limited character, but defining solemnly in his capacity of Successor of S. Peter and Pastor of the universal Church.

The addition of the words, "*a doctrine regarding faith or morals,*" signifies that the Pope is believed to be infallible only when he teaches a doctrine concerning *faith or morals,* that is to say, in matters relating to revealed truth, or to principles of moral conduct in life.

These limitations show that Catholics are not, according to the definition, bound to believe that the Pope cannot err in matters other than faith or morals, or even in matters of faith or of morals, when he is speaking as a private individual, and not in his official capacity *ex Cathedrâ.*

It is important here to remark that *infallibility,* as applied by Catholics to the Pope, differs from impeccability; for infallible, speaking of men, means preserved by God in certain cases from erring; and impeccable means either incapable of sin as God is, or preserved by God from sinning.

The Pope is not *impeccable;* on the contrary, any Pope may fall into sin; but nevertheless, every Pope is infallible in expounding Holy Scripture, in defining, that is, declaring in precise words revealed truth, and teaching points of faith or of morals, *when he does all this ex Cathedrâ.*

In a somewhat like manner in civil matters a Judge may be blamable in his private life, and yet eminent and faultless in his official duty of deciding points of civil law

Protestants are apt to make this objection. How can *a sinful man* be infallible? They should not, however, be astonished that the Successor of S. Peter, though liable to commit sin, should, by virtue of the all-powerful prayer and unfailing promise of *Jesus Christ*, be *preserved* under certain conditions by the Holy Ghost from expounding falsely the Word of God, when they see in Holy Writ that *sinful men*, as were Balaam, Solomon, and Jonas, have been made to speak infallibly, or to' put the Word of God into writing *free from all error*. Caïphas was unjust; and yet he was inspired by God to utter infallibly this prophecy : " *It is expedient for you that one man should die for the people.*" (S. John xi. 50); upon which the Evangelist, in the same place, makes this remark : " *And this he spoke not of himself: but being the High Priest of that year, he prophesied that Jesus should die for the nation.*"

Again, many of the Scribes and Pharisees were of sinful life, and yet our Lord, referring to them, says : "*The Scribes and the Pharisees have sat on the chair of Moses. All things therefore whatsoever they shall say to you, observe and do ; but according to their works do ye not ; for they say and do not.*" (S. Matth. xxiii. 2.) And S. Peter himself, though a sinner, is acknowledged by Christians to have been infallible in teaching the Church, both by word and by writing.

It seems hardly consistent that Protestants should find fault with Catholics for believing that the Pope has the special assistance of the Holy Ghost, since many of them go so far as to assume that assistance for every private individual. Again, those Protestants who hold that they are assisted by the Holy Ghost in the interpretation of Scripture, by a strange inconsistency, do not consider themselves to be infallible; for they admit that they are liable to err, liable to contradict themselves, and liable to contradict each other; whereas Catholics, consistent with their principles, hold that the Pope, for the very reason that he is *assisted by the Holy Ghost* when he teaches the whole Church, or any part, or even any member of it, *ex Cathedrâ*, in points of faith or of morals, cannot, within such defined limits, err in the interpretation of the Word of God, and cannot either contradict himself, or contradict the teaching *ex Cathedrâ* of another Pope, or the dogmatical definition of a rightly constituted General Council.

How is it, then, some may ask, that this Catholic dogma of the *Pope's infallibility* is so often clamoured against as impious and absurd? The honest inquirer will, I think, cease to be astonished at this if he will only observe that declaimers against the Pope's infallibility are not always careful accurately to state the terms and limitations of the solemn definition as just quoted, and that they then cry out against a phantom of their own imagining; thus condemning Catholics for a doctrine which they do not hold.

CHAPTER. X.

JUSTIFICATION.

Justification is a Divine act which conveys sanctifying grace, and by that grace communicates a supernatural life to the soul, which by sin, whether original or actual, had incurred spiritual death; that is to say, justification is a change or *translation* from the state of sin into a state of grace.

It is a gift of Almighty God, a ray, as it were, coming direct from the Divine goodness and filling the soul, which makes those who receive it pleasing to God and justified in His sight.

The grace of justification produces a change affecting the soul of the regenerate by its presence elevating and perfecting it. By this grace the likeness to God is brought out in them, and they are raised to a state of friendship with Him, and of Divine sonship.

The Catholic Church teaches that the grace of justification not merely *covers* sin, but *blots it out;* that is, blots out the guilt and stain arising from sin, and remits the *everlasting* punishment due to it.

Merely covering sin is a human way of forgiving, which consists in passing over the crime of a sinner, and in treating him outwardly as if he had not committed it, and as if no stain were in the soul in conseqence of it, though the guilt and the stain is still there.

God's way of pardoning a sinner is very different, and wholly divine. It is a way befitting His infinite goodness, sanctity, omnipotence, and the immense efficacy of Christ's Blood, and of His superabundant Redemption, and of His infinite merits.

God's way of pardoning is to erase entirely the guilt and stain of sin, so that instead of it, God sees in the pardoned sinner the "*charity of God poured forth in our hearts by the Holy Ghost*" (Rom. v. 5), and which, like a fire, has destroyed all the dross of sin, and rendered man pure, upright, and holy.

Hence the justification of a sinner is represented in Scripture as the putting on of the *new man*, who is "*created in justice, and holiness of truth*" (Ephesians iv. 24); the "*renovation of the Holy Ghost*" (S. Titus iii. 5).

In the case of grown-up persons, some dispositions are required on the part of the sinner in order to be fit to obtain this habitual and permanent grace of justification. A man can only dispose himself by the help of Divine Grace, and the dispositions which he shows do not by any means *effect* or *merit* justification, but only serve to prepare him for it; and for that reason are simply called dispositions or preparations. This is the teaching of the Council of Trent, which declares: "We are said to be justified gratuitously, because none of the things which precede justification, whether it be faith or good works, can *merit* this blessing for us". (Session VI. chapt. viii.) The same holy Council declares that sins are remitted *gratuitously* by the mercy of God through the merits of JESUS CHRIST. (Sess. VI. chapt. vii.)

The principal dispositions required for justification are the following acts, which can only be made by the assistance of God's actual grace, namely, an act of *faith*, or belief in revealed truths, of *fear of God*, of *hope*, and of *charity*; an act of *repentance* for past sins, with a *purpose* to avoid sin in future, and to keep the commandments : a desire of receiving *Baptism* for those who have not yet been baptized, and for those who have fallen into sin after Baptism, a *resolution* to approach the Sacrament of Penance. (Council of Trent, Sess. VI. chapt. vi.)

Justification may be lost by wilfully violating a commandment of God, either by doing what is forbidden, or by not doing what is commanded. Justification is a talent or gift which, unless made to bear fruit, will be taken away from us, and we shall be punished for this neglect.

By justification we are raised to the dignity of sons of God, heirs of His Kingdom; and this entails upon us the duty of acting in a way becoming to so high a dignity. "*If thou wilt enter into life, keep the commandments*," said our Lord. (S. Matt. xix. 17.) By justification we are incorporated with Christ, like a branch growing on a vine; but if the branch produces no fruit it will be cut off and cast into the fire. (S. John xv. 5.) Hence, the grace of justification is compared by our Saviour, not to a pond, but to a fountain, whose waters reach unto Heaven: "*But the water that I will give him shall become in him a fountain of water springing up into life everlasting*". (S. John iv. 14.)

ACTUAL GRACE.

After we are justified we still stand in need, in order to perform any meritorious good work, of another grace called *actual*. Justifying grace, called also *habitual* grace, is something in itself lasting; actual grace is something that passes, and extends only to individual acts for the time it is needed. Actual grace is a passing, supernatural, Divine help enlightening our understanding, and moving our will, and enabling us to perform any single good action; for instance, to accept any supernatural revealed truth, or to perform any good work, considered *good in the supernatural order*.

Grace does not force man's free-will, but respects it, and leaves man free to act with it or not. Grace, therefore, does not destroy our free-will, but only helps it, and our own working with grace is required. "God who has created thee without thee, will not save thee without thee," says S. Augustine; and in Holy Scripture it is repeatedly stated that God will render to everyone according to his works.

We stand in continual need of actual graces to perform good acts, both before and after being justified. The good acts, however, done by the help of grace before justification are not, strictly speaking, meritorious, but serve to smooth the way to justification, to move God, though merely through His mercy and condescension, to help us and render us better disposed for the same. But if, with the assistance of actual grace, good works are done by a person who is justified, then they are acceptable to God, and merit an increase of grace on earth and an increase of glory in Heaven.

Hence S. Paul says: "*God is not unjust that He should forget your work, and the love which you have shown in His name.*" (Hebrews vi. 10.)

Writing to S. Timothy, he declares that "*a crown of justice*" was laid up for him . . . and not only for him, "*but to them also that love His* (Christ's) *coming.*" (2 S. Timothy iv. 8.) And in his second Epistle to the Corinthians, he says, "*for that which is at present momentary and light of our tribulation, worketh for us above measure exceedingly an eternal weight of glory.*" (iv. 17.)

All our merits, however, without any exception, are grounded on the merits of *Jesus Christ*, and on His grace, without which no one can move a step towards Heaven.

The merit of a good action performed in a state of grace, as being in consequence of justification, and in union with our Lord, is truly our own merit, because that good action is really performed by us, by our cooperation with God's grace; but it is also, and principally, a merit of our Lord, as a grape is the fruit of the branch, and yet also and principally the fruit of the parent vine without which, or if not connected with which, the branch could not produce any fruit, or indeed have become a branch at all. Our merit, therefore, does not take away from Christ's merits, for *without Him we can do nothing.* We merit through Christ, Christ makes us merit; or still more properly, Christ merits in us, and therefore all the glory is His. "God forbid," says the Council of Trent, "that a Christian should confide or glory in himself and not in the Lord, whose goodness towards men is so great that He regards as their merits the very gifts which He

Himself bestows upon them." (Session VI., chap. xviii.) And S. Augustine had said long before, "*God crowns His own grace when He crowns our merits.*"

CHAPTER XI.

How Christ's Redemption is applied to Men, that they may be Justified and Sanctified.

Jesus Christ died for all mankind; He truly died that "*He might taste death for all*". (Hebrews ii. 9.) Yet we know that all men will not be saved, but only those who do His will; for we read in S. Paul: "*And being consummated, He became to* ALL THAT OBEY HIM *the cause of eternal salvation.*" (Hebrews v. 9.) And so, notwithstanding Christ's Redemption, it is stated in the Gospel that some "*shall go into everlasting punishment*". (S. Matth. xxv. 46.) Saint Paul did not say that God will save all men, but, "*Who will have all men to be saved*" (1 S. Timothy ii. 4), implying thereby that for salvation man's will and co-operation is required to fulfil the conditions, and use the means appointed by God Himself for the purpose.

Only those who "*have washed their robes and have made them white in the Blood of the Lamb*" (Apocalypse [Rev.] vii. 14), that is, who have the merits of Christ applied to them, and who persevere to the end in doing what is commanded, will be saved.

The direct means instituted by Christ Himself for applying His infinite merits to the souls of men are the Holy Sacraments, which are so many channels instituted by Jesus Christ to convey to men His grace purchased for us at the price of His most precious Blood: "*You shall draw waters with joy out of the Saviour's fountains.*" (Isaias xii. 3.)

CHAPTER XII.

The Holy Sacraments.

In the words of our Catechism, "A sacrament is an outward sign of inward grace, ordained by Christ, by which grace is given to our souls."

More fully, a Sacrament may be said to be an outward sign of a corresponding invisible grace, ordained by Jesus Christ as a permanent means in the Church, which, by virtue of Christ's infinite merits, has power to confer on the worthy receiver the grace which it signifies.

The object of the Sacraments is to apply the fruit of our Saviour's Redemption to men, by conveying through their means to our souls either the "*habitual grace*" of justification, or an increase of the same, and a pouring in of other graces, or the recovery of justification when lost.

The Catholic Church teaches that there are truly and properly seven, and only seven Sacraments of the New Law, instituted by Jesus Christ our Lord, and necessary for the salvation of mankind, though not all of them necessary for every person, as, for instance, Holy Order and Matrimony.

These seven Sacraments are : *Baptism*, by which we are made Christians, children of God, and members of His Holy Church; *Confirmation*, by which we receive the Holy Ghost, to make us strong and perfect Christians and soldiers of Jesus Christ; The *Holy Eucharist*, which is the true Body and Blood, with the Soul and the Divinity, of Jesus Christ, under the appearances of bread and of wine; *Penance*, by which the sins that we commit after Baptism are forgiven; *Extreme Unction*, which in serious or dangerous illness, comforts the soul, remits sin, and restores health of body, if God sees it to be expedient; *Holy Order*, by which Bishops, Priests, and other Ministers of the Church are ordained; and *Matrimony*, the Sacrament which sanctifies the union by marriage between man and woman.

Each of these has the three conditions necessary for a sacrament understood in the strict sense of the word, namely, *the outward sign, the inward grace*, and *the institution by Jesus Christ*, Who alone has the power to institute Sacraments; that is, outward signs as means of grace.

CHAPTER XIII.

Holy Baptism.

We have seen, in speaking of original sin, how the loss of original justice or grace produces a stain on the soul of man which we call original sin, and which forms the misery of man's fallen state.

It was therefore the part of our Saviour not only to purchase our Redemption by His death on Calvary, but to apply to each man the saving fruit of His Redemption by bestowing upon man a gift that would make up for this dire calamity.

Jesus Christ applies His most precious Blood freely, and not for any merit or work in the receiver, by bestowing upon him in Baptism justifying grace, pardon of original sin, and in the case of a grown-up person, of actual sins, if he be guilty of any, and sorry for them. The stains of these sins are washed away in holy Baptism and he becomes a friend and child of God and heir to the Kingdom of Heaven.

Baptism is a sacrament absolutely necessary for all,

without which no man can enter into the Kingdom of God, for *Jesus Christ* has said: "*Amen, amen, I say to thee, unless a man be born again of water and the Holy Ghost, he cannot enter into the kingdom of God.*" (S. John iii. 5.)

Hence it was not enough for Saul of Tarsus, converted on the road to Damascus (Acts ix. 18); and for the Chamberlain of Queen Candace, met on the road by Philip the Deacon (Acts viii. 38), to believe; they had to be baptised in order to obtain remission of their sins, and thus be in the way of salvation; therefore in the Nicene Creed we say: "I acknowledge one Baptism for the remission of sins".

So all-important is this sanctifying grace given in Holy Baptism, that God affords to man everywhere the utmost facility in obtaining it. Water is at hand almost always, and in case of *necessity*, a layman, a woman or even a child having the intention to baptise, can administer Baptism, by pouring common water on the head of the child or grown-up person, and saying at the same time in any language: "*I baptise thee in the name of the Father, and of the Son, and of the Holy Ghost.*"

Martyrdom supplies the place of ordinary Baptism by water; this is called *Baptism of Blood*. God indeed grants this justifying grace to every one who, believing the necessary Christian truths, sincerely desires Baptism, and does his best to procure it, but who dies before he can receive it. This is called *Baptism of desire*.

Baptism, as also Confirmation and Holy Order, can be received only once, because each of these Sacraments impress a *Character* or *Mark* on the soul which will remain for ever.

To receive this Holy Sacrament worthily and profitably, grown-up persons having the use of reason must believe and profess their belief in the necessary Articles of the Christian Faith—they must have trust in the Mercy and Merits of Christ, and be sorry for their sins; being assisted in so doing by actual grace, which grace God grants to everyone, and without which no one can move a single step towards Heaven.

In Baptism all infants, without any disposition on their part being required, are cleansed from the stain of original sin, taken into God's favour, made members of Christ's mystical Body, and heirs of the Kingdom of Heaven. They are thus regenerated, that is, in our Saviour's own words, they are "*born again of water and the Holy Ghost.*" (S. John iii. 5.) They have contracted the stain of original sin without their knowledge and personal co-operation, and they are freed from sin without their knowledge; and the dispositions necessary for grown-up persons are not required from them; for infants are incapable of any reasoning act. As infants are made heirs to earthly property before they are capable of consenting to receive it, so also in Holy Baptism infants are made heirs of heaven before they are capable of consenting to be baptised; their consent in both cases is justly presumed.

But, though Baptism suffices to save a child in the state of infancy, yet as soon as it comes to the use of reason, the Baptism which it received will not by itself suffice for its salvation: it must, besides, have proper dispositions—that is, it must believe and profess to believe the principal Articles of Faith, must hope in God, and must love Him with the whole heart.

This is making what are called acts of Faith, of Hope, and of Charity; and for any sins a person has committed since Baptism, an act of contrition is also required. (For these acts, see Appendix, No. 13.)

CHAPTER XIV.

ON SIN. (NATURE AND CONSEQUENCES OF SIN.)

Sin is of two kinds, namely, Original Sin and Actual Sin.

Original sin is that sin which we contract in our origin or conception, and which we inherit from our first parents Adam and Eve. See Chap. iii.

Actual or *Personal* sin is every sin which we ourselves commit.

Having already in the third chapter treated on original sin, I will here speak only of actual sin.

Actual sin is any wilful thought, word, or deed, or voluntary omission which violates the law of God, and is therefore an offence against God.

Actual or personal sin is of two kinds, either mortal or venial. S. John (1st Epistle v. 16) speaks of "*a sin which is not to death*": this is what we call *venial*; and "*a sin unto death*": this is what we call *mortal*.

Mortal sin is a thorough violation or breaking of a commandment of God with full knowledge and deliberation. It is a turning away from God, who should be the supreme object of our love, and a turning to a created object instead. *It is a grievous offence against God*, by which we lose His friendship and His grace, which loss is the death of the soul.* On this account it is called *mortal*—that is, *deadly* sin.

Venial sin is either a slight infringement of the law, or it may be in some cases a great violation of the law,

---

* *Anima amissa mors est corporis,*
Deus amissus mors est animae.
The soul gone is the death of the body,
God lost is the death of the soul.
—(St. Augustine, Serm. 28.)

but rendered slight in the person who commits it, through his want of sufficient knowledge, deliberation, or freedom.

Venial sin is not a complete breaking of the law, but a tendency towards breaking it. It is not a downright turning of one's back against God, but a turning aside or slackening of our tendency to Him as the supreme object of our desires or last end. It is not abandoning God for a creature, but it is, in some degree, dallying with created objects, whilst still adhering to God. It is a sin which does not grievously offend God as mortal sin does.

Venial sin, although an offence against God, does not cause the forfeiture of God's friendship, nor the loss of justifying grace, as mortal sin does, but it diminishes God's love towards us, and checks the flow of His choicest gifts and actual graces. In short, it does not inflict, like mortal sin, death on the soul, but a wound, which, in those who are well disposed, is easily healed; it causes a stain and a guilt in the soul, of which we can *easily obtain pardon;* and therefore it is in that sense called *venial*.

From this simple statement of the difference between mortal and venial sin, it follows that if we ought to be careful to avoid venial sin, because it is always an offence against God, we ought to be much more careful to avoid with horror mortal sin, which offends God grievously, causes death to the soul, and merits everlasting punishment.

Mortal sin is beyond comparison more dreadful than venial sin. No number, indeed, of venial sins can reach the malice and guilt of a mortal sin. All bodily evils in the world are as nothing compared with the evil of mortal sin. Mortal sin is the greatest of evils. It is in itself so hideous and detestable, that even were there no hell to punish it, it ought to be shunned on account of its own intrinsic foulness.

To give a clearer idea of this, I will touch upon some points which show the grievous malice of mortal sin, and the sad effects of it upon the soul.

The grievousness of an offence is increased by the dignity of the person offended, and by the claims which that person has upon our love and service.

Applying this principle, it follows that mortal sin, which is a grievous offence against God, Who is infinitely exalted above the highest of His creatures, and Whose claim to our love infinitely surpasses all other claims, is an offence incomparably greater than an offence against any creature, and manifests an infinite malice.

Sin, moreover, is most opposed to God.

God is		Sin is
	goodness itself	absence of all good.
,,	essential order..	,, thorough disorder.
,,	the supreme good	,, utter evil and corruption.
,,	essential beauty	,, monstrous deformity.
,,	diffusive love	,, narrow, mean selfishness.
,,	essential wisdom	,, blind madness.
,,	justice and holiness	,, injustice and wickedness.
,,	everlasting life	,, everlasting death.
,,	unfading glory	,, endless shame.

Hence, mortal sin is of necessity infinitely hateful to God, and He therefore punishes it everlastingly; in other words, God exacts for sin a complete satisfaction. The love that God of necessity has for His own infinitely perfect being is the reason and the measure of the hatred He has to sin.

Sin is a desertion, an abandonment of God: "*Know thou, and see that it is an evil and a bitter thing for thee to have left the Lord thy God.*" (Jeremias ii. 19.) And Moses says to the sinner: "*Thou hast forsaken the God that begot thee, and hast forgotten the Lord that created thee."* (Deuteronomy xxxii. 18.)

Mortal sin is a horrible disorder. It is placing one's good in a created object, instead of fixing it in God, Who is the ocean of all goodness, beauty, happiness, and glory.

Mortal sin is a dethroning of God from one's heart. It banishes God from the soul. Isaias says: *"Your iniquities have divided between you and your God"* (lix. 2.)

It is an injustice, for by it man refuses to give to God what by many titles he owes to Him. Hence sin is often called in Holy Scripture *iniquity*, that is, injustice.

Mortal sin is an act of insubordination, a revolt, an open rebellion against God, Who declares: *"Thou hast broken my yoke, thou hast burst my bands, and thou saidst, I will not serve."* (Jeremias ii. 20.)

It is a base contempt of God, of His authority, majesty, and friendship. It is preferring the slavery of the devil to the glorious service of God. *"He that committeth sin,"* says St. John, *"is of the devil."* (1 S. John iii. 8.)

It is a daring insult which man, who is *"dust and ashes,"* offers to a Being Who is infinitely great, infinitely powerful, infinitely wise, infinitely good, and infinitely holy.

It is a black ingratitude of a man towards his greatest Benefactor, his Creator and Redeemer, Who has loaded him with natural and supernatural gifts. It dishonours the image of God in the soul, and casts it down in the mire of base passion and vice.

It is in reality preferring misery to bliss; hell to heaven; Satan to God. *"To whom have you likened me?"* says the Lord (Isaias xlvi. 5): to a base passion at which you blush, to a little pleasure that passed so quickly, to a little gold which has melted in your hands. "*Be astonished, O ye Heavens, at this* . . . *For my people have done two evils. They have forsaken me, the fountain of living water, and have digged to themselves cisterns, broken cisterns, that can hold no water.*" (Jeremias ii. 12, 13.)

By sin man outrages God in all His titles—he outrages Him as *Creator*, by revolting against His supreme dominion; as *Legislator*, by violating His laws; as *Redeemer*, by despising His grace; as a *Friend*, by provoking His enmity; as a *Father*, by resisting His loving authority; as a *King*, by banishing Him from the possession of his heart.

By sin man outrages in a special manner each of the three Divine Persons—God the Father, the adopted sonship of Whom he renounces; God the Son, Whom he hath "*trodden under foot*" (Heb. vi. 6), and Whom, according to S. Paul, he "*crucifies again;*" God the Holy Ghost, Whom he is said to "*grieve,*" "*resist,*" and "*extinguish*". (1 Thess. v. 19.)

Let us now notice some of the *bad effects* that mortal sin produces in the soul.

Mortal sin causes a man to forfeit the friendship of God.

It turns God from a friend into an enemy.

It destroys the beauty of the soul, and covers it with a hideous leprosy.

It so degrades and debases man as to lead him to seek happiness in muddy waters, in feeding on husks fit only for the swine. "*How exceeding base,*" says God in Jeremias, "*art thou become, going the same ways over again!*" (ii. 36.)

It renders man more grovelling than the irrational animals themselves. "*Man when he was in honour,*" we read in the Psalms, "*did not understand; he is compared to senseless beasts, and is become like to them.*" (Psalm xlviii. 13.)

It leaves a hideous stain in the soul, deforms it, and makes it hateful in the sight of Heaven. It was one single mortal sin of thought which changed thousands of bright Angels into monstrous demons.

Mortal sin spreads bitterness, remorse, shame, disquietude and fear in the soul. It is a poison that tortures the conscience, and works destruction: "*By what things a man sinneth, by the same also he is tormented.*" (Wisdom xi. 17.)

By mortal sin man forfeits the right to his heavenly inheritance.

Mortal sin entirely extinguishes justifying grace in the soul.

It destroys the value of all acquired merits: "*All his justices which he had done shall not be remembered.*" (Ezechiel xviii. 24.)

It deprives the soul of all power of meriting. So long as any one remains in a state of mortal sin, all the good works he does are useless to obtain any reward in Heaven. S. Paul writes: "*If I have not charity, I am nothing.*" (1 Corinth. xiii. 2.)

It renders a man the slave of sin, and of his evil desires. (Romans vi. 16.) His passions tyrannise over him. Our Lord likewise says: "*Whosoever committeth sin, is the servant of sin.*" (S. John viii. 34.)

By sin a man sells himself, and enslaves himself to the devil: "*He that committeth sin is of the devil.*" (1 John iii. 8.)

Mortal sin causes the death of the soul. "*All iniquity,*" says Ecclesiasticus, "*is like a two-edged sword*" (xxi. 4), with which a man attacks God, and at the same time kills his own soul. In the same Book of Ecclesiasticus we read, "*The teeth thereof,*" that is of sin, "*are the teeth of a lion killing the souls of men*". (xxi. 3.) And in S. James it is said: "*But sin when it is completed begetteth death.*" (i. 15.)

Finally, mortal sin closes the gates of Heaven, and unless remitted before death, entails a punishment of "*everlasting fire, which was prepared for the devil and his angels.*" (S. Matth. xxv. 41.)

[*Prayer.*] Through Thy great mercy, O God, and through the merits of Jesus Christ, forgive us our sins. From all sin, Lord Jesus, deliver us.

CHAPTER XV.

The Sacrament of Penance.

Man, even though regenerated and justified, is still liable to fall into sin, on account of the depravity of his fallen nature, and also on account of the many temptations that surround him: therefore our loving Lord, in His infinite Mercy, instituted another Sacrament for the forgiveness of sin committed after Baptism. This is the Sacrament of Penance, in which, by the absolution of the Priest, joined with the *contrition*, *confession*, and *satisfaction* of the penitent, his sins are forgiven by God, through the application of the merits of Jesus Christ.

Contrition is an interior grief, horror and detestation of sin committed, with the firm resolve never more to relapse into our evil habits. (See Council of Trent, Session xiv., chap. 4.) Contrition thus includes in itself two acts: sorrow of the heart for sin committed, and the purpose of the will to avoid sin in future.

Confession is an express, contrite, but secret self-accusation, to a duly authorised Priest, of, at least all grievous sins committed after Baptism, or of all the mortal sins committed since the last confession when absolution was received, as far as we can recall them to memory, and an accusation of sins made.*

Satisfaction means doing the penance enjoined by the Priest in confession, repairing the scandal if any was given, and restoring the property and good name to our neighbour in case of his having been injured by us.

Almighty God certainly can, if it so pleases Him, depute a man to forgive sins in His Name. That He did depute certain men to forgive sins is plain from what our Blessed Lord said to His Apostles, and in the persons of the Apostles to their legitimate successors to the end of the world: "*Peace be to you. As the Father has sent me, I also send you. When He had said this, He breathed on them; and He said to them: Receive ye the Holy Ghost; whose sins you shall forgive, they are forgiven them; and whose sins you shall retain, they are retained.*" (S. John xx. 21-23.)

This divine commission to forgive sins in Christ's Name was always understood to mean what the words just quoted from St. John naturally and plainly signify; namely, that God has commissioned certain men to grant and also withhold the forgiveness of sin in His name; and these words have thus been understood from the time of the Apostles until now by the Catholic Church, and have thus been understood also by the separated Greek and other Oriental schismatical churches, in which the Sacrament of Penance is also believed and practised.

It is of course always God Who forgives when

---

* See Method of Confession, Appendix No. 15.

forgiveness is granted through the instrumentality or ministration of a Priest who acts as Minister of God. As in Holy Baptism, it is God Who forgives, yet it is done through the medium of the Minister who dispenses that Sacrament of regeneration, for whether it be Paul or Cephas who baptises, it is always *Jesus Christ* Who baptises; so in the Sacrament of Penance, when the Priest forgives, it is God Who forgives through His appointed authorised Minister.

From the words of S. John, lately quoted, it is evident that the Priest has, by the commission of Christ, sometimes to *forgive*, and sometimes to *retain*, that is, to withhold forgiveness of sin; therefore it is necessary that the penitent sinner should make known to the Priest in Confession the state of his conscience, in order that the Priest may give or withhold absolution with *knowledge* and prudence, and not grant or deny it unduly or at hazard; which Jesus Christ never intended.

The Priest, in fact, who is called upon to dispense the sacrament of Penance, and to remit sin, has to decide whether the person who comes to him as a penitent is really guilty of sin or not,—whether if guilty, the sin is grievous or is venial,—whether reparation to a neighbour is required or not;—he must judge what instruction, admonition, advice, or penance is necessary; he must form an opinion whether the penitent has or has not the dispositions which render that person fit to receive absolution.

In short, the Priest in the tribunal of penance is a judge, and as such he must, as a rule, have full knowledge of the case upon which he has to pronounce judgment; and this knowledge he can only receive from the penitent himself.

That it is a good thing to confess our sins appears from the following passages of Holy Writ: "*He that hideth his sins shall not prosper; but he that shall confess, and forsake them, shall obtain mercy."* (Proverbs xxviii. 13.) S. James writes: *"Confess therefore your sins one to another"* (v. 16.) If open confession is good for the soul, how much more advantageous is it to confess to a Priest who has power from God to forgive our sins. We must bear the shame of showing our wounds and bruises, and festering sores, if we wish to be cured. To humble ourselves is some reparation for the evil we have done; it pleases God, and procures for us many great blessings.

CHAPTER XVI.

THE HOLY EUCHARIST.

The Holy Eucharist is the true Body and Blood of Jesus Christ under the outward appearances of bread and wine.

This Sacrament surpasses in excellence all the other Sacraments, because under the *appearances** of bread and wine, and under *each* of these appearances, or species, that is to say, under the species of bread and under the species of wine, this most Blessed Sacrament contains *really*, *truly*, and *substantially*, though not perceptibly to our senses or with their natural accidents, the Body and Blood of our Lord Jesus Christ, together with His Soul and Divinity, which cannot possibly ever be separated from His Body and Blood.

Our Saviour said: *" My Flesh is meat indeed; and My Blood is drink indeed."* (S. John vi. 56.) And

---

* Those appearances which are outwardly perceived by the senses, as colour, taste, or shape, are also called *species* and *accidents*.

when He instituted this Sacrament He said: "*This is My Body which is* GIVEN *for you. Do this for a commemoration of Me.*" "*This is the chalice, the New Testament in My Blood which shall be shed for you.*" (S. Luke xxii. 19, 20.)

The words: "*Do this in commemoration of Me,*" should not be taken as irreconcilable with the real presence of our Lord in this Blessed Sacrament. At a banquet in commemoration of a battle, the presence of the victor does not render the commemoration impossible, but the more striking. It may also be said that the presence of Jesus Christ in this most Holy Sacrament renders the commemoration of His death more vivid.

The change or passing of one *substance* into another is called *Transubstantiation.* The co-existence of one substance together with, or mingled with, another is called consubstantiation.

To understand the word *Transubstantiation,* it is well to remark that in all bodies there are two things to be noted: 1st, the *outward appearance,* such as taste, smell, shape, colour; and 2d, the *matter* or *substance* in which these qualities reside. The sensible qualities are objects of knowledge which we can acquire by the testimony of the senses; but we cannot form any notion of the nature or elementary structure of the inward substance. We know for certain that in a body there must be the substance, or that thing upon which the accidents rest, and that the substance is the essential part in a body: as to the nature of substance itself it is beyond the reach of science and of our conception.

When a change in the *substance* of anything takes place in which thing all the outward appearances remain as they were before, but only the inward *im-*

perceptible substance is entirely changed, this is called Transubstantiation. Transubstantiation, therefore, is the entire change of the inward imperceptible substance, while all the outward appearances of that substance remain as they were before, unchanged.

The Catholic Church teaches that before consecration what on the altar appears to be bread and wine is simply bread and wine, and that after the consecration of that bread and of that wine that which still appears to be bread and wine is no longer bread and wine, but the Body and Blood of Jesus Christ. Something remains, namely, the outward appearances or *species* of bread and of wine, and something is changed, namely, the inward invisible *substance* of that bread and of that wine into the Body and Blood of Christ; this inward change or conversion is what is called *Transubstantiation*.

Catholics believe that in the Holy Eucharist Transubstantiation, and not consubstantiation, takes place, for the simple reason that our Saviour, at the Last Supper, did not say, 'IN this' or 'WITH this is My Body,' 'IN this' or 'WITH this is My Blood.' But He said: "*THIS is My Body*," "*THIS is My Blood*," which words, in their natural meaning, imply a *change of substance;* for, if what Jesus held in His hands was truly His Body and His Blood, it must have ceased to be the *substance* of bread and of wine.

And this is still more apparent from the New Testament as written in the Syro-Chaldaic, Greek, and Latin languages, in which the word *this* in the expression, "*This is My Body*," is *neuter*, and cannot be referred to *bread* which in those languages is of *masculine* gender, so that, according to the force of these languages, the only plain meaning is—this thing which I hold in My hand is My Body.

If we were to interpret the said expressions to mean "This *bread* is My Body," "This *wine* is My Blood," that would be a downright contradiction; and if we were to stretch those expressions to mean, "In this bread there is My Body," "In this wine there is My Blood," it would be an open violence to the text.

To believe in Transubstantiation, therefore, is in plain words to believe the assertion of Christ without hesitation or demur, without seeking for an escape, and without a doubt. To Christ asserting: "*This is My Body,*" "*This is My Blood,*" it is to answer with simplicity of faith: 'Yes, Lord, I believe what Thou sayest; *It is Thy Body, it is Thy Blood.*'

Transubstantiation takes place when the words of consecration, "*This is My Body,*" "*This is My Blood,*" used and ordered by Christ, are pronounced over the elements of bread and wine in the Holy Sacrifice of the Mass by a Priest, rightly ordained.

All persons who are capable of being instructed in this Holy Mystery, are bound by the command of Christ to receive this adorable Sacrament; and the Catholic Church, which allows to the faithful, and even recommends, the daily reception of the Blessed Eucharist, commands the reception of It, "at least once a year."

This solemn precept is based on the words of Jesus Christ: "*Amen, amen, I say unto you; Unless you eat the flesh of the Son of Man, and drink His Blood, you shall not have life in you.*" (S. John vi. 54.)

CHAPTER XVII.

THE HOLY SACRIFICE OF THE MASS.

Sacrifice is the highest act of Religion, because other

acts with which we worship God may also be used, though in a limited sense, in honouring the Angels, the Saints, Kings, and other high personages, while Sacrifice is so exclusively due to God, that it can only be offered to Him; for the natural end of Sacrifice is to show, by the destruction or notable change of the Victim, the sovereign dominion over creation which belongs to God alone.

From the beginning of the world the servants of God were accustomed to offer Sacrifice to the Most High God. And in all ancient Religions, true or false, this worship of sacrifice was always looked upon as the most solemn act of Religion.

It was therefore proper, that as in the Law of nature, and in the Mosaic Law, there were sacrifices instituted by the Almighty, there should also be in the Law of grace a continual sacrifice whereby to worship God in a manner worthy of Him, besides the One Sacrifice offered by our Lord Jesus Christ on Mount Calvary.

As the sacrifices with shedding of Blood of the Old Law were figures of the sacrifice offered by Christ on Calvary with the shedding of His most Precious Blood, so those sacrifices of the Old Law that were without the effusion of blood were types of another sacrifice in the New Law, which also was to be without bloodshedding.

The Prophet Malachias foretold in plain words this daily sacrifice of the New Law when he said: "*For from the rising of the sun, even to the going down, my name is great among the Gentiles, and in every place there is sacrifice, and there is offered to my name a clean oblation: for my name is great among the Gentiles, saith the Lord of hosts.*" (Malachias i. 11.)

What it was reasonable we should have, what was foreshadowed by the figures of the Old Testament, and, moreover, what was even foretold, our Lord Jesus Christ accomplished at the Last Supper. For the Holy Eucharist which He then instituted is not only a sacrament but also a true sacrifice offered up then by the same Jesus Christ to His Eternal Father, and offered also by Himself daily through the ministry of the Priest whenever the Priest celebrates Holy Mass at the Altar: the faithful who are present uniting in the Oblation.

The Holy Sacrifice of the Mass is a commemorative sacrifice, regarded as a true sacrifice by the Apostles and their Successors, and by the whole Catholic Church in all centuries. It is still so regarded even by all ancient schismatical churches, who separated themselves from the Catholic Church in communion with Rome between the fifth and ninth century, and who have, up to the present, preserved among them he Sacrifice of the Mass as an institution of Christ.

To complete a commemorative sacrifice, the *actual* putting to death of the victim is not necessary, but only the real presence of the victim, accompanied by a mystical death, or by such a notable change in the thing offered, as may *represent* death.

Jesus Christ "*dieth now no more*" (Romans vi. 9), and yet He offers Himself to His Eternal Father as one dead, though alive, "*a Lamb standing as it were slain*" (Apocalypse [or Revelation] v. 6), showing continually to God the Father His five most precious wounds, the marks of His Immolation on Calvary. In like manner His having died once, never to die again, does not prevent Jesus Christ from being offered a true Victim in the Holy Sacrifice of the Mass as an Immolation with only a mystical death.

Some of the sacrifices of the Old Law were of this kind, as, for example, the typical sacrifice of Isaac by

Abraham; and in the offering of the sparrow. Of these we read in the Book of Leviticus (xiv. 6): "*The other* (sparrow) *that is alive he* (Aaron) *shall dip with the cedar-wood and the scarlet and the hyssop in the blood of the sparrow that is immolated ;*"—"*he shall let go the living sparrow.*" Another instance is the "*Emissary-goat* (Azazel, the goat to go off, or scape-goat), "*he shall present* ALIVE *before the Lord, that he may pour out prayers upon him, and let him go into the wilderness.*" (Leviticus xvi. 8.)

Moreover, there are sacrifices of inanimate things, in which therefore actual death is not possible. Such were *the loaves* of proposition or shew-bread, called in Leviticus (xxiv. 9) "*most holy of the sacrifices of the Lord by a perpetual right.*" Such likewise were the sacrifices described in the 2d chapter of Leviticus in verses 2-9-16, where it is ordered that a handful of the flour offered by the people should be offered by the Priest in sacrifice upon the *Altar*, and there burnt by the *Priest Aaron or his sons.*

This sort of *sacrifice* was regarded by the Jews as a *true sacrifice*, called *Mincha*, which word is translated by the Seventy Interpreters (in the old Greek version called the Septuagint), and by the Latin Vulgate simply *Sacrifice.*

Now it is clear that in this kind of sacrifice neither an actual nor even a mystical death took place, but only a very notable *change*, which is enough for the nature of a sacrifice.

In the Holy Eucharist, the Victim, namely, Jesus Christ, is truly present, therefore He can be offered up, and He is truly offered up, as an Oblation to His Eternal Father; and although the death of the victim does not occur in *reality*, yet it takes place *mystically;* the Body of Christ being made present, as though separated from the Blood, since, by the power of the consecrating words, first, the Body of Christ is caused to be present under the *species* (or what appears to the senses) of bread, and then His Blood is caused to be present under the *species* of wine. This *mystical death*, by *seeming* separation of the Blood from Christ's Body, joined with the true *offering* of Jesus Christ, Who is truly present, living and entire under each *species*, can and does constitute a real sacrifice commemorative of that of the Cross.

This double consecration is by Christ's institution so essential for the Sacrificial Act that if there were *only* a consecration of the bread, or *only* a consecration of the wine, our Lord would be present, but not as a *Sacrifice*, because in these cases the mystical immolation would be incomplete.

Jesus Christ is called by the Royal Psalmist, "*A Priest for ever according to the order of Melchisedech*" (Psalm cix. 4), because the only Sacrifice Melchisedech, as "*the Priest of the Most High God*" (Genesis xiv. 18), offered, was that of bread and wine, which was not a direct figure of the Sacrifice offered up on Calvary with *spilling of blood*, but of the Sacrifice of the Mass, which is offered under the species of *bread and wine, without the shedding of blood*, and offered for ever; "*the clean oblation*" spoken of by the Prophet Malachias (i. 11).

It seems plain that it is also in reference to the Sacrifice of the Mass that mention is made by St. Paul of an *Altar* as belonging to the Christian Dispensation; an *Altar* always denoting a *Sacrifice* (Hebrews xiii. 10).

The Holy Sacrifice of the Mass does not differ *in its essence* from the Sacrifice offered up upon Mount Calvary. The two Sacrifices are essentially the same; for both on Calvary and in the Mass we find the *same identical Victim*, and the *same principal Offerer*, Jesus Christ; though the manner of offering be different. It is a repetition of the same Sacrifice, but made in a mystical manner, that is, without suffering, shedding of blood, or death of the Victim really present, except in appearance, and made by the same High Priest Jesus Christ. Therefore the Priest, at the time of the consecration, does not say: "This is the Body of Christ," but acting in the Person of Christ, says: "*This is my Body*," according to the Divine command, "Do THIS," or as these words might be rendered, OFFER THIS. It is on account of this Sacrifice offered daily on our Altars by Christ that He is called "*A Priest for ever according to the order of Melchisedech.*" (Psalm cix. 4; Hebrews vii. 17.)

CHAPTER XVIII.

THE HOLY SACRIFICE OF THE MASS SERVES TO APPLY CHRIST'S REDEMPTION TO MEN.

St. Paul affirms that Christ offered himself only *once*, meaning by *suffering, blood shedding and death*; as he compares Christ's oblation to the oblations of animal victims of the Old Law which were made by a real destruction of their animal life.

There is nothing in the Mass which is opposed to this teaching of S. Paul. So far from it, the Mass is a perpetual witness to the fact of that single death in blood; it is one of the most striking attestations we can make that Christ died for the World; there cannot be a more conspicuous testimony to the *one death of the one Victim* than the Holy Sacrifice of the Mass; that august Act, which, instituted by Christ Himself, "*shows forth the Lord's death till He come*," that death, without which the Mass would have neither a meaning nor even an existence.

What is, then, the chief purpose of the Mass? The chief purpose of the Holy Sacrifice of the Mass is to apply *practically* to our souls individually those merits and graces which the Sacrifice of the Cross had already gathered and prepared for all mankind; it is a channel or secondary fountain of the effects of Redemption, not the original source; not adding value or merit to the Sacrifice of Christ offered once for all on Calvary. It is not a sacrifice totally distinct from, and independent of that of the Cross, as the different victims and Sacrifices of the Old Law were independent of, and additional to each other; but it is a renewal and repetition of the 'once offered' oblation, by being a renewed sacrificial presentation of the same Victim in another and unbloody manner through the ministry of the Priest. It is renewed and repeated that we may have an opportunity of practically joining in that Sacrifice; repeated not for the sake of redeeming mankind afresh, or adding to the merits of the Redemption, but to apply Christ's satisfaction and merits gained on Calvary, to the Church in general, and to each soul in particular.

The following illustration will perhaps assist in making this more plain.

If some one had defrauded the Government, and a rich man should offer to pay the amount stolen on condition that the guilty person should be forgiven; should the Government accept the terms, on the understanding that the guilty person should first make a special application to the Government, signed by the rich man and by himself, no one would call this second requirement a disparagement to the first. It seems easy to conceive that this second demand is neither unreasonable, nor unjust, nor disparaging to the former; and why? Because it is based on the same agreement and presupposes it; it is only something required for properly carrying out the transaction in its details; a condition reasonably exacted in order to have the promised forgiveness in an orderly and profitable manner, and not with the intention of adding to the sum already laid down.

Thus the Sacrifice of the Mass cannot be considered to detract from the Sacrifice offered up "*once for all*" on Calvary, because the Sacrifice of the Mass rests upon it, derives all its value from it, and presupposes it; and yet the Mass is a true Sacrifice, because *Jesus Christ is truly offered up*, though in another form; and offered, not in the sense of adding new Merits, as if wanting to the first, but because it is a means appointed by the Eternal Father and the Incarnate Son, for *applying* the Merits of the first Sacrifice to the whole Church in general, and to each soul in particular.

To illustrate the same thing with another example, I will suppose that in a certain empire an orator, by a prodigy of eloquence, had obtained the freedom of a certain province; suppose, however, that the granting of that favour by the Emperor should be with this condition, that such freedom should be granted only to those inhabitants who were present at the recital of that oration by a deputy of the said orator. It is clear that this condition, far from being a disparagement to the original oration, would only tend to increase the honour of the orator and of his oration, by causing each inhabitant of that province to appreciate it more fully, and feel more deeply indebted to that orator.

The same may be said of the Holy Sacrifice of the Mass, for it gives an opportunity to each of us in particular :

1stly, To join our Lord, and the Priest in offering the Divine Victim present on our Altars to the Eternal Father ;

2ndly, To feel more deeply indebted to Christ by commemorating with a deep sense of gratitude and love the great sacrifice of Calvary ;

3rdly, To reap the fruit of that great Sacrifice by having it practically and personally applied to us. All these benefits, as is evident, redound entirely to the greater honour of Christ and of His great sacrifice on Mount Calvary.

The Mass no more detracts from Christ's Passion and Death, than the offering which Christ Himself made at His first entering into the World, or at His Presentation in the Temple, or at His Last Supper, or than Baptism or any other Sacrament does; for by all of them Christ applies to us the Merits of His Passion and Death.

In fact, Holy Mass is but one of the means left by our Saviour for applying His Merits to man. He Himself instituted Holy Mass when He said, "*Do this for a commemoration of Me.*" (S. Luke xxii. 19.)*

CHAPTER XIX.

Ceremonies and Ritual of the Catholic Church.

In the administration of the Sacraments and in the celebration of the Mass and other sacred services, the Church makes use of ceremonies ; that is, she employs

---

* See Appendix, No. 14, Method of hearing Mass.

CEREMONIES AND RITUAL OF THE CHURCH. 75

certain forms and rites for the purpose of administering the things of God in a becoming and dignified manner, and proper to impress the faithful with sentiments of faith and piety befitting the occasion.

Ceremonies do not form an essential part of the institution of Christ, most of them having been added by the Church in the time of the Apostles or in subsequent ages. Consequently they may, by the direction of authority, be changed or omitted (as in fact in cases of necessity they are omitted), without affecting the validity of the Sacraments. But as they are prescribed by the Church acting under the guidance of the Holy Spirit, in order the better to show forth the dignity and the effects of the Sacraments, and to dispose us to receive them in a more devout manner, it would be wrong to omit them, except in case of necessity.

That it is proper and dutiful, and therefore important, that Divine service and the administration of the Sacraments should be accompanied by ceremonies, may be gathered from the fact that not only the Latin Church, but also all the ancient Churches of the East, abound in ceremonies from a very remote period, and many of them traceable to Apostolic times. Thus the Greek, Armenian, Chaldean, Syro-Chaldean, and Eutychian Churches in the East have at all times used ceremonies as well as the Roman Catholic Church. Long experience testifies to the good effect which the use of ceremonies produces on the people.

If solemn ceremonies were not used in the celebration of the Mass, Catholic belief in the real presence of Christ upon our altars would not be fitly represented. If the faithful saw the altar stripped of ornaments, and the officiating Priests without distinctive vestments, not bending the knee, and not giving any outward token of worship before the consecrated elements, their

Catholic instinct would be shocked, and some of them would perhaps be tempted to say: "Surely the Priests themselves do not believe that Jesus is really present; for if they did, they would act very differently." On the other hand, when they see the great pains taken and the great cost often incurred for the becoming adornment of the house of God, for making the altar, the tabernacle, and the throne gleam with rich ornaments; when they see that the Priests and their assistants are robed with distinctive emblematic vestments, and especially when they see them bend the knee in humble adoration before the consecrated Host and the consecrated Chalice, their faith and devotion are strengthened, and the practical lesson they receive is likely to do them more good than any sermon on the subject.

What we say of the ceremonies of the Mass may be applied in due proportion to those also used in the administration of the Sacraments, and in all the services of the Church.

It is objected that there is danger that ceremonies may lead to mere *formality;* but I venture to say that the ceremonies used by the Roman Catholic Church, especially those used in the Holy Sacrifice of the Mass, far from leading people to *formality,* draw them on to greater *spirituality* and fervour.

Let us consider these externals, first, with regard to the officiating Priest, and afterwards with respect to the people.

The Mass generally consists of the following things:— The 42nd Psalm, beginning "*Judica me, Deus,*" Judge me, O Lord—the *Confiteor*—the *Introit,* or entrance prayer—the "*Kyrie Eleison,*" Lord have mercy— "*Christe Eleison,*" Christ, have mercy, repeated nine times—the "*Gloria in excelsis,*" or Glory to God in the highest—the *Collect*—the *Epistle* for the day—the prayer "*Munda cor meum*," or Cleanse my heart, O God—the *Gospel* for the day—the *Nicene Creed*—the *Offertory*—part of the 25th Psalm, beginning at the verse "*Lavabo*," that is, "I will wash"—*Oblation* prayer—the prayer called *Secret*—the *Preface*—the Sanctus, or Holy, Holy, Holy—the *Canon*, or prayers according to solemn unvarying rule—Consecration of the Host—Consecration of the wine—prayers after Consecration—the Lord's Prayer—*Agnus Dei*, Lamb of God— three prayers before Communion—Communion of the Priest—prayers after Communion—the blessing of the people—the last Gospel, most frequently from the first chapter of St. John, "In the beginning was the Word".

Now it is clear that all this is purely spiritual, and without any ceremonial formality, especially when we consider that the greatest part of this is said or done by the Priest in secret, that is, in a low tone of voice.

What is less important in the Mass, and what may strictly be called ceremonial, consists in the Priest changing his position; in his reverently bowing the head and genuflecting, that is, bending the knee; in kissing the Altar and paten, or silver plate on which the host is placed; in joining or in raising his hands; in looking up towards heaven, or to the crucifix on the Altar; in making repeatedly the sign of the Cross; and in turning towards the people when addressing them, as when he says, "*Dominus vobiscum*," (The Lord be with you) and "*Orate, fratres*," (Brethren, pray).

But men are struck at the reflection that nearly all these things Jesus did, and that, therefore, they cannot be called valueless formalities, unless indeed we were to say that the Priest does these things without the proper interior spirit, which would be an accusation our

Lord forbids us to make under pain of sin: "*Judge not, that you may not be judged*". (S. Matt. vii. 1.)

If we consider, now, the Mass with regard to the people present who assist at Mass, the more ground is there to convince us that no tendency to mere formality exists in the Mass, but that everything in it leads rather to spirituality.

First of all, in the Mass there is no set form of prayers to be repeated after the Priest in a formal way by the people, but the people are left free to follow the Mass in spirit, either meditating on the Passion of our Lord, or making some acts of repentance, love, praise, adoration, and like acts of devotion; or reciting some prayers, each in his own way, in keeping with his capacity, needs and desires; or following the Mass according to the direction of the book of devotion which each reader has chosen as adapted to his taste and devotional preference.

The different ceremonies, far from leading him to formality, serve to keep alive his attention and his devotion,

When in the beginning of the Mass the Priest bends his body and strikes his breast thrice saying the *Confiteor* or Confession, this calls him to make acts of contrition for his sins. The intoning of the *Gloria in excelsis* raises his soul to God. The chanting of the *Gospel* and *Creed* makes him stand up for the faith. The singing of the "*Sanctus*" invites him to join the choirs of the Angels in praising the sanctity of God. The uplifting of the Host and of the Chalice, and the repeated genuflections of the Priest, draw him to worship God on his knees; and so we may say of the rest. Every act tends to keep up the attention, the devotion, and the fervour of pious persons attending Mass.

The ceremonies, therefore, of the Mass, far from

inducing formality, are a good and powerful preservative against it.

But perhaps some may say: What need is there for holy water, for lighted candles in the day-time, and for such costly vestments? Why make so many changes of position, so much kneeling and standing? Why so much singing and playing of the organ and of other instruments? Why make so often the sign of the Cross? Why use incense?

I will endeavour to reply briefly to all these questions.

With regard to *holy water*, there is no *obligation* for the laity to use it; but the Church provides it and recommends all her children to use it. If S. John the Baptist, in his Baptism of penance, and our Lord in His Baptism of regeneration, have made use of the element of water to signify the purification of the soul, surely we cannot make objection if the Church at the threshold of the House of God or in the beginning of the Mass makes use of the same element to remind the people that they must follow after purity of soul by repentance if they would that their prayers should be answered by God.

The use of *holy water* is very ancient. S. Justin the Martyr, who lived in the second century, says in the second book of his Apology, that every Sunday in their assemblies the faithful were sprinkled with holy water.

As to *lighted candles* in the day-time, I would say that they are used chiefly as seemly emblematic ornament; and as such need not serve any other purpose. A lighted candle is an ornament most suited for the Altar, 1st, because exceedingly primitive and purely ecclesiastical, which many other ornaments are not; 2dly, because the light, the burning and self-consuming of the candle, can be taken as a beautiful emblem of our faith, which must be lively; of our charity, which must be burning and diffusive; of our devotion, which, [like that of Mary Magdalene, must not spare sacrifices.

As to *rich vestments,* Holy Church is glad to use them, when convenient, in Divine functions, because it redounds to the honour of God. If it is considered dutiful and honourable towards a prince that people should appear at his court in their best distinctive robes and ornaments, surely it cannot but be right that Priests, the Ambassadors and Ministers of God, should in public functions appear before the Altars of God in His sanctuary with their rich distinctive emblematic vestments. This was prescribed by God in the Old Law, though the Priests then made offerings of no intrinsic value, but only figurative ones. There is still more reason for the use of them now in the presence of the reality.

As to *bowing down the body,* and *bending the knee,* in sign of reverence, the Patriarchs and the Prophets, and even Jesus Christ Himself on earth also did the same repeatedly, and this S. John saw in a vision done by the twenty-four elders worshipping in heaven.

As to *music and singing,* it is what the Prophet David repeatedly recommends (see Psalms xcvii., cl.) And why shall we not make music as well as other things serve to the praises of God? Music, when good and properly adapted, gives expression, grandeur and solemnity to our sacred services, and to the offering of our praises to God. If sometimes it has not that effect upon some persons the cause is probably due to early prejudice or perhaps to the defect or absence of the musical sense, or when the music is not adapted to the words and to the religious feelings the subject should inspire; or, lastly, when the people do not attentively or intelligently follow the words and their respective musical expression.

As to the *sign of the Cross* (see Chap. XXXIV.), the Church makes frequent use of it, especially during the Mass, because it is the sign of our Redemption.

We cannot be reminded too often that we must be meek and patient and ready to suffer, because we profess to be followers of the Cross, that is, of our crucified Saviour. The Cross is a memorial of the sufferings and death of Christ. It speaks to us strongly of the malice and terrible consequences of sin, and of the immense love of God towards us.

The primitive Christians, as Tertullian and other ancient writers testify, were accustomed to make the sign of the Cross very often during the day.

Since, in this age, Christians make this sign less often, let us use it willingly, and rejoice to see it still frequently used, at least by the Priests in their priestly ministrations, to teach us not to be ashamed of the Cross of Christ, but to glory in it, as S. Paul gave us the example: "*But God forbid that I should glory, save in the Cross of our Lord Jesus Christ*". (Galatians, vi. 14.)

As to *incense*, it is a thing which the common sense of man has reserved to do honour to God with. Hence the wise Kings offered incense to the Child Jesus to honour His Divinity. In Leviticus (ii. 1) it was commanded that incense should be placed on the sacrifice called *mincha*. There was in the Temple of Solomon a special altar called the altar of incense, upon which, every day at a certain hour, incense was offered to God. (S. Luke i. 9-11.) Incense is a symbol of charity and of prayer. Holy David says: "*Let my prayer be directed as incense in Thy sight*" (Psalm cxl. 2); and S. John saw "*the four and twenty elders and the angels offering up to God odours and incense, which were the prayers of the saints"*. (Apocalypse or Revelation v. 8, viii. 4.)

Incense may also be taken to mean the fragrance of virtue, as also the inferior honour given to things which relate to God. In this sense the altar, the crucifix, the missal, the Priest, the assisting ministers, and the faithful themselves, are also incensed.

Some may object: How is all this consistent with those words of Christ to the Samaritan woman, "*But the hour cometh, and now is, when the true adorers shall adore the Father in spirit and in truth*"? (S. John iv. 23.)

Externals are perfectly consistent with these words of our Lord, for Christ by this expression did not exclude externals. The very words "adorer" and "adore" imply external action of the body.

The body is a part of man, created and redeemed by God; it owes, as well as the soul, and together with the soul, its tribute of worship to God.

When a ceremony, a genuflection for example, is made, and it is done not as a mere matter of form, but accompanied by, or as an expression of, the mind and heart, then it is a ceremony done in spirit and in truth, because it is then dictated by the spirit; it is an effect of the spirit, it is an outward expression of the spirit; and therefore it is a worship in spirit and in truth; the outward expression then corresponds to the inward feelings, and is a real worship and not a formal, hypocritical, or merely material action.

When our Saviour in the Garden of Gethsemane prostrated Himself with His face to the ground before His Eternal Father, He was truly adoring in spirit; and so likewise when He attended the sacrifices and other holy functions in the Temple.

We must not suppose that Christ's words to the Samaritan woman imply any slight of the Jewish rite as though only a formal, material worship. Can we suppose that the Patriarchs, that David, other Prophets, and all just men of the Old Law, were not adorers in spirit? Christ compares the new adorers with the Jews as they were then for the most part, not as they ought to have been, according to the spirit of the law. God has expressed strongly in Isaias (i. 11) and other places how in the Old Law He hated mere externals, and even prayer itself done without spirit and with a heart attached to sin. Therefore Christ by His words to the Samaritan woman would show that the true adorers of the New Law, who possess not mere emblems and figures, as the Jews had, but enjoy the advantage of having realities, will also be more careful to worship with a purer heart and with a purer intention, with better will, and more attention and spirit than the generality of the Jews did then.

Thus Catholic prayer-books are full of beautiful prayers to accompany every act of worship performed by the Priest at the Altar; and nothing is more recommended in Catholic Theology, Sermons, Catechisms, and books of devotion, than the necessity of assisting at Mass and other holy functions with a heart detached from sin, and with attention and fervour.

If then, outward demonstrations of veneration, faith, love, and zeal, when dictated by the inward spirit, are spirit and truth, it is all the better if a ritual should abound with externals, provided they spring from and are accompanied by the inward devotion of spirit?

Some Protestants might perhaps observe: What you say may be right, but this system puzzles me. I think that I should hardly feel myself at home in it.

I would answer—It is not astonishing, my friend, that

the Catholic system of worship should somewhat puzzle you as a Protestant. This system is new to you, and not very easily understood, and perhaps your mind has been prejudiced against it from childhood. But it would be unreasonable, on that account, for you to turn your back upon it with despondency or contempt. Would you act in this manner if a good business were offered to you, which at first you might find somewhat difficult to understand or conduct? Surely you would not act so, especially if you saw engaged in it happy little children well up to the work and quite at their ease. So if the Catholic worship appears at first sight strange or perplexing, be not disheartened; a little goodwill, a little instruction, a little explanation, a little study, and above all a little practice, will enable you to overcome every difficulty, and you will soon find yourself as much at home in it and enjoy it too as much as Catholics themselves.

Look at the Catholic children; they find it quite easy to follow the Mass, or Benediction; they understand well what seems so difficult to you; and you can easily understand it too, if you only condescend to be as they are, and allow yourself to be taught as they do.

CHAPTER XX.

BENEDICTION OF THE BLESSED SACRAMENT.

The real presence of Jesus Christ in the Blessed Sacrament by transubstantiation implies that Jesus Christ is present there so long as the *species* (appearance or natural accidents) of the bread or of the wine remain unaltered. And therefore the Blessed Sacrament, that is to say, *Jesus Christ* there present in the Blessed Sacrament, can and ought to be adored by the faithful.

This is what the Catholic Church teaches, and she provides that in most Churches, consecrated 'particles,' that is the Blessed Sacrament, be kept permanently (generally in the tabernacle on the Altar) : 1st, That It may be ready at any time to be administered to sick and dying persons; for, as the consecration of the Blessed Sacrament can only take place during Mass, which is celebrated only once a day by each Priest, and only in the morning, if the Blessed Sacrament were not reserved many Christians would die without the great advantage of then receiving this Sacrament, which when administered in the extremity of life is called *Viaticum*, or *food for the journey;* 2dly, In order to afford to the faithful the great consolation of *having Jesus Christ* always in the midst of them in the Tabernacle on the Altar, to receive their visits and prayers, and to dispense His graces.

Thus is literally fulfilled the Prophecy of Isaias that the Saviour was to be, and to be called, *Emmanuel*, that is, *God with us* (vii. 14). And also the promise of Jesus Christ Himself that He would not leave us orphans.

The Churches where the Blessed Sacrament is reserved, as is the case in all Parish Churches and in those of Religious Orders, are generally open ; some the whole day long, others some hours—morning and evening. Thus the faithful can all through the day visit the Blessed Sacrament, and pass some precious minutes in silent supplication before God, and in adoration of their Lord and Saviour Jesus Christ.

But to Kings of this world we are not satisfied to offer our homage in private, we also like occasionally to make a public demonstration of our allegiance and attachment to them. So besides this private and silent devotion of the faithful, the Church has provided special solemn rites to show forth our faith, giving us the opportunity of pouring out the innermost love of our hearts, and of expressing publicly our devotion towards our Lord God and King present in the Blessed Sacrament.

This she does by public processions, by the '*forty hours' exposition of the Blessed Sacrament,*' specially during Lent, and more frequently by the simple Rite called Benediction.

Benediction, as a rule, takes place in the afternoon or evening; less solemnly on week-days, more solemnly after Vespers and Sermon on Sundays and Festivals.

When the hour to give Benediction is come, all, or the greater part of the candles about the altar are lighted. This may seem strange to those who are not acquainted with the Catholic belief in the real presence of our Lord Jesus Christ in the Blessed Sacrament. If Jesus Christ were not present this display of pure wax candles might justly be looked upon as a mere show, a mere waste, and a profusion of lights to no purpose; but it will not appear so to those who enter into the spirit of the Catholic belief in the real presence of Jesus Christ in the Blessed Sacrament. Surely what we do for our Lord God and King, who is present, can never be too much. And as lighted candles and beautiful flowers are the most seemly ornaments for the Altar during divine worship, the faithful gladly bear the expense not heeding those who may say—"*Why this waste?*"

When the Altar is made ready and everything prepared, the officiating Priest, in his vestments, accompanied, if convenient, by other Priests, and preceded by servers and the censer-bearer in their surplices, comes to the Altar, at the foot of which all kneel. One of the Priests takes the Blessed Sacrament (or consecrated Host) out of the Tabernacle and reverently places It within the round crystal frame in the centre of the '*monstrance*,' which is made of gold or silver, finely wrought and often adorned with precious stones; and he thus exposes It on an elevated throne above the middle of the Altar, when the hymn beginning "*O Salutaris Hostia*"—"O Saving Host,"—is sung by the choir and people.

The clergy then profoundly adore the Blessed Sacrament, and the officiating Priest rising puts three times a small spoonful of incense (that is, sweet-smelling aromatic gum) into the burning censer or 'thurible,' and waving it thrice offers the ascending fragrance to God; as we read in the Apocalypse (or Revelation) of St. John, the Angels were seen to do in Heaven.

The Litany of Loreto commencing with invocations to each Person of the Blessed Trinity, is sung or other prayers recited after "*O Salutaris Hostia*," and then the "*Tantum ergo Sacramentum*," which hymn is never omitted; followed by a prayer said by the officiating Priest standing.

After the second offering of incense, a rich silk veil is placed upon the shoulders of the officiating Priest, who then ascends the Altar-steps, takes in his hands with the veil the monstrance which contains the Blessed Sacrament, previously taken down from the throne, and turning to the people, makes with It the sign of the cross over them, and thus blesses the faithful with the Most Holy.

This is done in silence, except that a small bell, and sometimes the tower bell of the Church, is sounded to call the attention not only of those who are in the Church, but also of those who are detained at home, that they all may prepare themselves kneeling to receive the blessing of God. Then the Blessed Sacrament is replaced in the Tabernacle, whilst the 116th Psalm, "*Laudate Dominum, omnes Gentes*"—"*O praise the Lord, all ye Nations*," is sung, and some concluding prayer is recited.

After another profound adoration by the clergy, the Blessed Sacrament is replaced in the Tabernacle, which is then locked. The Priests and servers then rise, make a genuflection, and return in order to the sacristy.

This is a most impressive rite, naturally connected with Catholic belief in the real presence. "Can there be a more touching rite, even in the judgment of those who do not believe in it? How many a man, not a Catholic, is moved, on seeing it, to say: 'Oh, that I did but believe it!' when he sees the Priest take up the Fount of Mercy, and the people bent low in adoration! It is one of the most beautiful, natural, and soothing actions of the Church."—"Cardinal Newman's Present Position of Catholics in England," ed. 4, p. 256.

Pious Ejaculation. } Blessed and praised every moment be the most holy and most divine Sacrament.

HYMNS AND PRAYERS COMMONLY SAID AT THE EXPOSITION AND BENEDICTION OF THE MOST HOLY SACRAMENT.

When the Priest opens the Tabernacle and incenses the Blessed Sacrament, is sung the Hymn,

O Salutáris Hostia,	O saving Victim, opening wide
Quae coeli pandis ostium :	The gate of Heaven to men below !
Bella premunt hostilia,	Our foes press in from every side ;

Da robur, fer auxilium.	Thine aid supply, Thy strength bestow.
Uni Trinoque Domino	To Thy great name be endless praise,
Sit sempiterna gloria,	Immortal Godhead, One in Three!
Qui vitam sine termino	Oh, grant us endless length of days
Nobis donet in patria.	In our true native land, with Thee.
Amen.	Amen.

After which generally follows the Litany of the Blessed Virgin, *and frequently also a prayer and, response. Then is sung the Hymn,* " Tantum ergo Sacramentum," *all present making a profound inclination of the body, while the words* " Veneremur cernui " *are being said.*

Tantum ergo Sacramentum Venerémur cernui; Et antiquum documentum	Down in adoration falling, Lo! the sacred Host we hail; Lo! o'er ancient forms departing,
Novo cedat ritui; Praestet fides supplementum Sensuum defectui.	Newer rites of grace prevail; Faith for all defects supplying Where the feeble senses fail.
Genitóri, Genitóque Laus et jubilatio,	To the everlasting Father, And the Son who reigns on high,
Salus, honor, virtus quoque	With the Holy Ghost proceeding
Sit et benedictio; Procedenti ab utroque Compar sit laudatio.	Forth from each eternally, Be salvation, honour, blessing, Might and endless Majesty.
Amen.	Amen.

Then are sung the following Versicle and Prayer:

V. Panem de Coelo praestitisti eis (Alleluia).
R. Omne delectamentum in se habentem (Alleluia).

V. Thou didst give them bread from Heaven (Alleluia).
R. Containing in itself all sweetness (Alleluia).

90 BENEDICTION OF THE BLESSED SACRAMENT.

Alleluia is said in Paschal time, and during the octave of Corpus Christi.

Orémus.	Let us Pray.
Deus qui nobis sub Sacraménto mirábili, passiónis tuae memoriam reliquisti ; tribue, quaésumus, ita nos córporis et sanguinis tui sacra mysteria venerári ; ut redemptionis tuae fructum in nobis júgiter sentiámus. Qui vivis. Amen.	O God, Who, under a wonderful Sacrament has left us a memorial of thy passion ; grant us, we beseech thee, so to venerate the sacred mysteries of thy body and blood, that we may ever feel within us the fruit of thy redemption, who livest, &c. Amen.

Here the Benediction is given with the Blessed Sacrament, all bowing down in prófound adoration and beseeching His blessing on themselves, and on the whole Church, and upon the world.

Then is often sung in Latin thrice, followed by the Laudate: Psalm 116.

Adorémus in aeternum Sanctissimum Sacramentum.	May we for ever adore The most Holy Sacrament.

*An Act of Spiritual Communion.**

I believe in thee, O my Jesus, present in the most holy sacrament of the Altar ; I love thee above all things ; and I desire to receive thee into my soul. Since I cannot now receive Thee *sacramentally*, come at least *spiritually* into my heart. I embrace thee, and I unite myself to thee as if thou wert already within my heart. O, never let me be separated from

---

* I would, with Saint Alphonsus, exhort all who seek to advance in the love of Jesus Christ to make a *spiritual communion* each time they visit the Blessed Sacrament or hear Mass. It would be better to make a spiritual communion three times on these occasions ; namely, at the beginning, middle, and end of the visit, and of the Mass.

thee! O Lord Jesus Christ, let the sweet and consuming force of thy love absorb my whole soul, that I may die for the love of thee, who wast pleased to die upon the Cross for the love of me.

CHAPTER XXI.

CONFIRMATION.

Besides Baptism, Holy Eucharist and Penance, the Catholic Church holds four other sacred Rites as Sacraments, namely, Confirmation, Extreme Unction, Holy Orders, and Matrimony.

Confirmation is a Sacrament instituted by our Lord, by which the faithful, who have already been made children of God by Baptism, receive the Holy Ghost by the prayer, unction, or anointing with holy oil called *Chrism*, and the laying on of the hands of a Bishop, the successor of the Apostles. It is thus that they are enriched with gifts, graces, and virtues, especially with the virtue of fortitude, and made perfect Christians and valiant soldiers of Jesus Christ, to stand through life the whole warfare of the world, the flesh, and the devil.

The first instance of Confirmation being administered to the faithful is recorded in the eighth chapter of the Acts of the Apostles, where S. Peter and S. John confirmed the Samaritans who had already been baptised by S. Philip. "*They prayed for them that they might receive the Holy Ghost. . . . Then they laid their hands upon them, and they received the Holy Ghost.*" (vers. 15, 17).

By this Sacrament a certain dedication and consecration of the soul to God is made; the *mark* of which is left for ever on the soul. This mark is called a *character*, and can never be effaced. Hence this Sacrament can only be received once.

All Christians are bound to receive Confirmation. The want of opportunity only can excuse from sin for not receiving it.

It must be received in a state of grace; and therefore if a Christian is conscious that he is in a state of mortal sin, he must first come to the Sacrament of Penance.

The time to receive Confirmation is from about seven years to any older age. "All must make haste to be confirmed by a Bishop; that is, to receive the sevenfold *grace of the Holy Ghost*" (S. Clement, Epistola ad Julium).

CHAPTER XXII.

Extreme Unction.

The Sacrament of Extreme Unction consists in the anointing, by the Priest, of those in danger of death by sickness, with holy oil, accompanied with prayer. It is called *Extreme*, because administered to sick persons towards the close of life.

It is a true Sacrament, because it possesses all the requisites for a Sacrament. 1st, It has the outward sign, which consists in the anointing with a little oil the seat of the senses, as the lips, the eyes, the ears, the hands, and the feet, accompanied by special prayers. 2nd, It has the promise of grace, as recorded by the Apostle S. James: "*Is any man sick among you? Let him bring in the Priests of the Church; and let them pray over him, anointing him with oil in the name of the Lord. And the prayer of faith shall save the sick man; and the Lord shall raise him up; and if he be in sins, they shall be forgiven him"* (v. 14, 15). 3rd, That it has been instituted by Christ is gathered from this, that none but God can give to an outward rite the power of forgiving sins, and of imparting inward grace.

This Sacrament can be received several times during life, but only once in the same dangerous illness.

Christians should not be negligent and postpone to the last moment of life the reception of this Sacrament, for there is a danger of dying without it, and thus they would be deprived of special graces, and of a more thorough purification of the soul, which would have rendered them better prepared for death and more fit to meet their Judge.

A slight danger, or as St. Alphonsus Liguori expresses it, "a danger of danger," that the illness might become serious may justify the reception of this Sacrament.

By postponing, one may also lose the blessing of recovery. For, as experience confirms, when God sees it to be good, Extreme Unction, besides purifying the soul, gives health to the body. *"The prayer of faith shall save the sick man, and the Lord shall raise him up"* (S. James, v. 15).

CHAPTER XXIII.

HOLY ORDER.

For carrying on Divine worship, ruling the Church, and administering the Sacraments, a Priesthood is required, and it belongs to God alone to institute the Priesthood.

In the Old Law, God chose and raised to the Priesthood Aaron, his children and their descendants, and they were to be assisted in their priestly functions by the members of the tribe of Levi; and thus the Priesthood was transmitted to posterity simply by family descent. In the New Law the means instituted by Christ for the transmission of the Priesthood was not by limiting it to one family or tribe, but by having the Sacrament of Holy Order conferred on those Christians whom the Apostles and their Successors should see fit to choose among the baptised that are willing, and should ordain for that dignity and office.

Holy Order, then, is a Sacrament by which Bishops, Priests, and other Ministers of the Church are ordained, and receive power and grace to perform their sacred duties.

The Sacramental character of Holy Order is manifest in Holy Scripture. S. Paul, in his Epistles to S. Timothy, says: "*Neglect not the grace that is in thee, which was given thee by prophecy, with imposition of the hands of the Priesthood.*" (1 S. Timothy iv. 14.) "*I admonish thee that thou stir up the grace of God which is in thee by the imposition of my hands.*" (2 S. Timothy i. 6.)

Here we have all the essentials of a Sacrament,—the outward sign—the inward grace annexed—and divine appointment; for, as we have before said, God alone can make outward signs to be means of grace.

CHAPTER XXIV.

HOLY MATRIMONY.

Marriage, also called Matrimony, is the conjugal union of man and woman who are naturally and legally fit to marry.

HOLY MATRIMONY. 95

It was raised by Christ to the dignity of a Sacrament, and is a bond only to be dissolved by death.

The marriage state is charged with many responsibilities, and has many difficulties to meet, many duties to fulfil, many burdens to bear, many temptations to overcome, and many offices to discharge.

Jesus Christ, in raising Christian marriage to a higher order, to a supernatural dignity, imposed stricter and nobler duties on the married couple. They were to be subject one to another in the fear of Christ, and the women "*subject to their husbands as to the Lord*". (Ephesians v. 22.) They were to love, nourish, and cherish each other, as Christ loved the Church (ver. 25), and to train up their children in the fear of God. "*Provoke not your children to anger: but bring them up in the discipline and correction of the Lord*" (vi. 4).

It is therefore clear that for the marriage state there is needed not merely an ordinary, but a very great and special grace, such as is received in a Sacrament.

Jesus Christ ennobled and blessed marriage by assisting personally at the nuptials of Cana in Galilee: He sanctioned the marriage bond with those sacred and plain words: "*What therefore God hath joined together, let not man put asunder*" (S. Mark x. 9), and raised it to the dignity of a Sacrament of the New Law.

S. Paul, in fact, calls it not only a Sacrament, but a "*great Sacrament*," because it is a Sacrament in a twofold manner; firstly, in the ordinary sense of a Sacrament of the New Law, being an outward sign of a holy and indissoluble union fortified by grace; secondly, because marriage itself, when lawful, is a mystical sign and an emblem of Christ's union with the Church: "*This is a great Sacrament*," he says: "*but I speak in Christ and in the Church.*" (Ephesians v. 32.)

Hence S. Cyril says: "Christ sanctified wedlock, and

gave grace to marriage ". (Cap. ii. in Johannem xxii.) Tertullian, S. Irenæus, S. Augustine, and S. Ambrose style marriage a Sacrament. The Nestorians, Copts, Armenians, and Greeks, though separated from the Catholic Church, are unanimous in recognising marriage as a Sacrament; agreeing in this with the Roman Catholic Church, which has always regarded marriage as a Sacrament of the New Law.

It is the teaching of the Church that legitimate matrimony between baptized people can never be a mere contract, but is always also a Sacrament. Though not defined as a point of faith, it is more generally held that the ministers of this Sacrament are the contracting parties themselves, when by word or outward signs they mutually accept each other as husband and wife.

In those parts of the world where the Decrees of the Council of Trent respecting Matrimony have not yet been promulgated (as in England), the presence of the Parish Priest is not essential for the validity of the Sacrament; but in those parts where the Council of Trent is officially published his presence is required to render the contract valid as well as lawful in the eyes of the Church.

The words which the Priest pronounces upon the contracting parties—"I join you together in matrimony, in the name of the Father, and of the Son, and of the Holy Ghost," are only intended to acknowledge and solemnly ratify the sacred engagement just effected by the contracting parties. The other prayers which he recites afterwards serve to implore more abundant blessings upon the couple just married.

Hence it follows that both parties ought to be in a state of grace when they contract the Sacrament of marriage, for two reasons, 1st, because they themselves administer, and 2ndly, because they receive that Sacrament.

As the union of Christ with the Church cannot be broken, so the bond between husband and wife is indissoluble. There is no cause that can justify, or power upon earth that can authorise the breaking of a legal and true marriage-bond between Christians after the marriage has been consummated.

Separation even is forbidden; and if, for grave reasons, it is sometimes permitted to the innocent party to live separately, this separation would only improperly be called divorce, as in such case the marriage-bond is not broken, and neither party can marry again during the known lifetime of the other; if ever, therefore, the word divorce is used, this word is understood to mean only *a separation from bed and board;* but *divorce*, properly and strictly so called, in the sense that a divorced person may re-marry during the lifetime of his or her respective partner, is forbidden by the law of God: and there is no reason that can justify, or authority on earth that can sanction it.

This has been the teaching of the Catholic Church in all ages, as proved from passages of the Fathers and Doctors of the Church.

For the first five centuries the indissoluble nature of marriage is testified by Hermas, Justin, Athenagoras, Tertullian, S. Leo of Alexandria, Origen, S. Basil, S. Ephrem, S. Chrysostom, S. Cyprian, Lactantius, S. Hilary, S. Jerome, and S. Augustine.

Jesus Christ was too explicit on this point to allow of being misunderstood. His words are as follows: "*Every one that putteth away his wife, and marrieth another, committeth adultery: and he that marrieth her that is put away from her husband committeth adultery.*" (S. Luke xvi. 18.) S. Paul teaches that nothing but death can dissolve the marriage-bond. "*To them that are married,*" he says: "*not I, but the Lord commandeth, that the wife depart not from her husband. And if she depart, that she remain* UNMARRIED, *or be reconciled to her husband. And let not the husband put away his wife.*" (1 Corinthians vii. 10, 11.)

The impression that the Church or the Pope has occasionally sanctioned divorce or the breaking of the marriage-bond, allowing one or both of the parties to re-marry during the lifetime of the other, is a mistake and without foundation.

It should be noticed that there are some cases which render a marriage invalid and null, as for example, default of consent, close affinity, illegality of contract, defect of age, and other invalidating causes.

In these cases the Church can, after inquiring into the matter, declare the marriage to have been null and void from the beginning; and this has been done, and may be done again. Strictly speaking, however, this is not dissolving an existing marriage, but in reality only declaring that a marriage never existed between certain parties, on account of some impediment which made the contract void. But a valid marriage completed between baptized people can in no case be lawfully dissolved. God has joined them together, and that sacred bond no one, not even a Pope, can rend asunder.

Society in general, and Catholics especially, ought to be most thankful to Jesus Christ for having established this inviolable sanctity of marriage, by which numberless scandals, and family strifes, and miseries, are prevented, family happiness more universally secured, and the weaker sex and children are greatly protected.

If in some particular case this law may happen to be burdensome, especially to persons who have not been wanting either in prudence in the choice they made, or in justice and kindness towards their partners, this hardship to the few is small compared with the immense good derived from it by society at large.

The sufferer must not on account of his special grief revolt against God, but bear patiently this like any other misfortune, and adore the general dispensation of the Creator and Lord of Nature.

CHAPTER XXV.

Only One true Church.

"*Come, and I will shew thee the bride, the wife of the Lamb.*" (Apocalypse [Rev.] xxi. 9.)

In the Old Law, only in the Temple of Jerusalem could sacrifices be offered to God. That was a figure of the Church of Christ, that is, of that special body of Christians which Christ recognises as His own, and to which it is necessary to belong in order to be acceptable to God, as a member of the mystical body of Christ.

The Church of Christ on earth is that permanent, visible, Society of Christians which forms one body with that which Christ, whilst on earth, principally founded on S. Peter, and also on the other Apostles, who were, as a ruling body, to continue in their lawful successors to rule the same until the end of the world. This ruling body in the Church Jesus Christ established with the intention of providing, through them, all men with the proper means to obtain eternal salvation.

As there is but *one* God, *one* Baptism, *one* Truth, *one* Faith, *one* Fold, *one* Shepherd, *one* Way, so there can be but *one* true Church of God on earth, the *Spouse*, as S. Paul and S. John call her, of Jesus Christ.

This Church is the Catholic Church, under the government of S. Peter's Successor, the Bishop of Rome; because this Church alone possesses, enjoys, and shows forth all the *four marks* of God's true Church, as pointed out in Scripture, and declared in the Nicene Creed in the words: "*I believe One, Holy, Catholic, and Apostolic Church.*"

CHAPTER XXVI.

First Mark—Oneness of Faith, of Worship, and of Sacraments.

The true Church of Christ must not be a mere medley of disconnected parts, but the parts must be so well connected together as to form a whole, like different members forming a compact body, and this we understand when we say that the true Church must be *one* (Ephesians iv. 16).

Protestants hold and proclaim as a right for all, the *private* interpretation of the Bible. This principle, *if it were from God*, should make them all agree in what they believe and teach; but they are divided by this principle into hundreds of denominations, opposed in various points of belief one to the other.*

Catholics, however, *are all united in one body*, holding one faith everywhere the same; in having the same Sacraments and Sacrifice, and all submitting to the same one, visible, universal chief Pastor.

Catholics all agree in acknowledging *Jesus Christ* to be their only Redeemer, and in believing all that Jesus Christ taught and continues to teach by His Church,

* See Appendix, Nos. 21, 22, 23, Statistics of Protestant Sects.

especially whenever that Church declares and defines any doctrine of faith or of morals; so that every one can know exactly what he must believe, and what he must do in order to be saved.

They also share in a common sympathy, and are in perfect communion with one another all over the world.

They share one with another their prayers, and all good works. They communicate also in worship; for Catholics admit everywhere their fellow-Catholics to the participation of the Sacraments; in the case of Priests, they are allowed by the local Bishops and by their fellow-Priests to celebrate Holy Mass in their Churches in every land. But above all, Catholics are united under the guidance of the same one visible chief Pastor, the Bishop of Rome, the lawful successor of S. Peter, to whom Jesus Christ committed the care of His whole flock, as may be seen in the following chapter on the Supremacy of the Roman Pontiff.

CHAPTER XXVII.

The Supremacy of the Bishop of Rome.

This supremacy or chief authority does not mean that the Pope has a higher degree of Priesthood than other Bishops. Of the various degrees of Priesthood, that of Bishop being the highest, the Pope is, in that respect, no higher than any other lawfully ordained Bishop. But, by the Pope's supremacy is meant that, as among the Bishops there is a difference in authority and jurisdiction, some being Bishops, others Archbishops, others Primates, and others Patriarchs, so the Bishop of Rome is, in authority and jurisdiction, above all Bishops, as well as above all the faithful of the universal Church on earth.

It is essential to the constitution of the Church that one of her Bishops should be recognised supreme in authority, otherwise it would be impossible to stay threatening abuses which local Bishops might be unwilling or unable to correct; to apply a remedy if a Bishop of any Diocese has become perverted in faith or morals; to settle matters in dispute which might arise between Bishop and Bishop, or between Bishops and laymen. Without this supreme authority there would not be union or sympathy between one part of Christendom and the other;—to assemble General Councils would be almost impossible; to found new Bishoprics, to fill up vacant Sees, and to transfer a Bishop from one See to another, would naturally fall into the hands of lay persons, or at least be dependent on them; and the sending of Missionaries to remote countries would either not be attended to, or done in a lax, irregular, and inefficient manner.

Besides, if such supreme spiritual authority did not exist, there would be instead of one Church many Churches opposed one to another, some of them being kept together only in an unreal union by temporal power. It could not in that case be said that the Church of Christ is one, nor could she then be compared to a human body with many members and one visible *head;* nor could she be called a *Kingdom,* unless a Kingdom divided against itself, and a Kingdom without a King.

Suppose, for example, that one of the British Colonies were to withdraw itself from the jurisdiction of the British Crown: from that time, even though the inhabitants were of British race, tongue, and customs, and had similar laws, that colony would evidently cease to form part of the British Empire. In like manner any part of Catholicity withdrawing itself in spiritual matters from the supreme centre of ecclesiastical authority, would from that time cease to be part of the heaven-born Kingdom of the Catholic Church. Such a community of Christians would become independent, or denominational, or national; but a living branch or part of the one visible Catholic body it could not be.

It being essential, then, that one of the Bishops should preside over the visible Church of God on earth, which of all the Bishops in the world should we naturally think ought to be invested with that supremacy? Should it be the Bishop of Jerusalem, of Antioch, of Constantinople, of Alexandria, of Paris, of London, or of Rome?

S. Peter, as appears from the first twelve chapters of the Acts of the Apostles, exercised, at the beginning of Christianity, a supremacy over the other Apostles and over the whole Church; it therefore seems just that the See permanently chosen by S. Peter, and in which he died, should be regarded as enjoying that privilege. Now, it is a well attested fact, as is proved by history and monumental evidence, that the permanent See chosen by S. Peter was Rome, then the Capital of the Roman Empire, and that there he suffered martyrdom by being fastened to a cross with his head towards the earth at his earnest entreaty, deeming himself unworthy to suffer crucifixion in the same manner as his divine Master.*

The Bishops of Rome, in fact, always claimed and still claim that supremacy, and no other Bishop in the world claims it, or ever did claim it.

---

* For proofs that S. Peter was in Rome as First Bishop, see Appendix, No. 36.

Some have indeed pretended to see an exception in Pope S. Gregory the Great, because in his Letter (iv. 20) to John the Patriarch of Constantinople, he rejects the title of *universal* Bishop. We must observe, however, that though S. Gregory repudiated that title and was satisfied, like other Popes, with the title of Bishop of Rome, he did not, however, reject the supremacy of jurisdiction, but asserted it in plain words for himself, as other Popes had done, and he asserted it in that very Letter: for, speaking in it of the See of Constantinople, he says: "Who doubts that it is subject to the Apostolic See?" and again, he says, "When Bishops commit a fault, I know not what Bishop is not subject to it" (that is, to the See of Rome). S. Gregory moreover repeatedly exercised the supremacy. Let it suffice here to mention what we read in the instruction he gave to the Benedictine Monk, S. Augustine (or Austin, as he is often called), when he sent him to England, in which instruction he says: "*We give you no jurisdiction over the Bishops of Gaul. . . . but we commit to your care all the Bishops of Britain.*" (History of Venerable Bede, i. 27.) No Pope has exercised universal jurisdiction over every country in Christendom more than S. Gregory, justly styled the Great.

In all ages the Bishop of Rome has been regarded by all Bishops, Kings, and Nations that were Catholic, as the successor of St. Peter, and as the supreme ruler and administrator of the Catholic Church; and whenever any one rejected the Pope's Supremacy, from that moment he was not regarded as a Catholic.

The very names of Romanist, Papist, and Ultramontane, so freely given to Catholics by those outside the Church, show that they see that the essential feature in Catholicism is, that Catholics, although belonging to different nations, yet form one compact body with their common centre of authority in Rome. They see that it is this that makes Catholics what they really are, *one Fold, one Body, one Kingdom* in spiritual matters, *one Church*. They can see that, in default of this supremacy, Catholics would cease to be Catholics, and would be throughout the world like stray sheep at the mercy of any who might take advantage of their division.

Protestants for the most part are under the impression that this supreme authority of the See of Rome is a usurpation, that it did not exist originally, but was introduced in course of time.

History proves, however, that the Pope's Supremacy was as firmly believed by Catholics in the first ages of Christianity as in those that followed. So far from there being any difference on this head, the fact is, that whilst in later ages the supremacy of the Pope has been denied by the schismatical Churches of the East, and by Protestant communities which have separated themselves from the Catholic Church, for the first seven hundred years the whole of Christendom united in believing and proclaiming the supremacy of the Roman See.

The Fathers of the Primitive Church had no doubt whatever that the Roman Pontiff was, by God's appointment, the Supreme Pastor of "sheep" and "lambs"; that is, as interpreted by the Fathers of the Church, of the whole flock of Christ, and the source of all spiritual jurisdiction. To reject this truth was, in their judgment, to ruin the whole fabric of the Church; to deny His Vicar was to deny Christ. No one ever pretended to create this majestic office, the divine institution of it was always taken for granted. The Councils did not invent it, but bore witness to it as older than themselves.

"The Roman Church always had the Primacy," said

the Fathers of Nicæa in the year of our Lord 325. This was the confession of the first Œcumenical Council.*

* Though these words are not to be found in the exemplars now extant of the Acts of the Council of Nicæa, there is no doubt that they did exist, at least in some copies of those Acts at the time of the Chalcedonian Council (451), for in the Acts of the 16th Session of this Council it is stated that the Roman Legate, the Bishop Paschasinus, read before that general Assembly the VI. Canon of the Council of Nicæa, beginning with these words, "The Roman See always had the Primacy".

It cannot be reasonably supposed that Pope S. Leo the Great would have entrusted forged exemplars to his Legates, or that Bishop Paschasinus would have dared to read a forged copy of the Acts of the Nicene Council before such an assembly over which he presided ; much less could it have been possible to do so without provoking some contradiction on the part of the Fathers. Yet ecclesiastical historians and theologians agree in stating that when the Roman Legate Paschasinus read the said passage, no one contradicted. See *Labbe*, Act I., Col. 93, tom. IV. *Bellarmine de Rom. Pontif.*, Book II., Chap. 13. Hefele in his recent *Concilien Geshicte*, Vol. I., page 384. Cardinal Orsi *Eccles. History*, Book XXXIII., No. 79.

Of two writers who lately ventured to state that the Fathers of the Council of Chalcedon repudiated the assertion, one did so without producing any authority, the other grounded himself wrongfully on Fleury ; I say wrongfully because the reference given does not even allude to the matter in question, and where Monsignor Claude Fleury gives an account of the transactions of the Council of Chalcedon he asserts quite the contrary ; here are his words : "Paschasinus read the VI. Canon of Nicæa beginning with these words : The Church of Rome always had the Primacy, which are not in the Greek, and notwithstanding in this particular no objection was raised". *Ecclesiastical History* of Monsignor Claude Fleury, Vol. IV., Book 28, No. XXX.

I think it important to notice here that as it was the custom in that age for each Bishop who wished it to have his own notary to write down the transactions of a Council, it should not surprise that differences occurred in various reports of the Acts ; and it should not also be forgotten that a positive assertion has a great deal more weight than mere silence.

THE SUPREMACY OF THE BISHOP OF ROME. 107

Twenty-two years later the great Council of Sardica, in 347, wrote to Pope JULIUS I., that it was "most fitting that the Bishops of the LORD make reference from all the Provinces *to the head, that is, the See of the Apostle Peter*".

The Council of Chalcedon, in 451, not only deposed Dioscorus in obedience to Pope S. LEO I., called "the Great," whom the Fathers inscribed as "the most blessed Apostle PETER, who is the rock and ground of the Catholic Church," but did so because Dioscorus had "dared to hold a Council without the authority of the Apostolic See". And this Council of Chalcedon was notably an Eastern Council. More than 600 Bishops attended it from the East, and only two Pope's Legates were from the West; yet in their Synodical letter the Council called the Roman Pontiff: "The interpreter to all of the voice of the blessed Peter". They say that he is entrusted by the SAVIOUR with the guardianship of the "Vineyard," and they humbly solicit him to confirm their Conciliar acts by his "supreme authority". All the Councils, one after another, say the same thing, and they all ground the doctrine which they all attest, upon the words of our divine LORD.

Many Protestants, following the "Book of Homilies," say that they accept the first six Councils. Should they, however, accept only the first four General Councils, they must accept the doctrine of the Supremacy of the Bishop of Rome, for to the Fathers of Ephesus and Chalcedon the opinion of those who denied the Primacy or Supremacy of the Pope would have seemed a detestable impiety, a denial of the Gospel, and a subversion of the Church of CHRIST.

The ancient Fathers agree with the early Councils in proclaiming the supremacy of the Bishop of Rome.

S. CYPRIAN (who died in the year of our Lord 258) says that the Pope is the only "fount of spiritual jurisdiction;" and S. MAXIMUS (who died 335), that "whoever anathematizes the Roman See, anathematizes the Catholic Church": and S. AMBROSE (397), "where Peter is there is the Church;" and S. INNOCENT I. (417), that "the very Episcopate and all the authority of this title sprung from the Apostolic See"; and S. JEROME (420), "whoso gathereth not with thee scattereth"; and S. AUGUSTINE (430), that "the See of Peter is the Rock against which the proud gates of hell prevail not".

That great Father, S. IRENAEUS, who flourished only a little more than a hundred years after the death of Christ, and had seen some of those who had seen our Lord, tells us expressly, "that all Churches and all the faithful of CHRIST are bound to agree with the Roman Church on account of her superior principality". (Against Heresies, book iii. chap. 7.)

The Roman See is the supreme Tribunal before which the saints have always pleaded. S. Cyprian (who died in the year 258) told Antonianus that "to be united with the See of Rome is to be united to the Catholic Church". S. Dionysius of Alexandria (271), accused of heresy, implores Pope DIONYSIUS I. to examine and judge his faith. S. Peter of Alexandria (312) has recourse to Pope DAMASUS I. S. Athanasius (373), driven from his See, appeals to the Roman Pontiff JULIUS I. S. Augustine (402) accepts the judgment of Innocent I. as that of Heaven. S. Cyril of Alexandria (444) wrote a letter to Pope CELESTINE I., praying him to judge the heresy of Nestorius. Everywhere the Roman Pontiff, whether a Victor, a Dionysius, a Damasus, an Innocent, or a Gregory, claims the same supreme authority, and everywhere the Saints confess with acclamation that he derives it from God.

In all these instances the cases submitted to the judgment of the Holy See were carefully investigated and judicially discussed, and ample justice was done to the contending parties. Ecclesiastical history is full of similar appeals, when the adverse parties manifested the most perfect acquiescence in the authority and equity of the judge.

Every part of Christendom bears witness, from the earliest ages, that the Church is built on PETER. A dispute having arisen in the Church of Corinth as to who should be regarded as the legitimate Pastor, the Corinthians did not apply to some Apostle then living, not even to S. John in Ephesus, but applied to Rome, to S. Clement, the third Successor of St. Peter. The Christian historian Socrates relates, that at one and the same time the Bishops of CONSTANTINOPLE, GAZA, ANCYRA, and ADRIANOPLE, driven from their Sees, commit their cause to Pope JULIUS. The Council of Antioch adopts the words of Juvenal, Bishop of Jerusalem, that "it is an Apostolic tradition that the Church of Antioch should be directed and judged by the Church of Rome". Churches in places the most distant from the Roman See proclaim the same truth as loudly as those which are situated nearer to it.

In 740 S. Boniface, the Englishman, and the seven English Suffragans in Germany, wrote to the English King and to Cuthbert, Archbishop of Canterbury, telling them what they had recently done in Synod.

"We declared," they say, "that we would preserve the Catholic faith, and unity and subjection to the Roman Church, to the end of our life; that we would be subject to S. Peter and his Vicar; that the Metropolitans should in all things strive to follow canonically the precepts of S. Peter, in order that they may be numbered among the sheep entrusted to his care; and this confession we all consented to, and subscribed, and sent to the body of S. Peter, the Prince of the Apostles."

About this time, it appears, the Pope made Lichfield into a Metropolitan See, detaching it, together with other Bishoprics, from the Metropolitan See of Canterbury. About fifty years later, the King of Mercia wrote a suppliant letter to the Pope then reigning, in his own name and in that of the Bishops and Dukes of England, saying: "No one presumes to gainsay your Apostolic authority"; but praying that Lichfield might again be subjected as a Suffragan to the See of Canterbury. Pope Leo III., "by his Apostolic authority," granted their petition, and restored Lichfield to be Suffragan to the See of Canterbury.

At the Council of Arles, held in 314, the British Bishops of LONDON, YORK, and LINCOLN, confessed, in the name of all their colleagues, the supreme rights and prerogatives of the Holy See.

When England had subdued Wales, and the Bishop of S. DAVID'S was summoned to do homage to the See of Canterbury, he replied that the British Bishops had never recognised any superior "except the Holy See". The Church of Scotland gave a similar answer to the Archbishop of YORK, when he claimed jurisdiction over it, and "the answer was approved," as Lingard observes, "by Pope CLEMENT III." These are only a few examples out of many that could be brought forward.

This office of the Roman Pontiff was given to him, not by men, but by GOD. It is God's provision, God's creation, "for the preservation of unity," as S. Thomas Aquinas remarks. It was not conferred on the Roman Pontiff by the Church; it comes directly from God.

It is inherited directly from S. Peter, to whom it was given by CHRIST.

This supreme authority was given to S. Peter under three most remarkable similitudes.

Christ compares the Church He is about to establish to a *building*, and makes S. Peter, after Himself, the foundation of it: "*Thou art Peter; and upon this rock I will build My Church, and the gates of hell shall not prevail against it.*" (S. Matthew xvi. 18.)* It is the

---

* "*Thou art Peter*, &c. As S. Peter, by divine revelation, here made a solemn profession of his faith of the divinity of Christ; so in recompense of this faith and profession, our Lord here declares to him the dignity to which He is pleased to raise him: *viz.*, that he, to whom He had already given the name of *Peter*, signifying a *rock* (S. John i. 42), should be a *rock* indeed, of invincible strength, for the support of the building of the Church; in which building he should be, next to Christ himself, the chief foundation stone, in quality of chief pastor, ruler, and governor; and should have accordingly all fulness of ecclesiastical power, signified by the keys of the kingdom of heaven. *Upon this rock*, &c. The words of Christ to *Peter*, spoken in the vulgar language of the *Jews*, which our Lord made use of, were the same as if He had said in *English: Thou art a rock, and upon this rock I will build My Church.* So that, by the plain course of the words, *Peter* is here declared to be the rock upon which the Church was to be built: Christ himself being both the principal foundation and founder of the same. Where also note, that Christ, by building His house, that is, His Church, upon a rock, has thereby secured it against all storms and floods, like the wise builder (S. Matthew vii. 24, 25). *The gates of hell*, &c. That is, the powers of darkness, and whatever Satan can do, either by himself or his agents. For as the Church is here likened to a house, or fortress, built on a rock, so the adverse powers are likened to a contrary house or fortress, the gates of which, *i.e.*, the whole strength, and all the efforts it can make, will never be able to prevail over the City or Church of Christ. By this promise we are fully assured, that neither idolatry, heresy, nor any pernicious error whatsoever shall at any time prevail over the Church of Christ."— *Footnote in Douay Bible on this passage.*

foundation which upholds and keeps a building solid; and in a body of men it is clearly the ruling authority which performs the same office.

Again, our Lord compares His Church to a *Town* or *Kingdom*, the keys of which He places in the hands of S. Peter, making him the master of it: "*And I will give to thee the keys of the Kingdom of Heaven*". S. Matt. xvi. 19.) This expresses in a forcible way the idea of chief authority, as it does also in Isaias, referring to the Messiah: "*I will lay the key of the house of David upon his shoulder, and he shall open, and none shall shut: and he shall shut, and none shall open*" (xxii. 22).

Thirdly, our Lord compares His Church to a *Sheepfold*, and makes S. Peter head-shepherd of it: "*Simon, son of John, lovest thou Me more than these? . . . Feed my lambs; . . . Feed my lambs. . . . Feed my sheep.*" (S. John xxi. 15, 17.)

These three comparisons all go to prove that our Lord conferred a supreme authority on S. Peter, whom He made the centre of unity, the ruler, and leader of His Kingdom, then about to be established upon earth.

Besides these passages, in which our Lord gives to S. Peter supreme authority under these striking comparisons, we find one in which Jesus Christ, having assured S. Peter that He had prayed for him, that his faith should *not fail*, in the plainest language entrusted to him this commission: "*Confirm thy brethren*". This was given at a most solemn moment, just when the bitter Passion of our Lord was about to commence. (S. Luke xxii. 32.)

These passages prove that our Lord Jesus Christ established S. Peter, and in the person of S. Peter, his legitimate Successors, as the chief Pastors of His Church upon earth. For it cannot be supposed that at the death of S. Peter the Church was to remain without its visible head-pastor, without its foundation.; therefore as S. Peter was to die, and the Church was to last to the end of the world, so the authority which Jesus Christ established for the purpose of keeping the whole Church together, like a compact body, was, of necessity, and according to Christ's will, to be transmitted to S. Peter's legitimate Successors, and was to last as long as the Church itself lasted.*

No one, then, should seek a pretext for denying this supremacy, essential to the Church, clearly instituted by Christ, and plainly intended for the good of the faithful. If the Pope's authority is great, the good derived from it to the Church is still greater. If this office is gigantic and seemingly beyond human power, the experience of eighteen centuries proves that it is practicable with the promised and never-failing assistance of God.

In the old law there was only one Supreme Pontiff or High Priest for the whole Jewish people, though the Jews in vast numbers were scattered over the world. We should not wonder therefore, that, in the new Dispensation, Christ should have established one, and only *one*, supreme Administrator of His Household on earth, that it might always be *one*, as He Himself is one. We should not wonder that He should have prepared a rock as the foundation of His *one* Church on earth based upon HIMSELF the Foundation of all, and the very Rock of ages.

Our Lord Jesus Christ being the *Foundation of foundations* (Isaias xxviii. 16), and *Chief Corner-Stone*, has the *fulness* of authority over the whole Church

* That S. Peter was the first Bishop of Rome, see Appendix No. 36.

whether in heaven or on earth, whether present or future, and is the original source of all authority and jurisdiction. Compared with the authority of Christ, that of the Pope over the Church is dependent, temporal, and, though ample, has its limits. The authority of the Pope is from Christ, under Christ, and for Christ.* He only possesses this authority over the Church on earth during the few years of his Pontificate. This is but a small portion of the immense flock of CHRIST, which consists of "*a great multitude which no man could number, of all nations, and tribes, and peoples, and tongues*" (Apocalypse vii. 9); and over the whole of which great multitude, when gathered together in the end of time from all the nations of the world, from all past ages, JESUS, the Eternal Shepherd of our souls, will Himself, without the ministry of any representative, visibly preside for ever and ever in heaven.

CHAPTER XXVIII.

LIST OF ALL THE GENERAL COUNCILS HELD IN THE CHURCH OF GOD FROM THE TIME OF THE APOSTLES TO A.D. 1880.

BY A GENERAL OR ŒCUMENICAL COUNCIL is understood a Council to which the Bishops of the whole world are lawfully summoned, though it is not necessary for the validity of the Council that all should attend.

A Council, in order to be Œcumenical, must be convoked by the Pope, or at least with his consent, and

---

* See "The Appeal to Antiquity." A Reply to the Protestant Bishop of Manchester, by the Bishop of Salford. 1877. (One Penny.) Burns & Oates.

be presided over by him, or by his Legates. The decrees of a Council must also have his approval.

A General Council headed by the Pope, by reason of its representing the whole Church, has the privilege of doctrinal infallibility and supreme authority. It is evident that even the largest assembly of Bishops without the Pope would be a body without a head, and could not represent the whole Church.

General Councils show the supernatural vitality which exists in the Church of God for her own preservation and purity. To the present time (A.D. 1880) the Œcumenical Councils are nineteen in number. The first eight were held in the *Eastern* part of Christendom, the remaining eleven were held in the *Western* part.

The following List of General Councils will place in a prominent light the fact that there has always existed in the Catholic Church *oneness of body*, that is, intercommunion between all the Catholic Bishops, and dependence upon their Visible Head the Roman Pontiff, and *oneness of faith*, which the Church, faithful to her office, never failed, when needed, boldly and clearly to state. And there is no instance of a doctrine on faith or morals defined by one General Council having been changed by another General Council or by a Pope :—

1. *The First Council of Nicaea (or Nice*, now called Isnick, in Anatolia, about 90 miles south-west of Constantinople), was held in the year 325, under Pope Sylvester I. There were present 318 Bishops; the Emperor Constantine the Great also assisting.

Arius was condemned for denying the Divinity of the *Word* and His consubstantiality with the Father; at this Council the greater part of what is commonly called the Nicene Creed was published.

2. *The First Council of Constantinople* was held in

381, confirmed by Pope Damasus I.; 150 Bishops, and the Emperor Theodosius attended.

The followers of Macedonius were condemned for denying the Divinity of the Holy Ghost and His consubstantiality with the Father and the Son.

3. *The Council of Ephesus* was held in 431, under Pope Celestine I. About 200 Bishops, and Theodosius the younger, were present.

Nestorius was deposed from his See of Constantinople and condemned for maintaining that in Jesus Christ there were two distinct persons; a human person, born of the Virgin Mary, and the Divine person, that is, the Eternal *Word* that became associated with the man Jesus. In consequence of this error he denied to the Blessed Virgin the title of *Theotokos* (or Mother of God), contrary to the Catholic doctrine, which confesses Mary to be the Mother of the ONE DIVINE PERSON, in whom are intimately and indissolubly united, by what is called *hypostatic* union, the Divine and the human nature.

4. *The Council of Chalcedon* (now called Scutari), in Asia Minor, under Pope Leo the Great, was held in 451. 630 Bishops, and the Emperor Marcian, were present. Papal supremacy acknowledged.

Eutyches, Abbot of Constantinople, and *Dioscorus*, Archbishop of Alexandria, were condemned for teaching that in JESUS CHRIST there was only one nature.

5. *The Second of Constantinople*, held in 553, under Pope Vigilius. 165 Bishops, and the Emperor Justinian, were present. Though neither the Pope nor his Legates attended, yet the Council is considered Œcumenical from its having afterwards received the sanction of the Popes.

The so-called Three Chapters or heretical writings of Theodórus of Mopsuesta, of Theodorétus and of Iba, favouring the already anathematized doctrines of Nestorius, were condemned.

6. *The Third Council of Constantinople*, held in the year 680 and 681, under Pope Agatho, attended by 170 Bishops.

The Monothelites, with their leaders Cyrus, Sergius, and Pirrhus, were condemned for maintaining that in JESUS CHRIST there was only one operation and one will. This heresy attempted to revive under a new form the error of Eutyches, which had been already condemned.

Pope Agatho dying before the Council came to a conclusion, it was confirmed by Leo II., his successor, who translated the Acts of this Council from the Greek into Latin.

7. *The Second of Nicaea*, held in 787, under Pope Adrian I., attended by 367 Bishops.

In this Council the Iconoclasts (or breakers of images) were condemned for rejecting the use of holy images, and the practice of paying them due respect. The last Session of this Council was held at Constantinople.

8. *The Fourth of Constantinople*, held in 869 and 870, under Pope Adrian II., attended by 102 Bishops.

The intruded Patriarch Photius, the author of the Greek Schism, was condemned and deposed, and S. Ignatius was restored to his See of Constantinople, which had been unjustly usurped by Photius. This is the last General Council held in the East.

9. *The First of Lateran*, held in Rome in 1123, under Pope Calistus II., attended by 300 Bishops and 600 mitred Abbots.

The contest regarding investitures, or appointment to benefices, was settled. The rights of the Church and of the Emperors in the serious business of the election of Bishops and Abbots were regulated.

10. *The Second of Lateran*, held in 1139, under Pope Innocent II., attended by 1000 Bishops, the Pope himself presiding.

The errors of the Albigenses and the heresies of Peter De Bruys and Arnold of Brescia were condemned and the schism of Peter Leo was repressed. One of the decrees of this Council anathematized those heretics who rejected Infant Baptism, the Holy Eucharist, the Priesthood, and Matrimony.

11. *The Third of Lateran*, held in 1179, under Pope Alexander III., who presided in person. It was attended by 300 Bishops.

The errors of the Waldenses were condemned and a better form of electing the Sovereign Pontiff was prescribed. Most beneficial rules were also framed for the election of Bishops, for regulating the rights of patrons, and for the gratuitous instruction of the people, especially of poor children.

12. *The Fourth of Lateran*, held in 1215, under the great Pope Innocent III., attended by 412 Bishops and upwards of 800 Abbots and Friars, besides the representatives of all the Princes of Christendom.

A short exposition of the Catholic Faith was drawn up in opposition to the errors of the time, especially those of the Albigenses and Waldenses. Ecclesiastical laws were framed for the Reformation of morals among Christians. The obligation of Confession for adults, instead of several times a year, was reduced to once a year at least; and holy Communion likewise to at least once a year, and that at Easter-time. A decree authorising an expedition (known as *Crusade*) for the recovery of the Holy Places was likewise published, and the election of Frederic II. as Roman Emperor was confirmed.

13. *The First of Lyons*, celebrated in 1245, under Pope Innocent IV., attended by 140 Bishops and many Abbots and Procurators of Chapters. There was also present Baldwin, Emperor of Constantinople, with other Princes and various Ambassadors.

The Emperor, Frederic II. (a noted persecutor of the Church, who, owing to the aid of the great Pope Innocent III., his Godfather, ascended the throne of the German Empire) was excommunicated and deposed after hearing the powerful defence made by his Imperial representatives and advocates.

14. *The Second of Lyons*, held in 1274, under Pope Gregory X., attended by 500 Bishops of the Latin and the Greek Rite, nearly 70 Abbots and about 1000 minor Prelates, the Pope presiding in person.

The schismatic Greeks returned to the unity of the Church, acknowledging again the Pope as the head of the whole Church, of the Greek as well as of the Latin Rite.

15. *The Council of Vienne in France* was held in the year 1311 and 1312, under Pope Clement V. There were 300 Bishops and many other Prelates present.

The Order of Knights-Templars abolished. The errors of the Begards, who pretended that man is capable of attaining such perfection in this life as to become impeccable (or incapable of sinning), even when freely gratifying the evil propensities of the body, were condemned.

[The *Council of Constance* was assembled in 1414; when, owing to the interference of States, there were three candidates contending for the Papal Chair—John XXIII., Gregory XII., and Benedict XIII. It was attended by about 200 Bishops and a number of other Prelates.

At this Council the serious schism caused by this usurpation which had so long distracted the Church of God ended, and the errors of John Wickliff and others were condemned.

In November 1417 Pope Martin V. was recognised by all as the lawfully elected Pope, and he presided over the Council until it closed. In the last Session Pope Martin V. approved and ratified all that the Council had defined "*conciliariter*," that is, according to the strict rules of defining in General Councils, and, therefore, in these definitions the Council was received as Œcumenical, although it does not rank among Œcumenical Councils, because in some of its Sessions it was not Œcumenical.]

16. *The Council of Florence, Italy*, held in 1438 and 1439, under Pope Eugenius IV. Attended by 200 Bishops of the Latin and of the Greek Rite, and by the Emperor of the Greeks, John Paleologus.

The Supremacy of the Pope over the whole Church was declared. Once more the Schismatic Eastern and Russian Bishops who were present submitted to the Supremacy of the Pope, and were thereby re-united to the Catholic Church.

17. *The Fifth Lateran, Rome*, A.D. 1512-1517, under the Popes Julius II. and Leo X., attended by 120 Bishops. Many representatives of Kings and Princes were also present.

It abolished the *Pragmatic Sanction*, that is, the collection of 38 decrees, which the Council of Bâle had published concerning the rights and privileges of the Roman Pontiff, the authority of Councils, the election of Prelates, and other ecclesiastical matters. The dogma relating to the immortality of the soul was defined. The Council of Pisa was condemned, and the ecclesiastical discipline reformed. An impulse was given to an expedition or Crusade against the Turks, who were at the time threatening to over-run Christendom.

18. *The Council of Trent, in the Austrian Tyrol*, held from 1545 to 1563, under the Popes Paul III., Julius III., Marcellus II., Paul IV., and Pius IV. It was attended by about 200 Bishops, 7 Abbots, and 7 Generals of Religious Orders, and by the Representatives of Kings and Princes. Including an adjournment of four years, and a suspension of ten years, this Council lasted eighteen years.

The Catholic doctrine regarding the Holy Scripture, Tradition, Original Sin, Justification, and the Seven Sacraments, was clearly explained; the contrary errors condemned; and abuses in morals and discipline reformed.

19. *The Vatican Council* was opened in the Basilica of S. Peter, Rome, on the 8th of December 1869, and continued up to the 18th of July 1870. It was summoned by Pope Pius IX., who presided, but generally by his Legates. The Patriarchs, Archbishops, and Bishops, present at the Council, at any time between December the 8th, 1869, and July the 18th, 1870, were 704. This number included 113 Archbishops and Bishops *in partibus infidelium* (in infidel regions), of whom all but 38 held the office of Administrator, Auxiliary, Coadjutor, Vicar-Apostolic, or Prefect-Apostolic.

In this Council the dogma of the *Supremacy* of S. Peter and his Successors, previously recognised in the First Council of Ephesus, A.D. 431, and more fully explained in the Council of Florence, A.D. 1438, was again solemnly affirmed. This dogma of faith teaches that on S. Peter was conferred a Primacy of jurisdiction over the other Apostles, and over the whole flock of Jesus Christ, and that the Bishop of Rome is the successor of Peter in that jurisdiction. It was also declared that this jurisdiction extends over the whole Church and over every member of the Church, and that all the faithful are bound to submit to it, not only in things that belong to faith or to morals, but also in things that belong to the discipline and the government of the Church.

At this Council the Pope's *infallibility*, when speaking *ex Cathedrâ* in matters of Faith or of Morals, was also solemnly defined. Besides the Primacy and the Infallibility of the Pope (see Chap. IX.), this Council also defined against the daring attacks of modern infidelity, the existence of a personal God.

Some people wrongly imagine that the dogma of the infallibility of the Pope is a *new* doctrine, because it was for the first time defined *as an article of faith* only at the Vatican Council; but they who argue thus might with as much show of reason assert that the dogma which teaches the existence of a personal God is therefore also a new doctrine because that article of the faith was for the first time defined as dogma (in order to oppose modern heresy) in this Council.

This Council issued likewise some very important decrees relating to Discipline.

CHAPTER XXIX.

Second Mark—Holiness.

The Catholic Church is *Holy*, because, as our Catechism says, "she teaches a *holy doctrine*, offers to all the *means of holiness;* and is *distinguished by the eminent holiness* of so many thousands of her children."

Catholics see clearly, and non-Catholics themselves for the most part admit, that among the various Protestant sects there are grave errors, divisions, and losses to deplore.

These may be contradictions, or unsound, unscriptural tenets, or the loss of Sacraments, the abandonment of the Evangelical Counsels of perfection, or it may be, some faulty principles, inconsistent with holiness, which, if carried out into practice in their natural consequences, would certainly prove to be opposed to God's Perfections, to man's salvation, and to the well-being of Society.

The following enumeration of some of the tenets held by various denominations, though not all by each, may serve to exemplify this remark : *

That the grossest sins do not hurt the elect, who do not forfeit thereby the grace of adoption and the state of justification. This *Luther* taught.

That God is the author of sin, and at the same time the avenger of it. This *Calvin* taught.

That there is no falling from the grace of God, but that "once in grace one is always in grace, how grievous sins soever he may commit." (Calvin "Book of Institutions," chapter ii.)

That there is no freewill in man. (Luther on slave will.)

That God sees no sin in believers.

That "no sin, unbelief alone excepted, can cause damnation." (Luther on Captivity of Babylon.)

That several Books of Holy Scripture are to be rejected, although they are sanctioned by the same authority that has in the sixth Council of Carthage

---

* See Bp. Bossuet ("*Variations*"), and Bp. Milner's "*End of Controversy.*"

A.D. 419, sanctioned all the Books of the New Testament.

That a man has a right to prefer and maintain his own interpretation of Scripture, in opposition to the judgment of all the Fathers and Bishops of the Catholic Church.

That man is *justified* by *faith only*, without anything else; understanding by faith, a mere reliance on Christ for pardon.

That repentance, love of God, and of our neighbour, are not *necessary* for justification or for salvation.

That good works are not only not necessary, but hurtful to justification. (See *Mosheim.*)

That man is totally depraved, and that all his works are sinful.

That all sins are of equal guilt.

That "works of supererogation cannot be taught without arrogancy and impiety."*

That the exact observance of the Commandments of God is impossible.

That all religions are good, and that it is a matter of indifference which is professed.

That God (so Calvin taught) has predestined and consigned some men, independently of their acts, and without any fault of their own, to everlasting perdition.

And many more tenets hurtful and unsound. These fruits show of what sort the tree (the right of private

---

* See 14th Article of Religion, Book of Common Prayer of Church of England. By works of supererogation are meant works not *commanded* but only *counselled* by Christ, called counsels of perfection, or virtues not absolutely commanded, such as voluntary *poverty*, voluntary state of *celibacy*, or chaste single life for God's sake, and voluntary *obedience*, which is, the putting of oneself under a legitimate superior to obey him in any matter which is not in violation of the Law of God.

SECOND MARK—HOLINESS. 125

interpretation of Scripture against legitimate authority) is, for "*by their fruits you shall know them.*" (S. Matt. vii. 20.)

Notwithstanding these faulty principles, a high moral standard is often found amongst Protestants of various denominations. This is because happily such Christians do not carry out their professed principles to their legitimate conclusions, but follow rather the dictates of natural sense of right and wrong, and adhere to certain portions of Catholic faith still surviving among them.

The Catholic Church is truly holy. Her teaching, both in faith and in morals, inspires her children with a love of perfection; leads them to holiness of life, to practise all virtues, to abhor all sin, to avoid the occasions of it, and to observe faithfully all God's commandments. This is all included in the idea of true holiness. She urges the use of prayer and of the holy Sacraments, and of all other means through which God's grace can be obtained. Holy Church commands her children to render to all whatever is their due; loyal allegiance to the ruling Civil Power in temporal concerns;[*] faithful obedience to Ecclesiastical superiors in spiritual matters; affection and ready submission to Parents, and to those acting in their stead; respect to all placed over us; consideration and kindness to all placed under us; respect and Christian love towards all, and even love in return for hatred.

The Church encourages us to devote ourselves, as much as our other duties will allow us, to spiritual and corporal works of mercy. Such are—to instruct the ignorant; to reclaim the sinner; to help those in danger and trouble on sea and on land; to relieve the poor;

---

[*] See Duke of Wellington on Catholic Loyalty, Appendix No. 35.

to shelter the homeless, the young, and the infirm; to visit the afflicted, the aged, the sick, and the dying, in workhouses, orphanages, hospitals, asylums, and prisons, or wherever they may be; to bury the dead, and to pray for them and for the spiritual and temporal wants of our neighbour in general.

We are taught by Holy Church to worship God, who is of infinite Majesty, Power, Truth, Mercy, and Goodness, by frequent acts of adoration, humility, faith, hope, contrition, and love; and by regular and devout attendance at the Services of the Church, which she celebrates not only on Sundays and Festivals but also on week-days, Holy Mass being celebrated daily in all Catholic Churches by each Priest, in order to *shew forth the death of the Lord*, and keep the faithful constantly in remembrance of Him and His all-availing Passion and Death.

She puts constantly before her children the life of JESUS CHRIST as the Perfect Model for their imitation, "*Put ye on the Lord Jesus Christ.*" (Romans xiii. 14.)

The lives of the Saints also are often placed before us that we may be encouraged by their bright example in the practice of humility, obedience, purity, charity, patience, self-denial, devotion, perseverance and zeal; which virtues the Saints possessed in a degree called heroic, that distinguished them from ordinary pious Christians.

The example of the martyrs who died for Christ, for the faith, and for virtue's sake, are also continually placed before us, that we may learn how to endure sufferings and even death rather than be unfaithful to God, and stain our conscience with sin. The Christian motto is: "*Malo mori quam foedari,*" that is, *Death before dishonour.*

The Church commands us to be continually watchful

over ourselves, so as not wilfully to allow for a moment even one bad thought to defile the mind.

Those who, unhappily, have fallen into sin, she encourages to repent and to return to God without delay, and to approach the Sacrament of Penance in order to have their souls cleansed in the Most Precious Blood of JESUS, which is applied to them in that life-restoring, healing, and comforting Sacrament.

The Catholic Church forbids the least injustice to any one, and strictly obliges us to make reparation and restitution, according to our ability, for any injury or injustice that we may have done to any one, even though our neighbour may not be aware of the wrong.

She presses us to approach frequently and devoutly the most Blessed Sacrament of Holy Communion, that our souls may be fed and strengthened by that Heavenly Food, our hearts more and more inflamed with the fire of Divine Love, and that thus we may continually grow in grace and piety.

In short, the Catholic Church forbids all that is wrong, even for the sake of obtaining the greatest temporal advantage; she commands all that is dutiful and encourages all that is good, holy, and perfect, even the striving after the attainment of those sublime virtues, for the observance of which Jesus Christ gave not *precepts* but only *counsels*, called "Counsels of perfection".

The Church cannot be held responsible for the conduct of bad Catholics, for they are bad, inasmuch as they *depart* from the Catholic teaching and rule. All Catholics who faithfully and humbly follow the guidance of the Church, whatever may be their nation, or lawful calling and position in life, will become exemplary Christians, and it may be, even Saints.

Here the question naturally arises: Are the fruits of

sanctity or virtue, which are attained through grace, and practised to the high degree called heroic, to be found among the members of the Catholic Church, or among the different new teachers who undertook to reform the Church in the sixteenth century?

The first thoughts that strike most people who consider this subject are, that not one of those leaders of the Reformation is regarded by any as a Saint, but that some of them are admitted, even by many Protestants, to have been quite the reverse of Saints, and, that all the Saints of Christendom, even those Saints retained in the Calendar of the State Church of England, and under whose names many Protestant Churches are dedicated, lived and died strict members of the Catholic Church in communion with the See of Rome, zealously attached to her doctrine and discipline.

In this calendar of the Church of England we still meet with Pope S. Gregory I., the zealous asserter of Papal Supremacy (March 12); S. Benedict (March 21) of Monte Cassino, the Patriarch of the Western Monks and Nuns; S. Dunstan of Canterbury (May 18), the vindicator of clerical celibacy; S. Augustine of Canterbury (May 26), who, after the Saxon Invasion, preached the Catholic Faith to the inhabitants of pagan England; and the name of Saint Bede, known as Venerable Bede (May 27), the Benedictine Monk of Yarrow, Northumberland, the faithful historian of those days of Catholic glory in England; the glorious Martyr S. Lawrence (Aug. 10), the devoted Deacon of S. Sixtus II., Pope and Martyr; S. Jerome (Sept. 30), who was so devoted to the Papal chair, in the fourth century; S. Clement, Pope and Martyr (Sept. 23), whose Apostolic letters still exist; Pope S. Sylvester (Dec. 31), (under whom the Christian Emperor Constantine the Great was converted to Christianity), who, empowered by the

Emperor, first built, in several parts of Rome, churche for public worship, which, history states, he adorned with sacred images.

The names of other Catholic Saints,—for example, S. David, S. Chad, S. Edward, S. Richard, S. Alphege, S. Martin, S. Swithin, S. Giles, S. Lambert, S. Leonard, S. Hugh, S. Remigius, S. Edmund, S. Agnes, S. Catherine, S. Etheldreda, S. Margaret,—are all retained in the Calendar of the State Church of England, and give name to many Churches of that Establishment.

Besides these there are very many other Saints in the Catholic Church, who, for the extraordinary purity and sanctity of their lives, many learned and candid Protestants admit were Saints. Even Luther acknowledges S. Anthony, S. Bernard, S. Dominic, S. Francis of Assisi, S. Bonaventure and others to be Saints, though they were avowed Roman Catholics, and defenders of the Roman Catholic Church against the heretics and schismatics of their times.

But, independently of this and of every other testimony, it is certain that the supernatural virtues and heroic sanctity of a countless number of holy persons of different nation, sex, rank, and profession, have wondrously adorned the Catholic Church in every age.

For three hundred years every Successor of the glorious S. Peter, almost without exception, numbering more than thirty, received, like S. Peter, the crown of Martyrdom in, or near, their beloved city of Rome. A great number of Popes, and an immense number of Bishops, are regarded by the Church as Saints, besides more than twelve millions of martyrs who are known to have nobly sealed their belief in the Catholic faith with their blood.

CHAPTER XXX.

List of some Saints.

Besides the Apostles chosen by our Lord, the names of a great number of Saints are familiar to Catholics. The following comparatively short list of *Saints* (for the number might readily be increased a hundred fold), and of some styled by the Church, "*Servants of God*," "*Venerable*," and when Canonised by the Church, "*Blessed*," and more familiarly known among Catholics in the United Kingdom and in Italy, has been carefully drawn up and arranged in the order of time.

The year and day on which the festival of each occurs in the Catholic Calendar is added, and this date, following for the most part that given by the learned Rev. Alban Butler, generally marks the day of their decease, and on which we may piously believe that their holy souls passed to the enjoyment of everlasting happiness.

ABBREVIATIONS HERE USED EXPLAINED.

A. Ap.—signifies Apostle.
Ab., Abs.—Abbot, Abbess.
Abp.—Archbishop.
A. D.—Anno Domini *(in the year of our Lord)*.
B., or Bp.—Bishop.
Bl.—Blessed.
C.—Confessor.
c.—*circa*; about.
Card.—Cardinal.
C. O.—Congregation of the Oratory of S. Philip Neri.
Comps.—Companions.
Congr.—Congregation.
D.—Doctor (or Teacher) of the Church.

Disc.—Signifies Disciple.
Emp., -ss.—Emperor, Empress.
F.—Father.
Fndr., ss.—Founder, -dress.
K.—King.
M.—Martyr.
O. M. C.—Order of Mount Carmel.
O. P.—Order of Preachers or Dominicans.
O. S. A.—Order of St. Augustine.
O. S. B.—Order of Monks of St. Benedict.
O. S. C.—Oblate of S. Charles Borromeo.

LIST OF SOME SAINTS. 131

O. S. F.—Signifies Order of the Friars Minor of St. Francis of Assisi.
O. S. M.—Order of Servites of B. V. Mary.
P.—Pope.
Pat., Patrs.—Patron, Patroness
Q.—Queen.
S., St., SS.—Saint, Saints.

S. J.—Signifies Society (or Company) of *Jesus*.
V.—Virgin.
Ven.—Venerable.
W.—Widow.
&—and.
&c.,—*et cætera* (and the rest).
i.e.—*id est* (that is).

NOTE.—This sign † placed before the name of a Saint in this list signifies that such name is still retained in the Calendar prefixed to the Book of Common Prayer of the State Church of England.

S. Linus, P.M. Rome. Sept. 23, A.D. 76.
S. Thecla, V.M. Iconium, Disc. of S. Paul. Sept. 23, 100.
† S. Clement, P.M. Rome. Nov. 23, 100 (Philipp. iv. 3).
S. Pudentiana, V. Rome. Disc. of S. Peter. May 19, 101.
S. Ignatius. M. Bp. of Antioch. Feb. 1. 107.
S. Pius I., P.M. Rome. July 11, 151.
S. Polycarp, M. Bp. of Smyrna. Jan. 26. 166.
S. Justin Martyr, Sichem, Palestine, Apologist of the Christian Religion. Apr. 13, 167.
S. Eleutherius. P.M. Rome, at the request of K. Lucius sent S. Fugatius and S. Damianus into Britain. June 1, 179, or Oct. 9, 182.
S. Irenæus, M. Bp. of Lyons, France. July 4, 202.
S. Victor, P.M. African, Rome. July 28, 202.
† S. Perpetua M. and comps. Carthage. Mar. 7, 203.
S. Zephyrinus, P.M. Rome. Aug. 26, 219.
S. Calistus, P.M. Rome. Oct. 14, 222.
† S. Cecily, V.M. Rome, patrs. Sacred Music. Nov. 22, 230.
S. Victoria, V.M. Rome. Dec. 22, 250.
† S. Agatha, V.M. Sicily. Feb. 5, 251.
S. Sixtus II., P.M. Rome. Aug. 6, 258.
† S. Lawrence, M. Deacon of Rome. Aug. 10, 258.
S. Cyprian, M. Africa, Bp. of Carthage. Sept. 16, 258.
S. Eugenia, V.M. Rome, formerly named in the Canon of the Mass. Dec. 25, about 258.
† S. Denis (or Dionysius), P.M. Rome, defended the faith in the Divinity of *Jesus Christ*, and of the Holy Ghost. Dec. 26, 269.

† S. Valentine, M. priest, Rome, devoted to serve the martyrs under Emp. Claudius II. Feb. 14, 270.
S. Denis, M. Rome, first Bp. of Paris. Oct. 9, 272.
† S. Prisca (or Priscilla), V.M. Rome. Jan. 18, 275.
† S. Margaret, V.M. Antioch, Pisidia. July 20, 278.
S. Maurice, M. Gaul, captain of a Legion. Sept. 22, 286.
† S. Fabian, P.M. Rome. Jan. 20, 288.
S. Sebastian, M. Narbonne, France, soldier under Rom. Emp. Jan. 20, 288.
† S. Crispin, M. Soissons, France, cordwainer. Oct. 25, 288.
† S. Faith, V.M. Agen, Aquitaine. Oct. 6, 290.
† S. George, M. Cappadocia, Asia Minor, pat. England and Russia, styled by the Greeks, *The Great Martyr*. Apr. 23, 303.
S. Victoria, V.M. Abitina, near Carthage, martyred with forty-eight other Christians. Feb 11, about 303.
† S. Alban, M. Verulam, St. Albans, first martyr in Britain. June 22, 303.
S. Philomena, V.M. Rome. Aug. 11, 303.
† S. Agnes, V.M. Rome, of Patrician family. Jan. 21, 304.
† S. Vincent, M. Deacon, Saragossa, Spain. Jan. 22, 304.
S. Pancratius (or Pancras), M. Rome, Patrician youth much revered in England. May 12, 304.
S. Eugenia, V.M. Egypt. Sept. 22, 304.
S. Quiricus (or Cyr), M. Tarsus, Cilicia, brave boy of three years, Patron of great military College near Versailles, France, killed for the faith, with his mother, S. Justine. Sept. 26, 304.
S. Barbara, V.M. Nicomedia. Dec. 4, 306.
S. Chrysogonus, M. Rome, named in Canon of the Mass. Nov. 24, about 304.
† S. Lucy V.M. Syracuse, Sicily. Dec. 13, 304.
S. Anastasia, M. Rome, Disc. of S. Chrysogonus. Dec. 25, 304.
† S. Catherine, V.M. Alexandria, Egypt. Nov. 25, 307.
S. Theodosia, V.M. Tyre, Palestine. Apr. 2, 308.
S. Helen, Emps. Britain (Colchester), Mother of Emp. Constantine the Great. Aug. 18, 328.
† S. Sylvester, P.C. Rome. Dec. 31, 337.
† S. Nicholas (S. Claus), C. Bp. of Myra (Lycia, Asia Minor), patr. children. Dec. 6, 352.
S. Anthony, Ab. Egypt, *Patriarch of Monks*. Jan. 17, 356.
† S. Hilary, C.D. Gaul, Bp. of Poitiers. Jan. 13, 368.

LIST OF SOME SAINTS. 133

S. Eusebius, M. Isle of Sardinia, Bp. of Vercelli, Piedmont. Sept. 26 and Dec. 15, 370.

S. Athanasius, C.D. Egypt, Patriarch of Alexandria, one of the four great Doctors of the East. May 2, 373.

S. Basil, C.D. Cappadocia, *The Great*, Abp. Cæsarea, one of the four great Doctors of the East, June 14, 379.

S. Cyril, C.D. Bp. of Jerusalem, was present at the first Council of Constantinople, 381. Mar. 18, 386.

S. Monica, W. Tagaste, Africa, Mother of S. Augustine, Bp. of Hippo. May 4, 387.

S. Gregory Nazianzen, C.D. *The Theologian*, Abp. of Constantinople, one of the four great Doctors of the East, chosen friend of S. Basil, and teacher of S. Jerome. May 9, 389.

S. Martin, C. Bp. of Tours, France. Nov. 11, 397.

† S. Ambrose, C.D. Gaul, Abp. of Milan, one of the four great Doctors of the West. Dec. 7, 397.

S. Ives, C.B. Persian missionary to Britain. June 10, c. 400.

S. Alexius, C. pilgrim, patrician, Rome. July 17, c. 400.

S. Simplicius, C. Bp. of Milan after S. Ambrose. Aug. 16, 400.

S. Pelagia, penitent, Antioch, formerly an actress. Oct. 11, c. 400.

S. Paula, W. of Patrician family, Rome. Jan. 25, 404.

S. John Chrysostom, C.D. Antioch, patriarch of Constant., one of the four great Doctors of the East. Jan. 27, 407.

† S. Jerome, C. Stridon, Dalmatia, Card., one of the four great Doctors of the West; Author of the Latin version of Holy Scriptures called the "Vulgate," from the original Hebrew and Greek. Sept. 30, 420.

† S. Augustine, C. Bp. of Hippo, Africa, one of the four great Doctors of the West. Aug. 28, 430.

S. Cyril, C. patriarch of Alexandria. Jan. 28, 444.

S. Germanus, C. Bp. of Auxerre, France, *Apostle of Britain*, with comps. S. Lupus of Troyes, and afterwards with S. Severus of Treves. July 30 and Aug. 11, 448.

S. Vincent, C. of Lerins, Provence. May 24, 450.

S. Peter Chrysologus, C.D. Imola, Abp. Ravenna. Dec. 2, 450.

S. Ursula, V.M. and comps. Britain, shot with arrows by the Huns in Bas Rhin, Germany, Patr. of education and of the Sorbonne, Paris. Oct. 21, 453.

S. Patrick, B.C. Britain, or Brittany, Abp. of Armagh, *Apostle of Ireland*. Mar. 17, 460.

LIST OF SOME SAINTS.

S. Leo I., P.C.D. "*The Great,*" Rome, staved Attila, "the Scourge of God," from invading South Italy. Apr. 11 and Nov. 10, 461.

S. Germanus, B.M. France, *Apostle of Scotland.* May 2, 480.

S. Genevieve, V. Nanterre, Putrs. of Paris. Jan. 3, 512.

S. Brigid, V. ab. (Kildare), Patrs. of Ireland. Feb. 1, 523.

S. Fulgentius, c. D. Carthage, Bp. of Ruspa, Africa. Jan.1,533.

S. Remigius (or Remy), c. Abp. of Rheims, France, Apostle of the Franks. Jan. 13 and Oct. 1, 533.

* S. Scholastica (O.S.B.), V. Abs. Italy. S. Benedict's sister, Fndrs. of the Benedictine Nuns. Feb. 10, 543.

† S. Benedict, c. Abbot, Nursia, Italy, Monte Cassino, *Patriarch of the Western Monks.* March 21, 543.

† S. David, c. Abp. of Menevia, Patr. of Wales, Disciple of S. Paulinus. Mar. 1, 544.

S. Finian, c. Leinster, Ireland, Bp. of Cluain-Iraird (or Clonard). Dec. 12, 552.

† S. Leonard, c. hermit, Orleans, France. Nov. 6, 559.

S. Cloud (or Clodoald), priest, son of Clodomer, K. of Orleans, and St. Clotilde. Sept. 7, 560.

S. Columb (or Columbkill), c. Scotland, Disciple of S. Finian, Ab. of Durrogh, Ireland, *Apostle of the Picts, Scotland.* June 9, 567.

† S. Gregory I. (O.S.B.) P.C.D. "*The Great,*" one of the four great Doctors of the West, *Apostle of England.* Mar. 12, 604.

† S. Augustine (O.S.B.), c. Abp. of Canterbury, *Apostle of England,* sent by Pope Gregory the Great to convert the Anglo-Saxons. May 26, 604.

S. John Climacus, c. Egypt, "*The Scholastic.*" Mar. 30, 605.

S. Ethelbert, c. K. of Kent, England. Feb. 24, 616.

S. Columban, c. Leinster, Ab. of Fontaines, France. Nov. 21, 617.

S. Lawrence (O.S.B.), c. Abp. of Canterbury. Feb. 9, 619.

S. Benno, c. Shrewsbury, Ab. of Cluunoc, Carnarvon, Wales. April 21, about 620.

S. Winefrid, V.M. Patrs. of Wales, Holywell. Nov. 3, 630.

S. Aidan, c. Iona, Apostle of Northumbria. Sept. 20, 631.

---

* Many of the Saints (after A.D. 543) in this list belong to the Venerable Order of S. Benedict, to which Order the United Kingdom is indebted for the foundation of so many of her noble Abbeys, Cathedrals, and Colleges.

- S. Edwin, M. K. of Northumbria, Fndr. of Edinburgh. Oct. 12, 633.
- S. Oswald, M. K. of Northumbria. Aug. 5, 642.
- S. Sigebert, K. of the East Angles, Fndr. of Westminster Abbey. Oct. 29, 642.
- S. Bees (or Bega), v. Ireland, Fndrs. of Abbeys at Durham, Hartlepool, and Tadcaster. Sept 6, Nov. 22. o. 650.
- S. Bavon, o. hermit, Liege, Gand (Ghent). Oct. 1, 653.
- S. Botolph, M. Ab. England, Norwegian, starved in the Chersonese (Crimea). June 17 and Nov. 12, 655.
- S. Martin, P.M. Tuscany. June 17 and Nov. 12, 655.
- S. Gertrude (O.S.B.), v. first Abs. of Nivelles, Belgium. Mar. 17 (Brabant, May 8), 659.
- † S. Chad (O.S.B.), o. Whitby, Bp. of Lichfield. Mar. 2, 673.
- † S. Etheldreda (or S. Audry), (O.S.B.), v. Abs. of Ely, Cambridge, of Royal descent. June 23, 679.
- S. Erconwald, o. Bp. of London, of royal descent, brother of S. Edelburga. April 30, 686.
- S. Cuthbert (O.S.B.), o. Kells, Meath, Ireland. Bp. of Lindisfarne, Northumbria, Patr. of Durham. Mar. 20, 687.
- S. Bennet Biscop (O.S.B.), Ab. of Wearmouth. Jan. 12, 690.
- S. Wereburge (O.S.B.), v. ab. Patrs. of Chester. Feb. 21, 690.
- S. Mùnde or Mungo, o. Ab. Scotland, Patr. of Argyleshire. April 15, 692.
- † S. Lambert, M. Bp. of Maestrich, Patr. Liège, Brabant. Sept. 17, 709.
- S. Wilfrid (O.S.B.), o. Bp. of York. Oct. 12, 709.
- † S. Giles, o. Ab. of Arles, France. Sept. 1, 724.
- † S. Bede, styled *The Venerable* (O.S.B.), o. Father & Doctor of the Church, Jarrow, England. May 27, 735.
- † S. Boniface (O.S.B.), M. England, Bp. of Mayence, Ap. of Germany and Denmark. June 5, 755.
- S. Walburge (O.S.B.), Abs. Dorset, niece of S. Boniface. Feb. 23, 779.
- S. Ida, w. Munster, Germany. Sept. 4, 830.
- † S. Swithin (O.S.B.), o. Bp. of Winchester. July 15, 862.
- S. Ebbe, V.M. and Comps., Scotland, burned by Danes under Hinguar & Hubba. April 2 & Oct. 5, o. 870.
- † S. Edmund, M. K. of the East Angles. Nov. 20, 870.
- Bl. Alfred, "*The Great*," o. K. of England. Oct. 26, 900.
- S. Odo (O.S.B.), o. styled "*The Good*," England, Abp. of Canterbury. Sept. 1, 958.
- † S. Edward, M. K. of England. Mar. 18, 979.

S. Edith, v. Wilton, nat. daughter of K. Edgard. Sept. 16, 984.
† S. Dunstan (O.S.B.), c. Abp. of Canterbury, Ab. of Glastonbury, nephew of S. Alphege. May 19, 988.
S. Oswald (O.S.B.), c. Abp. of York, nephew of S. Odo. Feb. 29, 992.
S. Adelaide, w. Burgundy, wife of Otho I., Emp. of Germany. Dec. 16, 999.
Bl. Bernard of Menthon, c. Savoy, Fndr. of Hospice of Great & Littl' St. Bernard. May 28 & June 15, 1008.
† S. Alphege (O S.B.), M. Abp. of Canterbury. April 19, 1012.
S. Henry II. (O.S.B.), c. "*The Pious*," Bavaria, Emp. of Germany, obtained from the Pope that Nicene Creed should be sung at High Mass. July 15, 1024.
S. Edward, named *The Confessor*, c. K. of England, Patr. of Westminster. Jan. 5 and Nov. 13, 1066.
S. Canute IV., M. K. of Denmark, nat. son of K. Suenon II. Jan. 19, 1086.
† S. Margaret, w. Q. of Scotland, wife of K. Malcolm, who built Durham Cathedral & Dunfermline Abbey. S. Margaret's head rests at Douay, France. June 10, 1093.
S. Wulstan (O.S.B.), c. Bp. of Worcester. Jan. 19, 1095.
S. Bruno, c. Fndr. of Carthusians, Cologne. Oct. 6, 1101.
S. Anselm (O.S.B.), c.D. Aoste, Piedmont, Abp. of Canterbury. April 21, 1109.
S. Robert (O.S.B.), c. Ab. of Molesme, France, Fndr. of Cistercians. April 29, 1110.
Bl. Ida, w. Lorraine, mother of Godfrey de Bouillon. April 13, 1112.
S. Hugh, c. Bp. of Grenoble, France. April 1, 1132.
S. Stephen Harding (O.S.B.), c Ab. Dorset. April 17, 1134.
S. Norbert, c. Abp. of Magdeburg, Fndr. of the *Order of Premonstratensians*. June 6, 1134.
S. Leopold, c. Austria, son of K. Leopold III. and Ita. Nov. 15, 1136.
S. William (O.S.B.), c. Ab. Lombardy, Fndr. of *Congr. of Monte Vergine*, near Naples. June 25, 1142.
S. Malachy, c. Abp. Armagh, Primate of Ireland and Papal Legate. Gifted with the spirit of prophecy. Died in Clairvaux Abbey, in S. Bernard's arms, aged 54. Nov. 2, 1144.
S. Bernard (O.S.B.), c. Ab. of Clairvaux, France. Aug. 20, 1153.

LIST OF SOME SAINTS. 137

S. William, c. Abp. of York. June 8, 1154.
S. Robert (O.S.B.), c. Fountains Abbey, York, Ab. of Newminster, Northumberland. June 7, 1159.
S. Matilda, v. Abs., Bavaria. May 30, 1160.
S. Aelred (O.S.B.), c. Ab. of Rievaulx, York. Jan. 12, 1156.
S. Thomas (O.S.B.), M. Abp. of Canterbury. Dec. 29, 1170.
S. Albert, M. Bp. of Liege. Nov. 28, 1192.
✝ S. Hugh, c. Burgundy, Bp. of Lincoln, Carthusian, First Prior of Witham Abbey, Somerset. Nov. 17, 1200.
Bl. Albert (O.M.C.), c. Parma, Bp. of Vercelli, Italy, Latin Patriarch of Jerusalem. Sept. 14, 1214.
S. Dominic, c. Spain, Fndr. of *Order of Friars-Preachers, or Dominicans.* Taught the Rosary of the Blessed Virgin. Aug. 4, 1221.
S. Francis of Assisi, c. Umbria, Italy, styled *The Seraphic*, marked with the *stigmata* (or scars of the five wounds) of Our Lord, Fndr. of *Order of Friars-Minor or Franciscans.* Oct. 4, 1226.
S. Anthony of Padua, Italy (O.S.F.), Lisbon, great preacher and worker of miracles. June 13, 1231.
S. Elizabeth, w. Princess of Hungary, Founded many Orphanages and Hospitals. Nov. 19, 1231.
S. Edmund (O.S.B.), c. Abp. of Canterbury, Patr. of pious, studious youth. Nov. 16, 1242.
S. Hedwige, w. Patrs. of Poland. Oct. 17, 1243.
S. Theobald, c. Ab. France. Dec. 8, 1247.
✝ S. Richard, c. Bp. of Chichester. April 3, 1253.
S. Clare (O.S.F.), v. Abs. of Assisi, Italy, Fnds. of the *Poor Clares.* Aug. 12, 1253.
S. Julienne, v. of Mt. Cornillon, Liège, obtained from Pope Urban IV. the institution of the Feast of *Corpus Christi.* April 9, 1258.
S. Rosa of Viterbo. v. Italy. Sept. 4, 1258.
Bl. Bonfiglio Monaldi, c. (O.S.M.), Florence, first of the seven founders of the *Order of Servites of Mary.* Jan. 1, 1262.
S. Simon Stock, c. Sixth Carmelite General. England, died at Bordeaux, France. May 16, 1265.
S. Louis IX., c. K. Patr. of France. Aug. 25, 1270.
S. Zita, v. Lucca, Italy, model for domestic servants. Her body, still uncorrupted, is venerated in the Basilica of S. Frigidian at Lucca. April 27, 1272.

- S. Thomas Aquinas, Italy (O.P.), C.D. called "*The Angelic Doctor*," famous Author of the "*Summa*," and of other great Theological Works. Mar. 7, 1272.
- S. Bonaventure, C.D. (O.S.F.), Tuscany, Card. Bp. of Albano, called *The Seraphic Doctor*. July 14, 1274.
- Bl. Albert (O.P.), c. Cologne, Bp. of Ratisbon., surnamed *The Great*, Dec. 17, 1280.
- S. Thomas, c. Lancashire, Bp. of Hereford. Aug. 23 and Oct. 2, 1282.
- S. Philip Benizi, c. Bologna, Italy, first General of the *Order of Servites of Mary*. Aug. 23, 1285.
- S. Gertrude (O.S.B.), v. Abs. of Saxony, surnamed *The Great*. Nov. 15, 1292.
- S. Margaret of Cortona, Italy, penitent. Feb. 26, 1297.
- S. Ivo (or Ives). c. Brittany, France (O.S.F., 3rd Order), Patr. of Parish Priests and of the Poor. May 19, 1303.
- S. Brigit, w. Princess of Sweden, Fndrs. of *Brigitines*. Oct. 8, 1313.
- S. Elzear, c. (O S.F.) Provence, France. Sept. 27, 1325.
- S. Roch (or Rock), c. Montpellier, France. Aug. 16, 1327.
- Bl. Imelda Lambertini, v. Bologna, Italy. Sept. 16, 1333.
- S. Elizabeth (O.S.F.), w. Aragon, Spain, Q. of Portugal, great niece of S. Elizabeth, of Hungary. July 8, 1336.
- S. Juliana Falconieri, v. Florence, Fndrs. of third Order of Women *Servites of Mary*. June 19, 1340.
- S. Pelegrino, c. (O.S.M.), Forli, Italy, *Apostle of Emilia*. May 1, 1345.
- Bl. Delphina (O.S.F.), v. Digne, France. Sept. 26, 1360.
- S. Catherine of Sienna (O P.), v. April 30, 1380.
- S. John Nepomucen, M. Canon of Prague, Bohemia, Martyr to the "Seal of Confession". May 16, 1383.
- S. Vincent Ferrer, c. (O.P.), Valencia, Spain. April 5, 1419.
- S. Frances (O S.B), w. of Rome, Fndrs. of *Collatines*. Mar. 9, 1440.
- Bl. Gabriel Ferretti, c. (O.S.F.) Ancona, where his body remains uncorrupted. Dec. 22, 1456.
- S. Catherine of Bologna, Italy, v. (O.S.F.) Her body still intact. Mar. 9., 1463.
- Bl. Amedeus, c. Duke of Savoy. Mar. 30, 1472.
- S. Casimir, c. son of Casimir III., K. of Poland and Elizabeth of Austria. Mar. 4, 1483.
- S. Bernardine of Sienna, Italy, c. (O.S.F.), great missionary, great worker of miracles, and great prophet. May 20, 1483.

LIST OF SOME SAINTS. 139

Bl. John Angelo Porro, c. (O.S.M.), Milan, introduced the method of *Christian Doctrine.* Oct. 24, 1506.
S. Francis of Paula, c. Calabria, great worker of miracles, Fndr. of *Friars Minims.* April 2, 1507.

And in later times, since poor England was torn away from Catholic unity:

S. Jerome Emilianus of Venice, c. Fndr. of the *Somasky,* for educating youth. July 20, 1537.
S. Angela of Merici, v. Brescia, Italy, Fndrs. of *Order of St. Ursula.* Jan. 27, 1540.
S. John of God, c. Fndr. of *Order of Charity for the Sick.* Mar. 11, 1550.
S. Francis Xavier (S.J.), c. Apostle of the Indies and Japan. Dec. 3, 1552.
S. Thomas of Villanova, c. Spain, Abp. of Valencia. Sept. 8, 1555.
S. Ignatius of Loyola, c. Guipuscoa, Spain, Fndr. of the *Society* or "*Company of Jesus*". July 31, 1556.
S. Stanislas Kostka (S.J.), c. Poland, Patr. of Youth. Nov. 13, 1568.
S. Puscal Babylon (O.S.F.), c. Aragon, Spain. May 17, 1582.
S. Teresa of Jesus, v. Avila, Castille, Spain, Reformer of the Carmelites, styled *The Seraphic Mother.* Oct. 15, 1582.
S. Pius V., P.C. (O.P.)., of Bosco, near Alessandria, Piedmont. May 5, 1572. He crushed the power of the invading Turks, of Emp. Selim II., in the Gulf of Lepanto, Ionian Sea. His uncorrupted body is seen in the Basilica of St. Mary Major, at Rome.
S. Charles Borromeo, c. Card. Abp. of Milan, once capital of Lombardy, Fndr. of *Oblates of S. Charles.* Nov. 4, 1584.
S. Catherine Ricci of Florence. v. Feb. 13, 1590.
S. Louis Gonzaga, or St. Aloysius (S.J.), c. Royal Prince, Castiglioni, Mantua. June 21, 1591.
S. John of the Cross (O.M.C.), c. Avila, Spain, co-adjutor of S. Teresa in reforming O.M.C. Nov. 24, 1591.
Bl. Alexander Sauli, c.B. Lombardy, Bp. of Pavia, Sup. Gen. of *Barnabites.* April 23 & Oct. 12, 1592.
Bl. Felix, c. Capuchin, Rome. May 18, 1595.
Bl. Peter Canisius, c. (S.J.) of Cologne. Dec. 21, 1597.
S. Philip Neri, c. Florence, Fndr. of the *Fathers of the Oratory,* surnamed *Apostle of Rome.* May 26, 1595.

LIST OF SOME SAINTS.

S. Mary Magdalen of Pazzi, Florence, v. Teresian Carmelite. May 27, 1607.
S. Andrew Avellino, c. *Theatine Father.* Nov. 10, 1608.
S. Camillus of Lellis, c. Fndr. of the *Clerks Regular (Servants of the Sick).* July 21, 1614.
S. Rose of Lima (O.P.), v. first canonised saint of South America. Aug. 30, 1617.
S. Francis of Sales, c. Bp. of Geneva, Fndr. of Order of *Nuns of the Visitation.* Jan. 29, 1622.
S. Sebastian Valfré, c. (C.O.) Piedmont, called the *Apostle of Turin.* Jan. 30, 1629.
S. Michael de Sanctis, c. Priest, Catalonia. April 10 1625.
S. Hyacintha Mariscotti, v. Rome. Feb. 6, 1640.
S. John Francis Regis (S.J.), Narbonne, France, wrought many miracles. June 16 and Dec. 31, 1640.
S. Jane Frances of Chantal, w. of Dijon, France, First of *Nuns of the Visitation.* Aug. 21, 1641.
S. Joseph Calasanctius, c. Aragon, Spain, Priest, Fndr. of the *Regular Clerks for the Instruction of Youth.* Aug. 27, 1648.
S. Catherine of Genoa, w. Mar. 22, 1650.
Bl. Peter Claver (S.J.) Carthagena, Spain, *Apostle of the Negroes,* called himself *Slave of the Slaves.* Sept. 9, 1654.
S. Vincent of Paul, c. Landes, France, Fndr., "*Congregation of Lazarists*" & "*Sisters of Charity.*" July 19, 1616.
S. Joseph of Cupertino, Italy, Friar-Minor, c., marvellous for his raptures, humility, and zeal. Sept. 18, 1663.
Bl. Margaret Mary Alacoque of the Incarnation, v. of Autun, and Paray-le-Monial, France, Nun of the *Visitation*; promoter of the Devotion to the SACRED HEART of JESUS. Oct. 17, 1690.
Ven. Margaret Bourgeois, Montreal, Lower Canada, Established Missions in Illinois, Vermont, and Connecticut; Fndrs., Order of Sisters of Congregation of Notre Dame, at Ville-Maria, Montreal. Died Jan. 12, 1700, aged 80.
Bl. Crispin (O.S.F.), Viterbo. May 23, 1710.
S. Leonard, c. Port Maurice, Genoa. Nov. 26, 1751.
S. Paul of the Cross, c. Ovada, near Alessandria, Piedmont, Fndr. of *Passionist Fathers.* April 28, 1775.
Bl. Joseph Benedict Labré, c. Mendicant, Boulogne, France. April 16, 1783.

S. Alphonsus Liguori, c.d. Bp. of St. Agatha, Naples. Fndr. of *Redemptorist Fathers*, Doctor of the Church. Aug. 2, 1787.

Ven. John Baptist de la Salle, Theologian, Canon of Rheims, France, Fndr. of the Institute of *Christian Brothers*, declared Venerable May 8, 1840. Died April 7, 1719.

Ven. Gaspare del Bufalo, c. Rome, Fndr. of the *Congregation of the Most Precious Blood*. Dec. 28, 1837.

Servant of God, Vincent Pallotti, Rome, Fndr. of the *Pious Society of Missions*, departed this life in the odour of sanctity, Jan. 22, 1850.

Ven. John B. Marie Vianney, Curé of Ars, near Lyons, France, departed this life in the odour of sanctity, Aug. 4, 1859, and declared Venerable Oct. 3, 1872.

Ven. Anne (de Lobera), of Jesus O.M.C. of Medina del Campo, Spain. *Companion of St. Teresa.* Founded Convents in France and Belgium. Departed this life in the odour of sanctity, at Brussels, Mar. 4, 1621. Declared Venerable by Pope Leo XIII., April 13, 1878;

and a host of other Saints of all nations, whom no man can number, and of *whom the world was not worthy, a glorious cloud of witnesses,* who lived and died strict members of the Catholic and Roman Church, and whose sanctity God has made known by many miracles, according to His promise:

"*Amen, amen, I say to you, he that believeth in Me, the works that I do, he also shall do, and greater than these shall he do: because I go to the Father.*" (S. John xiv. 12.) See also S. Mark xvi. 17, 18.

Thus it may be seen that the Roman Catholic Church has the doctrine of Holiness, the means of Holiness, the fruits of Holiness, and the divine testimony of Holiness.

CHAPTER XXXI.

Third Mark—Catholicity.

Catholics believe, as expressed in the Nicene Creed,

that the true Church of God is *Catholic*, that is to say, *universal*, or *spread throughout all nations*.

Jesus Christ sent His Apostles to teach, not only *one* nation, but *all nations;* therefore the true Church of Christ cannot be merely a *National Church*, separated in its teaching and discipline from all other Churches, but must be the Church which, everywhere one and the same, is spread throughout all the world.

Catholics are truly *Catholics*, in *fact* and in *name*. In *fact*, from their being not of one nation only, but of all nations of the earth; in *name*, because whenever and wherever *Catholics* are mentioned, without any additional designation, all persons, excepting a few who make a point of calling themselves Catholics, understand that Christians in communion with the See of Rome are meant and not others.

In all times Heretics, to avoid the force of this Mark, so strikingly in favour of Catholics, have endeavoured to change the name of *Catholics* into that of *Romans* and Romanists. S. Gregory of Tours relates of the Arians, that they persistently called the Catholics *Romans*. "Romanorum nomine vocitant nostræ Religionis homines?" (Hist., book xvii. chap. 25), but never succeeded in depriving the Catholics of their name.

The Protestants of the present day have somewhat departed from the old method. Seeing that it is useless to attempt to deprive us of this MARK of *Catholicity*, which throughout all ages distinguishes the true Church of God, they endeavour to weaken the force of it by qualifying it and saying: "We grant that you are Catholics, but you are not simply Catholics, you are *Roman* Catholics." They thus hope to establish for themselves a right to share with us this luminous

Mark and to call themselves Catholics or Anglican Catholics.

The addition, however, of *Roman* is unnecessary, because by the word Catholic is commonly understood the very same body of Christians they intend to describe by the additional name of Roman.

This way of speaking is calculated to mislead incautious people, by making them suppose that there can be more than one Church Catholic, or that the term *Roman* implies that the Catholic Church is only National, thus making nothing of the glorious *marks* of *Oneness* and of *Catholicity*.

A little reflection, however, might convince any one that the Catholic Church is not a human Institution, created by the State. It does not depend upon any earthly power for spiritual authority,—for rights,—for the free exercise of spiritual jurisdiction,—or for support, as Churches which are only National do; but is by Divine institution throughout all States and Kingdoms of the world free and independent.

It should be remembered that the Pope, the Successor in the Chair of S. Peter, whether exercising temporal power or not, remains from age to age the *visible* Head of the Church of God on earth, with the full authority, jurisdiction, and privileges granted to him by our Lord; and therefore Catholics are *Roman* because Rome is the centre, and the Bishop of Rome is the visible Head of Catholicity, and no one is really a Catholic unless he is in communion with the See of Rome.

To call Catholics *Roman* in this sense, does not alter the fact that they are Catholic in *name* and in *truth;* for the Catholic Church is truly universal, and spread among all Nations, although the Church is also *Roman* in having the Roman Pontiff for her visible Head. In this sense the word Roman marks the unity of the

Church and points to the Bishop of Rome as the one visible Shepherd. In this sense "the Catholic Church" and "the Roman Catholic Church" is the same thing: for both names, though one more fully than the other, express one and the same reality.

But when, owing to the remnant of the ancient faith yet lingering with them, Protestants in repeating the Apostles' Creed say: "*I believe the Holy Catholic Church*," they surely cannot mean, "I believe the particular denomination to which I belong," or, "I believe my National Church, to be the Catholic Church," if they reflect that local and limited as their denomination or church is, and separated from all other churches and nations of the world, they cannot in truth be called *Catholic*.

Again, it is not reasonable for Protestants to say that they believe the *Catholic* but not the *Roman* Catholic Church. Such a mode of interpreting this passage of the Nicene Creed seems but a poor way of appropriating to themselves this glorious mark of *Catholicity* by confusing the minds of simple people, and mystifying the sense of the word *Catholic*, and of the word *Roman*.

I will here endeavour to show the error of this interpretation.

When Protestants say: "*We believe the Catholic but not the Roman Catholic Church*," they may be taken to argue with Catholics in this manner: "We admit that you are *Catholics*, because in fact your Church is spread throughout all nations, but still you are also *Roman*, because you acknowledge the Bishop of Rome to be the visible Head of your Church, and therefore we are justified in calling you Roman; and we are careful to call you by this name, because this word *Roman* makes it appear to unreflecting people that you are only National Catholics like ourselves."

THIRD MARK—CATHOLICITY.

After having called us *Roman* Catholics, they also tell us that they themselves are not *Roman* Catholics, for the simple reason that they reject the Pope of Rome. And though they are members of a church which is only *National*, or of a denomination *only limited*, and therefore not *Catholic* in the proper sense of the term, they yet call themselves Catholics in *some other particular sense of their own*, and they say therefore that they are *Catholics*, though not *Roman* Catholics.

It is easy, however, to see that this is not fair reasoning. Surely it would not be fair dealing if a Mahommedan were to maintain that he was a *Christian* on the ground that, although he did not believe Christ to be God and Saviour, yet he believed a great deal that is related about Him, and therefore had a right to call himself a Christian, and to say, "*I am a Christian, but not a thorough-going Christian*". The least you would say of such a man, I imagine, would be, that he acts unfairly, and deceives himself, not taking the word *Christian* in the common meaning, but attaching to it a meaning of his own, which no one, unless told his particular views, could possibly understand.

Nor does it avail such Protestants to say that by professing to believe the Catholic Church, *they mean the Universal invisible Church;* for this would amount to believing in a Church that does not and cannot come forward and speak out, and therefore *does not teach*. This would bring to nought the essential office of *teaching* committed by Christ to His Church, and the corresponding duty on the part of the faithful to *believe what she teaches*. The Church on earth is essentially and perpetually *visible*. She is that "*mountain . . . on the top of mountains*," (Isaias ii. 2; Daniel

ii. 35), that "*city seated on a mountain*," a city that "*cannot be hid*" (S. Matth. v. 14).

Some Protestants answer in this manner—When we say, "*I believe the Catholic Church,*" we do not mean, "*I believe my Denomination or National Church.*" We do not mean, "*I believe an invisible Church,*" but we mean, "*I believe a visible Church, spread throughout the world, composed of different National Churches, Greek, Roman, Lutheran, Anglican, American, and others, which, though disagreeing in certain things, yet agree with each other in essentials, and are so many branches of one tree, forming one universal Church*".

It should be observed however, first, that such *interpretation* of this passage of the Creed was never admitted in the Church. Such an interpretation was *implicitly* (that is in an implied manner) rejected in all centuries, as is evident from the fact that the Catholic Church has always regarded as *schismatical* any Christian community not in communion with herself, and as *heretical* any community rejecting any of her defined articles of faith.

Secondly, that this interpretation is universally and openly rejected not only by Roman Catholics, but also by the separated Greek and other schismatical Churches, and is held only by some Protestants, and by a human tradition of the Anglican State Church, who make use of this explanation to justify their position with regard to this Article of the Creed.

Thirdly, that this interpretation or theory cannot stand, for these different Communities are, in fact, not united in essentials. On the contrary, they disagree in some doctrine which one Community considers *essential* to profess and another considers *essential* to deny. They cannot, therefore, be compared to branches of the one only tree, having the same stem and root, and partaking of the same sap, whatever resemblance they may have in certain features.

Perhaps by the words, "agree in essentials," they mean that the said Communities, though differing from one another in points considered *vital* by some of them, yet that they all agree in the things defined by the first six General Councils, which are admitted in the "Homilies" of the State Church of England to be binding upon all Christians. But the early Church, and those six General Councils, based their right of making any definition on this fundamental principle *admitted* by all the members of the said Church, namely, that "everything which the Church in communion with the See of Rome should ever define as an article of faith was to be believed by all".

It is self-evident that without this previous general admission of the duty of believing whatever the Church teaches and should teach as an article of faith, any assembling of General Councils for the sake of setling disputes of religion would have been of no use.

I said, "in communion with the See of Rome". The necessity of this is manifest. The very Bishops themselves of those six General Councils were convoked, and presided over by the Pope through his Legates. They submitted to the Pope's orders. The Canons framed by the Council had to receive the final sanction of the Pope before their validity would be recognised. Moreover, the Bishops expressed in plain words in those very Councils the Primacy or Supremacy of the Roman See.

Thus, in the First General Council, that of Nicaea, the Fathers said, as quoted by the Council of Chalcedon (Fourth General Council, Act 16), "*The Roman Church always had the Primacy*" (See page 106).

In the Second General Council (the First of Constantinople), in the letter which the Fathers wrote to Pope Damasus I., as recorded by Theodoret in the fifth book of his "Ecclesiastical History" (chap. 9), the Fathers or Bishops of that Council acknowledged that the Roman Church is the HEAD and they the MEMBERS.

In the Fourth General Council, that of Chalcedon (in the 1st, 2nd, and 3rd Acts), the Fathers several times called Pope S. Leo, the then reigning Pontiff, "*The Bishop of the universal Church,*" "*To whom the Saviour has entrusted the guardianship of the Vineyard,*" as they add in their letter to the same holy Pontiff.

With the exception, therefore, of the Catholics in communion with Rome, who, to this day, adhere to the said fundamental principle, all Schismatical Churches or Christian Communities which repudiate that principle are convicted of not adhering either to that early Church, or to ALL the Definitions of those first six General Councils; and, with regard to those Definitions which they do accept, they do not agree with the spirit with which they were made, nor with the above-stated fundamental principle upon which they were based.

To say that the Church, called in the Gospel the *Kingdom of God*, is made up of a number of discordant Churches which have no real inter-communion, and no visible connection, and each of which considers the other schismatical, or heretical, would be as strange as to say that Europe forms one Empire, though composed of different nations independent one of another; and that, though disunited as they are, though rivals, and though at times even at war, yet that they are one, because they agree with each in some points of law, custom, or civilisation. This would be like saying that the Church of God is a Society composed of disconnected and clashing elements, without any visible head, without unity, order and proportion, and without that intercommunion, harmony, and sympathy between the members of it, which a well-regulated Society should have, and which on this account is compared by S. Paul to a perfect human body. This would be like supposing that the Church is only a *Church of disunion* or *no Church at all*, and that her office of teaching tends only to puzzle or to mislead people by continual contradictions.

CHAPTER XXXII.

FOURTH MARK—APOSTOLICITY.

The Catholic Church is Apostolic. This means that she is a Church which has not sprung up in modern times, nor ever separated herself from any other Church, but is the very Church founded by *Jesus Christ* and the Apostles, although now become more unfolded, like a nobly spreading tree which once was but a small plant.

Apostolicity, more accurately defined, consists in *an unbroken succession of Pastors, who from the time of the Apostles down to the present day, have been rightly ordained, lawfully sent*, and who in succession have taught the *same unchanging doctrines.*

By this *right ordination, legitimate mission*, and *pure doctrine*, the Catholic Church of to-day is the continuation of that Church founded by *Jesus Christ* and the Apostles; forms with it but one living identical body, which carries on the Mission of the Apostles, and is the only true abiding messenger sent by Christ for the guidance of men to eternal salvation.

The Roman Catholic Church alone is all this. Her doctrine has never changed; it has from time to time been unfolded and made more clear, especially when heresy or some other necessity has called for a solemn and precise definition; but there is no case of the Roman Catholic Church holding a doctrine which was previously declared heretical, or declaring heretical what was formerly defined by the Church as a dogma of faith; so much so that it is a proverbial saying even among Protestants that the Roman Church *(semper eadem)* never changes.

In the Catholic Church *alone*, from the time of the Apostles until now, has there been an unbroken succession of Pastors, lawfully *ordained and sent.** The Catholic Church never separated herself from any other Church, and there never was a time from the foundation of Christianity when she did not exist.

Protestant denominations, on the contrary, are all

---

* The Greek Schismatic Church having by separation in the ninth century (879) under Photius, Patriarch of Constantinople, rejected the lawful authority of the Church of Christ, though possessing rightful ordination, has not lawful mission, nor continuity of the whole deposit of Catholic doctrine. That the Holy Ghost does not proceed from the Son as well as from the Father is a heresy anathematized by S. Cyril of Alexandria in a Provincial Synod held in that city; and this condemnation of S. Cyril against Nestorius was confirmed by the General Council of Ephesus in 431, and yet the Greek Church, since her separation from the Catholic Church in 879, adheres to this heresy. True, in the General Council of Lyons, 1274, the Greek Bishops retracted their error, and together with the Latin Bishops condemned it, and caused the words, "*Who proceeds from the Father and the Son,*" to be inserted in the Nicene Creed, but soon relapsed into that heresy. Again, in the General Council at Florence, held in 1439, which was attended also by the Schismatical Greek Bishops, this heresy was condemned (Session xxv.), but on returning home the Greek Bishops relapsed into their Schism and Heresy, and still adhere to it.

modern; the oldest of them having only a few centuries of existence. They saw no sect quite like themselves at the time of their separating from the Catholic Church, or probably they would have joined it. These sects, in fact, only began when their several founders gave them existence; hence they are often distinguished by the name of their founder or by some special feature of their new doctrine;* and far from being Apostolic,

*See List of Sects in Appendix, No. 21.

they reject Apostolical Tradition and the testimonies of the first Successors of the Apostles, either in profession or in practice, or in both. Cardinal Bellarmine has enumerated a score of Protestant doctrines, which are but old heresies, condemned in the early centuries of the Church (*De Notis Ecclesiæ*, book iv. chap. 9).

The following historical series of all the Bishops of Rome, Successors of S. Peter, to the present time confirms the fact that this luminous MARK of APOSTOLICITY belongs to the Roman Catholic Church alone.

CHAPTER XXXIII.

LIST OF THE SOVEREIGN PONTIFFS WHO, BY AN UNBROKEN LINE, HAVE SUCCEEDED ST. PETER IN THE SEE OF ROME.

CENTURY I.—4 Popes. *Vulgar Era.*

NO. A.D.
1. SAINT PETER, native of Bethsaida in Galilee, became Pope on the Ascension of JESUS CHRIST; that is, in the year 29 of the Vulgar Era,* and BISHOP of ROME in 42, where he died Martyr in the year...................................... 67

*The Vulgar Era is designated by the initials A.D. from the Latin *Anno Domini* (in the year of our Lord). It is the Era of which all Western Catholics make use in the designation of years. It was introduced by Dionysius Exiguus about the year A.D. 540, and sometime after was universally adopted. A more diligent examination, however, of ancient monuments has caused many learned writers to consider this calculation

LIST OF SOVEREIGN PONTIFFS.

	Vulgar Era.
NO.	A.D.
2. S. Linus, native of Volterra, Martyr............Succeeded	67
3. S. Cletus, Rome, Martyr..	80
4. S. Clement I., Rome, Martyr......................................	92

CENTURY II.—11 Popes.

5. S. Anacletus, Athens, Greece, Martyr........................	101
6. S. Evaristus, Bethlehem, Martyr.................................	112
7. S. Alexander I., Rome, Martyr...................................	121
8. S. Sixtus I., Rome, Martyr...	132
9. S. Telesphorus, Greece, Martyr, confirmed the Lenten Fast, introduced the *Gloria in Excelsis* in the Mass, and allowed three Masses to be celebrated on Christmas Day............	142
10. S. Hyginus, Athens, Greece, Martyr, instituted Subdeaconship and the Minor Orders....................................	154
11. S. Pius I., Aquileia, Martyr..	158
12. S. Anicetus, Syria, Martyr...	167
13. S. Soter, Naples, Martyr..	175
14. S. Eleutherius, Epirus, Martyr...................................	182
15. S. Victor I., Africa, Martyr..	193

CENTURY III.—15 Popes.

16. S. Zephyrinus, Rome, Martyr....................................	202
17. S. Calistus, Rome, Martyr...	219
18. S. Urban I., Rome, Martyr..	224
19. S. Pontianus, Rome, Martyr......................................	231
20. S. Anterus, Greece, Martyr..	235
21. S. Fabian, Rome (at his election a dove rested on his head) Martyr..	240
22. S. Cornelius, Rome, Martyr.......................................	251
23. S. Lucius I., Lucca, Martyr..	253
24. S. Stephanus I., Rome, Martyr...................................	255
25. S. Sixtus II., Athens, Greece, Martyr.........................	257
26. S. Dionysius, Turin..	259
27. S. Felix I., Rome, Martyr, prescribed the rite for the dedication of Churches..	269
28. S. Eutychianus, Tuscany, Martyr...............................	275
29. S. Caius, Dalmatia, Martyr..	283
30. S. Marcellinus, Rome, Martyr...................................	295

CENTURY IV.—11 Popes.*

31. S. Marcellus I., Rome, Martyr..................................	304
32. S. Eusebius, Calabria...	309
33. S. Melchiades, Africa...	311

inexact. According to them our Lord was born in the seventh year before the first year of the Vulgar Era. Therefore, strictly speaking, the Christian Era commences when Christ was between six and seven years of age. So that, adding seven years to the date of the Vulgar Era put down, gives the real date from the real epoch of the birth of our Lord.

* The dates of accession of several Popes before the time of Constantine somewhat differ in some of the early catalogues.

LIST OF SOVEREIGN PONTIFFS. 153

	Vulgar Era. A.D.

34. S. Sylvester I., Rome, commanded that the altars be of stone. Received the Emperor Constantine into the church as Catechumen. Constantine was baptised and died near Nicomedia...*Succeeded* 314
35. S. Marcus, Rome.. 336
36. S. Julius I., Rome... 341
37. S. Liberius, Rome... 352
38. S. Felix II., Rome, during the exile of Pope Liberius............ 363
39. S. Damasus I., Spain, commanded the *Gloria Patri* to be added in the end of every Psalm....................................... 366
40. S. Siricius, Rome... 385
41. S. Anastasius I., Rome, prescribed that at the reading of the Gospel in the Mass all should stand........................... 398

CENTURY V.—12 Popes.

42. S. Innocent I., Albano... 402
43. S. Zosimus, Greece, condemned Pelagius and Celestius........... 417
44. S. Boniface I., Rome.. 418
45. S. Celestine I., Rome.. 423
46. S. Sixtus III., Rome.. 432
47. S. Leo I., the Great, Tuscany. He stayed Attila and Genseric from further invading Italy.................................... 440
48. S. Hilarius, Sardinia.. 461
49. S. Simplicius, Tivoli... 468
50. S. Felix III., Rome.. 483
51. S. Gelasius I., Africa. He decreed the Canon of Scripture with which the Tridentine Canon agrees............................. 492
52. S. Anastasius II., Rome.. 496
53. S. Symmachus, Rome.. 498

CENTURY VI.—13 Popes.

54. S. Hormisdas, Frosinone.. 514
55. S. John I., Tuscany, Martyr....................................... 523
56. S. Felix IV., Benevento.. 526
57. Boniface II., Rome... 530
58. John II., Rome... 532
59. S. Agapetus I., Rome.. 535
60. S. Silverius, Frosinone, Martyr.................................... 536
61. Vigilius, Rome.. 538
62. Pelagius I., Rome, condemned the "Three Chapters."........... 555
63. John III., Rome.. 560
64. Benedict I., Rome.. 574
65. Pelagius II., Rome... 579
66. S. Gregory I., the Great, Rome, instituted the plain chant, Apostle of England. Through humility styled himself *servant of servants*, yet he exercised supreme Pontifical jurisdiction like any other Pope.. 590

CENTURY VII.—20 Popes.

67. Sabinianus, Volterra, introduced the use of bells............... 604
68. Boniface III., Rome.. 607

LIST OF SOVEREIGN PONTIFFS.

		Vulgar Era.
NO.		A.D.
69.	S. Boniface IV., Valeria in the Marsi. Instituted All-Saints' Day. Obtained the *Pantheon* from the Emperor Phocas, which he dedicated to God in honour of the Blessed Virgin and all the holy Martyrs..................................*Succeeded*	608
70.	Deodatus I., Rome...	615
71.	Boniface V., Naples..	620
72.	Honorius I., Capua. He was greatly censured for having been remiss in condemning heretics................	625
73.	Severinus, Rome..	640
74.	John IV., Dalmatia...	640
75.	Theodore I., Greece..	642
76.	S. Martin I., Todi, Martyr....................................	649
77.	S. Eugenius I., Rome...	654
78.	S. Vitalianus, Segni, introduced the use of organs in churches...	657
79.	Deodatus II., Rome..	672
80.	Donus I., Rome...	677
81.	S. Agatho, Greece...	679
82.	S. Leo II., Sicily. Improved the Church chant.................	682
83.	S. Benedict II., Rome..	685
84.	John V., Antioch...	686
85.	Conon, Thrace..	687
86.	S. Sergius, Sicily...	688

CENTURY VIII.—13 Popes.

87.	John VI., Greece...	701
88.	John VII., Greece..	705
89.	Sisinnius, Syria...	707
90.	Constantinus, Syria..	708
91.	S. Gregory II., Rome...	715
92.	S. Gregory III., Syria...	731
93.	Zachary, Greece..	741
94.	Stephen II., Rome, died before his consecration.............	752
95.	Stephen III., Rome, called by some Stephen II. Pepin gave him the Italian Provinces which he had conquered from the usurper King of Lombardy, Astulphus....................	752
96.	S. Paul I., Rome...	757
97.	Stephen IV., Syracuse, called by some Stephen III..........	768
98.	Adrian I., Rome (Colonnae)....................................	772
99.	S. Leo III., Rome, consecrated Charles the Great, Emperor of the West, and thus restored the Roman Empire after 300 years cessation..	795

CENTURY IX.—19 Popes.

100.	Stephen V., Rome, called by some Stephen IV................	816
101.	S. Paschal I., Rome..	817
102.	Eugenius II., Rome..	824
103.	Valentinus, Rome..	827
104.	Gregory IV., Rome...	827
105.	Sergius II., Rome..	844
106.	S. Leo IV., Rome, fortified the Vatican against Saracens........	847

LIST OF SOVEREIGN PONTIFFS.

NO.		Vulgar Era. A.D.
107.	*Benedict III., Rome .... Succeeded	855
108.	S. Nicholas I., the Great, Rome.........................	858
109.	Adrian II., Rome..	867
110.	John VIII., Rome..	872
111.	Martin II., or Marinus I., Gallese...................	882
112.	Adrian III., Rome.......................................	884
113.	Stephen VI., Rome, called by some Stephen V.............	885
114.	Formosus, Ostia...	891
	Boniface VI., Rome, reigned only fifteen days; doubtful if legitimately elected.	
115.	Stephen VII., Rome, called by some Stephen VI...........	897
116.	Romanus, Gallese..	898
117.	Theodorus II., Rome.....................................	898
118.	John IX., Tivoli..	898

CENTURY X.—24 Popes.

119.	Benedict IV., Rome......................................	900
120.	Leo V., Ardea...	903
121.	Christophorus, Rome.....................................	903
122.	Sergius III., Rome......................................	904
123.	Anastasius III., Rome...................................	911
124.	Lando, Sabina...	913
125.	John X., Ravenna..	915
126.	Leo VI., Rome...	928
127.	Stephen VIII., otherwise VII., Rome.....................	929
128.	John XI., Rome..	931
129.	Leo VII., Tusculum......................................	936
130.	Stephen IX. or VIII., Rome..............................	939
131.	Martin III., or Marinus II., Rome.......................	943
132.	Agapetus II., Rome......................................	946
133.	John XII., Rome...	956
	Leo VIII., antipope.................................... 963	
134.	Benedict V., Rome.......................................	964
135.	John XIII., Rome..	965
136.	Benedict VI., Rome......................................	972
137.	Donus, or Domnus II., Rome..............................	974
138.	Benedict VII., Rome.....................................	975
139.	John XIV., Pavia..	984
	Boniface VII., antipope, French, lasting 8 months.	
	John XV., antipope, Rome, who died in 4 months.	

* Between S. Leo IV. and Benedict III. is placed by comparatively recent detractors of the Papacy the name of Joan or Johanna. A female Pope is a thing not only improbable and absurd, but also impossible; for, according to Catholic belief, a woman cannot even be a Priest, much less a Bishop and a Pope. Her name, in fact, is not found in any of the ancient chronologies of Popes, nor is it mentioned by any of the contemporaries, nor by any trustworthy historian, during the seven centuries that followed the epoch of the pretended reign. Leibnitz, Blondell, Boxhorn, Cave, and other Protestants have proved that the whole thing is absolutely false. It appears that this story has no other foundation than a false rumour by Frederick Spenheim eagerly received by people disaffected to the Papal Chair.

156   LIST OF SOVEREIGN PONTIFFS.

		Vulgar Era.
NO.		A.D.
140.	John XV. or XVI., established rules for solemn canonisation of Saints... *Succeeded*	985
141.	Gregory V., before called Bruno, of royal blood, Germany. He was interrupted for a short time by an intruded John XVII. of Placentia..	996
142.	Sylvester II., Auvergne, France (Gerbert). Gave to Stephen, Ruler of Hungary, the title of King........................	999

CENTURY XI.—18 Popes.

143.	John XVIII., Rome..	1003
144.	John XIX., Rome...	1003
145.	Sergius IV., the first Pope who changed his name on ascending the Papal throne. His baptismal name was Peter.....	1009
146.	Benedict VIII., Rome..	1012
147.	John XX., Rome..	1024
148.	Benedict IX., Rome...	1033
149.	Gregory VI., Rome, abdicated in 1046..........................	1045
150.	Clement II., Saxony..	1046
151.	Damasus II., Bavaria...	1048
152.	S. Leo IX., Alsace, Bavaria, Germany............................	1049
153.	Victor II., Servia...	1055
154.	Stephen X. or IX., Germany..	1057
	Benedict X., antipope	1058
155.	Nicholas II., Burgundy, France (Gherard). Ordered that in future Popes be elected by the Cardinals in Conclave......	1059
156.	Alexander II., Milan...	1061
157.	S. Gregory VII., Soana; (Aldobrandeschi) withstood the encroachments of Cæsarism. Absolved Henry IV. at Canossa, who ungratefully afterwards invaded Rome................	1073
158.	Victor III., Benevento..	1087
159.	Urban II., Rheims...	1088
160.	Paschal II., Tuscany..	1099

CENTURY XII.—15 Popes.

161.	Gelasius II., Gaeta...	1118
162.	Calistus II., Burgundy..	1118
163.	Honorius II., Bologna...	1124
164.	Innocent II., Rome..	1130
165.	Celestine II., Città di Castollo......................................	1143
166.	Lucius II., Bologna..	1144
167.	B. Eugenius III., Montemagno, Pisa. He had been disciple of S. Bernard. He was thrice compelled to emigrate from Rome on account of seditions............................	1145
168.	Anastasius IV., Rome...	1153
169.	Adrian IV. (Nicholas Brakspear), Langley, England..........	1154
170.	Alexander III., Siena..	1159
171.	Lucius III., Lucca..	1181
172.	Urban III., Milano...	1185
173.	Gregory VIII., Benevento...	1187
174.	Clement III., Rome..	1187
175.	Celestine III., Rome...	1191
176.	Innocent III., Anagni...	1196

CENTURY XIII.—17 Popes.

NO.		A.D.
177.	Honorius III., Rome .... Succeeded	1216
178.	Gregory IX., Anagni	1227
179.	Celestine IV., Milan.	1241
180.	Innocent IV., Genoa................................	1243
181.	Alexander IV., Anagni	1254
182.	Urban IV.. Troyes, instituted the Feast of "*Corpus Domini*".	1261
183.	Clement IV., Narbonne, France	1265
184.	Gregory X., Piacenza...............................	1271
185.	Innocent V., Savoy	1276
186.	Adrian V., Genoa...................................	1276
187.	John XXI., Lisbon.	1276
188.	Nicholas III., Rome................................	1277
189.	Martin IV., Champagne, France......................	1281
190.	Honorius IV., Rome.................................	1285
191.	Nicholas IV., Ascoli...............................	1288
192.	S. Celestine V., Terra di Lavoro, Naples (resigned the Pontificate) hermit..	1294
193.	Boniface VIII., Anagni.............................	1294

CENTURY XIV.—10 Popes.

194.	B. Benedict XI., Treviso...........................	1303
195.	Clement V., Bordeaux, ordered the election of Popes to be made in conclave ; removed to Avignon..............	1305
196.	John XXII., Cohors, France.........................	1316
197.	Benedict XII., Foix, France........................	1334
198.	Clement VI., Limoges, France.......................	1342
199.	Innocent VI., Limoges, France......................	1352
200.	B. Urban V., Mende, France.........................	1362
201.	Gregory XI., Limoges, France, returned to Rome, 1377	1370
202.	Urban VI., Naples..................................	1378
203.	Boniface IX., Naples, published the Crusade against Bajazet	1389

CENTURY XV.—13 Popes.

204.	Innocent VII., Sulmona.............................	1404
205.	Gregory XII., Venice, resigned in 1409	1406
206.	Alexander V. Bologna...............................	1409
207.	John XXIII., Naples, resigned in 1415	1410
208.	Martin V., Rome....................................	1417
209.	Eugenius IV., Venice...............................	1431
210.	Nicholas V., Sarzana...............................	1447
211.	Calistus III., Valentia, Spain.....................	1455
212.	Pius II., Siena....................................	1458
213.	Paul II., Venice...................................	1464
214.	Sixtus IV., Savona.................................	1471
215.	Innocent VIII., Genoa..............................	1484
216.	Alexander VI., Spain	1492

CENTURY XVI.—17 Popes.

217.	Pius III., Siena...................................	1503
218.	Julius II., Savona.................................	1503
219.	Leo X., Florence...................................	1513
220.	Adrian VI., Utrecht................................	1522
221.	Clement VII., Florence.............................	1523

5A

LIST OF SOVEREIGN PONTIFFS

NO.		*Vulgar Era.* A.D.
222.	Paul III., Rome, convoked the Council of Trent....Succeeded	1534
223.	Julius III., Tuscany...	1550
224.	Marcellus II., Montepulciano.................?.............	1555
225.	Paul IV., Naples..	1555
226.	Pius IV., Milan, *ended* and confirmed the Council of Trent...	1559
227.	S. Pius V., Bosco, near Alessandria, Piedmont...............	1566
228.	Gregory XIII., Bologna, corrected the Calendar.............	1572
229.	Sixtus V., Ancona, Franciscan. He procured a more correct Latin (or Vulgate) edition of the Bible................	1585
230.	Urban VII., Rome..	1590
231.	Gregory XIV., Cremona.......................................	1590
232.	Innocent IX. Bologna..	1591
233.	Clement VIII., Florence.......................................	1592

CENTURY XVII.—11 Popes.

234.	Leo XI., Florence..................................Succeeded	1605
235.	Paul V., Rome...	1605
236.	Gregory XV., Bologna..	1621
237.	Urban VIII., Florence..	1623
238.	Innocent X., Rome,...	1643
239.	Alexander VII., Siena..	1655
240.	Clement IX., Pistoja...	1667
241.	Clement X., Rome..	1670
242.	Innocent XI., Como..	1676
243.	Alexander VIII., Venice.......................................	1689
244.	Innocent XII., Naples...	1691

CENTURY XVIII.—8 Popes.

245.	Clement XI., Urbino...	1700
246.	Innocent XIII., Rome..	1721
247.	Benedict XIII., Rome. Praised the Thomistic School.......	1724
248.	Clement XII., Florence. Declared that the praises bestowed by his predecessor to the Thomistic School do not detract from other Catholic Schools.............................	1730
249.	Benedict XIV., Bologna..	1740
250.	Clement XIII., Venice..	1758
251.	Clement XIV., Sant' Angelo in Vado.........................	1769
252.	Pius VI., Cesena...	1775

CENTURY XIX.

253.	Pius VII., Cesena...	1800
254.	Leo. XII., Spoleto..	1823
255.	Pius VIII., Cingoli..	1829
256.	Gregory XVI., Bellimo...	1831
257.	Pius IX., John Mary Mastai-Ferretti, born in Senigallia (March) Italy, May 13, 1792. Died Feb. 7, 1878. Reigned nearly 32 years. Created Pope, June 16................	1846
258.	His Holiness Leo XIII., Vincent Joachim (Gioacchino) Pecci* Bishop of Perugia. Born in Carpineto, Velletri, March 2, 1810. Thirteen days after the death of his glorious Predecessor he was created Pope, Feb. 20, 1878, whom may God long preserve...	1878

* Pronounced *Petshee*.

NOTE.—*The Roman Pontiffs.*—The number of Popes from S. Peter to Leo XIII. inclusively, without counting the Antipopes, is commonly said to be 258. Of this number, 82 are venerated as Saints, 33 were martyred; 104 have been Romans, and 103 natives of other parts of Italy; 15 Frenchmen; 9 Greeks; 7 Germans; 5 Asiatics; 3 Africans; 3 Spaniards; 2 Dalmatians; 1 Hebrew; 1 Thracian; 1 Dutchman; 1 Portuguese; 1 Candiot; and 1 Epglishman. Nine Pontiffs have reigned less than 1 month, 30 less than 1 year, and 11 more than 20 years. Only 6 have occupied the Pontifical Chair over 23 years. These are S. Peter, who was Supreme Pastor in Rome (besides the years of his Pontificate in Antioch), 25 years, 2 months, 7 days; Sylvester I., 23 years, 10 months, 27 days; Adrian I., 23 years, 10 months, 14 days; Pius VI., 24 years, 6 months, 3 days; Pius VII., 23 years, 5 months, 6 days; and Pius IX., who reigned 31 years, 7 months, 21 days, and who celebrated his 30th year in the Pontifical Chair June 19, A.D. 1876.

CHAPTER XXXIV.

THE SIGN OF THE CROSS.

This holy sign, called the "*Sign of the Son of Man*" (S. Matt. xxiv. 30), is made use of by the Catholic Church in all the Sacraments to show us that they derive all their virtue from the CROSS; that is, from the death and Passion of our Saviour JESUS CHRIST.

The pious custom of signing oneself with the sign of the CROSS is in frequent use among Catholics.

The sign of the CROSS is made upon ourselves in the the following manner :—

You put the fingers of your right hand on your forehead and say: *In the name of the Father;* then, putting them on your breast, you say, *and of the Son;* then on the left shoulder, and immediately after on the right shoulder, while you say, *and of the Holy Ghost.* You may then join both hands before your breast, and say, *Amen.*

It is honourable thus to disregard human respect, to profess outwardly what we are, namely, followers of *Jesus Christ.* This is what we do when we make the sign of the Cross, as this sign recalls to the mind of all persons present the mystery of our Redemption wrought by our Lord and Saviour on the Cross, and in which Redemption we believe and trust.

The Cross is the natural emblem, and, as it were, the distinguishing banner, of Christians. Every Christian, therefore, like S. Paul, ought not to be ashamed to sign himself with it, but to *glory in the Cross of Christ*, (Galatians vi. 14.)

Should a feeling of shame come over you whilst making this sign, shake it off by recalling to mind those words of Jesus Christ: "*For he that shall be ashamed of Me and of My words, of him the Son of man shall be ashamed, when He shall come in His majesty, and that of His Father, and of the holy Angels.*" (S. Luke ix. 26.)

For these reasons, and also for the edification of others, it is commendable and useful for Christians to make the sign of the Cross.

The sign of the Cross is also an excellent Act of Faith in the two fundamental truths of the Christian Religion, namely, in the mystery of the Holy Trinity, one God in three Persons, and in the mystery of the Incarnation.

For, by saying, In the "*name*," in the singular number, we profess to believe that there is only one God. By saying, "*of the Father, and of the Son, and of the Holy Ghost*," we profess to believe that in one God there are three Divine Persons. By the form of the Cross, which we trace with our right hand from our forehead to our breast, and then across from shoulder to shoulder, we profess to believe that the Son of God is our Redeemer, who wrought out Redemption by dying for us upon the Cross.

By the word, *Amen* (so be it), we mean to confirm

and seal, as it were, our belief in the said fundamental truths.

The sign of the Cross was used in the first five centuries even more frequently than it is now. Passages could be quoted from Lactantius, from Eusebius of Cæsarea, from S. Athanasius, S. Basil, S. Ephrem, S. Cyril of Jerusalem, S. Ambrose, and from S. John Chrysostom, all of them Fathers of the fourth century, to prove it. But I will quote only two passages.

Tertullian, who wrote in the second century, says: "At every fresh step and change of place, whenever we come in or go out, when we put on our sandals, or wash, or take our meals, or light our lamps; whether we are about to recline or to sit down, and whenever we begin a conversation, we impress on our forehead the sign of the Cross. "*Ad omne progressum atque promotum, ad omnem aditum et exitum, ad calceatum, ad lavacra, ad mensas, ad lumina, ad cubicula et sedilia, quandocumque nos conversatio exercet, frontem, crucis signaculo terimus.*" (De Corona Militis, chap. iii. 4.)

St. Jerome, a Father of the fourth century, addressing the Roman Lady Eustachia, writes: "*Before every action, at every step, let your hand form the sign of the Cross.*" (Epistola xviii. ad Eustachiam, titulo iv.)

St. Basil asserts as a noted fact that the practice of making the sign of the Cross was introduced by the Apostles. (Book on the Holy Ghost, chap. 37.)

Let us, therefore, in imitation of the ancient Christians, be fond of making the sign of the Cross before doing anything of any consequence. It will be like directing our intention to do that thing for God. It will be the token of putting our whole trust in the Merits of *Jesus Christ* which He earned on the Cross, and of our invoking God's help through those Merits.

CHAPTER XXXV.

On Prayer.

Prayer is "a raising up of the mind and heart to God," begging His aid and blessing. It forms a considerable part of the worship we owe to God. It is needful that we should give an outline of the Catholic teaching on this subject.

Although God gives some graces without being asked, such as the first moving graces of faith, and the grace of prayer, He has other graces necessary for salvation in store only for those who humbly ask for them. It is therefore necessary for us who have the use of reason to pray.

To make use of prayer is not only a counsel but a precept: "*Watch ye and pray,*" says our Lord, "*that ye enter not into temptation.*" (S. Matt. xxvi. 41.) "*We ought always to pray and not to faint.*" S. Luke xviii. 1.)

Therefore, to neglect prayer altogether for any great length of time would not only be dangerous but a grievous sin.

There are certain occasions in life in which we are especially bound to pray; as when pressed by a strong temptation which we feel we have not the strength to overcome; or when in evident danger of death; or when we have to receive a Sacrament, for the due reception of which Sacrament prayer is necessary by way of preparation ; or in time of great public calamity ; and, in general, when there is a particular need of Divine assistance.

Let us not say, God is infinite goodness, He knows all our wants, He will grant us what is needful without our asking for it. God requires that we should ask, not because He knows not our wants, or because He is not ready to help us, but that we may, by asking show our humility and dependence on Him, and enjoy the advantage and honour of praying to Him.

It is a part of the duty of princes and princesses to present themselves morning and evening to their royal parents, to converse with them, to show them their filial love and respect, affection, and gratitude, and make known their wants and wishes to them. Few would object to be a prince merely on account of the trouble he would have in presenting himself dutifully every day to his parents. Surely, if it be a task, it is a sweet one.

Prayer rightly regarded should be a sweet duty, and it is a great honour to be allowed to present ourselves before our Creator, the immortal King of Heaven, to be allowed to call Him Father, to be permitted to communicate with Him, to show Him our reverence, gratitude, and love, and to put our wants before Him. By it we enjoy an opportunity of dutifully acknowledging Him as the source of all good, the Author of our salvation ; and of kindling in our hearts love towards Him by that sweet intercourse which prayer procures to us, and by the benefits that prayer obtains.

Indeed, to render the duty of prayer sweeter still, God does to us what Kings and Queens do not do to their children. He encourages us to approach Him with confidence, by pledging His word that our petitions shall never be rejected, even if we be in a state of sin like the poor publican or the penitent thief; for, though the prayer of the just is more acceptable to God, according to S. James: "*The continual prayer of a just man availeth much*" (v. 16), yet Christ says in general, without excluding the sinner: "*Every one that asketh, receiveth.*" (S. Matt. vii. 8.) For as S. Thomas Aquinas teaches: "The efficacy of prayer does not depend on the merit of the person who prays, but on the mercy of God, and on His faithfulness to His promise."

This promise of God, however, does not extend to petitions for things that are not for our spiritual good; as these could not be asked in the name of *Jesus Christ*, and because God, as a loving Father, could not grant what would be hurtful to us. Such petitions God refuses, as He refused that of the mother of the sons of Zebedee, saying: "*You know not what you ask*" (S. Matt. xx. 22); but He grants something better instead.

Therefore, when we ask for temporal favours, it should always be with resignation to God's will, and on condition that what we ask is profitable to our souls. Our Saviour gave us an example of this resignation when, in the Garden of Gethsemane He besought His Eternal Father to take from Him the bitter chalice that was prepared for Him, and then added: "*But yet not my will, but thine be done*". (S. Luke xxii. 42.)

Prayer, such as it should be, is always favourably heard. If sometimes our prayers are not answered, it is because we pray amiss, as S. James reminds us. Either because we pray with some lingering attachment to sin, or without attention and devotion; or because we pray without confidence and without humility.

Therefore prayer should be made:—

1st, With *devotion* and *attention;* such an attention, at least, as would discourage wilful distractions. To this effect it is good before prayer to *remain some moments silent,* and consider in WHOSE presence we are, the suitable attitude in which we should place ourselves, and with what dispositions and feelings we should pray. This is the advice of Ecclesiasticus (or the Preacher): "*Before prayer, prepare thy soul; and be not as a man that tempteth God*" (xviii. 23).

2ndly, With *confidence:* "*Nothing wavering; for he that wavereth is like a wave of the sea, which is moved and carried about by the wind,*" (S. James i. 6.) "*All things whatsoever you ask when ye pray,*" says our Lord, "*believe that you shall receive: and they shall come unto you.*" (S. Mark xi. 24.) Distrust or diffidence dishonours God; confidence honours God's goodness and His faithfulness to fulfil His promises.

3rdly, With *humility.* For it is written, "*God resisteth the proud, and giveth grace to the humble.*" (S. James iv. 6.) The parable of the Pharisee and the Publican is an instance of it. And it is also written, "*The prayer of him that humbleth himself shall pierce the clouds.*" (Ecclesiasticus xxxv. 21.)

If our prayer is made with these conditions, it is infallibly heard with favour.

Sometimes, however, either to try us, or to cause us to value more what we ask for, or to make us pray more earnestly, so that God might afterwards reward us more abundantly, God delays to grant what we ask, as we learn from the parable of the unjust Judge (S. Luke xviii. 1), and from the persevering woman of Canaan. (S. Matt. xv. 22.)

Therefore we should not be disheartened when the favour is delayed, but recalling to mind those words of

Christ: "*Ask, and it shall be given you; seek, and you shall find; knock, and it shall be opened to you*" (S. Matt. vii. 7), we should, full of confidence, persevere in prayer; for that delay is for our good.

We should also pray for others; and this sort of prayer, whilst it will do good to our neighbour, will not be less beneficial to us than if we were praying for ourselves alone, but even more. The reason is, because our prayer is then grounded on charity. In the *Lord's Prayer*, which is the model of all prayers, we are taught to pray to our Heavenly Father for all others as well as for ourselves.

Therefore, besides praying for ourselves in particular, let us also pray for the conversion of sinners, for the enlightenment of Jews and of all unbelievers, for the unity of all Christians in the true faith, and for final perseverance in it,—for those who are sick or dying, or in any danger,—for our parents and relatives, friends and enemies,—for those who rule the Church and Nation,—for those who suffer persecution, crosses, distress of mind or body, or any other kind of hardship and misery, and this, whether they are near to us or far away; and God the Giver of all good gifts will bestow His blessings both upon them and upon us in abundance, *through Jesus Christ our Lord*, in Whose blessed name we always are to pray.

CHAPTER XXXVI.

WORKS OF PENANCE.

In the case of those who have fallen into mortal sin after Baptism, when the guilt of such sin and the everlasting punishment due to it are forgiven through the

Merits of Christ in the Sacrament of Penance, there still very often remains a *debt of temporal punishment*, to be paid by the sinner. This *debt* remains not from any imperfection in the power of absolution in the Sacrament of Penance, nor from any want of efficacy in the atonement of Jesus Christ, more than sufficient of itself to atone for the sins of the whole world, but because by God's will chastisement for past sins helps us to supply for the imperfection in our repentance, and serves as a correction. The fear of temporal punishment often helps to strengthen the resolution of amendment, it acts as a check to prevent us from again falling into sin, and excites us to make reparation for the scandal given.

From this we see that, whilst the God-man, Jesus Christ, has, by atoning for our sins, done what we could not possibly do for ourselves, He has not dispensed us from doing with the help of His grace what we can to punish ourselves for the outrages offered to God. Good sense tells us that this is but right and just.

Our first Parents, after the *guilt* of their sin had been forgiven, had to undergo a long course of temporal chastisement for their sin. This was also the case with Aaron, Moses, his sister Miriam, and the people of Israel in the desert. (See the Book of Numbers, chapters xii., xiv., xx.) David, in like manner, upon repenting of his sin, and humbly saying: "*I have sinned,*" heard from the Prophet Nathan these words: "*The Lord also hath taken away thy sin: thou shalt not die; nevertheless because thou hast given occasion to the enemies of the Lord to blaspheme, for this thing the child that is born to thee shall surely die.*" [2 Kings (2 Samuel) xii. 13, 14.] Again, David says of himself: "*I have laboured in my groanings, every night I will wash my bed; I will water my couch with my tears*". (Psalm vi. 7.)

The Catholic Church has ever taught that after sin has been remitted in the Sacrament of Penance, penitential works, such as prayers, fastings, alms, and other works of piety must still be performed. These penitential works *of themselves*, however, do not satisfy the justice of God for any sin, but only inasmuch as they derive all their value from that all-availing atonement which JESUS CHRIST made upon the Cross, and in virtue of which *alone* all our good works find acceptance in the sight of God.

Thus it was that in the primitive Church the *penitential Canons* were established, and the *forty days' Fast of Lent* was observed from the time of the Apostles. S. Jerome says: "According to the *Apostolical Tradition* at the proper season of the year we observe Lent". (Epistola 27, ad Marcellum). And S. Leo says: "Let the Apostolical institution of forty days be spent in Fasting," (3rd Sermon on Lent.)

The great General Council of Nicæa, celebrated in the year 325, not only alludes to the penitential discipline then in vigour throughout the whole Church of God, but further establishes certain penitential works to be performed by some kind of sinners in Canon IX. and following. This ought to be especially noticed by those Protestants who profess veneration for antiquity, and notably for the first six General Councils.

The pardon granted to the penitent thief in the saving words: "*Amen, I say to thee, this day thou shalt be with Me in Paradise*" (S. Luke xxiii. 43), cannot be taken as a proof that we are dispensed by God from doing works of Penance. *That* was a wonderful and special grace granted under extraordinary circumstances; namely, when the Blood of Redemption was actually being shed upon the Cross; moreover, the dying thief, besides bearing testimony to the Divinity of Jesus Christ, confessed his guilt, and in the spirit of penance suffered the torment of his crucifixion, and the cruel breaking of his legs, as penalties justly due to his sins; and probably it was the *first time* that he received pardon.

The Catholic Church, which teaches the necessity of penitential works in general, holds also that grown-up persons who receive pardon of actual sins for the *first time* in Baptism, and even those who having fallen again into sin after Baptism *die martyrs*, or who come to the Sacrament of Penance with a very intense *perfect contrition*, or who approaching that Sacrament with imperfect contrition, afterwards obtain the benefit of a plenary indulgence, have no remaining *debt of temporal* punishment to pay.

CHAPTER XXXVII.

INDULGENCES.

It is a pity that many Protestants should have been so ill-informed about Indulgences as to suppose that it means the forgiveness of a sin, or a permission to commit a sin.

By an indulgence is meant not a permission to commit a sin, nor the forgiveness of a sin, but the *remission*, through the merits of *Jesus Christ, of the whole or part, of the debt of temporal punishment due to a sin,* the *guilt* and *everlasting punishment* of which sin have, through the merits of *Jesus Christ*, been already forgiven in the Sacrament of Penance.

Indulgences do not secure Heaven, but only hasten

the time of entering it to those who have already secured Heaven by having obtained forgiveness of their sins and put themselves in a state of grace before death.

Catholics believe that the power of granting Indulgences was left by Christ to the Church. It is included in the promise made by Jesus Christ to S. Peter: *"And whatsoever thou shalt loose upon earth shall be loosed also in Heaven"* (S. Matt. xvi. 19), for these words contain an ample and universal power given to S. Peter and his Successors of loosing a properly disposed person from everything that may hinder him from going to Heaven; and the debt of temporal punishment does hinder for a time even a justified soul from going into eternal bliss; that is, until that debt be paid or remitted.

It may be said, at least according to their principles, that Protestants give a kind of plenary or full indulgence to every one, when they say that works of penance are not necessary; but Catholics believe that from all of us poor sinners works of penance are required, and that the power of binding and loosing, which includes that of granting an Indulgence, was left only to the legitimate Successors of the Apostles, in whom alone this power is still vested.

Thus the criminal Corinthian was subjected to a very severe penance by S. Paul. At length, however, upon the solicitation of the Brethren, the Apostle granted to that repentant sinner an Indulgence, suspended the punishment inflicted upon him, and re-admitted him to the communion of the Faithful. (1 Corinth. v. and 2 Corinth. ii.)

Experience proves that this granting of an Indulgence is very useful: it encourages the Faithful to deeper repentance, to have more frequent recourse to the Holy Sacraments of Penance and Communion, and to exercise works of charity and devotion : for it is the doctrine of the Catholic Church that, in order to obtain any indulgence the soul must be *in a state of grace*, that is, must be *free from mortal sin;* and the conditions for gaining a Plenary Indulgence almost always are, that the applicant should worthily receive the Sacraments of Penance and the Holy Eucharist, as a preparation for the reception of the Indulgence, and perform some outward works of piety. Therefore an Indulgence granted only *under such conditions*, far from being an inducement to sin, encourages us to repent and to do penance and other works of piety, and is a happy corrective of sin and a preservative against the " occasions " by which one may be led into sin.

CHAPTER XXXVIII.

On Purgatory.

Purgatory is a state of suffering after this life, in which those souls are *for a time detained* which depart this life after their deadly sins have been remitted as to the *stain and guilt*, and as to the *eternal pain* that was due to them ; but which souls have on account of those sins still some debt of *temporal* punishment to pay ; as also those souls which leave this world guilty only of *venial* sins. In Purgatory such souls are purified and rendered fit to enter into Heaven, where nothing defiled enters.

Catholics believe that a Christian who dies after *the guilt and everlasting punishment* of mortal sin have been forgiven him, but who, either from want of opportunity or through his negligence, has not discharged the debt of temporal punishment due to his sin, will have to discharge that debt to the Justice of God in Purgatory.

They believe also that those Christians who die with the guilt of venial sin [*] only upon their soul do not immediately enter Heaven, where " *nothing defiled* " can enter, but go first to Purgatory *for an allotted time*, and after being purified there from the stain of these venial or lesser faults, are admitted into Heaven.

As works of penance have no value *in themselves* except through the Merits of Jesus Christ, so the pains of Purgatory have no power *in themselves* to purify the soul from sin except in virtue of Christ's Redemption; or, to speak more exactly, souls in Purgatory are able to discharge the debt of temporal punishment demanded by God's Justice, and to have their venial sins remitted only through the Merits of Jesus Christ, " *yet so as by fire* ".

The Catholic *belief in Purgatory* rests on the authority of the Church and her Apostolic Traditions recorded in ancient Liturgies, and by the ancient Fathers, Tertullian, S. Cyprian, Origen, Eusebius of Cæsarea, Arnobius, S. Basil, S. Ephrem of Edessa, S. Cyril of Jerusalem, by the Fourth Council of Carthage, by S. Gregory of Nyssa, S. Ambrose, S. Epiphanius, S. John Chrysostom, S. Jerome, S. Augustine, and by many other authorities of antiquity.

That this tradition is derived from the Apostles S. John Chrysostom plainly testifies in a passage, which shall be quoted presently, when speaking of suffrages or help for the departed.

St. Augustine says of Aerius, that he was the first who dared to teach that it was of no use to offer up

---

[*] See Chapter XIV. on mortal sin, in which a notion of venial sin is also given.

prayers and sacrifices for the dead; and this doctrine of Aerius he reckoned among heresies. (Book of Heresies, Heresy 53rd.)

There are also passages in Holy Scripture from which the Fathers have confirmed the Catholic belief on this point.

St. Paul, in his first Epistle to the Corinthians says: *"For other foundation no man can lay, but that which is laid; which is Christ Jesus. Now if any man build upon this foundation, gold, silver, precious stones, wood, hay, stubble: every man's work shall be manifest: for the day of the Lord shall declare it, because it shall be revealed in fire: and the fire shall try every man's work, of what sort it is. If any man's work abide, which he has built thereupon: he shall receive a reward. If any man's work burn, he shall suffer loss: but he himself shall be saved, yet so as by fire."* (Chapt. iii. 11.)

The ancient Fathers, Origen in the third century, S. Ambrose and S. Jerome in the fourth, and S. Augustine in the fifth, have interpreted this text of S. Paul * as relating to venial sins committed by Christians, which S. Paul compares to "*wood, hay, stubble,*" and thus with this text they confirm the Catholic belief in Purgatory, well known and believed in their time, as it is by Catholics in the present time.

In S. Matthew (chap. v. 25, 26) we read, "*Be at agreement with thy adversary betimes, whilst thou art in the way with him; lest perhaps the adversary deliver thee to the judge, and the judge deliver thee to the officer, and thou be cast into prison. Amen, I say to*

---

* Origen, Homily xiv. on Leviticus, and in Homily xvi. (in some editions xii.) on Jeremias; S. Ambrose in his comments on 1 Corinthians; S. Jerome in his second book against Jovinian, title 4, part 2; S. Augustine in his *Enarratio* on Psalm xxxvii. title 4.

thee, thou shalt not go out from thence till thou repay the last farthing."

On this passage S. Cyprian, a Father of the third century, says: "It is one thing to be cast into prison, and not go out from thence till the last farthing be paid; and another to receive at once the reward of faith and virtue; one thing in punishment of sin to be purified by long suffering and purged by long fire, and another to have expiated all sins by suffering (in this life); one in fire, at the day of judgment to wait the sentence of the Lord, another to receive an immediate crown from Him". (Epistle lii.)

Our Saviour said: *"He that shall speak against the Holy Ghost, it shall not be forgiven him neither in this world, nor in the world to come."* (S. Matt. xii. 32.)

From this text S. Augustine argues, that "It would not have been said with truth that their sin shall not be forgiven, *neither in this world nor in the world to come,* unless some sins were remitted in the next world". (De Civitate Dei, Book xxi. ch. 24.)

On the other hand, we read in several places of Holy Scripture that God will render to every one (that is, will reward or punish them) according as they deserve. (See for example in S. Matt. xvi. 27.) But as we can hardly suppose that God will punish everlastingly a person who dies burdened with the guilt of one venial sin only, it may be an "*idle word,*" it seems reasonable to infer that the punishment rendered to that person in the next world will only be temporary.

The Catholic belief in Purgatory does not clash with the following sayings of Holy Scripture, which every Catholic firmly believes, namely, that it is *Jesus who cleanseth us,* that *Jesus bore "the iniquity of us all,"* that *" by His bruises we are healed"*. For the departed souls in Purgatory are able to satisfy there for the debt of temporal punishment, and are there cleansed from the stain of their venial sins *through the Redemption of Christ alone.*

Likewise the Catholic belief in Purgatory is not in opposition to those texts of Scripture in which it is said that a man when he is justified is *translated from death to life; that he is no longer judged, that there is no condemnation in him.* For these passages do not refer to souls transferred to glory when the natural death occurs, but they refer to people in this world, who from the death of sin pass to the life of grace. Nor does it follow that, dying in that state of grace, that is, in a state of spiritual life, they must go at once to Heaven. A soul may be justified and yet have something to suffer for a time; thus also in this world many are justified and yet are not exempt from suffering.

Again, it is not fair to bring forward against the Catholic doctrine on Purgatory that text of the Apocalypse (Rev. xiv. 13): "*Blessed are the dead who die in the Lord. From henceforth now, saith the Spirit, that they may rest from their labours: for their works follow them,*" for this text applies only to those souls who die perfectly in the Lord, that is, entirely free from every kind of sin, and from the *stain*, the *guilt*, and the *debt of temporal punishment* of every sin: for Catholics also believe that these souls have no pain of Purgatory to suffer, as was the case with the Martyrs and many Saints who died in a perfect state of grace.

It is usual to bring forward against the Catholic belief in Purgatory that text which says: "*If the tree fall to the south, or to the north, in what place soever it shall fall, there shall it be*". (Ecclesiastes xi. 3.)

This text confirms and illustrates the truth that when death comes the *final doom* of every one is fixed, and that there is no more possibility of changing it, so that one dying in a state of mortal sin, will always remain in a state of sin, and consequently be rejected for ever; and one dying in a state of grace and friendship with God, will for ever remain accepted by God, and in a state of grace and in friendship with Him.

But this text proves nothing against the existence of Purgatory; for a soul, although in a state of grace, may still have to suffer for a time before being perfectly fit to enter upon the eternal bliss of Heaven, and to enjoy the vision of God.

Some might be disposed notwithstanding to make this text tell against Purgatory by saying that the two places alluded to in the texts are Heaven and Hell. But this interpretation Catholics readily admit, for at death either Heaven or Hell is the final place to which all men are allotted, Purgatory being only the passage to Heaven.

This text surely does not tell against those who died long before Christ came to save the world, and who, though sure of Heaven, could not go there, but had to wait in some state, called by S. Peter "*Prison*," until after the Ascension of Jesus Christ; neither therefore does it tell against Purgatory.

Christ's Redemption is abundant, "*plentiful*," as Holy Scripture says (Psalm cxxix. 7), and Catholics do not believe that those Christians who die guilty only of venial sins unrepented of and unforgiven are condemned to the everlasting pains of Hell, as Protestants must believe, if consistent with their principles. Catholics believe that for such there is still a way, although painful, of being cleansed from these *lesser* faults after this life, through the *merits of Jesus Christ*. And this is in Purgatory, where they can be purified like gold in the fire, and made fit to enter into the *Heavenly*

Jerusalem, wherein "*there shall not enter anything defiled*" (Apocalypse [Revelation] xxi. 27); or, to use the language of St. Paul, "*he himself shall be saved, yet so as by fire*". (1 Corinth. iii. 15.*)

Catholics also believe that the souls in Purgatory continue to be members of the Church of Christ, and that they are relieved by the sacrifice of the Mass, by prayer, pious works, such as almsdeeds, and other helps called *suffrages*, which are applied to them by the Faithful here on earth, with the intention of helping them. Indulgences may also be applied to them.

The living can pray for each other efficaciously, according to S. James the Apostle: "*Pray for one another that you may be saved*". (v. 16.) Why then should not we be able to pray also with efficacy for the dead, especially since the souls in Purgatory departed this life in the state of grace and love which, according to S. Paul, "*never falleth away*". (1 Corinth. xiii. 8.) If death does not break their ties of love towards us, the same should not sever our bonds of love towards them, nor prevent us from doing what we can in their behalf.

This Catholic belief is comprised in those words of the Apostles' Creed, "*I believe in the Communion of Saints*". The natural meaning of this declaration being that we are in communion of spiritual goods with the Saints, whether in Heaven, in Purgatory, or on earth. It has always been the practice of the Catholic Church to offer prayers and other pious works in suffrage for the dead, as is amply testified by the Latin Fathers; for instance, Tertullian, S. Cyprian, S. Augustine, S. Gregory; and amongst the Greek Fathers, by S. Ephrem of Edessa, St. Basil, and S. John Chrysostom.

* See note on this passage in the Douay Catholic version.

St. Chrysostom says: "It was not without good reason ordained by the Apostles that mention should be made of the dead in the tremendous mysteries, because they knew well that these would receive great benefit from it." (On the First Epistle to Philippians, Homily iii.) By the expression "tremendous mysteries" is meant the holy Sacrifice of the Mass.

S. Augustine says: "It is not to be doubted that the dead are aided by the prayers of the Holy Church, and by the salutary Sacrifice, and by the alms which are offered for their spirits; that the Lord may deal with them more mercifully than their sins have deserved. For this, which has been handed down by the Fathers, the universal Church observes." (Vol. v., Sermon 172.)

The same pious custom is proved also from the ancient Liturgies of the Greeks and other Eastern Churches, in which the Priest is directed to pray for the dead during the celebration of the Holy Mysteries.

CHAPTER XXXIX.

ON THE INVOCATION OF THE SAINTS.

Rightly to understand the Catholic doctrine of the Invocation of Saints, it is necessary that Protestants should bear in mind that the word *worship* has different significations, according as it is applied to God or applied to creatures. When applied to God, it means the *highest* degree of honour due to God as God, and to God alone. When applied to things created, it means *inferior*, that is, less honour, justly paid to them, either on account of their exalted position among

ON THE INVOCATION OF THE SAINTS.

creatures, or on account of a special reference they bear to God.

Catholics believe that the Saints reigning with Christ are to be honoured and invoked, that they offer prayers to God for men, and that their relics are to be held in veneration. We read in Holy Scripture that angels were *worshipped* by Abraham and Josue (Genesis xix. 1; Josue v. 15); that the prophet Samuel and Eliseus were *worshipped*, that is, treated with marks of honour and reverence [1 Book of Kings (or 1 Samuel) xxviii. 14]. And in the First Book of Paralipomenon (or 1 Chronicles) xxix. 20, we read: "*And all the assembly blessed the Lord God of their fathers: and they bowed themselves, and worshipped God, and then the king.*" In the Protestant version it reads: "*worshipped God and the king.*"

"*The continual prayer of a just man availeth much*" (S. James v. 16); and we find St. Paul earnestly asking the prayers of the Roman Christians, saying: "*I beseech you, therefore, brethren, through our Lord Jesus Christ, and by the charity of the Holy Ghost, that you help me in your prayers for me to God.*" (Romans xv. 30.) All Christians allow that it is right and useful to ask the prayers of holy persons who are upon earth, it cannot surely be wrong or useless to ask the prayers of the Saints in Heaven, now that they are so near to God, and in no danger of offending Him.

That the Saints can know something of what passes on earth, and can sympathise with us, may be inferred from what our Saviour says in S. Matthew (xxii. 30), that the Saints "*shall be as the Angels of God in Heaven*"; and from what He said in S. Luke (xv. 7, 10), "*I say to you, there shall be joy before the Angels of God upon one sinner doing penance*". If angels see a sinner doing penance, the Saints, who are like the Angels of God, are able to see the same.

The Holy Prophets, enlightened by God, could see what was passing in distant places, and could even foresee future things. We have a striking instance in Exodus (xxxii. 7, 14). When Moses was on the mountain with God, out of sight of the people below, God told him that the people had fallen into idolatry, and that He would therefore destroy them. But Moses at once prayed God to spare them, and God did so. If Moses, far away and out of sight, but with God, was allowed to know what was passing *elsewhere*, and to pray, as he did, for the idolatrous Israelites, we may naturally suppose that the Saints in Heaven are allowed to know something of what takes place on earth, and to pray for sinners. Surely the Saints in the glory of Heaven are not less enlightened than the Prophets; nor can it be said that they have lost the power of praying, being nearer to the throne of God. If charity prompts us to pray one for another here on earth, may not the Saints pray for us in Heaven, where "*Charity never falleth away*?" (1 Corinth. xiii. 8.) Shall it not be permitted to us who "*are fellow-citizens with the Saints*" (Ephesians ii. 19), to ask their intercession, that they may, *through the Merits and Mediation of Jesus Christ*, obtain for us what we stand in need of? We naturally feel that these blessed souls, being bound to us by ties of nature and grace, must have a zealous desire to help us in our necessities,* and that God will not withhold from them this satisfaction.

The power which the Blessed Virgin and all the Saints enjoy of interceding for us is a privilege com-

---

* The rich man in Hell felt sympathy for his brothers (S. Luke xvi. 27) on earth; we must suppose that the Saints in Heaven have no less sympathy for their relatives and friends.

municated to them by Christ and based on His Divine Merits.

An objection often raised against the Invocation of Saints is—that it places them between God and men, making them mediators in the same way as *Jesus Christ* is the Mediator. This objection has no real foundation, because JESUS is the only Mediator of *Redemption*, and also *of intercession by His own rights and Merits;* whereas the mediation of the Saints is *not* a mediation of Redemption but only a mediation *of intercession through the Merits of* JESUS CHRIST, *their Divine Saviour and ours.*

In the sense of intercessor, through JESUS CHRIST, a Saint, or any one even here on earth who prays for his neighbour, may be considered and be called a mediator; as Moses was, who could say of himself: "*I was the Mediator, and stood between the Lord and you.*" (Deuteronomy v. 5).

CHAPTER XL.

THE BLESSED VIRGIN MARY JUSTLY CALLED MOTHER OF GOD.

The Blessed Virgin Mary is rightfully called *Mother of God;* for *Jesus Christ*, God Incarnate (that is, God made man), is truly her son, as St. Luke (i. 35) expressly states: "*The Holy which shall be born of thee shall be called the Son of God.*" St. Elizabeth calls the Blessed Virgin "*the mother of my Lord*" (S. Luke i. 43.) And the Blessed Virgin called our Saviour "Son". (S. Luke ii. 48).

The General Council of Ephesus (held A.D. 431) condemned Nestorius as a heretic for denying this title of *Mother of God* (in the Greek Theotok'os) to the Blessed Virgin. Those, therefore, who refuse to her this title of *Mother of God* show that they do not realise the Incarnation of the Son of God. They thus virtually deny the personal Divinity of the Redeemer and the efficacy of the Redemption; for the blood which was shed on Calvary would not have been the Blood of a God-man, but simply the blood of a man. It would be like falling in with the heresy of Nestorius, who (contrary to the Catholic Faith, which teaches that in Jesus Christ there are two natures but only one Divine Person) taught that in Christ, besides the two natures there are also two persons, the Divine Person and the human; and that the Eternal Son of God did not become man in the sense of assuming to Himself our human nature, but only in the sense of residing in the humanity as in a temple, or of being united to it, not in one person but in some other mysterious way only; and consequently that the Blessed Virgin was merely the mother of that human person, but not of that Divine Person which was in Christ.

The reason why Protestants refuse to join in that affection due to our Lady, Mother of God, is because they do not properly comprehend and realise in their hearts the import of this title "*Mother of God*". Let us then see what this title means.

It does not mean that Mary is the *mother of the Divinity*, if by Divinity be understood the Divine nature, for the Divine nature is *uncreated, eternal before all worlds*. Nor does it mean that Mary is the mother of the Second Person of the Blessed Trinity, God the Son according to His *Divine nature*, which would be the same as being mother of the Divinity, to assert which would be indeed not only absurd but *blasphemous*. Nor does it mean that Mary became the mother of a new person, one that did not exist before, as is the case naturally with all mothers, for God the Son who became the Son of Mary is in His Divine nature co-eternal with the Father. But it means that Mary is the Mother of God the Son according to His *human nature*, which human nature He had not before He took it from Mary, for until then He possessed only one nature, the *Divine*.

After His Incarnation God the Son possessed two natures, the Divine and the human. In other words, Mary gave birth to a perfect and complete human nature which, from the very first instant that she conceived it of the Holy Ghost, God the Son made His own, assumed it, and united to it His Godhead, and thus God the Eternal Word *was made flesh and became man*.

Hence the Fathers speak of a twofold birth or nativity of the *Word*, that is, God the Son ; the one, His being born of God the Father from all eternity, " *ex Patre natum ante omnia saecula* " ; and the other, which is in time, His being born man of the Blessed Virgin, " *ex Maria Virgine, et homo factus est.*"

God the Son, by assuming this perfect human nature, which He took from the Blessed Virgin, was born in the flesh, and became the real and true son of Mary according to His human nature. Therefore the Blessed Virgin, the Mother of Jesus Christ, is properly and justly called " *Mother of God*," that is, Mother of God the Son *from the time that He became also man*. True that the Blessed Virgin Mary is simply a *creature*, deriving all her graces, privileges, and glory from God, and is wholly dependent upon Him ; but it is no less true that God chose her to be the Mother of the Word Incarnate, that the Divine Infant Whom she bore and brought forth into the world was a Divine Person, clothed indeed with human nature, but in Whom no human *personality* existed, because two persons could not so exist in the Mystery of the Incarnation. If Mary were not truly the Mother of the Eternal Word made man, neither would the Eternal Word be truly Incarnate, nor truly the Son of man.

The Blessed Virgin Mary therefore is justly styled "*Mother of God*," because she is the Mother of Jesus Christ, Whose humanity is assumed by and united to a Divine Person, that is, God the Son. No wonder, then, that the Blessed Virgin Mary should exclaim in her great Hymn of praise to God known as the *Magnificat*: "*For He that is mighty hath done great things to me; and holy is His name.*" (S. Luke i. 49.)

CHAPTER XLI.

HONOUR AND DEVOTION TO THE BLESSED VIRGIN MARY.

Because the Blessed Virgin Mary is "*full of grace*," as the Archangel Gabriel declared, and because of her incomparable dignity of being the chosen Mother of Jesus Christ, the Catholic Church regards her as the most highly favoured of all creatures, as a creature highly exalted above all men and angels: and consequently believes that she is to be honoured as the most blessed among women, according to the admonition of St. Paul: "*Render therefore to all their dues, . . . honour to whom honour*". (Romans xiii. 7.)

All the honour given to the Blessed Virgin by men does not equal the least one of those countless acts of honour given to her by her Divine Son our Lord during the time that He lived with her and St. Joseph at Nazareth; when, as we learn from the Gospel, He "*was subject to them*". (S. Luke ii. 51.) We need not therefore be afraid of honouring her whom the *Word* Incarnate so greatly honoured. We are encouraged by the Church to do so, and to frequently recommend ourselves to her prayers.

This honour and this recourse to her intercession, far from detracting from the worship due to God and to the Mediation of Jesus Christ, are felt by Catholics to be really tokens of respect to our Blessed Saviour, on Whose account chiefly we honour her; in fact, we honour her whom He Himself has so wonderfully honoured, and whom He must wish all to honour. To dishonour Christ's Mother would be to dishonour Christ; to honour and to love her is to honour and to love Christ, since it is above all for *His sake* that we show such affection and reverence to her.

This is sweetly expressed by the Very Rev. Father Faber in a Hymn to our Blessed Lady, beginning :—

> "Mother of mercy,* day by day
>   My love of thee grows more and more;
> Thy gifts are strewn upon my way
>   Like sands upon the great sea-shore.
>
> . . . .
>
> "But scornful men have coldly said
>   Thy love was leading me from God;
> And yet in this I did but tread
>   The very path my Saviour trod.
>
> "They know but little of thy worth
>   Who speak these heartless words to me,
> For what did JESUS love on earth
>   One half so tenderly as thee;
>
> . . . .

* Being Mother of the Redeemer, she can but feel compassion for those for whom her Son died.

"Jesus, when His three hours were run,
  Bequeathed thee from the Cross to me;
And Oh! how can I love thy Son,
  Sweet Mother! if I love not thee?"

The parable in the Gospel of the poor Publican, who "*standing afar off, would not so much as lift up his eyes towards heaven; but struck his breast, saying, O God, be merciful to me a sinner*" (S. Luke xviii. 13), proves *humility* to be the best disposition to render our prayers availing; and our recourse to Mary is the effect of humility and of a sense of our unworthiness.* Moreover, Catholics see clearly that in asking the Blessed Virgin to *pray* for them, they thereby affirm that she is not herself the fountain of grace or of merit, since she herself, in order to obtain graces and merits for us, must, as well as we, have recourse to *God, her and our Creator and Saviour;* and that when she prays she prays only through the Mediation and Merits of her Divine Son.

In asking the Blessed Virgin Mary to *pray* for us to Jesus, we thereby openly declare that *Jesus Christ* is our *only* Redeemer.

CHAPTER XLII.

The Immaculate Conception of the Blessed Virgin Mary.

The Immaculate Conception of the Blessed Virgin Mary, or her Conception without the stain of original sin, refers to her soul, not to her body; for it is an admitted principle in theology that a human *body* is

---

* See the beautiful lines by Professor Longfellow, Appendix, No. 41.

not in *itself* capable of guilt and of the stain of sin, as sin causes a *moral* and not a material stain. The Catholic Church teaches that in all other human beings descended from Adam, the soul, when created and united by God to the infant body yet unborn, (which union is called *passive* Conception, and in which parents have no part), necessarily contracts, by thus becoming a child of fallen Adam, the stain of original sin, which can afterwards be washed away by having the Merits of *Jesus Christ* applied to it; but that with the Blessed Virgin Mary it was otherwise, for her soul, at the very instant in which it was created and infused into her body, was *preserved* from contracting the stain of original sin, by having sanctifying grace bestowed upon her in the very first moment of her existence, and this *through the foreseen Merits of Jesus Christ*, which were applied to her in the way of *prevention*, and therefore in a special and more perfect manner.

The soul of the Blessed Virgin was of itself liable to contract the stain of original sin like any other child of Adam, and therefore in need of Redemption, but *in view of and through the Merits of Jesus Christ*, Whose Virgin Mother she was to be, (and in whose favour some other general laws, as that a woman cannot be mother and virgin at the same time, were suspended), she was, by exception, preserved from contracting this stain.

The belief in the exemption of the Blessed Virgin Mary from all sin is not confined to the Catholic Church. Even the Koran of Mahomet, written twelve centuries ago, declares that Mary the Mother of Jesus was always protected from all the attacks of Satan.

All Christians admit that God could preserve the Blessed Virgin immaculate, and most persons will feel that it would redound to the honour of Christ that His

Mother should never have been defiled by sin, never have been the slave of the devil, nor ever *even for an instant* have been an object hateful to God; for the christian mind shudders at the thought that the one who was to be the living Temple of God Incarnate should have been permitted by God, who could prevent it, to be first the abode of the devil.

That which some Protestants think possible, just, reasonable, and strongly demanded by the honour of Christ, Catholics hold as an article of faith.

It is true that before the solemn definition of this doctrine a diversity of opinion was tolerated by the Church and maintained by some Catholic theologians, who were not on that account accused of heresy, but this was because the Church had not yet given an explicit definition on the subject, and some of the terms employed in debate in the Divinity Schools of that time were not sufficiently precise and definite, and a clear distinction between *active* and *passive* conception was not made.

This doctrine was solemnly defined as an article of faith by Pope Pius IX., speaking *ex Cathedrâ* on the 8th December, 1854, as follows:—"*Auctoritate Domini
" Nostri Jesu Christi, beatorum Apostolorum Petri et
" Pauli ac Nostri declaramus, pronunciamus et defini-
" mus, doctrinam, quæ tenet, beatissimam Virginem
" Mariam in primo instanti suæ Conceptionis fuisse
" singulari omnipotentis Dei gratia et privilegio, intuitu
" meritorum Christi Jesu Salvatoris humani generis, ab
" omni originalis culpæ labe præservatam immunem,
" esse a Deo revelatum, atque idcirco ab omnibus fideli-
" bus firmiter constanterque credendam.*

"*Quapropter si qui secus ac a Nobis definitum est,
" quod Deus avertat, præsumpserint corde sentire, ii
" noverint, ac porro sciant, se proprio judicio condem-*

"*natos, naufragium circa fidem passos esse, et ab unitate Ecclesiæ defecisse.*"

This extract from the solemn Definition may be translated as follows :—"By the authority of Our Lord Jesus Christ, of the blessed Apostles Peter and Paul, and by Our own authority, We declare, pronounce, and define, that the doctrine, which holds that the most Blessed Virgin Mary, in the first instant of her Conception, by a special grace and privilege of Almighty God, in view of the merits of Jesus Christ, the Saviour of mankind, was preserved free from all stain of original sin, has been revealed by God, and therefore is to be firmly and steadfastly believed by all the Faithful.

"Wherefore, if any shall presume, which may God avert, to think in their heart otherwise than has been defined by Us, let them know and moreover understand that they are condemned by their own judgment, that they have made shipwreck as regards the Faith, and have fallen away from the unity of the Church."

That this doctrine is in accordance with Holy Scripture and the ancient Tradition of the Church, may be seen in books* that treat on this subject, as also in the Apostolic Letter of His Holiness Pope Pius IX., "*Ineffabilis Deus*" (so named from the Latin words with which the said Encyclical Letter begins), of the 8th December, 1854, which contains the dogmatical definition of the Immaculate Conception. In this document is also clearly explained how this doctrine, far from detracting from the Redemption of Christ,

* See F. Passaglia, S.J., and Bishop Ullathorne, O.S.B., on the Immaculate Conception.

adds to it a new lustre, inasmuch as it shows Christ's Merits to be so efficacious, as not only to have power to efface the stain of sin after it is contracted, but also, what is more wonderful and beneficial, to preserve the soul from contracting it.

To treat this important subject in a satisfactory manner would require an entire volume, but for the satisfaction of some I will here quote one text of Holy Scripture, and a few passages from the ancient Fathers in confirmation of the Catholic belief in the Immaculate Conception.

In the Book of Genesis (iii. 15) God said: "*I will put enmities between thee and the woman, and between thy seed and her seed*".

According to all ancient interpreters this is a prophecy. The woman mentioned is Mary the Mother of Jesus Christ, and the seed of the woman is Jesus Christ Himself, the Redeemer of mankind.

Certainly the enmity which exists between Jesus Christ and the evil spirit is a *perpetual* one, and excludes sin of all kind.

But the *same enmity* it is here declared by God should exist between the woman (that is, the Blessed Virgin Mary and the serpent [that is, the devil]).

Therefore the deduction is, that the enmity which exists between Mary and the devil is a *perpetual* one, and also necessarily excludes all sin, and therefore also original sin, which of itself suffices to enslave a person to the devil.

Consequently from this text it is proved that the Blessed Virgin Mary, through the merits of her Son Jesus Christ, is from the first moment of her existence Immaculate: that is, she was preserved from contracting the stain of original sin in the first moment that her soul was united to her body and began to exist as a human being, that is, at the time of her passive Conception.

St. Cyprian, a Father of the third century, says: "The Holy Spirit overshadowing her (Mary), the original fire of concupiscence became extinct, and therefore it was not fit that an innocent one should endure pain, nor could justice allow that that vase of election should be prostrated by the usual pains of childbirth. Because being *very different from the rest of mankind, human nature, but not sin, communicated itself to her.* (De Nativitate Christi.)

Theodorétus, a Father who lived in the fifth century, says, that Mary "surpassed by far the Cherubim and Seraphim in purity". Had Theodorétus believed that Mary was born in sin he would not have used such an expression.

St. Ephrem, a Father of the fourth century, says, that Mary was "entirely free from every defilement and stain of sin". (Oratio ad Beatam Virginem.)

St. Maximus, Bishop of Turin, a Father of the fifth century, says: "Mary clearly was a worthy dwelling-place for Christ, not on account of the beauty of her person, but because of original grace". (Homilia v. ante Natalem Domini.)

In the Greek Liturgy of S. Chrysostom, a Father of the fourth century, which Liturgy is still used by United Catholic Greeks and the Schismatic Greeks, the following words are directed to be chanted by the choir during the Canon of the Mass: "It is truly meet that we should praise thee, O Mother of God, who art always to be blessed, and *who art exempt from every fault:* thou art the Mother of our God, to be venerated in preference to the Cherubim; thou art beyond comparison more glorious than the Seraphim." (Goar, Euchologium, p. 78.)

Theodorus, Patriarch of Jerusalem, said in the second Council of Nicæa that Mary "is truly the Mother of God, and Virgin before and after childbirth; and she was created in a condition more sublime and glorious than that of all natures, whether intellectual or corporeal." (Labbe, vol. viii.)

Add to all this, that disbelief in the Immaculate Conception of the Blessed Virgin Mary would imply belief in the following revolting consequences: that He Who is holiness itself, and has an infinite horror of sin took human nature from a corrupt human source, whilst He might have taken it from an incorrupt one: that the Infinite Purity was enshrined in the Ark of the maternity which had been sullied by original sin, whilst He might have avoided it: that the Divine Person drew the Precious Blood of His Humanity from a source which was not always immaculate, whilst He might have preserved it immaculate, and this without diminishing, but rather enhancing, the efficacy of His Redemption.

Who can believe that it being in the power of God the Son to exempt the Blessed Virgin, who was to be His Mother from contracting the stain of original sin, should not have done so?

Who can believe that it being in the power of God the Son to prepare a spotless holy temple wherein to dwell Incarnate for nine months, should have preferred to have one which was first profaned by sin?

Who can imagine that God Who could become Incarnate by preparing to Himself an Immaculate Mother, should have preferred to have one who had first been defiled by sin and had been once in the power and slavery of Satan?

These things shock too much Christian ears. Christian sense, grounded on theological reasons, sees at a glance that the Mother of God Incarnate *must* have always been immaculate : that without this the enmity of Mary to sin would not have been perpetual and complete : that it having been in the power of God to preserve Mary unstained from original sin, therefore He did it. *Potuit ergo fecit.* We cannot conceive how the Incarnation could have taken place, unless the Mother had been preserved unstained.

CHAPTER XLIII.

REVERENCE TO RELICS AND OTHER RELIGIOUS OBJECTS.

The Catholic Church teaches that the images or representations of Jesus Christ, of His Blessed Virgin Mother, and the Saints in general, are to be honoured with "*due* honour"; not indeed for what they are in themselves, but for what they represent. This honour is called *relative* honour, because it *relates* or refers to the person represented. Thus it would be simply a token of affection towards our parents if we were to kiss the likeness of a dear father or mother. At the English Court it is a customary mark of respect to Her Most Gracious Majesty the Queen to bow before her *empty chair* of State. Again, men honour Her Majesty by putting her *portrait* in a distinguished place and in bowing before it. It would be dishonouring the Queen herself to treat her portrait with any disrespect.

The reverence paid by Catholics to holy images does not offend against the Commandment of God. It is true that the latter part of the first Commandment declares : "*Thou shalt not make to thyself a graven thing,*" but this is explained by the words that follow : "*Thou shalt not adore them* (non adorabis ea), *nor*

6A

serve them." (Exodus xx. 4 and Deuteronomy v. i.) *
The meaning therefore clearly is: "Thou shalt not make unto thyself a graven thing or idol for the sake of adoring it as a false god or idol. The words "bow down" in the Protestant version, instead of "adore," are unhappily calculated to mislead unreflecting persons. This Commandment does not condemn the use of images intended to promote the honour and worship of our Lord Jesus Christ, the true living God, or the inferior honour due to the Holy Angels and the Saints, as this is in no way idolatry or worship of strange gods.

It was thus understood by the Jews, who by the command of God placed *two graven images of the Cherubim* on the ark of the Covenant (3 Kings vi. 23), and *other images of angels in the Temple of Solomon.* (2 Paralipomenon, or Chronicles iii. 10, 11.) It is, in fact, thus practically understood also by those Protestants who have no scruple in making graven images, and even in setting them up in their places of worship.

No Christian certainly could find in his heart to treat the crucifix, that affecting image and appealing likeness of our crucified Saviour, as an *idol*, and trample it under his foot. Christian feeling would prompt him

---

* An eminent Protestant—the late Archdeacon Paley (author of "The Evidences of Christianity") in a sermon on the Commandments (Works, Ed. Edinb., 1826, page 655) says:—"The prohibition of the Commandment is pointed against the particular offence of idolatry and no other. The first and second * Commandments may be considered as one, inasmuch as they relate to one subject, or nearly so. For many ages, and by many Churches, they were put together and considered as one commandment. The subject to which they both relate is false worship or the worship of false gods. This is the single subject to which the prohibition of both Commandments relates—the single class of sins which is guarded against."

* According to Protestant division.

to respect it, as he respects and reveres the precious *word*, the *sound*, the very *letters*, of the Holy *Name* of JESUS.

It would be idolatry to worship any Saint, or the image of any Saint *as God*, but it is not idolatry to honour the Saints *for what they are*, namely, the faithful servants of God, and to honour pictures of them *for what these pictures represent*. If we may pay respect to the likeness of a parent, child, or friend, living or departed, we may surely honour pictures of the Saints who are the special friends of God, and show our reverence for those who, now glorious in Heaven, are "*The spirits of the just made perfect*" (Heb. xii. 23), who are "*like to Him*" (1 S. John iii. 2), and who behold Him "*face to face*" (1 Corinth. xiii. 12).

The danger which some Protestants suppose to exist that any Christian might worship the image for the reality, in other words, make an idol of it, is very remote indeed; for every Christian, even the least educated, knows how to distinguish an image from what it represents. The very word *image* or *likeness* itself marks plainly this distinction. If any one, seeing a poor Catholic woman praying before an image or picture of the Blessed Virgin, were to say to her: "The Blessed Virgin is in Heaven and not there, my good woman,"—she would look at such a person with pity and surprise for thinking it necessary to remind her of that.

Josue and the "Ancients" did not break the Commandment of God when they remained a whole day prostrate before the Ark of the Covenant and the likenesses of the Cherubim, as stated in the Book of Josue (vii. 6) in these words: "*But Josue rent his garments, and fell flat on the ground before the Ark of the Lord until the evening, both he and all the ancients of Israel*".

In the Catholic penny Catechism, entitled "The Abridgment of Christian Doctrine," learnt amongst the first lessons by every Catholic child in England, is found in the fourth chapter the Decalogue or the Ten Commandments of God, taken from the twentieth chapter of Exodus, but following as to the last two commandments the order of the repetition of the Law of Moses in the fifth chapter (verse 21) of the Book of Deuteronomy. The division of the Commandments into ten adopted by the Catholic Church is that made by S. Augustine, Bishop of Hippo, in the fifth century in his Book of "Questions on Exodus" (Question 17). This is a philosophical arrangement worthy of remark and study, and naturally suggested by the different matter of each part. This division is followed by the Protestants in Germany, and generally, except by the English Protestants.

In the same chapter of the penny Catholic Catechism we are taught the kind of respect and honour we should pay to relics and pictures in the following questions:—
"*Qu. Is it allowable to honour relics, crucifixes, and holy pictures? Ans. Yes; with an inferior and relative honour, as they relate to Christ and His Saints, and are memorials of them.* Qu. *May we pray to relics or images?*" and the plain answer put in the mouth of the child is: "*No, by no means, for they can neither see, nor hear, nor help us.*"

That God wills we should bestow honour on the relics of His Saints, we gather from the marvellous virtue with which it pleases God sometimes to honour their bones and other relics. Thus in the Fourth Book of Kings (2 Samuel of Protestant version) we read: "*Some that were burying a man, . . . cast the body into the sepulchre of Eliseus* (Elisha). *And when it had touched the bones of Eliseus, the man came to life, and stood upon his feet*" (xiii. 21).

The woman of the Gospel who, full of faith and humility, trusted for her cure in the *touch* of the *hem of the garment* of our Lord (S. Matt. ix. 20), and those who had confidence in the *shadow* of S. Peter to cure their sick (Acts v. 15), and those who confided in the *handkerchiefs* and *aprons* that had touched the body of S. Paul, and brought them to the sick (Acts xix. 12), all these were not disapproved by our Lord nor by the Apostles, but rewarded by God.

The many celebrated miracles wrought at the tombs of the Martyrs prove that the honour we pay to them is agreeable to God. (See S. Augustine, Book xxii., City of God, chap. viii.)

CHAPTER XLIV.

Why the Catholic Church in the West uses the Latin Language.

The Church is *Apostolic.* She is the Church of S. Peter and of the other Apostles, and she has guarded with tenderness all the precious memories they left.

When the Apostles parted from each other for their mission to announce to all nations the Gospel of salvation, two languages chiefly were spoken and understood by the two great civilised divisions of mankind— the Latin language for the most part in the West, and the Greek in the East. They preached the faith chiefly in Latin and Greek; their teachings and their constitutions were written in those two rich languages, and the Church has preserved these monuments with a religious veneration. This is the reason why her language is for the most part Latin in the West, and Greek in the

East. Yet this which, in fact, is a testimony in favour of her antiquity, is made by some a theme of reproach against her.

Providence had already disposed all in advance. Latin and Greek became dead languages, and hence invariable, and wonderfully adapted to formulate (or express with precision) the doctrines of the Church which alters not because she is divine.

An interesting calculation made on the changes that have been made in the living languages shows, that had the Church in France adopted the French instead of the Latin language, she would have been obliged to modify the formula (or essential words) used in the administration of the Sacrament of Baptism a great many times ;* otherwise these formulas would not have expressed correctly the idea they should convey. By this we can judge of the many changes which the wording of the *Creed*, and Decrees of primitive Councils and those of the Popes, were they not in an unalterable (or dead) language, would have had to undergo.

Protestants have perhaps reason in preferring spoken modern tongues in their standard books of religion. Living languages, continually changing, are more suited to convey doctrines which are subject to frequent alteration.

The Church speaks Latin, not only because she is unchangeable, but also because she is *Catholic*, or universal, and has to address herself to all people in all times.

During the first four centuries Latin was the language of the civilised world, and although then a living language, it had that character of universality which the Church requires. When in course of time the

* See " *Causeries*," by Monseigneur de Ségur.

world was divided into many nationalities, the Church still preserved her beautiful primitive language, and thus remained unchanged in her speech as in her essence.

Thus the Church speaks Latin because she is *Apostolic, Unchangeable,* and *Catholic.*

St. Paul, it is true, in his first Epistle to the Corinthians (chap. xiv.), directed the Christians to use in their assemblies a language understood by all the faithful present; but many Protestants draw from this an objection which does not apply to the present question.

The Apostle confines himself to the preaching, exhorting, and instructing the assembled faithful, all which, he says, must be done in the vernacular or common language of the people. The word *prophecy* includes instructions—speaking on things divine. The Catholic Church follows this Apostolic command to the letter. Her bishops, priests, missionaries, and catechists always employ in their teaching a language understood by all. They speak when needed in the most obscure and poorest dialects, in order that the Word of God preached may reach all understandings.

The Catholic Church speaks not only the particular distinctive language of each country and tribe when instructing the people, but has also a special Catholic language, that her pastors belonging to every nation may readily communicate with each other, that they may minister together at the altar, and that her laity, of whatever tongue, may not, when in a foreign land, feel strange in the house of God, but feel at home in any Catholic place of worship, in any part of the world.

In this way the Church unites in one universal tongue to implore the mercy and sing the praises of God. This beautiful and sublime harmony of nations in one faith, with one voice, in the one Fold of the one Shepherd, is worthy of the Church of Christ, and of the unity which is her grand characteristic.

The Mass is a Sacrifice, and it is not necessary for the people to follow in the Latin the words of the priest. When the Catholic priest stands at the altar, though there may be persons present from every clime, so soon as he pronounces aloud any part of the Service, all understand, and take an intelligent part in his ministration; a fact which reminds one of the preaching of the Apostles on the Day of Pentecost, when all from every nation heard S. Peter, each in his own tongue. (Acts ii. 6.)

The Church speaks Latin, therefore, not only because she is *Apostolic, Unchangeable, and Catholic,* but also because she is *One.*

Change of language in the Liturgy seems to break the link with the past, and raise some suspicion of innovation in what is expressed in the Liturgy; while the having retained the same ancient language indicates that the Church which continues to use it is the very same as of old, and that she has not changed in any essential matter, having been so careful as not to change even her language, which, compared with doctrine, is of much less importance.

It is fairly presumed that the Church which possesses the language of antiquity has antiquity on her side; that being the inheritor of the language, she is also the inheritor of the faith. The fact of her still using the Latin language makes us feel the more sure that the Catholic Church is the one old unchangeable Church of God.

CHAPTER XLV.

Some Things that Catholics do not Believe.

We have already passed in review what seem to be the principal points of Catholic belief, and now, in order to meet the most common of the misapprehensions and misrepresentations on these matters, we will here state, though it may be in part a repetition, some things that Catholics do *not* believe.

1. They do *not* believe that there is any other Mediator of Redemption than our SAVIOUR JESUS CHRIST, "*For there is no other name under heaven given to men, whereby we must be saved*" than that of JESUS (Acts of the Apostles, iv. 12); and when they call the Blessed Virgin or any other Saint a mediator, it is *not* in the sense of Mediator of Redemption attributed to our Saviour, but in the sense of *intercessor* or *pleader*, in which sense any Christian may be called a mediator, whenever he intercedes between God and his fellow-man, as Abraham and Moses and St. Paul did, and thus prays for his neighbour. God Himself commanded Eliphaz and his friends to apply to the Patriarch Job that he should pray for them, and God promised to accept his prayers. "*Go to my servant Job, and offer for yourselves a holocaust: and my servant Job shall pray for you: his face I will accept, that folly be not imputed to you.*" (Job xlii. 8.) In this sense Moses could also say, "*I was the mediator, and stood between the Lord and you*". (Deuteronomy v. 5.)

2. They do not believe that the Blessed Virgin is in *any way* equal to God, for she, being a *creature*, although the most highly favoured, is *infinitely* less than God. Nor do they claim for her any power beyond that which she derives from Him; for she is

entirely dependent on God for her existence, her privileges, her grace, and her glory.

The strong, loving expressions used oftentimes by Catholics, which seem to attribute to the Blessed Virgin more than is here stated, are to be understood in the *limited sense* meant by Catholics themselves, as here explained; that is, in a way consistent with the Catholic teaching and spirit, and not in the unlimited, un-Catholic sense which persons not understanding that teaching may be led to apply to them. These tender expressions, however, ought not to be judged of by cold or hostile criticism, for they spring from fervent heartfelt devotion and unmeasured love.

If it were permitted to take offence at expressions which are only true in a limited sense, surely from those words of Scripture: "*I have said you are gods*" (Psalm lxxxi. 6), one might argue that Holy Scripture holds certain men to be really gods. From those words of the Gospel: "*If any man come to me, and hate not his father, and mother, and wife, and children, and brethren, and sisters, ... he cannot be my disciple*" (S. Luke xiv. 26), one might pretend that Christ encourages the hating of parents and other relatives. That direction of our Lord: "*If thy right hand scandalize thee, cut it off*" (S. Matth. v. 30), might be taken to justify self-mutilation. And from the words: "*How knowest thou, O man, whether thou shalt save thy wife?*" (1 Corinth. vii. 16), some might argue that according to Scripture a man can be the saviour of his wife.

If, therefore, even in the interpretation of Holy Scripture, it would be a wrong principle to take in the full extent expressions that were meant to be understood in a qualified sense only; so still more unjust it would seem to apply this wrong principle to expressions found in books of devotion or in religious poetical compositions, in which a certain latitude to the expansion of a warm heart is allowed.

It is a common practice among men to use expressions which are true only in a secondary and limited sense. For instance, mothers often call their children their little "*angels*," "*kings*," and "*queens*," and are said to "*adore*" or "*idolize*" them, and no one thinks of blaming such tender exaggerated expressions of heart-felt love. In like manner the title of "*Worshipful*" is given to every Company or Guild of the City of London, to Mayors and Magistrates, and Justices of the Peace. Thus again, in the Marriage-Service in the Book of Common Prayer of the Established Church of England, the bridegroom has to say to the bride: "With my body *I thee worship*".

No one should take offence at these expressions; indeed, it would seem captious to do so; more especially when the speaker declares his meaning.

3. Catholics do *not* believe that there is any authority upon earth or in Heaven that can give leave to commit any sin, even the least; or that a sin can be forgiven for money; or that a Priest can give valid absolution to a sinner who does not repent and truly purpose to forsake sin and amend his life.

4. They do *not* believe that a man can by his own good works, *independently of the Merits and Passion of Jesus Christ and of His grace*, obtain salvation, or make any satisfaction for the guilt of his sins, or acquire any merit.

5. They do *not* believe that it is lawful to break an oath, or tell a lie, or to do any other wicked thing whatever for the sake of promoting the supposed interest of the Church, or for any good, however great, likely to arise from it, or for any other cause at all. The

false and hateful principle that the end justifies the means, or that we may do evil that good may come, is *utterly condemned* by the Catholic Church.

6. They do *not* believe that it is in the power of the Church to add to the truths contained in the "*deposit of faith*," that is, to frame or enforce any doctrine which has not for its source the Written or Unwritten Word, or authority from the same. Nor do they believe, when the Church makes a *Definition* in matters of faith, that this definition or article of faith is a new doctrine, but only a solemn declaration and a clear definition of what was believed, at least implicitly, (that is, in an implied way), in the time of the Apostles.

7. Catholics do *not* believe that Protestants who are baptised, who lead a good life, love God and their neighbour, and are *blamelessly* ignorant of the just claims of the Catholic Religion to be the only one true Religion (which is called *being in good faith*), are excluded from Heaven, provided such Christians believe that there is one God in three Divine Persons;* that God will duly reward the good and punish the wicked; that Jesus Christ is the Son of God made man, Who redeemed us, and in Whom we must trust for our salvation; and provided they thoroughly repent of having by their sins offended God.

Catholics hold that Protestants who have such dispositions, and moreover have no suspicion of their Religion being erroneous, nor have the means to discover, or fail in their honest endeavours to discover, the true Religion, and who are so disposed in their heart that they would *at any cost* embrace the Roman

---

* A believer in one God who, without any fault on his part, does not believe that in God there are three divine Persons, is so far in a state of salvation, according to the opinion of most Catholic theologians of the present day.

Catholic Religion if they knew it to be the true one, are *Roman Catholics in spirit*, without knowing it. She holds that these Christians belong to, and are united to the "*soul*," as it is called, of the Catholic Church, although they are not united to the visible *body* of the Church by external communion with her, and by the outward profession of her faith.

Very different is the case of a Protestant who, having the opportunity, neglects to learn from authentic sources what the Catholic Religion is and really teaches, *fearing*, that were he to become convinced of the truth of the Catholic Faith, he would be compelled by his conscience to forsake his own Religion and bear the worldly inconveniences attached to this step. This very *fear* shows a want of good faith, and that he is not in that *insurmountable ignorance* which could excuse him in the sight of God, but that he is one of those of whom it is said in Psalm xxxv. 4, "*He would not understand that he might do well*".

Fairness, no less than common sense, teaches that a man should study and examine the teaching of the Catholic Church at Catholic sources before condemning her. Surely no man ought to reject Catholic doctrines if he has not made himself acquainted with them. Nor is it fair to form a judgment from *misrepresentations* made by interested and prejudiced persons; but he should rather, by the study of authorised Catholic works, judge of the truth with that calm and unprejudiced mind which the all-important subject of Religion deserves.*

Our Saviour gave no hope of salvation to the Samaritan woman unless she embraced the one true Church of that time, saying to her, destitute of a sure

* In No. 44 of the Appendix a list of selected useful Catholic books is given.

guide: "*You adore that which you know not: we adore that which we know; for* SALVATION IS OF THE JEWS". (S. John iv. 22.) So likewise there is no salvation for any one who, having by God's grace come to the knowlege of the truth, obstinately remains out of the one Fold of salvation, the true Church of God.

There was no safety out of the Ark of Noah during the Deluge, and no one can be saved who is in *no sense within* the true Church, prefigured by that Ark. According to S. Cyprian: "*No one can have God for his Father who has not the Church for his Mother. If any one could escape the Deluge out of Noah's Ark, he who is out of the Church may also escape*". (Book on the Unity of the Church.)

It is hard to understand how a Protestant can daily say in the Apostles' Creed, as many happily do still say: "*I believe the Holy Catholic Church,*" without at least a thought arising in his mind, that perhaps after all the Church which *alone* is truly Catholic or universal, both in *name* and in *fact*, has more claim on his love and obedience than his own denomination, which really is *not Catholic.*

CHAPTER XLVI.

CONCLUSION.

May the blessing of God accompany the reading of this short exposition of Catholic doctrine and practice!

May honest-hearted people, by the study of these few pages of plain and candid explanation, be helped to form a more correct idea of the real teaching of the Catholic Church, and to entertain a more favourable opinion of the Holy Catholic Faith!

"*The charity of* CHRIST *presseth us*" (2 Corinth. v. 14) to entreat such earnest-minded persons to pray heartily to God for *supernatural faith*, for *light* to lead them on to the truth, and for *strength* to tear themselves away from all attachments to any known sin.

If these earnest souls persevere in prayer and in avoiding sin and the occasion of sin, they shall find the truth—and *the truth shall make them free indeed*— "*For every one that asketh receiveth ; and he that seeketh findeth ; and to him that knocketh it shall be opened*". (S. Matt. vii. 8 ; S. Luke xi. 10.) JESUS said : "*Blessed are the clean of heart : for they shall see God*". (S. Matt. v. 8.) He also said : "*Other sheep I have, that are not of this fold ; them also I must bring, and they shall hear my voice, and there shall be one fold and one shepherd*". (S. John x. 16.) If, then, they are constant in prayer, they shall be guided into the *one* Fold of the Good Shepherd JESUS CHRIST, our Blessed Lord and Saviour, to Whom, with God the Father, and God the Holy Spirit, be all honour and glory for ever and ever. Amen.

A PRAYER.*

For light to find the true Church of Christ, and for grace to submit humbly and heartily to her guidance when found.

O GOD the *Father*, my Creator ; O GOD the *Son*, my Redeemer ; O GOD *the Holy Ghost*, my Sanctifier ; *Holy Trinity, One* God, have mercy upon me !

---

* It is strongly recommended to pray and to pray much, as conversion is a matter of God's light and grace. How many are thoroughly convinced of the truth of the Roman Catholic Religion, and yet have not the courage to embrace it, because they do not pray, or do not pray properly and enough. See Observations of Cardinal Newman on Faith, Appendix No. 12.

O Jesus, the Way, the Truth, and the Life, Who didst appoint Thy Apostles to act in Thy stead, with power to teach all revealed truth, and to dispense Thy Sacraments, give me light to know Thy one true Church visible here on earth.

Help me, dear Saviour, to submit myself humbly to her guidance, and let me not be tossed to and fro by every wind of doctrine.

Thou Who didst heal the sick, heal me. Thou Who didst give sight to the blind, grant that I may see. Let me find in Thy Church pardon and salvation, through the Merits of Thy most precious Blood.

Help me, a poor sinner, to follow after Thee, and to press forward to the full enjoyment of Thee for ever in Heaven. Amen.

Ejaculations, or little prayers, recommended to be repeated very often, humbly and fervently.

Jesus, meek and humble of heart, make my heart like to Thy Heart.

Dear Jesus, lead me into Thy one Fold, O God of my salvation.

O God the Holy Spirit, give me light to know, and courage to profess the true Religion.

Jesus, our God : Have mercy on us.

Maxim.

No security can be too great where *Eternity* is at stake.

PART II.

APPENDIX No. I.

ANSWERS TO SOME DIFFICULTIES, AND TO SOME QUESTIONS THAT A PERSON EARNESTLY SEEKING THE TRUE RELIGION MIGHT WISH TO ASK.

Question.—May we not consider that all Christian denominations are good for salvation, provided a man lives up to the principles of the religion he professes?

Answer.—No; for though under certain conditions, as explained at Chapter xlv. No. 7, some may be saved, who, *without any fault of their own*, are not outwardly, that is, visibly, united to the Body of the Church, yet it is a great mistake to say that all Christian religions are good, and leading to salvation.

The Church of Jesus Christ, as is explained in Chapter xxiv., can be but *one*, and Jesus Christ has threatened condemnation to any one who refuses to hear *this* one appointed Divine Teacher. (S. Mark xvi. 16.)

We are as much bound to submit our *intellect* to God as we are bound to submit to Him our *will*. But to give credit to opinions taught by persons not sent by God, or by interpreters not authorised by Him, is not submitting our intellect to God.

Again, as the law of God in morals excludes *vice*, so in intellectual matters it excludes *error in faith*, and forbids it under pain of exclusion from Heaven. (See Galatians v. 20-21.)

God, Who is essential truth, can only command true faith, therefore every one is bound to look for the true faith.

To suppose that God is indifferent as to whether we have the truth or the contradiction of it, which is error, whether we commit ourselves to the Guide appointed by Him, or rebel against that Guide, and commit ourselves to unauthorised teachers, would be to bring to naught the object of revelation, to nullify the office of the Church, to contradict Christ's declaration, and, if done wilfully, to offer an insult against the God of Holiness, Charity, and Truth.

Question.—I can scarcely suppose that really God does require of me to give up the religion of my fathers, in which I was born and brought up, for another religion, in which it may be difficult for me to feel at home. Does God require of me such a sacrifice as the ruin of my prospects, loss of my property, the opposition of parents and friends who will in all likelihood resent such a step and forsake me, leaving me as an outcast from society, and an object of pity and suspicion?

Answer—This must naturally be a painful thought, but, instead of regarding this step as abandoning the religion of your fathers, you should consider it, *as it really is*, a coming back to the faith of your forefathers, of which faith you and your parents have unconsciously been deprived; for it is a well-known historical fact that down to the time of the Reformation in the sixteenth century all Christian people in England were Catholics, that the people in England have been forced into Protestantism by the banishment of all Catholic Bishops and Priests, and by stringent penal laws against any one that absented himself from Protestant service, or attended Catholic worship.

If Protestantism had been introduced in a fair way (as by persuasion), Protestants would have built Churches of their own, leaving the Catholic churches in possession of their rightful owners. The simple fact that all Catholic churches, colleges, and other Catholic public edifices, have been taken away from Catholics by Protestants, and not one of them left in their hands, is a sign that Protestantism was introduced into this country in a violent way.*

The sacrifices entailed by embracing the true religion, were they even greater in number and more severe than they really are, ought not to be considered great when compared with the gain; and we ought to be ready to undergo them with a generous heart, out of a *sense of duty to God*, and in view of our *eternal interest*.

The sacrifice of any temporal advantage is never too great to secure everlasting salvation. No earthly advantage, which is but for a time, can make up for the loss of heaven. Our Lord expressed this truth in those searching and solemn words: "*What doth it profit a man, if he gain the whole world, and suffer the loss of his own soul?*" (S. Matt. xvi. 26.)

The example of so many millions of martyrs who died for the faith ought to stir up our courage and devotion.

Our Lord says: "*He that loveth father or mother more than Me, is not worthy of Me; and he that loveth son or daughter more than Me, is not worthy of Me. And he that taketh not up his cross, and followeth Me, is not worthy of Me.*" (S. Matt. x. 37, 38.) "*So likewise every one of you that doth not renounce all that he possesseth cannot be my disciple.*" (S. Luke xiv. 33.)

* See Appendix, No. 81.

"*For he that shall be ashamed of Me and of my words, of him the Son of Man shall be ashamed when He shall come in His majesty, and that of His Father, and of the holy angels.*" (S. Luke ix. 26.) "*Do not think that I came to send peace upon earth; I came not to send peace, but the sword.*" (S. Matth. x. 34.)

From all this it is plain that our Lord Jesus Christ expects sacrifices from us. We ought, therefore, not to be backward in making them for the love of Him who sacrificed Himself unsparingly for the love of us. We ought to be glad to have an opportunity of doing so. And our Lord will not be sparing in His rewards. (See S. Matth. xix. 29.)

Some are naturally much affected by the thought of having to leave the religion in which they were born and educated, and in which they passed so great a part of their life. But surely this is to allow oneself to be guided by feeling rather than by duty, by conscience, and by reason. If this were a good motive, in this case, all those who have the misfortune to be brought up in heresy would be justified in remaining in it. To have been born and bred in a certain religion is not a sound reason for retaining it, when you come to see clearly that it is not true. You will be answerable to God for *wilfully* persevering in a religion which, by God's grace, you have seen to be false, and for *wilfully* refusing to embrace that religion which, by God's grace, you feel convinced is the true religion founded by Jesus Christ.

The idea of changing your long-cherished convictions alarms you. You should observe, however, that though, on the one hand, you are required to give up all that is false in the religious belief you have professed until now, you will happily retain everything good and true that you possessed when a Protestant, to which you have only to add those necessary points of belief in which you are deficient. Whatever truth and whatever good there is in the religious belief you have hitherto professed, you will find in all their genuine simplicity and fulness in the Catholic Church. Instead of having less affection for your Parents and friends, your love for them will be deepened, and your sympathy ennobled and enlarged.

If what keeps you back were fear of not being able to surmount certain difficulties, you should consider that as it is a *strict duty* on your part to embrace the true religion, God will surely not fail to give you the necessary strength to that end. To doubt this and to distrust God's assistance would be more unreasonable, more offensive to God, and more fatal to yourself, than the distrust shown by the Jews in the desert, of being able to overcome the obstacles which opposed their taking possession of the promised land. (See Book of Numbers, chapts. xiii. and xiv.)

Question.—In order to become a member of the Catholic Church, is it necessary to be formally received by a Catholic Priest, or is it sufficient to be a Catholic in heart and spirit? If a person believes all that the Catholic Church teaches, and frequents Catholic services and fulfils other Catholic duties, is he not then a Catholic, without any need of a formal reception?

Answer.—No; for no Protestant is considered to be a convert to the Catholic Church until, being baptized, he is received into the Church according to the prescribed rite. No other way of admitting any Christian as a member of the Catholic Church was ever known except that of absolving him with an external rite from ecclesiastical censures (that is, certain spiritual disadvantages and penalties) resting on him, and of admitting him into the Church. This rite is performed only by a Catholic Priest in the name of the Church.*

A foreigner or alien is not considered a subject of the British Empire unless he has undergone the formalities of naturalisation making him a British subject; and a Christian estranged from the Church of God is not, as a rule, reckoned as belonging to the Church—the kingdom of God on earth—unless he is duly absolved and received. One must be within the Ark to be safe from the deluge ; one must be within the walls of the city to be safe from the enemy. The Church is that Ark, that City. S. Jerome says : " Whoever is not in the Ark of Noah will perish by the deluge." (Epistle to S. Damasus.) And in a passage of Isaias which refers to the Church it is said : " SALVATION *shall possess* THY WALLS ". (lx. 18.)

Question.— Nicodemus was a disciple of Christ, though secretly ; why cannot I in like manner be a Catholic in heart and in secret ?

Answer.—Nicodemus was a disciple of Jesus Christ, and in secret ; but he presented himself to our Lord. Begin therefore by presenting yourself to the Catholic Priest, to be instructed and received into the Church. After being received privately into the Church, if weighty reasons require it, such as loss of home, or property, or position, or employment (provided the retaining of these is not inconsistent with belief in the Catholic Religion), and so long as those weighty reasons last, you need not make your Catholicity public, but may attend to your Catholic duties privately. Circumstances, however, may occur in which either the sacredness of truth, or the honour of God, or the edification of neighbours may require of you " *to contend*

---

* See Conversion of Victorinus, Appendix No. 7.

earnestly for the faith" (S. Jude 3); and in such cases, as the holy Apostle S. Paul warns us, "*with the mouth confession is made unto salvation*". (Romans x. 10.)

Question.—What should a person do who is convinced of the truth of the greater part of Catholic teaching, but who is not quite satisfied about some points?

Answer.—Humbly beg God's aid and blessing; apply with confidence to a Catholic Priest; state your difficulties to him, and ponder well before God upon his explanations and advice.

As a father, he will be sure to receive you kindly, whoever you are, and will patiently hear what are your difficulties. He will gladly remove from your mind any mistaken notion about Catholic belief, and, it may be, remove your difficulties.

It is very important that you should hear for yourself an answer to your religious difficulties from one who, by study, training, and in virtue of his office, is fitted to deal with such matters; for it often happens that the particular objections you may have are not answered, or, perhaps, even so much as mentioned, in ordinary books of Catholic instruction.

Go then at once, as you value your immortal soul; for you may never be able by yourself to overcome your difficulties; and by delaying you may lose, through a mere crotchet perhaps, after all, the priceless joy and peace of living and dying in the embrace of your true Mother the Holy Catholic Church, the Church founded and protected by *Jesus Christ.*

Question.—What steps should be taken by any one who, after having thought on the matter well and prayed earnestly, has decided to become a Catholic?

Answer.—You must apply to a Priest, who will

judge of your dispositions and of your knowledge of the Catholic Faith. He will give you further instruction if needed, and explain your duties, and how you have to act after your reception into the Church. When he is satisfied that you are properly prepared, he will appoint the time for your being received.

Question.—What is the practice for the reception of a convert into the Catholic Church.

Answer.—On coming to be received, if it is certain that you have never been baptized, you will receive the Sacrament of Baptism, and that is a full reception into the Church without any other form. In such case, it may be useful to make a confession of your past sins; but you are in no way bound to do it, because Holy Baptism remits not only original sin, but also all actual sins.

For converts, who have been baptised in their Protestant Religion, coming to be received into the Church, the practice is—

1st, You go to the Altar or to the Sacristy, or other place convenient for your reception.*

* It has been the practice until of late to hear a *preparatory* confession from a Protestant *before* being received into the Church; which confession was completed and followed by Sacramental absolution after the conditional Baptism had been administered. This practice, I am authorised to state, is now, as a rule, superseded; for, by an instruction of the Holy See, which is printed in the Appendix to the 4th Provincial Council of Westminster (Chapter xviii.), it is required: (1) That those persons who, on being converted to the Catholic faith in England, are conditionally baptised, shall also make a full sacramental confession of the sins of their past life; and (2) that this confession, with conditional absolution, shall follow the conditional Baptism. I said, *as a rule*, because if a convert, of his own accord, wishes to open his mind and tell his sins beforehand to the Priest, completing his confession, and receiving absolution after having received conditional Baptism, there is nothing to prevent it.

2nd, The Priest who is with you says certain prayers appointed by the Church; you, in the meantime, kneel down and pray silently.

3rd, You will then read, or repeat aloud, after the Priest, the Profession of Faith, namely, that Summary of Catholic belief known as the Creed of Pope Pius IV., together with the short addition made at the last General Council in 1870, both given at Appendix, No. 3, or some other authorised form, as that placed, Appendix, No. 4.

4th, After this, the prayer called the General Confession or "*Confiteor*"* is said by the Priest, if no one else is there to say it for you. He will then release you from the ban and censures of the Church, under which, as a Protestant (by misfortune, probably, rather than by fault), you have hitherto been, and he will so receive you into the Fold of the Church. If you do not yourself say the "*Confiteor*," you will do well to repeat in a low voice with sorrow of heart those words of the Penitent in the Gospel: "*O God be merciful to me a sinner*". (S. Luke xviii. 13.)

5th, The Priest will then administer to you Baptism under condition, by pouring a little water thrice on your head or forehead, whilst he addresses you by your Christian name, and pronounces these words: "[Christian name] *If thou art not already baptised, I baptise thee in the name of the Father, and of the Son, and of the Holy Ghost. Amen.*"†

It should here be noticed that the conditional words, "*If thou art not already baptised*," makes this act to

---

* The *Confiteor* will be found a little further on.

† The Latin form used by the Priest is: "N.N. *si non es baptizatus, ego te baptizo in nomine Patris et Filii et Spiritus Sancti. Amen.*"

be no Baptism at all if the first Baptism was valid. In this way the danger and even the possibility of administering a second Baptism is effectually avoided.

Conditional Baptism is, as a rule, administered for safety's sake to all converts from Protestantism, on their reception into the Church, from the fear that, as sometimes has been the case, what they received before as Baptism was not really Baptism, either for want of intention, or on account of some defect in the element used, or in the words uttered, or on account of some serious fault in the administration; and to make full inquiries about every case is almost an impossibility.*

It is to be remarked, therefore, that *only* when there has previously been really no Baptism does this Baptism "*under condition*" take effect; for Holy Baptism is a Sacrament that can be received only once.

In Baptism under condition the ceremonies prescribed for Baptism are not required, nor are Sponsors needed.

6th, After the Baptism under condition the Priest recites the ancient Hymn of the Church, beginning: "*Te Deum laudamus*"—" We praise Thee, O God". See Appendix No. 11.

7th, Being now baptised and received into the Church, you will go to the Confessional to make your confession and to receive from the Priest the Sacramental absolution.† While receiving absolution, you must renew your sorrow and your hatred of sin, and

---

* Though a Priest is not bound under the said circumstances to make investigation about the validity of the Baptism of each convert, yet if, in some particular case, the Priest happens to be thoroughly convinced that a person has been validly baptised, the Baptism under condition is omitted according to directions from Rome.

† Directions how to approach the Sacrament of penance will be found in the Appendix, No. 15.

your resolution to amend, making a sincere Act of Contrition. (See Appendix, No. 13.)

As some converts feel a great deal of needless alarm and anxiety about confession, it may be well here to remark—

1st, That we are *bound* to confess only mortal sins (that is, grievous sins which "kill the soul," by depriving it of the grace of God), which after self-examination can be called to mind. Our venial sins (that is, lesser faults, which, "though they offend God, do not kill the soul "), we are not bound to confess, although it is recommended to do so. Holy Communion, an Act of contrition, or a fervent Act of the love of God, suffices through the Merits of Christ, without sacramental confession, to cleanse the soul from the stain of *venial* sin.

2nd, That it is not required of us to mention each sin of the same sort or kind in detail, but the sins of one kind may be all mentioned together : for example, the penitent confessing may say : " I accuse myself of having been guilty of grievous disobedience to my Father or Mother, or of having given way to great anger, about so many times," stating, according to the best of his belief, after careful examination, the number ; and thus also of other mortal sins.

3rd, That if we are not able to remember the exact number of our sins, it is enough to state the probab'e number to the best of our recollection and judgment, saying : about so many times a day, a week, or a month. In fact, we are bound to reveal our conscience to the Priest as we know it ourselves, there and then stating the things certain as certain, those doubtful as doubtful, and the probable number as probable ; for God does not require impossibilities, but only what we can offer, namely, sincerity and ordinary diligence.

Confession rightly explained is not so difficult as some imagine it to be.

Confession is the healing *medicine* of the soul, and we must not wonder that, in the Providence of God, it is somewhat bitter; yet we ought to be ready to use it for our soul's health, as we take a medicine for the good of the body, however distasteful that medicine may be.

If prisoners condemned to death were offered release on condition that they would make confession of their misdeeds in secret to one of the Judges, who would be bound, in honour only, never to reveal a word of what they had confessed, surely they would thankfully avail themselves of the offer, and would easily overcome their natural dislike to self-accusation in order to purchase life and liberty. So a Christian ought not to consider it too hard a condition of forgiveness to have to confess to any Priest he may choose, who has the authority, called "faculty," from his Bishop to hear confessions, and who is most solemnly bound, not only in honour but in conscience, by the law of God, and by the positive law of the Church, to the most sacred and inviolable secrecy with regard to what he has heard in sacramental confession. The penitent sinner will not think it too hard to make the confession of his sins if he only considers the punishment his sins have deserved, the sufferings they have caused to his Divine Saviour, the forgiveness he receives, his rescue from the slavery of Satan, and his restoration to the friendship of God.

Jesus Christ shed his Precious Blood to the last drop, in the midst of the most cruel torments on the Cross, to provide for us sinners an overflowing fountain of salvation in the Sacrament of Penance,—the Sacrament of reconciliation. To refuse to make use of this life-giving Sacrament, on the plea that to confess to a

Priest is disagreeable to nature, is unworthy of a Christian.

Let me add, that confession is not after all so hard in practice as some not accustomed to it may imagine. With God's grace and the assistance of your confessor, added to your own good dispositions, confession becomes surprisingly easy.

How many converts who were in alarm before making their confession have afterwards exclaimed : "And is that all ? Had I only known how easy it was, I would not have endured the burden of sin so long, and put off my reception into the Catholic Church. Thank God ! now I feel an unspeakable peace."

Oh ! that many, many more would thus readily obtain peace and happiness ! Why are there persons who endanger their salvation by choosing to remain in a state of uncertainty in matters necessary to be believed, having all the while their conscience burdened with sin and misery ? Hear Cardinal Newman on this point.

"How many are the souls in distress, anxiety, or loneliness, whose one need is to find a being to whom they can pour out their feelings unheard by the world ! Tell them out they must; they cannot tell them out to those whom they see every hour. They want to tell them and not to tell them ; and they want to tell them out, yet be as if they be not told ; they wish to tell them to one who is strong enough to bear them, yet not too strong to despise them ; they wish to tell them to one who can at once advise and can sympathise with them ; they wish to relieve themselves of a load, to gain a solace, to receive the assurance that there is one who thinks of them, and one to whom in thought they can recur, to whom they can betake themselves, if necessary, from time to time, while they are in the world. How many a Protestant's heart would leap at the news of such a benefit, putting aside all distinct ideas of a sacramental ordinance, or of a grant of pardon and the conveyance of grace! If there is a heavenly idea in the Catholic Church, looking at it simply as an idea, surely, next after the Blessed Sacrament, Confession is such. And such is it ever found in fact—the very act of kneeling, the low and contrite voice, the sign of the Cross hanging, so to say, over the head bowed low, and the words of peace and blessing. Oh, what a soothing charm is there, which the world can neither give nor take away! Oh, what piercing, heart-subduing tranquillity, provoking tears of joy, is poured almost substantially and physically upon the soul, the oil of gladness, as Scripture calls it, when the penitent at length rises, his God reconciled to him, his sins rolled away for ever! This is Confession as it is in fact." (Cardinal Newman, *Present Position of Catholics*, p. 351.)

Oh! if they only would, how many might joyfully exclaim, with the Royal Psalmist: *Our soul hath been delivered, as a sparrow out of the snare of the fowlers; the snare is broken, and we are delivered*" (Psalm cxxiii. 7); and why will they not?

"*O taste, and see that the Lord is sweet; blessed is the man that hopeth in him.*" (Psalm xxxiii. 9.)

THE "CONFITEOR" OR CONFESSION.

"Confiteor Deo omnipotenti, beátae Mariae semper Virgini, beáto Michaéli Archangelo, beáto Joanni Baptistae, sanctis Apostolis Petro et Paulo, omnibus sanctis, et tibi, Pater, quia peccávi nimis cogitatione, verbo

"I confess to Almighty God, to Blessed Mary ever Virgin, to Blessed Michael the Archangel, to Blessed John the Baptist, to the holy Apostles Peter and Paul, to all the Saints, and to you, Father,

et opere, meâ culpâ, meâ culpâ, meâ maxima culpâ.

Ideo precor beâtam Mariam semper Virginem, beâtum Michaélem Archangelum, beâtum Joannem Baptistam, sanctos Apostolos Petrum et Paulum, omnes sanctos, et te Pater, orâre pro me ad Dominum Deum nostrum."

that I have sinned exceedingly in thought, word, and deed, through my fault, through my fault, through my most grievous fault. [*Here strike your breast in sorrow thrice.*] *Humbly make the sincere confession of your sins, and then finish the form of the "Confiteor" thus:*—

Therefore I beseech Blessed Mary ever Virgin, Blessed Michael the Archangel, Blessed John the Baptist, the holy Apostles Peter and Paul, all the Saints, and you, Father, to pray to the LORD our GOD for me."

No. 2.—THE APOSTLES' CREED.

1, I believe in God, the Father Almighty, Creator of heaven and earth;—2, And in Jesus Christ, His only Son, our Lord;—3, Who was conceived by the Holy Ghost, born of the Virgin Mary;—4, Suffered under Pontius Pilate, was crucified, dead, and buried;—5, He descended into Hell; the third day He rose again from the dead;—6, He ascended into Heaven; sitteth at the right hand of God the Father Almighty;—7, From thence he shall come to judge the living and the dead.—8, I believe in the Holy Ghost;—9, The Holy Catholic Church; the communion of Saints;—10, The forgiveness of sins;—11, The resurrection of the body;—12, and the life everlasting. Amen.

No. 3.—Creed of Pope Pius IV.*

I, *(N, Christian Name)* with a firm faith, believe and profess all and every one of those things which are contained in that Creed which the Holy Roman Church maketh use of. Namely:—I believe in one God, the Father Almighty, Maker of Heaven and Earth, of all things visible and invisible. And in one Lord, Jesus Christ, the only-begotten Son of God, born of the Father before all ages. God of God: Light of Light: true God of true God; begotten, not made, consubstantial † with the Father; by ‡ Whom all things were made. Who, for us men, and for our salvation, came down from Heaven, and was incarnate by the Holy Ghost of the Virgin Mary, *and was made man.* He was crucified also for us, under Pontius Pilate, He suffered and was buried, and the third day He rose again according to the Scriptures. He ascended into Heaven, and sittteth at the right hand of the Father, and He shall come again with glory to judge the living and the dead :—of Whose kingdom there shall be no end. And I believe in the Holy Ghost, the Lord and Life-giver, who proceedeth from the Father and the

---

* This Creed was composed at the conclusion of the General Council of Trent (capital of the Austrian Tyrol), held from the year of our Lord 1545 to 1563, to meet the errors of the first Protestants, Luther, Calvin, and others, then spreading. A few supplementary words were added by Pope Pius IX., referring to the Supremacy and Infallibility of the Roman Pontiff.

† Of one substance with.

‡ Or through Whom, "per quem".

Son, Who, together with the Father and the Son, is adored and glorified; Who spoke by the Prophets.

And I believe One, Holy, Catholic, and Apostolic Church. I confess one Baptism for the remission of sins: and I look for the resurrection of the dead, and the life of the world to come. Amen.*

I most steadfastly admit and embrace Apostolical and Ecclesiastical Traditions,† and all other observances and constitutions of the same Church.

I also admit the Holy Scriptures, according to that sense which our Holy Mother the Church has held, and does hold, to which it belongs to judge of the true sense and interpretation of the Scriptures ‡ neither will I ever take and interpret them otherwise than according to the unanimous consent of the Fathers.§

---

* So far, this is, word for word, the Nicene Creed, which was mainly composed by the Council of Nicæa, held in the year of our Lord 325, against the Arians, who denied the Divinity of Jesus Christ.

† That is, I admit as points of *revealed truth* what the Church declares that the Apostles have taught as such, whether clearly or not clearly expressed or not even mentioned in the Written Word of God: as, for instance, that Baptism is to be conferred on infants, that Sunday instead of Saturday (called the Sabbath) is to be kept holy: and moreover, I admit those points of discipline which the Church holds as established by the Apostles, or by their Successors as lawful rulers of the Church in the early centuries of Christianity, such as points of Liturgy or of Church Government.

‡ This means:—I will not take the Holy Scripture in a *wrong sense;* as would be the case if one were to interpret a passage of Scripture in a sense opposed to that defined by the Church. (See Chapter viii.)

§ This regards points of *faith or morals* not yet defined by

I also profess that there are truly and properly seven Sacraments of the New Law, instituted by Jesus Christ our Lord, and necessary for the salvation of mankind, although not all of them necessary for every one. Namely, Baptism, Confirmation, the Eucharist, Penance, Extreme Unction, Order, and Matrimony; and that they confer grace; and that of these, Baptism, Confirmation, and Order cannot be repeated without the sin of sacrilege. I also receive and admit the received and approved ceremonies of the Catholic Church used in the solemn administration of the aforesaid Sacraments.

I embrace and receive all and every one of the things which have been defined and declared in the Holy Council of Trent, concerning Original Sin and Justification.

I profess likewise, that in the Mass there is offered to God a true, proper, and propitiatory Sacrifice for the living and the dead. And that in the most holy Sacrifice of the Eucharist, there is truly, really, and substantially the Body and Blood, together with the

---

the Church; and it means that when it is known that the Fathers (venerated Christian writers of ancient times) agree in the interpretation of any passage of Scripture on matters of *faith or of morals*, it would be rash and wrong to disregard their interpretation; as in such case their testimony represents the faith of the Church. It does not, however, imply that an obligation rests on a private person to consult the Fathers when reading the Holy Scripture for his own edification and instruction. To put such an interpretation on this passage would be mere cavilling.

Soul and Divinity of our Lord Jesus Christ, and that there is made a conversion of the whole substance of the bread into the Body, and of the whole substance of the wine into the Blood; which conversion the Catholic Church calls Transubstantiation. I also confess that, under either kind alone, Christ is received whole and entire, and a true Sacrament.

I steadfastly hold that there is a Purgatory, and that the souls therein detained are helped by the suffrages * of the Faithful. Likewise that the Saints reigning together with Christ are to be honoured and invoked, and that they offer prayers to God for us, and that their relics are to be held in veneration.†

I most firmly assert that the images ‡ of Christ, of the Mother of God, ever Virgin, and also of other Saints, ought to be had and retained, and that due honour and veneration is to be given them.§

I also affirm that the power of granting Indulgences was left by Christ in the Church, and that the use of

---

* That is, *spiritual helps*, such as pious works or prayers.

† This article does not enjoin as a *precept* the pious duty of invoking the Saints and the honouring of their relics, as this, except in the public services of the Church, is left by the Church to the discretion and devotion of each individual; but it intends to condemn the error of those who reject altogether as wrong the invocation of Saints and the honour paid to them and their relics.

‡ Or pious memorials.

§ In this passage also no *precept* is implied for us to keep holy images, but it only binds us to admit the *principle* of the lawfulness of the practice, and that it is right and good to use them.

them is most wholesome to Christian people. (See Chapter xxxvii.)

I acknowledge the Holy, Catholic, Apostolic, Roman Church for the Mother and Mistress of all Churches, and I promise true obedience to the Bishop of Rome, Successor of St. Peter, Prince of the Apostles, and Vicar of Jesus Christ. (See Chapter xxvii. on the Supremacy of the Bishop of Rome.)

I likewise undoubtingly receive and profess all other things which the Sacred Canons and General Councils, and particularly the Holy Council of Trent and the Œcumenical Vatican Council, have delivered, defined, and declared, and in particular, about the supremacy and infallible teaching of the Roman Pontiff.* And I condemn, reject, and anathematise all things contrary thereto, and all heresies which the Church has condemned, rejected, and anathematised.

I *(Christian name)*, do at this present freely profess and sincerely hold this true Catholic Faith, without which no one can be saved.† And I promise most

---

* "Et ab Œcumenico Concilio Vaticano tradita præsertim de Romani Pontificis Primatu et infallibili magisterio."

† This expression should not appear too strong, as it is only a repetition of what Christ said : "*But he that believeth not, shall be condemned.*" (S. Mark xvi. 16.) And, moreover, this condemnation is not intended to apply to the earnest Christian who has not the means of knowing the Catholic Faith, for he thus belongs *in some sense* to the Catholic Church, and is excused, on the plea of invincible ignorance. This remark applies also to those who are altogether out of the light of the faith, but who follow with fidelity the light of the natural law they possess written in their hearts. (See Chapter xlv., Some things that Catholics do *not* believe, No. 7.)

constantly to retain and confess * the same entire and unstained, with God's assistance, to the end of my life.

No. 4.—SHORT FORM OF PROFESSION OF FAITH.

I *(Christian name)*, do sincerely and solemnly declare that, having been brought up in the Protestant Religion *(or other Religion as the case may be)*, but now, by the grace of God, having been brought to the knowledge of the Truth, I firmly believe and profess all that the Holy Catholic and Roman Church believes

---

* This condemns the opinion of some, that for salvation it is enough to believe the Catholic faith only *inwardly*; for, not professing habitually the Religion of Christ is equivalent to being ashamed of Christ; and regarding those who are ashamed of Him, Christ declared He would be ashamed of them when He shall come in the *glory of His Father*. (S. Mark viii. 38, and S. Luke ix. 26.) St. Paul declares, "*with the heart we believe unto justice but with the mouth confession is made unto salvation*". (Romans x. 10.) From the moment that one is convinced that the Catholic faith is the true faith, and the Catholic Church the true Church of Christ, it is his duty to become a member of it, and be added to it also *exteriorly* by an outward reception; as otherwise he would belong neither implicitly nor explicitly to it, that is, neither to the *Soul* nor to the *Body* of the Church. Not to the *Soul*, because that is the privilege only of a person in *good faith*, as explained in Chapter xlv. No. 7. Not to the *Body*, because, as we suppose, he refuses to join it outwardly in the manner appointed by the Church. Thus it was not enough for St. Paul or for Cornelius the Centurion to believe *inwardly*, though enlightened by a supernatural light, but the former had, by God's direction, to apply for that purpose to the priest Ananias, and Cornelius to St. Peter. (See example of Victorinus, Appendix, No. 7.)

and teaches, and I reject and condemn whatever she rejects and condemns.*

No. 5.—DIFFICULTIES OF PRIVATE INTERPRETATION, BY FATHER G. BAMPFIELD, B.A., OXON (ST. ANDREW'S MAGAZINE, APRIL, 1879, FROM PAGE 65).

I was a young man when my enquiry into Truth began. I wished to save my soul—to know the truth and do the right; I asked myself and others how I was to find the truth; the answer was ever the same,—"Search the Scriptures".

But here came a difficulty.

I knew that the Scriptures were the Word of God—but I knew also that God's Writings are then only of use to us when we know what God meant by that which He wrote. God's Word, if we put to it the Devil's meaning, or man's meaning, is not God's word at all. "The letter killeth"; it is "the spirit" which "quickeneth".† What we need is God's meaning of God's Word. The same Holy Ghost who wrote the Scriptures, He only can interpret them.

Was it possible for me to miss this meaning? I read in the Gospels that the Scriptures could be so misused. The Devil tempted our Lord with Scripture texts, using God's Word with the Devil's meaning; S. Matthew, c. 4: the Pharisee rejected our Lord by

---

* This profession of Faith was approved by His Holiness Pope Gregory XVI., and attested by His Eminence Cardinal Wiseman. It may be used instead of the Creed of Pope Pius IV., when weighty circumstances render it advisable.

† II. Cor. iii. 6. "The letter killeth, but the spirit giveth life."—Prot. version.

Scripture;* "Search the Scriptures, and see that out of Galilee a prophet riseth not" (S. John vii. 52), using God's Word, indeed, but perverted by man's sin: of the Sadducees our Lord said that though they read the Scriptures, they knew them not (S. Mark xii. 24); and the Apostles were "foolish and slow of heart to believe in all things which the Prophets have spoken". (S. Luke xxiv. 25.) It was not the multitude who "knew not the law," who condemned our dearest Lord, but the Pharisee, the scribe, and the lawyer, whose whole study was in the sacred Writ.

Nay, the Scriptures themselves told me plainly, † "that no prophecy of the Scripture is made by private interpretation." (2 S. Peter, i. 20.) And, again, that in S. Paul's Epistles at least there ‡ "are certain things hard to be understood, which the unlearned and unstable wrest, *as they do also the other Scriptures*, to their own destruction." (2 S. Peter, iii. 16.) The Scriptures, then, can be used to our destruction, and who was I that I should think myself learned or stable? "Thinkest thou," said Philip to Queen Candace's eunuch, § "that thou understandest what thou readest?" who said, "And how can I, unless some man show me?" (Acts viii. 30, 31.)

It was then, I concluded, possible for me to miss the true meaning of God's Word; and if I missed it, I

---

* "Search and look, for out of Galilee ariseth no Prophet."—Prot. version.

† "No Prophecy of the Scriptures is of any private interpretation."—Prot. version.

‡ "Are some things hard to be understood, which they that are unlearned and unstable wrest, as they do also the other Scriptures, unto their own destruction."—Prot. version.

§ "Understandest thou what thou readest? And he said, How can I, except some man should guide me."—Prot. version.

missed it "to my own destruction". The fault lay not in the Scriptures, which are holy, but in my wretchedness, who misinterpreted.

When I stated this difficulty to others, I received always the same answer, "Pray to God the Holy Ghost, and He will guide you". But here arose two or three difficulties.

A. I knew that without God's help no man can understand the Scriptures; but I knew also, that God's help is given more or less in proportion to the fervency of prayer and the righteousness of him who prays. It is the "continual prayer of a just man"; or, as the Protestant translation renders it, "the effectual fervent prayer of the righteous man" (S. James v. 16), not the lukewarm prayer of the unrighteous that "availeth much." Dared I " trust in myself that I was righteous?" (Luke xviii. 9)—my prayer "fervent and effectual?" If conscience did not compel, humility would exhort me to think otherwise ; and, if so, how could I tell that the true meaning of Scripture was given me in answer to such worthless prayers as mine? The fault lay not in God, who is ever ready to give to them that ask, but in the poverty of the asking and the asker.

B. But I found that on this view not only must I "trust in myself that I was righteous, but despise others also." (S. Luke xviii. 9.) For I found that others did the very same thing which I did—viz., pray to the Holy Ghost, and yet explained Scripture in a sense wholly opposite to mine. If I learned from the Scripture that Baptism was necessary to salvation, another from the very same Scripture would teach that Baptism was not necessary to salvation, and that my doctrine was soul-destroying and hateful to God. If I prayed to the Holy Spirit, so did he ; if I was fully convinced, so was he : if to my spirit I hoped that "the Holy

Spirit gave testimony that I was a child of God" (Rom. viii. 16),* the same claim also did he make. How could I tell that he was wrong and I right? My prayers answered and his not? Was I holier than he? I dared not think so.

Of one thing I was certain, that the Holy Ghost could not teach to me that a doctrine was true, and to him that the same doctrine was not true. One of us was wrong, and teaching, what God hates, a lie; but by what sure sign could I say which was wrong?

Sometimes I was told that these differences were not essential points; but I could not understand this. Men certainly differ, for example, on the question whether Baptism is necessary to Salvation or not. Surely a debate about a necessity is an essential point. In no wordly business, I am certain, in no question about the life of our bodies should we say, "such a thing may be necessary, but it is not essential for us to know whether it is necessary or not."

Moreover, who would dare to tell us which part of our Lord's teaching was essential and which not. "Such a truth will save us, but such another truth He need not have brought from heaven." This I knew that not one jot or tittle of His words shall pass away (S. Matt. v. 18; S. Matt. xxiv. 35), and that to His words we dare not add nor take from them (Rev. xxii. 18, 19), but I knew not who was to be the Judge of our Lord's teaching, and tell us which part we must believe and which we might reject.

It is a marvel to me how men can believe that Christ, who is Love, has so left Christianity in the world, that nearly nineteen centuries have passed away,

---

* "The Spirit itself beareth witness with our spirit that we are the children of God."—Prot. version.

and men are still in doubt about the very necessities of salvation. In the Catholic Church alone is no doubt.

C., The third difficulty which came to me, when I was told to pray to the Holy Spirit and He would guide me, was this. I asked of my instructors, "Do you mean that the Holy Spirit will guide me infallibly, so that I shall make no mistakes?" They laughed at the idea. "Of course not," they answered, "no man is infallible; infallibility is one of the errors of Rome." "But then," was my reply, "if I can be mistaken when I interpret Scripture, how am I to tell when I am mistaken and when not?" To this question I have to this day been unable to obtain an answer, except in the Catholic Church. I propose it once more for solution.

The answer which I made to myself was that if our interpretations of Scripture are little more than guesses in which we might be mistaken, we could *never* tell if we were right or not; and that, as a result, the possession of truth was to us impossible: truth, I argued, is *certain*; that which we know as true cannot by possibility be false; if we once admit doubt we cease to know it as a truth. Most of all should this be the case with religious truth: if heaven is not a *certainty* it were hard to struggle for it; if it be doubtful that there are Three Persons in God, who could worship them? What martyr would bleed for an opinion which was possibly false?

Truth, then, is certain; but our interpretations of Scripture are *not* certain, therefore they are not truth. Our interpretations are fallible opinions, and opinions, however probable, are not truth. It seemed to me, then, that we had the choice of two evils, either to hold that each individual interpreter of Scripture is infallible, or to acknowledge that all interpretations of Scripture are fallible, and therefore all religious doctrines uncertain, or, in other words, not truth. I need not show the absurdity of the first alternative ; for the upholders of private judgment are the very men who deny infallibility. I fear, then, we must accept the second, and own that there is no religious truth on earth, unless, indeed, the Catholic Church be right, and God has provided, in His mercy, a guide whom He has made infallible.

No. 6.—EARNEST APPEAL TO PROTESTANTS, SUGGESTED BY THE AFFECTING WORDS OF ST. AUGUSTINE, BISHOP OF HIPPO, TO THE DONATISTS.

Let me beg of you, my brethren, to consider how beautiful is the Catholic Unity in doctrine by which the Faith is preached, without shadow of change and with authority, in each Catholic cathedral and church ; and how reverenced by the Faithful. See how the Catholic teaching is set high in our colleges above the assaults of infidelity and the contradictory wranglings of so-called scientific theories; how striking is the Catholic Unity in government, by which spiritual jurisdiction, issuing from Christ, flows in fair subordination through Bishop and Priest, so that each Pastor knows his own flock, while his flock knows him and hears his voice.

What a contrast between this blessed vision of peace within the Church and the scene of disorder and tumult that oppress you outside ! There, nearly every pulpit is made the centre of a different teaching, which, delivered without authority, is heard without submission; there, sometimes the very foundations of Christianity are uptorn to be shaped anew, according to individual bias or the caprice of an excited assembly ; there, the flock strays at will after strangers *whose own the sheep are not.*

Here seasonably come those words of S. Augustine: "*Doctrines resound, various heresies arise. Fly to the tabernacle of God—namely, the Catholic Church; here you will be protected from the contradictions of tongues.*"[*]

I will also appeal to you in the affectionate words which the same holy doctor and Father of the Church addressed to the Donatists of his day: "*Come, brothers, come! that you may be engrafted on the true vine. You yourselves cannot but perceive what the Catholic Church is, and what it is to be cut off from the stem. If then there be among you any who have care of themselves, let them arise, and come and draw vigour from the root. Let them come before it be too late; before they lose the little Catholic sap that yet remains to them, and become dry wood fit only for the fire. Come, then, brothers, if you will, and be engrafted on the vine. It grieves us to see you lying as you are, lopped off from the tree. Reckon, then, one by one, the Pontiffs who have sat from his time downwards on Peter's very seat, and mark the regular succession in that order of Fathers. That seat is the rock, which the proud gates of hell overcome not.*"[†]

---

[*] "*Diversae doctrinae personant, diversae haereses oriuntur. Curre ad tabernaculum Dei, id est, Ecclesiam Catholicam! ibi protegeris a contradictione linguarum.*"

[†] "Scitis ecclesia Catholica quid sit et quid sit esse præcisum a vite.
Si qui sunt inter vos cauti, veniant, vivant in radice
Ante-quam nimis arescant, jam liberentur ab igne.
Venite, fratres, si vultis, ut inseramini in vite.
"Dolor est cum vos videmus præcisos ita jacere.
Numerate Sacerdotes vel ab ipsa Petri sede,
Et in ordine illo patrum quis cui successit videte.
Ipsa est petra, quam non vincunt superbæ inferorum portæ."
Psalm. Contra partem Donati, Coll. 5.

No. 7.—Conversion of Victorinus.*

To encourage timid souls to apply at once to a Catholic Priest for instruction when the truth of the Catholic Religion begins to dawn in their minds, and not to allow themselves to be kept back by human respect from frankly applying to be received into the Church when thoroughly convinced of the truth of her Divine claim to their obedience, I might here mention many illustrious examples of our own time of conversion to the Catholic Faith in England.

Foremost among these would stand the honoured names of Manning (now Cardinal Archbishop of Westminster), of Newman (now Cardinal Prince of the Church), of Addis, Akers, Allies, Anderdon, Angus, Anstey, Antrobus, Arden, Arkell, Arnold, Ashburnham, Aspinall, Badeley, Bagshawe, Ballard, Bampfield, Barff, Bathurst, Beaumont, Belaney, Bellasis, Beste, Bethell, Blair, Bliss, Bowden, Bowyer, Boycott, Brady, Bridges, Britten, Brownlow, Buchan, Buckler, Bury, Bute, Campbell, Caswall, Chambers, Chatto, Chisholm, Christie, Clarke, Clifton, Clutton, Coffin, Coghlan, Coleridge, Coventry, Crispin, Dalgairns, Dayman, Deane, Denbigh, Digby, Dodsworth, Douglas, Dunraven, Earle, Emly, Fairlie, Fincham, Formby, French, Fortescue, Lane-Fox, Galton, Gainsborough, Garside, Gladstone, Goldsmid, Gordon, Granard,

---

* His full name was FABIUS MARIUS VICTORINUS. He was of "Consular Dignity," and is supposed to have been one of the teachers of S. Jerome. He flourished in the time of the Emperor Constantius, son of Constantine the Great, about A.D. 352. S. Jerome (De Scriptoribus Eccl. cap. 101) gives this short notice: "Victorinus, of African origin, taught Rhetoric under Constantius, and, when already much advanced in years, he embraced the faith of *Jesus Christ*. He wrote some books against Arius . . . and commentaries upon the Apostle S. Paul."

Grant, Grimshaw, Grindle, Harper, Hathaway, Herbert, Hibbert, Howard, Humphrey, Hutchison, Hutton, Jerrard, Kenyon, Keogh, Kerr, Knox, Laing, Towry-Law, Leeds, Leigh, Lennox, Leslie, Lindsay, De Lisle, Lloyd, Lockhart, Louth, Lucas, Luck, Macmullen, Madan, Manners, Marshall, Maskell, Maude, Maxwell, Mayo, Mivart, Molesworth, Montagu, Monteith, Mordaunt, Morell, Morris, Scott-Murray, Nelson, Newdigate, Norman, Norreys, North, Northcote, Oakeley, Orford, Ormsby, Ornsby, Osborne, Paley, Palmer, Parkinson, Patmore, Patterson, Peel, Phillips, Pollen, Pope, Procter, Wegg-Prosser, Purbrick, Pye, Radcliffe, Ram, Ranken, Rawes, Rhodes, Richardson, Ripon, Robertson, Ross, Roscommon, Rowe, Watts-Russell, Ryder, St. John, Hope-Scott, Seager, Sellon, Orby-Shipley, Sibthorpe, Simeon, Spencer, Stanton, Stokes, Sutton, Swift, Talbot, Healy-Thompson, Thynne, Todd, Turnbull, Urquhart, Vaughan, De Vere, Vincent, Walker, Walpole, Ward, Wenham, Wilberforce (three brothers), Winchester, Woodward, Warmoll, Wrey, Wynne, Yard, and others; and of noble women not a few; best known to God and to the poor, but some whose names cannot be unknown to many an English poor Mission, as Argyll, Atchison, Athole, Buccleuch, Chisholm, Coleridge, Fullerton, Gladstone, Hamilton, Hastings, Herbert, Holland, Kenmare, Lockhart, Londonderry, Lothian, Queensbury, Stanley, Thynne, Waterford, Wilberforce, who, with many more of either sex, in every condition of life, some highly distinguished in their profession, have shown great moral courage and loftiness of mind, undaunted by the frown of the world, or by any personal or public loss. These all have cheerfully submitted to the Catholic Church, and have humbly sought and found reception into her Fold, in lasting joy and peace.

CONVERSION OF VICTORINUS. 239

But passing over our own day, I prefer to relate a truthful and affecting history of early Christian times—the conversion of Victorinus, a celebrated Orator and Poet of Rome, which occurred in the fourth century. It is recorded by the illustrious African Bishop and Doctor of the Church, St. Augustine, in his deeply interesting work called " *Confessions*." *

From this historic account it will be seen that the formal reception by an authorised Priest, now required of a convert on becoming reconciled, and formally admitted a member of the Catholic Church, is not anything new, but is a practice which has been the universal custom of the Church from very early times.

This narrative by S. Augustine, translated for me by my kind friend, Mr. William Hutchison, from the beautiful Latin (*Confessiones*, Book VIII, Chap. 2), is as follows:—

"Therefore (O Lord), I went straightway to the Priest, Simplicianus, who, in the conveying of Thy grace, was the spiritual father of Ambrose, then Bishop, and whom Ambrose really loved as his father.†

"To Simplicianus I disclosed the mazy wanderings of my errors. When, however, I told him that I had read certain books of the Platonic School, which Victorinus, formerly Professor of Rhetoric in the city of Rome, and who, as I had heard, died a Christian, had translated (from the Greek) into Latin, he rejoiced with

---

* St. Augustine wrote his "*Confessions*" about the year of Our Lord 400.

† St. Augustine calls Simplicianus the spiritual father of St. Ambrose, because it was at the hands of this holy Roman Priest Simplicianus, that St. Ambrose received the grace of Holy Baptism. Simplicianus was sent from Rome by Pope Damasus I. to Milan, to aid St. Ambrose, whom he succeeded in that bishopric. (See St. Augustine's *Retractations*, Book II., chap. 1.)

me that I had not fallen in with the writings of those other philosophers that are *full of fallacies and deceits, according to the principles of this world ;* * whereas the Platonic writings tend, in every way, to suggest God and His Divine Word.†

"To encourage me, then, in the love of *Christ's* humility, *hid from the wise, and revealed to little ones,*‡ he recalled to mind the same Victorinus, with whom he, when living at Rome, had been most intimately acquainted ; and he took occasion to relate to me an account of his friend that I will not pass over in silence, because it redounds to the great glory of Thy grace, O Lord.

"Simplicianus related how this aged and most learned man, thoroughly versed in all the liberal sciences, who had read and judged and explained so many works of the philosophers, who had taught so great a number of noble senators, and who also had merited and gained for himself, in acknowledgment of his remarkable success as a teacher, the rare honour, so highly prized by the citizens of this world, of having his statue set up in the Roman Forum ; how he, even to that old age, had been a worshipper of idols, taking part in those profane rites which nearly all the nobility as well as the people of Rome at that time were so full of ; for they worshipped all kinds of monstrous divinities, even the barking (dog-headed) Anúbis of Egypt ; monsters, who all in former days had, as enemies to the Romans, fought against Neptune, Venus, and Minerva ; § so that, indeed, Rome was then supplicating the very demons she had vanquished.

---

* See Colossians ii. 8.   † *Logos, Sermo,* or *Verbum.*
‡ St. Matthew xi. 25.
§ See *Æneid* of Virgil, Book VIII., line 698.

CONVERSION OF VICTORINUS.

"How this aged Victorinus, who, by his thunder-like eloquence, for so many years had been defending these hateful idols, yet who now, old as he was, did not blush, O God, to become the child of Thy *Christ*, the new-born babe of Thy Baptismal Font, submitting his neck to the yoke of humility, and his subdued forehead to the reproach of the Cross.

"O Lord, my Lord, Thou *who didst bow the heavens and didst come down, who didst touch the mountains, and they gave forth smoke,** by what winning ways didst Thou make entrance for Thyself into that heart ?

"Victorinus, as Simplicianus told me, used to read Holy Scripture, and most diligently examine and most profoundly study all Christian writings; and one day he said to Simplicianus, not publicly, but in a more confidential and friendly way: 'You must know that now I am a Christian ?' To this Simplicianus replied: 'I will not believe it, nor shall I account you as a Christian unless I see you among the faithful in the Church of Christ'.

"Victorinus turning it into jest, with a smile replied: 'Do the walls then make people Christians ?' And often would he say that now he was a Christian, and Simplicianus as often made the same reply as before, to which Victorinus would always return the jest about the walls; for he was afraid of offending his friends, those haughty worshippers of demons, from the lofty height of whose Babylonian dignity, as from the *cedars of Libanus* † which the Lord had not yet *broken in pieces*, he feared that a heavy storm of enmity would fall upon him.

"But, after a while, by reading, and by a thirst for truth, he gained inward strength, and feared to be dis-

---

* Psalm cxliii. 5. † Psalm xxviii. 5.

owned by *Christ* before the holy Angels if he should be afraid to confess Him before men; and he seemed to himself guilty of a great crime in being ashamed of the mysteries of the humiliation* of Thy eternal *Word*, and of not having been ashamed of the sacrilegious rites of proud demons, in which, as a haughty worshipper, he had taken part.

"Emboldened to cast off false shame in quitting vanities, he took shame to himself for not having stood by the truth; so that suddenly and unexpectedly he said to Simplicianus, who told me so himself: '*Come, let us go to the Church, for a Christian I will be*'.

"Simplicianus, beside himself for joy, at once went with him. When there, after he had received the first instructions in the Christian mysteries, he soon also gave in his name that he might be regenerated in Holy Baptism, to the wonder of Rome and joy of the Church. *The proud saw and were angry, they gnashed with their teeth and pined away.*† *But as for Thy servant, the Lord God was his hope, and he had not regard to vanities and lying follies.*‡

"At last, when the hour came for his making profession of the faith, which, at Rome, it is the custom for those who come to receive Thy grace to pronounce in a set form of words learnt by heart, from a raised place, in the sight of the faithful, Simplicianus told me that it was proposed by the Priests to Victorinus to make his profession privately, as it was customary to allow to some who seemed likely to be troubled through bashfulness; but that he chose rather to make his profession of the saving faith in the presence of the holy congregation.

"What he had been accustomed to teach from his

* St. John i. 14.   † Psalm xci. 10.   ‡ Psalm xxxix. 5.

chair of rhetoric was not indeed a matter of salvation, and yet he had professed that science publicly; how much less reason could there be for him, who never had feared when speaking his own words to crowds of foolish men, now to be afraid to pronounce Thy words, O Lord, before Thy gentle flock?

"When, then, as he went up to make his profession of faith, all who knew him (and who was there that did not know him?) one and all, according to their acquaintance with him, uttered his name in an outburst of joy; and, from the mouths of all rejoicing together, in a hushed voice on all sides, resounded—*Victorinus! Victorinus!*

"Quickly the people broke silence at the joy of seeing him, and quickly were all again still in order to hear him speak.

"He pronounced the truthful Christian faith with admirable confidence, and all were longing to carry him off into their innermost heart; and this, O Lord, they did by the embrace of *joy* and *love*—these two affections were the hands that took him prisoner."

No. 8.—DISTINGUISHED AMERICAN CONVERTS.

Among the many illustrious men who have left the ranks of Protestantism for the Catholic Church in America are the most Rev. James Roosevelt Bayley, D.D., Archbishop of Baltimore; the Most Rev. James Frederick Wood, D.D., Archbishop of Philadelphia; the Right Rev. Josue Young, D.D., late Bishop of Erie; the late Bishop Tyler, of Hartford; Bishops Becker, of Wilmington; Gilmour, of Cleveland; Rosecrans, of Columbus; and Wadhams, of Ogdensburg; L. S. Ives, D.D., Protestant Bishop of North

Carolina, who, having recognised the truth of Catholicism, renounced everything to become a layman in her fold; the Very Rev. George H. Doane, Vicar-General of the Diocese of Newark, and son of the Protestant Bishop of that name; the Rev. James Kent Stone, late President of Hobart and Kenyon College, now a Paulist Father; the Very Rev. I. T. Hecker, Francis A. Becker, A. F. Hewitt, Edward Dwight Lyman, Episcopal clergymen of distinction, and now Catholic priests; Generals Rosecrans, Pike, Graham, Newton, James A. Hardy, and others; Orestes A. Brownson, LL.D., the distinguished reviewer, whom Lord Brougham styled "the master-mind of America"; General D. W. Clark, of Vermont; the Rev. Dr. Rodgers; the Rev. Fr. David Hudson, O.S.C., of Notre-Dame (Indiana); Dr. Joshua Huntington, the well-known author of "Rosemary," "Gropings after Truth," &c.; the Hon. Thomas Ewing, Senator from Ohio, and for some time Secretary of the United States Treasury; the Hon. Henry May, one of the leaders of his party in the House of Representatives; Homer Wheaton, Esq., late of Poughkeepsie, N.Y., at first a lawyer, afterwards a Protestant minister, until he was led into the Catholic Church. Besides these, there are the Hon. Thomas B. Florence, of Philadelphia, for sixteen years a member of the United States House of Representatives; the Hon. Judge T. Parkin Scott, of Baltimore, and a great number of others eminent in the different walks of life.

No. 9.—ADDRESS OF SOME OF THE PRESBYTERIES OR CLERGY-HOUSES IN AND NEAR LONDON AND ABROAD (1880).

Strangers in London may be glad to know the

address where they can easily find, any morning or evening, a Priest with whom to converse on religious matters.

Pro-Cathedral, Our Lady of Victories—Kensington Road, W. (near High Street, Kensington, not far west from Metropolitan Station). *Clergy-House*—1 St. Leonard's Place.
Carmelite Fathers (English, French, Italian, and Spanish)—47 Church Street, Kensington, W.
Fathers of the Oratory of St. Philip Neri—Adjoining the South Kensington Museum, Brompton, S.W.
St. Mary's—Cadogan Terrace, Sloane Street, Chelsea, S.W.
The Servite Fathers (Italian and English)—St. Mary's Priory, 264 Fulham Road, West Brompton, near the Union House, S.W.
Fathers Oblates of St. Charles Borromeo — (St. Mary's of the Angels) Westmoreland Road, Bayswater, W.
St. James—6 Spanish Place, Manchester Square, W.
St. Aloysius—49 Clarendon Square, Somers Town, N.W.
The Dominican Fathers—The Priory, Southampton Road, Haverstock Hill, N.W.
St. Mary's Help of Christians—Fortess Place, Junction Road, Kentish Town, N.W.
The Passionist Fathers—St. Joseph's Retreat, Highgate Hill, N.
St. John the Evangelist—Duncan Terrace, Islington, N.
The Augustinian Fathers — St. Monica's Priory, Hoxton Square, N.
The Jesuit Fathers—Farm Street Church (near Hill Street), Berkeley Square, W. *Clergy-House*—111 Mount Street, Grosvenor Square, and at Roehampton, S.W.
The same Fathers—St. Mary's, Horseferry Road, S.W. *Clergy-House*—12 Earl Street, Westminster.
Bavarian Church—Warwick Street, Regent Street, W. *Clergy-House*—24 Golden Square, W.
Marist Fathers (French and English) — 5 Leicester Place, Leicester Square, W.C.
The same Fathers—(St. Anne's Church), Albert Place, Spicer Street, Spitalfields, E.
Corpus Christi Church—Maiden Lane, Southampton Street, Strand, W.C.
Sardinian Church—Duke Street, Lincoln's Inn Fields. *Clergy-House*—54 Lincoln's Inn Fields, W.C.

St. Patrick's—Sutton Street, Soho Square, W. *Clergy-House*—21A Soho Square.

The Franciscan Fathers—(St Francis' Church and Friary), The Grove, Stratford, London, E. Confessions heard in English, Irish, Italian, French, and Dutch.

St. Mary's—Tottenham Road (near Dalston Station), Kingsland, N. *Clergy-House*—170 Culford Road.

The Fathers of Charity—(St. Etheldreda), 14 Ely Place, Holborn Viaduct, E.C.

Fathers of the Pious Society of the Missions—(Italian and English)—St. Peter's Italian Church, Hatton Garden, E.C. Open from seven in the morning till ten at night. Confessions heard in Italian, English, French, and Polish. *Clergy-House*—St. Peter's Retreat, 4 Back Hill, Clerkenwell Road, Hatton Garden.

Oblate Fathers of Mary Immaculate—(Church of the English Martyrs) 23 Great Prescot Street, Tower Hill, E.

St. Mary's—Moorfields, Bloomfield Street, E.C. *Clergy-House*—22 Finsbury Circus.

St. Mary's and St. Michael's—Commercial Road, East, E.

St. Mary's of the Rosary—209 Marylebone Road, N.W. *Clergy-House*—184 Marylebone Road.

St. George's—(Southwark Cathedral) Westminster Bridge Road, S.E.

Franciscan Capuchin Fathers—(St. Mary's Church) Lower Park Road, Peckham, S.E.

The Redemptorist Fathers—(St. Mary's) Clapham, S.W., and Fulham.

ENGLISH PRIESTS HEARING CONFESSIONS ABROAD.

Selected from the List of about two hundred given at page 82 in the "Catholic Directory" for 1880 (Burns & Oates), 1/6.

ROME—Fr. Bonaventure Doyle (O.S.F.), S. Peter's—English, Scotch, Irish, and American Colleges — Franciscans S. Isidoro—Fr. Douglas, S. Alphonso on the Esquiline.

FLORENCE—Fr. Weld (S.J.), Chapel of Palazzo Strozzini.

GENOA—Padre Casabuona, Oratory of S. Philip.

NAPLES—Padre Guerritore (Saturdays from 9 to 12), Sta Caterina a Chiaja.

PALERMO—Abbate Casano, 56 Via Bara Olivella.

TURIN—Abbate Grossi, S. Filippo.

PARIS—Passionist Fathers, 50 Avenue de la Reine Hortense.
,,   Jesuit Fathers, 35 Rue de Sèvres, near St. Sulpice.
,,   Monsignor Rogerson, 19 Rue de Chaillot—Redemptorists, 57 Boulevard Ménilmontant.
BOULOGNE-SŪR-MER—Redemptorist Church.
CANNES—Chaplain of the Hôpital.
LOURDES—Fr. Carton (S.J.), Notre Dame.
LYONS—Père Irenée, Dominican Convent.
MARSEILLES—Père Bion, Dominican Convent, 53 Rue Montaux.
MALTA, Valetta—Canon Debono, 176 Strada S. Paolo.
EINSIEDELN (Switzerland)—Benedictine Monastery.
LUCERNE—Canon Suter, 9 Hof.
SUEZ—Franciscan Fathers, near Suez Hotel.
JERUSALEM—Rev. F. Guido, Casa Nova.
BUENOS AYRES—Canons Dillon and Miller, Cathedral.
NICE—Dr. Novello, 11 Rue S. François de Paule.
PAU—Curé of S. Jacques.
BRUGES—Abbe Isacq, English Convent.
BRUSSELS—Capuchin, Carmelite, and Jesuit Churches.
GHENT—Carmelite and Franciscan Churches.
OSTEND—Abbé Thomas, Capuchin Church.
SPA (Belgium)—Abbé Gilissen, Institut Selessin.
VIENNA (Austria)—Fr. Eskell, Dominican Convent, 4 Postgasse.
COLOGNE—Dr. Bellesheim, Cathedral.
FRANKFORT-ON-THE-MAIN—Rev. Hof Baur, Notre Dame.

The person who applies for instruction to any of the above-named addresses, or, indeed, at any Catholic Church or Clergy-House, may simply say to the Sacristan or to the Servant: " I should like to have a little conversation with a Priest ". He need not tell his name, unless he wishes it, either to the servant or to the Priest. This reserve will readily be excused under the circumstances.

No. 10.—THE LORD'S PRAYER.

Our Father who art in heaven, hallowed be Thy name; Thy kingdom come; Thy will be done on earth, as it is in heaven. Give us this day our daily bread;

and forgive us our trespasses, as we forgive them that trespass against us; and lead us not into temptation; but deliver us from evil. *Amen.*

THE HAIL MARY.

Hail Mary, full of grace, the Lord is with thee; blessed art thou among women, and blessed is the fruit of thy womb, JESUS. Holy Mary, Mother of God, pray for us sinners, now and at the hour of our death. *Amen.*

GLORIA PATRI.

Glory be to the Father, and to the Son, and to the Holy Ghost. As it was in the beginning, is now, and ever shall be, world without end. *Amen.*

A DAILY PRAYER.

O my God, I hope that I shall not be so base and wicked as to offend Thee this day; yet knowing my weakness, I fly to Thee for help. Give me courage to avoid sin, and whatever may be to me an occasion of offending Thee; give me strength to withstand every temptation, and grace to do Thy will in all things; give me patience, and help me to keep in charity with all my neighbours.

O Mary, My Mother, pray for me; Saint Joseph, pray for me; my Guardian Angel, protect me in all dangers; all ye Saints and Angels, pray for me.

ROSARY OF THE BLESSED VIRGIN.

By the Rosary (or beads) is meant an excellent devotional practice devised by the Wisdom of God, made known by the Blessed Virgin herself to S. Dominic, and commenced in the thirteenth century. It consists of fifteen *decades*. Each decade (or *ten*) is made up of one '*Our Father*' and ten '*Hail Mary's*,' followed by one '*Glory be to the Father*'. No other prayers whatever form part of the Rosary : those that are said before or after it, or after each decade, are merely pious additions.

During each decade we consider a Mystery ; that is, we think over one of the events of the life of our Lord or of His holy Mother. These Mysteries are divided into three series of five each, called the *Joyful*, the *Sorrowful*, and the *Glorious*.

JOYFUL MYSTERIES.

1. The Annunciation to the Blessed Virgin.
2. Visitation of the B. Virgin to S. Elisabeth.
3. Birth of Jesus at Bethlehem.
4. Presentation of Jesus in the Temple.
5. Finding of the child Jesus in the Temple.

SORROWFUL MYSTERIES.

1. The Agony of Jesus in the Garden of Gethsemane.
2. Scourging of Jesus at the pillar.
3. Crowning of Jesus with thorns.
4. Carrying of the cross by Jesus to Mount Calvary.
5. Crucifixion of Jesus on Mount Calvary.

GLORIOUS MYSTERIES.

1. The Resurrection of Jesus.
2. Ascension of Jesus.
3. Descent of the Holy Ghost upon the Apostles.
4. Assumption of the B. Virgin into Heaven.
5. Crowning of the Blessed Virgin in Heaven.

THE ANGELUS.*

I. V. Angelus Domini nuntiavit Mariæ.

R. Et concépit de Spiritu Sancto.

Ave Maria, gratia plena Dominus tecum ; benedicta tu in muliéribus, et benedictus fructus ventris tui, Jesus. Sancta Maria, mater Dei, ora pro nobis peccatoribus, nunc et in hora mortis nostræ. Amen.

II. V. Ecce ancilla Domini.

R. Fiat mihi secundum verbum tuum.

Ave Maria, &c.

III. V. Et Verbum caro factum est.

R. Et habitávit in nobis.

Ave Maria, &c.

V. Ora pro nobis, Sancta Dei Genitrix.

R. Ut digni efficiámur promissionibus Christi.

Oremus.

Gratiam tuam, quæsumus, Domine, mentibus nostris infunde ; ut qui, angelo nuntiante, Christi Filii tui incarnationem cognóvimus, per Passionem ejus et Crucem ad resurrectionis gloriam perducámur ; per eumdem Christum Dominum nostrum. Amen.

I. The angel of the Lord announced unto Mary.

R. And she conceived of the Holy Ghost.

Hail Mary, full of grace, the Lord is with thee ; blessed art thou among women, and blessed is the fruit of thy womb, Jesus. Holy Mary, mother of God, pray for us sinners, now and at the hour of our death. Amen.

II. Behold the handmaid of the Lord.

R. Be it done unto me according to thy word. (S. Luke i. 38.)

Hail Mary, &c.

III. And the word was made flesh.

R. And dwelt among us. (S. John i. 14.)

Hail Mary, &c.

V. Pray for us, O holy Mother of God.

R. That we may be made worthy of the promises of Christ.

Let us Pray.

Pour forth, we beseech thee, O Lord, Thy grace into our hearts ; that we, to whom the incarnation of Christ Thy Son was made known by the message of an angel, may, by His Passion and Cross, be brought to the glory of His resurrection; through the same Christ our Lord. Amen.

---

* At Easter time, instead of the "Angelus," the "Regina Coeli laetare, Alleluia," is said, standing.

From Compline on Holy Saturday till Trinity Eve.

Regína Cœli, lætáre! alleluia.

Quia quem meruisti portare; alleluia.

Resurrexit sicut dixit; alleluia.

Ora pro nobis Deum; alleluia.

V. Gaude et lætare, Virgo Maria: alleluia.
R. Quia surrexit Dominus vere; alleluia.

Oremus.

Deus, qui per resurrectionem Filii tui Domini nostri Jesu Christi mundum lætificare dignátus es; præsta, quæsumus, ut per ejus Genitricem Virginem Mariam perpetuæ capiámus gaudia vitæ. Per eumdem Christum Dominum nostrum.
R. Amen.
V. Divinum auxilium maneat semper nobiscum.
R. Amen.
V. Fidelium animæ, per misericordiam Dei, requiescant in pace.
R. Amen.

Joy to thee, O heavenly Queen! alleluia.

He whom thou wast meet to bear; alleluia.

As He promis'd, hath arisen; alleluia.

Pour for us to Him thy prayer; alleluia.

V. Rejoice and be glad, O Virgin Mary; alleluia.
R. For the Lord hath risen indeed; alleluia.

Let us pray.

O God, who didst vouchsafe to give joy to the world through the resurrection of Thy Son our Lord Jesus Christ; grant, we beseech Thee, that, through His Mother, the Virgin Mary, we may obtain the joys of everlasting life. Through the same Christ our Lord.
R. Amen.
V. May the divine assistance remain always with us.
R. Amen.
V. May the souls of the faithful departed, through the mercy of God, rest in peace.
R. Amen.

PRAYERS IN BEHALF OF THE DYING.

Let us say three "Our Fathers" in honour of the agony of Jesus, and three "Hail Marys" in honour of our Lady's Dolours, for the faithful who are this day throughout the world in their last agony.

Indulgences: 300 days every recital. Plenary once a month. both applicable to the holy souls in Purgatory.

THE DIVINE PRAISES, *said after Mass and Benediction in most Churches, the People repeating each portion after the Priest.*

1. Blessed be God.
2. Blessed be His Holy Name.
3. Blessed be Jesus Christ, true God and true man.
4. Blessed be the Name of Jesus.
5. Blessed be Jesus in the most Holy Sacrament of the Altar.
6. Blessed be the great Mother of God, Mary Most Holy.
7. Blessed be her holy and Immaculate Conception.
8. Blessed be the Name of Mary, Virgin and Mother.
9. Blessed be God in His Angels and in His Saints. Amen.

ACT OF RESIGNATION TO THE WILL OF GOD.

May the most just, most high, and most amiable will of God be done, praised, and eternally exalted in all things. Amen.

May the most sacred Heart of JESUS be loved by all.

PRAYER IN OUR LAST AGONY.

Into Thy hands, O Lord, I commend my spirit (S. Luke xxiii. 46). Lord JESUS, receive my soul.

PRAYER TO OUR CRUCIFIED LORD,
while we contemplate on what He suffered for us.

Behold, O kind and most sweet JESUS, I cast myself upon my knees in Thy sight, and with the most fervent desire of my soul I pray and beseech Thee to impress upon my heart lively sentiments of *Faith, Hope,* and *Charity,* with true repentance for my sins, and a most firm purpose of amendment; while with deep affection and grief of soul I call to mind and ponder on *Thy five most precious Wounds,* having before my eyes that which the Prophet David spoke of Thee, O good JESUS: " *They have dug my hands and feet; they have numbered all my bones* ". (Psalm xxi. 17.)

NOTE.—To the devout reciting of this foregoing Prayer, " Behold, O kind," &c., in any language, is annexed, by Pope Pius VII., April 10, A.D. 1821 (in a decree of the Sacred Congregation of Indulgences), a plenary indulgence, and which may be obtained by all the faithful who, after having confessed their sins with contrition, and received Holy Communion, shall devoutly recite it before any representation of *Christ Crucified*. This indulgence is also applicable to the souls in Purgatory.

A PRAYER FOR OUR HOLY FATHER THE POPE.

" *The Lord preserve him and give him life; and make him blessed upon the earth; and deliver him not up to the will of his enemies.*" (Psalm xl. 3.)

A Prayer in Sickness or Affliction.

O Lord Jesus Christ, I receive this affliction with which Thou art pleased to visit me as coming from Thy fatherly hand. It is Thy will, and therefore I submit;—"Not my will, but Thine be done." May it be to the honour of Thy holy name, and for the good of my soul. I here offer myself with an entire submission to all Thine appointments; to suffer whatever Thou pleasest, as long as Thou pleasest, and in what manner Thou pleasest: for I Thy creature, O Lord, have often and most ungratefully offended Thee, and Thou mightest justly have visited me with Thy severest punishments. Oh, let thy justice be tempered with mercy, and let Thy heavenly grace come to my assistance, to support me under this affliction! Confirm my soul with strength from above, that I may bear with true Christian patience all the uneasiness, pains, and troubles under which I labour; preserve me from all temptations and murmuring thoughts, that in this time of affliction I may in no way offend Thee; and grant that this and all other earthly trials may be the means of preparing my soul for its passage into eternity, that, being purified from all my sins, I may believe in Thee, hope in Thee, and love Thee above all things, and finally through Thy infinite merits, be admitted into the company of the blessed in heaven, there to praise Thee for ever and ever. Amen.

O God, who hast doomed all men to die, but hast concealed the hour of their death, grant that I may pass my days in the practice of holiness and justice, and that I may be able to quit this world in the peace of a good conscience, and in the embrace of Thy love, through Jesus Christ our Lord. Amen.

The Fourth Penitential Psalm.

Psalm 50. (Protestant Version, 51.) *Miserere.*

1. David prays for remission of his sins ; 8. for perfect sanctity. 17. God delights not in sacrifice, but in a contrite heart. 19. David prays for the exaltation of the Church.

Miserére mei, Deus :* secundum magnam misericordiam tuam.

Et secundum multitudinem miseratiónum tuárum :* dele iniquitátem meam.

Amplius lava me ab iniquitate mea :* et a peccáto meo munda me.

Quoniam, iniquitátem meam ego cognosco :* et peccátum meum contra me est semper.

Tibi soli peccávi, et malum coram te feci :* ut justificéris in sermonibus tuis, et vincas cum judicáris.

Ecce enim in iniquitatibus conceptus sum :* et in peccátis concépit me mater mea.

Ecce enim veritátem dilexisti :* incerta et occulta sapientiæ tuæ manifestasti mihi.

Asperges me hyssópo et mundábor :* lavábis me, et super nivem dealbábor.

Audítui meo dabis gaudium et lætitiam :* et exultábunt ossa humiliáta.

1 Have mercy upon me, O God ; according to Thy great mercy.

2 And according to the multitude of Thy tender mercies : blot out my iniquity.

3 Wash me yet more from my iniquity : and cleanse me from my sin.

4 For I acknowledge my iniquity : and my sin is always before me.

5 Against Thee only have I sinned, and done evil in Thy sight : that Thou mayest be justified in Thy words, and mayest overcome when Thou art judged.

6 For behold, I was conceived in iniquities : and in sins did my mother conceive me.

7 For behold, Thou hast loved truth : the uncertain and hidden things of Thy wisdom Thou hast made manifest to me.

8 Thou shalt sprinkle me with hyssop, and I shall be cleansed ; Thou shalt wash me, and I shall be made whiter than snow.

9 Thou shalt make me hear of joy and gladness : and the bones that have been humbled shall rejoice.

Averte faciem tuam a peccátis meis : * et omnes iniquitátes meas dele.

Cor mundum crea in me, Deus : * et spiritum rectum innova in viscéribus meis.

Ne projicies me a facie tua : * et Spiritum sanctum tuum ne áuferas a me.

Redde mihi lætitiam salutáris tui : * et spiritu principáli confirma me.

Docébo iníquos vias tuas : * et impii ad te convertentur.

Líbera me de sanguinibus, Deus, Deus salútis meæ : * et exultábit lingua mea justitiam tuam.

Domine labia mea aperies : * et os meum annuntiábit laudem tuam.

Quoniam si voluisses sacrifícium, dedissem útique : * holocaustis non delectáberis.

Sacrificium Deo spiritus contribulátus : * cor contrítum et humiliátum, Deus, non despícies.

Benigne fac Domine, in bona voluntate tua Sion : * ut ædificentur muri Jerusalem.

Tunc acceptábis sacrificium justitiæ, oblationes, et holocausta : * tunc impónent super altáre tuum vítulos.

Gloria Patri, et Filio, et Spiritui Sancto. Sicut erat in principio, et nunc, et sem-

10 Turn away Thy face from my sins : and blot out all my iniquities.

11 Create in me a clean heart, O God : and renew a right spirit within my bowels.

12 Cast me not away from Thy face : and take not Thy Holy Spirit from me.

13 Restore unto me the joy of Thy salvation : and strengthen me with a perfect spirit.

14 I will teach the unjust Thy ways : and the wicked shall be converted unto Thee.

15 Deliver me from bloodguiltiness, O God, Thou God of my salvation : and my tongue shall extol Thy justice.

16 Thou shalt open my lips, O Lord : and my mouth shall declare Thy praise.

17 For if Thou hadst desired sacrifice, I would indeed have given it : with burnt-offerings Thou wilt not be delighted.

18 A sacrifice to God is an afflicted spirit : a contrite and humbled heart, O God, Thou wilt not despise.

19 Deal favourably, O Lord, in Thy good will with Sion : that the walls of Jerusalem may be built up.

20 Then shalt Thou accept the sacrifice of justice, oblations, and whole burnt-offerings : then shall they lay calves upon Thine altars.

Glory be to the Father, and to the Son, and to the Holy Ghost. As it was in the be-per, et in sæcula sæculorum. Amen.

ginning, is now, and ever shall be, world without end. Amen.

The Sixth Penitential Psalm.

Psalm cxxix.—*De Profundis.*

The cry of a contrite heart imploring the Divine mercy.

De profundis clamávi ad te, Domine:* Domine, exaudi vocem meam.
Fiant aures tuæ intendentes* in vocem deprecatiónis meæ.

Si iniquitátes observaveris, Domine:* Domine, quis sustinébit ?
Quia apud te propitiátio est:* et propter legem tuam sustinui te Domine.

Sustínuit anima mea in verbo ejus:* sperávit anima mea in Domino.
A custodia matutína usque ad noctem:* speret Israel, in Domino.
Quia apud Dominum misericordia:* et copiósa apud eum redemptio.
Et ipse rédimet Israel,* ex omnibus iniquitatibus ejus.*
Requiem aeternam dona eis Domine.
Et lux perpetua luceat eis.

Requiescant in pace. Amen.

1 Out of the depths have I cried unto Thee, O Lord: Lord, hear my voice.
2 Oh, let Thine ears consider well: the voice of my supplication.
3 If Thou, O Lord, wilt mark iniquities: Lord, who shall stand it ?
4 For with Thee there is merciful forgiveness: and because of Thy law I have waited for Thee, O Lord.
5 My soul hath relied on His word: my soul hath hoped in the Lord.
6 From the morning watch even until night: let Israel hope in the Lord.
7 For with the Lord there is mercy: and with Him is plentiful redemption.
8 And He shall redeem Israel from all his iniquities.†
Eternal rest give to them, O Lord.
And let perpetual light shine upon them.
May they rest in peace. Amen.

† This psalm is often said by Catholics for the souls in Purgatory, in which case instead of ending it with the "Glory be to the Father," it is ended as here laid down.

Prayer for Another's Conversion.

O Divine and adorable Saviour, Thou Who art the way, the truth, and the life, I beseech Thee to have mercy upon N., and bring him [or her] to the knowledge and love of Thy truth. Thou, O Lord, knowest all his darkness, his weakness, and his doubts; have pity upon him, O merciful Saviour; let the beams of Thy eternal truth shine upon his mind; clear away the cloud of error and prejudice from his eyes, and may he humbly submit to and embrace with his whole heart the teaching of Thy Church. Oh, let not his [or her] soul be shut out from Thy blessed fold! Unite him to Thyself in the communications of Thy love, so that, partaking of the blessings of Thy grace in this life, he may come to the possession of those eternal rewards which Thou hast promised to all those who believe in Thee and who do Thy will. Hear this my petition, O merciful Jesus, Who, with the Father and the Holy Ghost, livest and reignest ever and ever. Amen.

For a Friend in Distress.

O merciful Lord, give the sweetness of Thy comfort to Thy afflicted servant N., and remove, according to Thy accustomed mercy, the heavy burden of his calamities. Give him, I humbly beseech Thee, patience in his sufferings, resignation to Thy adorable will, and perseverance in Thy service.

For the Sick.

V. Heal Thy servants, O Lord, who are sick, and who put their trust in Thee.

R. Send them help, O Lord, and comfort them from Thy holy place.

O Almighty and everlasting God, the eternal salvation of them that believe in Thee, hear us in behalf of Thy servants who are sick; for whom we humbly crave the help of Thy mercy; that, their health being restored to them, they may render thanks to Thee in Thy Church; through *Jesus Christ Our Lord.*

Prayer for a Bishop or Priest.

O God, Who amongst Thy Apostolic Priests hast raised up Thy servant (N.——) to the dignity of Bishop (or Priest), grant, we beseeech Thee, that he may also be admitted in Heaven to Thy everlasting fellowship, through *Jesus Christ Our Lord.* Amen.

For the Dead.

O Almighty and eternal God, Who hast dominion over the living and the dead, and art merciful to all whom Thou foreknowest shall be Thine by faith and good works; we humbly beseech Thee, that they for whom we offer up our prayers may, by Thy clemency and goodness, obtain pardon and full remission of their sins; through our Lord Jesus Christ, Thy Son, who, with Thee and the Holy Ghost, liveth and reigneth one God, world without end. Amen.

Prayer for a Departed Father and Mother.

O God our Heavenly Father, Who hast commanded us to honour our Father and our Mother, have mercy on the souls of my dear Father and Mother, and grant that, if they are not yet with Thee, they may soon come to enjoy Thy blessed vision in Heaven; through *Jesus Christ Our Lord.* Amen.

Other Prayers for the Dead.

The Psalm *Miserere* and the Psalm *De Profundis* may be used, saying, at the end of each, instead of " Glory be to the Father," &c., the Versicle:

V. Eternal rest give unto them, O Lord.
R. And let perpetual light shine upon them.

A Prayer for the Faithful Departed.

O God, the Creator and Redeemer of all the faithful, grant to the souls of Thy servants departed the remission of all their sins, that, through pious supplications, they may obtain the pardon which they have always desired. Who livest and reignest with God the Father, in the unity of the Holy Ghost, world without end. Amen.

On the Day of a Person's Decease or Burial.

O God, whose property is always to have mercy and to spare, we humbly beseech Thee for the soul of Thy servant N.———, which Thou hast this day commanded to depart out of this world, that Thou wouldst not deliver it into the hands of the enemy, nor forget it unto the end, but wouldst command it to be received by Thy holy angels, and conducted to Paradise, its true country; that, as in Thee it hath hoped and believed, it may not suffer the pains of hell, but may take possession of eternal joys. Through Christ Our Lord.

For the Patronage of St. Joseph.

O God, who by Thy adorable Providence didst vouchsafe to choose the blessed Joseph for the spouse of Thy most Holy Mother, grant, we beseech Thee, that he whom we venerate as our protector on earth may be our intercessor in heaven; who livest and reignest for ever and ever. Amen.

No. 11.—Hymns.

Hymn to Jesus.

(From the Latin of St. Bernard, " Jesu, dulcis memoria.")

Jesus, the only thought of Thee,
   With sweetness fills my breast;
But sweeter far it is to see,
   And on Thy beauty feast.

No sound, no harmony so gay
   Can art or music frame;
No thought can reach, no words can say,
   The sweets of Thy blest name.

Jesus, our hope when we repent,
   Sweet source of all our grace;
Sole comfort in our banishment,
   Oh! what when face to face!

Jesus, that name inspires my mind,
   With springs of life and light;
More than I ask in Thee I find,
   And languish with delight.

No art or eloquence of man
   Can tell the joys of love,
Only the saints can understand
   What they in Jesus prove.

Thee then I'll seek retired apart,
   From world and business free;
When these shall knock, I'll shut my heart,
   And keep it all for Thee.

Before the morning light I'll come,
   With Magdalene, to find,
In sighs and tears, my Jesu's tomb,
   And there refresh my mind.

My tears upon His grave shall flow,
   My sighs the garden fill;
Then at His feet myself I'll throw,
   And there I'll seek His will.

Jesus, in Thy blest steps I'll tread,
   And walk in all Thy ways,
I'll never cease to weep and plead
   To be preserved in grace.

O King of Love, Thy blessed fire
   Does such sweet flames excite,
That first it raises the desire,
   Then fills it with delight.

Thy lovely presence shines so clear
  Through every sense and way,
That souls which once have seen Thee near,
  See all things else decay.

Come then, dear LORD, possess my heart,
  Chase thence the shades of night ;
Come, pierce it with Thy flaming dart,
  And ever-shining light.

Then I'll for ever JESUS sing,
  And with the saints rejoice ;
And both my heart and tongue shall bring
  Their tribute to my dearest King,
In ever-ending joys. Amen.

THE PRECIOUS BLOOD.*

(*From the Italian.*)

BY FATHER FABER.

[*Oratory Hymn 14.*]

HAIL, Jesus ! hail ! who for my sake
Sweet Blood from Mary's veins didst take,
  And shed it all for me ;
Oh ! blessed be my Saviour's Blood,
My life, my light, my only good,
  To all eternity !

To endless ages let us praise
The Precious Blood, whose price could raise
  The world from wrath and sin ;
Whose streams our inward thirst appease
And heal the sinner's worst disease
  If he but bathe therein.

O sweetest Blood, that can implore
Pardon of God, and heaven restore—
  The heaven which sin had lost ;
While Abel's blood for vengeance pleads,
What Jesus shed still intercedes
  For those who wrong Him most.

---

* To all the faithful who, being in a state of grace, say or sing this hymn, Pius VII. granted an indulgence of one hundred days, also applicable to the souls in purgatory.

Oh! to be sprinkled from the wells
Of Christ's own Sacred Blood, excels
   Earth's best and highest bliss;
The ministers of wrath divine
Hurt not the happy hearts that shine
   With those red drops of His!

Ah! there is joy amid the Saints,
And hell's despairing courage faints,
   When this sweet song we raise;
Oh! louder then, and louder still,
Earth with one mighty chorus fill,
   The Precious Blood to praise.

Hymn to the Holy Ghost.

Veni, Creator Spiritus,
Mentes tuórum visita,
Imple superna gratia,
Quæ tu creasti péctora.

Qui díceris Paráclitus,
Altissimi donum Dei,
Fons vivus, ignis, charitas,
Et spiritális unctio.

Tu septiformis munere,
Digitus Paternæ dexteræ,
Tu rite promissum Patris,
Sermóne ditans guttura.

Accende lumen sensibus,
Infunde amorem cordibus,
Infirma nostri córporis
Virtúte firmans pérpeti.

Hostem repellas longius,
Pacemque dones prótinus;
Ductore sic te prævio
Vitémus omne noxium.

Per te sciámus da Patrem,
Noscámus atque Filium,
Teque utriusque Spiritum
Credámus omni tempore.

Deo Patri sit gloria,
Et Filio, qui a mortuis
Surrexit, ac Paráclito,
In sæculorum sæcula.
        Amen.

Come, Holy Ghost, Creator come,
   From Thy bright heavenly throne;
Come take possession of our souls,
   And make them all Thy own.

Thou Who art call'd the Paraclete,
   Best gift of God above;
The living Spring, the living Fire,
   Sweet Unction and true Love.

Thou Who art seven-fold in Thy grace,
   Finger of God's right hand;
His promise, teaching little ones
   To speak and understand.

O! guide our minds with Thy blest light,
   With love our hearts inflame;
And with Thy strength, which ne'er decays,
   Confirm our mortal frame.

Far from us drive our fiendish foe,
   True peace unto us bring;
And through all perils lead us safe
   Beneath Thy sacred wing.

Through Thee may we the Father know,
   Through Thee the eternal Son,
And Thee the Spirit of them both,
   Thrice blessed Three in One.

All glory to the Father be,
   With His co-equal Son,
The like to Thee, great Paraclete,
   'Till time itself is done.
        Amen.

ADESTE FIDELES—*Hymn for Christmas.*

Adeste fidéles,	Ye faithful, approach ye,
Læti triumphantes ;	Joyfully triumphing ;
Venite, venite in Bethlehem :	O come ye, O come ye, to Bethlehem :
Natum videte	Come and behold ye
Regem angelorum :	Born the King of angels :
Venite adorémus,	O come, let us worship
Venite adoremus,	O come, let us worship,
Venite adoremus Dominum.	O come, let us worship Christ the Lord.
Deum de Deo,	God of God.
Lumen de lumine,	Light of Light,
Gestant puellæ viscera ;	Lo, He disdains not the Virgin's womb :
Deum verum	
Genitum, non factum :	Very God,
Venite adoremus, &c.	Begotten, not created :
	O come, let us worship, &c.
Cantet nunc Io !	Sing, choirs angelic,
Chorus angelorum :	Sing with exultation ;
Cantet nunc aula cœlestium,	Sing, all ye citizens of heaven above,
Gloria	Glory to God
In excelsis Deo !	In the highest !
Venite adoremus, &c.	O come, let us worship, &c.
Ergo qui natus	Yea, Lord, we greet Thee,
Die hodierna,	Born this happy morning ;
Jesu tibi sit gloria ;	Jesu, to Thee be glory given ;
Patris æterni	Word of the Father
Verbum caro factum !	In our flesh appearing :
Venite adoremus, &c.	O come, let us worship, &c.

HYMN—(BY THE VERY REV. F. FABER, D.D.)

On the Love of Jesus.

O JESUS, JESUS, dearest Lord,
    Forgive me if I say
For very love Thy Sacred Name
    A thousand times a day.
I love Thee so, I know not how
    My transports to control ;
Thy love is like a burning fire
    Within my very soul.

O wonderful ! that Thou should'st let
    So vile a heart as mine
Love Thee with such a love as this,
    And make so free with Thine.

The craft of this wise world of ours
  Poor wisdom seems to me ;
Ah, dearest JESUS, I have grown
  Childish with love of Thee.

For Thou to me art all in all,
  My honour and my wealth,
My heart's desire, my body's strength,
  My soul's eternal health.
Burn, burn, O Love, within my heart,—
  Burn fiercely night and day,
Till all the dross of earthly loves
  Is burned, and burned away.

O Light in darkness, Joy in grief,
  O Heaven begun on earth !
JESUS ! my Love ! my Treasure ! who
  Can tell what Thou art worth ?
O JESUS, JESUS, sweetest Lord,
  What art Thou not to me ?
Each hour brings joys before unknown,
  Each day new liberty.

What limit is there to Thee, love ?
  Thy flight where wilt Thou stay ?
On, on ! our Lord is sweeter far
  To-day than yesterday.
O love of JESUS ! blessed love !
  So will it ever be ;
Time cannot hold Thy wondrous growth,
  No, nor eternity.

LITANY OF THE PASSION OF JESUS.

By the blood that flowed from Thee
In Thy bitter agony,
By the scourge so meekly borne,
By Thy purple robe of scorn,—

    CHORUS—

Jesu, Saviour, hear our cry !
  Thou wert suffering once as we ;
Hear the loving Litany
  We Thy children sing to Thee.

By the thorns that crowned Thy head,
By Thy sceptre of a reed,
By Thy footsteps, faint and slow,
Weighed beneath Thy cross of woe,—

Jesu, Saviour, &c.

By the nails and pointed spear,
By Thy people's cruel jeer,
By Thy dying prayer, which rose
Begging mercy for Thy foes,—

Jesu, Saviour, &c.

By the darkness thick as night,
Blotting out the sun from sight,
By the cry with which, in death,
Thou didst yield Thy parting breath,—

Jesu, Saviour, &c.

By Thy weeping Mother's woe,
By the sword that pierced her through,
When, in anguish, standing by,
On the cross she saw Thee die,—

Jesu, Saviour, &c.

"THE STABAT MATER."

Stabat Mater dolorosa
Juxta crucem lacrymosa,
  Dum pendebat Filius.
Cujus animam gementem,
Contristatam, et dolentem,
  Pertransivit gladius.

At the Cross her station keeping ;
Stood the mournful Mother weeping
  Close to Jesus to the last :
Through her heart, His sorrow sharing,
All his bitter anguish bearing,
  Now at length the sword had passed.

O quam tristis et afflicta
Fuit illa benedicta
  Mater Unigeniti.
Quæ mœrebat, et dolebat,
Pia Mater, dum videbat
  Nati pœnas inclyti.

Oh, how sad and sore distressèd
Was that Mother highly blessèd
  Of the sole-begotten One !
Christ above in torment hangs :
She beneath beholds the pangs
  Of her dying glorious Son.

Quis est homo qui non fleret,
Matrem Christi si videret
  In tanto supplicio ?

Is there one who would not weep,
Whelmed in miseries so deep
  Christ's dear Mother to behold ?

Quis non posset contristari,
 Christi Matrem contemplari
   Dolentem cum Filio?
 	
 Pro peccatis suæ gentis
 Vidit Jesum in tormentis,
   Et flagellis subditum.
 Vidit suum dulcem Natum
 Moriendo desolatum,
   Dum emisit spiritum.
 	
 Eia Mater, fons amoris,
 Me sentire vim doloris
   Fac, ut tecum lugeam.
 Fac ut ardeat cor meum
 In amando Christum Deum,
   Ut sibi complaceam.
 	
 Sancta Mater, istud agas,
 Crucifixe fige plagas
   Cordi meo valide.
 Tui Nati vulnerati,
 Tam dignati pro me pati,
   Pœnas mecum divide.
 	
 Fac me tecum pie flere,
 Crucifixo condolere,
   Donec ego vixero.
 Juxta Crucem tecum stare,
 Et me tibi sociare
   In planctu desidero.
 	
 Virgo virginum præclara,
 Mihi jam non sis amara;
   Fac me tecum plangere.
 Fac ut portem Christi mortem,
 Passionis fac consortem,
   Et plagas recolere.
 	
 Fac me plagis vulnerari,
 Fac me Cruce inebriari,
   Et cruore Filii.
 Flammis ne urar succensus,
 Per te, Virgo, sim defensus
   In die judicii.
 	
 Christe, cum sit hinc exire
 Da per Matrem me venire
   Ad palmam victoriæ.
 Quando corpus morietur,
 Fac ut animæ donetur
   Paradisi gloria.
           Amen.
	Can the human heart refrain
	 From partaking in her pain,
	   In that Mother's pain untold?
	
	 Bruised, derided, cursed, defiled,
	 She beheld her tender Child
	   All with bloody scourges rent:
	 For the sins of His own nation,
	 Saw Him hang in desolation,
	   Till His spirit forth He sent.
	
	 O thou Mother! fount of love!
	 Touch my spirit from above,
	   Make my heart with thine accord:
	 Make me feel as thou hast felt,
	 Make my soul to glow and melt
	   With the love of Christ my Lord.
	
	 Holy Mother! pierce me through,
	 In my heart each wound renew
	   Of my Saviour crucified:
	 Let me share with thee His pain,
	 Who for all my sins was slain,
	   Who for me in torments died.
	
	 Let me mingle tears with thee,
	 Mourning Him who mourned for me
	   All the days that I may live:
	 By the Cross with thee to stay,
	 There with thee to weep and pray,
	   Is all I ask of thee to give.
	
	 Virgin of all virgins best!
	 Listen to my fond request:
	   Let me share thy grief divine;
	 Let me, to my latest breath,
	 In my body bear the death
	   Of that dying Son of thine.
	
	 Wounded with His every wound,
	 Steep my soul till it hath swooned
	   In His very blood away:
	 Be to me, O Virgin, nigh,
	 Lest in flames I burn and die,
	   In His awful judgment day.
	
	 Christ, when Thou shalt call me hence,
	 Be Thy Mother my defence,
	   Be Thy cross my victory;
	 While my body here decays,
	 May my soul Thy goodness praise,
	   Safe in Paradise with Thee.
	           Amen.

Te Deum Laudamus.

Te Deum laudámus: * te Dominum confitémur.

Te æternum Patrem, * omnis terra venerátur.

Tibi omnes ángeli, * tibi cœli, et universæ protestátes:

Tibi Chérubim, et Séraphim,* incessábili voce proclámant:

Sanctus, sanctus, sanctus, * Dominus Deus Sábaoth:
Pleni sunt cœli et terra, * majestátis gloriæ tuæ.
Te gloriosus * Apostolórum chorus.
Te Prophetárum * laudábilis númerus.
Te Mártyrum candidátus * laudat exércitus.
Te per orbem terrárum * sancta confitétur Ecclesia.

Patrem * immensæ majestátis.
Venerandum tuum verum * et únicum Filium.
Sanctum quoque * Paráclitum Spiritum.
Tu Rex gloriæ, * Christe.

Tu Patris * sempiternus es Filius.
Tu ad liberandum suscepturus hominem, * non horruisti Vírginis úterum.

Tu devicto mortis aculeo, * aperuisti credentibus regna cœlórum.

We praise Thee, O God: we acknowledge Thee to be the Lord.
All the earth doth worship Thee: the Father everlasting.
To Thee all angels cry aloud: the heavens and all the powers therein.
To Thee Cherubim and Seraphim: continually do cry:
Holy, holy, holy: Lord God of Sabaoth.
Heaven and earth are full: of the majesty of Thy glory.
The glorious choir of the Apostles: praise Thee.
The admirable company of the Prophets: praise Thee.
The white-robed army of Martyrs: praise Thee.
The Holy Church throughout all the world: doth acknowledge Thee.
The Father: of an infinite majesty.
Thy adorable, true: and only Son.
Also the Holy Ghost: the Comforter.
Thou art the King of Glory: O Christ.
Thou art the everlasting Son: of the Father.
When Thou tookest upon Thee to deliver man: Thou didst not abhor the Virgin's womb.
When Thou hadst overcome the sting of death: Thou didst open the kingdom of heaven to all believers.

Tu ad dexteram Dei sedes, * in gloria Patris.	Thou sittest at the right hand of God: in the glory of the Father.
Judex créderis * esse ventúrus.	We believe that Thou shalt come: to be our Judge.
† Te ergo quǽsumus, tuis fámulis súbveni, * quos pretióso sanguine redemisti.	We pray Thee, therefore, help Thy servants: whom Thou hast redeemed with Thy precious blood.
Ætérna fac cum Sanctis tuis,* in gloria numerári.	Make them to be numbered with Thy Saints: in glory everlasting.
Salvum fac populum tuum, Domine, * et benedic hæreditáti tuæ.	O Lord, save Thy people: and bless Thine inheritance.
Et rege eos, et extolle illos, * usque in æternum.	Govern them: and lift them up for ever.
Per singulos dies * benedicimus te.	Day by day: we magnify Thee.
Et laudámus nomen tuum in sæculum, * et in sæculum sæculi.	And we praise Thy name for ever: yea, for ever and ever.
Dignáre, Domine, die isto, * sine peccáto nos custodíre.	Vouchsafe, O Lord, this day: to keep us without sin.
Miserére nostri, Domine, * miserére nostri.	O Lord, have mercy upon us: have mercy upon us.
Fiat misericordia tua, Domine, super nos: * quemádmodum sperávimus in te.	O Lord, let Thy mercy be showed upon us: as we have hoped in Thee.
In te, Domine, sperávi; * non confundar in æternum.	O Lord, in Thee have I hoped: let me not be confounded for ever.

No. 12.—Observations on Faith, by Cardinal Newman.

"Faith is not a mere conviction in reason; it is a firm assent, it is a clear certainty, greater than any other certainty; and this is wrought in the mind by the grace

---

† Here it is usual to kneel.

of God, and by it alone. As then men may be convinced, and not act according to their conviction, so may they be convinced and not believe according to their conviction. They may confess that the argument is against them, and that they have nothing to say for themselves, and that to believe is to be happy; and yet, after all, they avow they cannot believe, they do not know why, but they cannot; they acquiesce in unbelief, and they turn away from God and His Church. Their reason is convinced, and their doubts are moral ones, arising in their root from a fault of the will. In a word, the arguments for Religion do not compel any one to believe, just as arguments for good conduct do not compel any one to obey. Obedience is the consequence of willing to obey, and faith is the consequence of willing to believe; we may see what is right, whether in matters of faith or obedience, of ourselves, but we cannot will what is right without the grace of God. Here is the difference between other exercises of reason and arguments for the truth of religion. It requires no act of faith to assent to the truth that two and two make four; we cannot help assenting to it; and hence there is no merit in assenting to it; but there is merit in believing that the Church is from God: for though there are abundant reasons to prove it to us, yet we can, without an absurdity, quarrel with the conclusion; we may complain that it is not clearer, we may suspend our assent, we may doubt about it, if we will; and grace alone can turn a bad will into a good one."—*Discourses to Mixed Congregations, p. 226.*

No. 13.—ACTS OF FAITH, HOPE, CHARITY, AND CONTRITION.

AN ACT OF FAITH
(From the Penny Catechism of Christian Doctrine, for England.)

I firmly believe that there is One God; and that in this one God there are Three Persons, the Father, the Son, and the Holy Ghost; that the Son took to Himself the nature of man, from the Virgin Mary's womb, by the power of the Holy Ghost ; and that in this our human nature He was crucified and died for us ; that afterwards He rose again and ascended into heaven, from thence He shall come to repay the just with everlasting glory, and the wicked with everlasting punishment ; Moreover, I believe whatsoever else the Catholic Church proposes to be believed, and this because God Who is the Sovereign Truth, Who can neither deceive nor be deceived, has revealed all these things to this His Church.

An Act of Hope.

O my God, relying on Thy almighty power and Thy infinite mercy and goodness, and because Thou art faithful to Thy promises, I trust in Thee that Thou wilt grant me forgiveness of my sins, through the Merits of Jesus Christ Thy Son ; and that Thou wilt give me the assistance of Thy Grace, with which I may labour to continue to the end in the diligent exercise of all good works, and may deserve to obtain the glory which Thou hast promised in heaven.

An Act of Charity.

O Lord, my God, I love Thee with my whole heart, and above all things, because Thou, O God, art the sovereign Good, and for Thine own infinite perfections are most worthy of all love ; and for Thy sake I also love my neighbour as myself.

An Act of Contrition.

O my God, Who art infinitely good, and always hatest sin, I beg pardon from my heart for all my offences against Thee ; I detest them all, and am heartily sorry for them, because they offend Thy infinite goodness ; and I firmly resolve by the help of Thy grace never more to offend Thee, and carefully to avoid the occasions of sin.

It is the strict duty of every Christian to make sometimes these or similar *Acts* of Faith, Hope, Charity, and Contrition, and it is strongly recommended to repeat them *often*, because by an Act of *Faith* we worship God's Infinite Wisdom and Truth ; by an Act of *Hope* we worship God's Infinite Mercy, and honour our Saviour's Redemption by placing in that

Divine Redemption our full reliance for pardon, justification. and grace; by an Act of *Charity* we worship God's Infinite Goodness, Holiness, and all His Perfections in general; by an Act of *Contrition* we worship God's Infinite Justice and Mercy, and acknowledge Him as the Father of Mercies.

SHORT ACTS OF FAITH, HOPE, LOVE, AND CONTRITION, FOR LITTLE CHILDREN.

Act of Faith.—My God, I believe in Thee, and all Thy Church doth teach, because Thou hast said it, and Thy word is true.

Act of Hope.—My God, I hope in Thee, for grace and for glory, because of Thy promises, Thy mercy, and Thy power.

Act of Charity.—My God, because Thou art so good, I love Thee with all my heart, and for Thy sake, I love my neighbour as myself.

Act of Contrition.—O my God, because Thou art so good, I am very sorry that I have sinned against Thee, and I will not sin again.

HYMN OF REPENTANT SORROW.

(Frequently sung at Mission-Services, slowly.)

JESUS, my God, behold at length the time
When I resolve to turn away from crime.
   O pardon me, Jesus, Thy mercy I implore,
   I will never more offend Thee—no, never more.
Since my poor soul Thy precious Blood hath cost,
Suffer it not for ever to be lost.
   O pardon me, Jesus, Thy mercy I implore, &c.
Kneeling in tears, behold me at Thy feet—
Like Magdalen, forgiveness I entreat.
   O pardon me, Jesus, Thy mercy I implore, &c.

NO. 14.—A SHORT METHOD OF HEARING MASS.

(It is recommended that each of the following prayers should be said at the very time assigned in the "*Directions.*"

Just before the Mass begins, say:

O my God, give me grace to assist with attention and devotion at this solemn act of religion, by which the

Church intends to worship Thee in a manner worthy of Thee.

☞ *When the Priest at the foot of the Altar begins Mass, and the "Confiteor" or General Confession is recited, say:*

O God, who am I that I should dare to stand in Thy Temple before Thy altar, guilty, as I am, of so many sins ? Prostrate at Thy feet, O Lord, I will humbly repeat over and over again the words of the penitent publican in the Gospel, "*O God, be merciful to me a sinner.*"

☞ *When the Priest ascends the steps and kisses the Altar, then goes twice to his right, or the Epistle side, and shortly after, once to his left or the Gospel side, say:*

This reminds me, O Lord, of the beginning of Thy bitter Passion—1st, Thy agony in the Garden, where Thou wast betrayed by Judas with a kiss; 2ndly, Thy being taken and led captive to the different tribunals of Annas, Caiphas, Pilate, King Herod, and back again to that of Pontius Pilate; 3rdly, It reminds me how in these tribunals Thou wast ill-treated, falsely accused, and unjustly condemned. O Lord, give me patience in all my crosses and troubles, of whatever kind they may be.

☞ *At the Kyrie Eleison (Lord have mercy) say:*

Have mercy on me, O Lord, and forgive me all my sins. Have mercy on me, O Lord, have mercy on me.

☞ *At the Gloria in excelsis (Glory to God in the highest) say:*

Glory be to God on high, and on earth peace to men of goodwill. We praise Thee; we bless Thee; we adore Thee; we glorify Thee; we give Thee thanks for Thy great glory, O Lord God, heavenly king, God the Father Almighty. O LORD JESUS CHRIST, only-begotten Son; O Lord God, Lamb of God, Son of the Father, Thou who takest away the sins of the world, have mercy on us. Thou who takest away the sins of the world, receive our prayers. Thou who sittest at the right hand of the Father, have mercy on us. For Thou only art holy; Thou only art the Lord; Thou only, O JESUS CHRIST, with the Holy Ghost, art most high in the glory of God the Father. Amen.

APPENDIX NO. XIV.

☞ *When the Priest reads the Epistle, say:*

Thou hast taught us, O Lord, Thy sacred truths by Thy Prophets and Apostles; grant that we may so improve by their doctrine and example in the love of Thy holy Name and of Thy holy Law that we may show forth by our life that we are Thy disciples. May we no longer follow the corrupt inclinations of the flesh, but subdue all our passions. May we be ever directed by Thy light, and strengthened by Thy grace to walk in the way of Thy Commandments, and serve Thee with pure hearts, through our LORD JESUS CHRIST.

☞ *When the Priest reads the Gospel, and the people stand, say:*

O *Jesus*, the Way, the Truth, and the Life, I give Thee most hearty thanks for the heavenly truths Thou teachest us. I thank Thee also for having appointed Thy Holy Church on earth a sure guide to make known to us which are the inspired Books of Scripture, and the true sense in which they are to be understood. Never permit me to abandon Thy holy Word, nor Thy Church, the lawful interpreter of the same. It has pleased Thee, O LORD JESUS, to continue daily to teach us by Thy holy Gospel; grant me grace that I may not be wanting in any care needful for my instruction in Thy saving truths: let me be as industrious for my soul as I am for my body; that while I take pains in the affairs of this world, I may not, through stupidity or neglect, let my soul starve and perish everlastingly. Let the rules of the Gospel be the guide of my life, that I may not only know Thy will, but likewise do it. May I keep all Thy Commandments, and, resisting all the inclinations of corrupt nature, may I, as a true disciple, ever follow Thee Who art the Way, the Truth, and the Life.

☞ *When the Priest recites the Nicene Creed (see Appendix No. 3) say:*

O my God, I believe this Creed and all other definitions of faith made by the Holy Catholic Church, which Thou hast appointed to teach Thy revealed truth to all mankind, and which Thou dost assist in a special manner, that she never can lead us astray; and in this faith of Thy Saints I wish to live and die.

SHORT METHOD OF HEARING MASS.

☞ *When the Priest uncovers the paten and the chalice, and offers to God first the bread and then the wine about to be consecrated, say:*

O God, I offer Thee this holy Sacrifice for the same ends for which the Church offers it to Thee: namely,
1. To Thy honour and glory.
2. In thanksgiving for all the benefits we have received from Thee.
3. To obtain more graces for myself and for all others.
4. To obtain pardon for my sins and for the sins of all men.

(Dwell a while upon each of these four points, repeating them with devotion and fervour.)

☞ *At the Preface and Sanctus, say:*

O my God, I rejoice to see that the angels in heaven and men on earth are ranged, as it were, in two choirs to extol Thy glory, and to thank Thee for Thy countless benefits. Unworthy though I am, I wish to unite in heart and voice with them in thanking and glorifying Thee; and in exclaiming: Holy, Holy, Holy is the Lord God of Hosts. Heaven and earth are full of Thy Glory. Blessed is he that cometh in the name of the Lord. Hosanna in the highest!

☞ *Whilst the Priest reads the Canon in secret, call to mind the following points of the Passion of our Lord:*

JESUS terribly scourged at the pillar.
,, cruelly crowned with thorns.
,, unjustly condemned to death.
,, loaded with the heavy weight of the Cross.
,, sadly meeting His desolate Mother in the way.
,, falling down thrice under the weight of the Cross on His way to Calvary.
,, being there stripped of His clothes and nailed to the Cross.

☞ When the Consecration takes place, and the Priest raises above the level of his head the Host, and shortly afterwards the Chalice, the little bell is rung by the Server at each elevation to call special attention to this, the principal part of the Mass; call to mind when the Cross, with *Jesus* nailed thereon, was raised on Mount Calvary;—how He remained hanging there in agony in the midst of most excruciating torments for three long hours;—how at last He expired, the victim of immeasurable love for us;—and then say:

O *Jesus*, I adore Thee, I thank Thee with all my heart for having allowed Thy love to carry Thee to that excess as to die for me upon the Cross. In return, I wish to love Thee with all my heart and soul, and above all things. I repent most sincerely for having offended Thee. I am distressed and confused on account of my past ingratitudes to Thee; yet, full of confidence, I run to Thy sacred wounds for refuge. I thank Thee for having graciously given us this holy Sacrifice, and thus afforded us an opportunity of joining Thee, our High Priest, in offering Thyself to Thy Eternal Father as a most pure and most acceptable Divine Victim of expiation, able to call down upon us all blessings.

O Eternal Father, I offer to Thee the most precious Blood of Thy beloved Son JESUS CHRIST in expiation of my sins, for the wants of Holy Church, and in thanksgiving for all the benefits ever imparted to us.

☞ *At the Memento of the dead, say:*

I offer Thee again, O Lord, this holy Sacrifice of the Body and Blood of Thy only Son, in behalf of the faithful departed, and in particular for the souls of [*here name those you wish to pray for*]. To these, O Lord, and to all that died in Christ, grant, we beseech Thee, a place of refreshment.

☞ *When the Priest recites the "Pater Noster," that is, the Lord's Prayer, say with devotion:*

Our Father who art in heaven, hallowed be Thy name; Thy kingdom come; Thy will be done on earth, as it is in heaven. Give us this day our daily bread; and forgive us our trespasses, as we forgive them that trespass against us; and lead us not into temptation; but deliver us from evil. Amen.

☞ *Whilst the Priest says thrice* "AGNUS DEI" (*Lamb of God*), *and shortly after, thrice,* "DOMINE NON SUM DIGNUS" (*Lord I am not worthy*),*

---

* At this moment the Server again sounds the little bell, to give notice of this other principal part of the Mass, and to remind those who have to communicate (if Communion is then given) that it is time to approach

and whilst the Priest administers to himself the Body and the Blood of Christ, you will do well, if you are not among those happy ones who go up to the Altar-rails to receive your Saviour SACRAMENTALLY, to awaken in your heart a great desire to receive Christ SPIRITUALLY within you. This is called spiritual communion, and you will do well to say:

O *Jesus*, I firmly believe that Thou art truly present in this Blessed Sacrament. I see Thee therein full of love, willing to pardon us, and anxious to dwell within us, and to be very closely united to us. I wish most earnestly to answer to this Thy desire and love. I detest all my sins by which I have displeased Thee. Pardon me, O Lord, and purify my soul in Thy precious Blood; I love Thee, O Lord, and I wish to love Thee more and more. Come to me, O Lord, and dwell within me. I long to have Thee within my breast. Since I cannot now receive Thee Sacramentally, come at least Spiritually into my heart. I embrace Thee, and unite myself to Thee, as if Thou wert already there. With all the love I have, I cling to Thee. Guard me from falling into sin, that I may never be separated from Thee, but may remain united with Thee for ever.

☞ *When the Priest says, "*ITE MISSA EST*" (that is, "You may go, the Mass is said"), and then blesses the people, you will sign yourself with the sign of the Cross,** *saying:*

In the name of the Father and of the Son, and of the Holy Ghost. Amen. O Holy Trinity, one God, may Thy blessing remain with us for ever. Glory be to the Father, and to the Son, and to the Holy Ghost: as it was in the beginning, is now, and ever shall be, world without end. Amen. Eternal thanks to Thee, O Lord, for having given me the opportunity to be present at the

the Altar-rail, and kneel there to receive Holy Communion. Few go to Communion at High Mass, which is generally celebrated at a late hour in the morning. Most persons going to Holy Communion, and therefore fasting, prefer to go to an earlier Mass, called Low Mass, from having fewer ceremonies than High Mass.

* The sign of the Cross is made thus; You put the fingers of your right hand on your forehead, saying, *In the name of the Father;* you then lower the fingers on to your breast, saying, *and of the Son;* you then touch with the same right hand first your left shoulder, and then your right shoulder, while saying, *and of the Holy Ghost;* you may then join both hands before your breast, saying, *Amen.*

highest Act of Religion, and to unite in spirit and truth in that worship which thou didst institute, which alone is worthy of Thee, and in which Thy Father is well pleased. Amen.

No. 15.—Method of Confession.*

A person who wishes to receive the Sacrament of Penance has to do these five things—First, he has to examine carefully his conscience. Secondly, to be heartily sorry for having offended God. Thirdly, to make a firm resolution never to commit any sin again. Fourthly, to make a candid and humble confession of all his mortal sins to a priest. Fifthly, he must have an intention of doing the penance enjoined by the priest, and of satisfying his neighbour to the best of his power if he has done injury to any one.

Before all this, however, he should say the following or a similar prayer to obtain Divine aid to make a good Confession :—

O Almighty God, I long to return to Thee, the fountain of all good. I desire, like the prodigal son, to look seriously into my heart, and to forsake my evil ways without delay. I am wearied in pursuit of empty toys, seeking in vain to satisfy my thirst with muddy waters, and my hunger with husks fit only for swine.

But, O my God, though I can go astray from Thee by myself, I cannot make one step towards Thee without the help of Thy grace. This grace, then, I most humbly implore for the sake of Jesus Christ my Redeemer. And since I have now to examine my conscience, that I may call to mind my sins, in order to detest and bitterly deplore them and confess them, mercifully enlighten my understanding that I may clearly see the state of my conscience. Disclose to me, O my God, all those secret thoughts, irregular desires, criminal words and actions, or omissions of my duty, by which I have violated Thy

---

* Read the very useful, interesting "*Treatise on Auricular Confession,*" by Rev. Dr. Raphael Melia. (See List of Books, Appendix, No. 44.)

sacred laws, or given scandal to my neighbour. Do not permit self-love to deceive me, but help me that I may behold the true state of my heart, and weep bitterly over my sins, and now humbly and sincerely confess them to Thy minister.

You will then proceed to examine your conscience, and as you are bound to confess mortal sins, and not bound, although recommended, to confess lesser faults, called venial sins, your first care should be to find out the mortal sins, that is, the grievous sins you may have committed, and find out also the precise number of times each such sin was committed, or at least the probable number.

If you are not in the habit of making your examination of conscience, the following list of sins may be of some assistance to you.

SINS AGAINST GOD.

Have you been guilty of disbelieving an article of faith ?

———— rashly exposed yourself to the danger of infidelity by reading dangerous books or keeping bad company ?

———— abused the words of Holy Scripture by indecent or grossly irreverent application of them ?

———— been negligent in procuring the necessary instruction for those under your care in their duties to God ?

———— despaired of salvation or of the forgiveness of your sins ?

———— thought it impossible to avoid mortal sin or to be good ?

———— presumed on God's goodness without caring to amend ?

———— delayed repentance ?

———— murmured against the providence of God ?

———— thought God cruel or unjust, or indifferent to our doing good or evil ?

———— neglected to prevent evil, when it was your duty and in your power to do so ?

Have you said and maintained maliciously that all religions were good?

———— been wilfully negligent in the Church during Divine worship?

———— neglected prayer for several weeks?

———— said your prayers with great want of attention?

———— been irreverent in the church by talking, laughing, or making others laugh?

———— sworn to a lie, or sworn to do what was wrong?

———— broken your lawful oath?

———— taken the Holy Name of God in vain?

———— passed Sunday or a holy-day of obligation in idleness or sin, or have you been the occasion to others of so passing such time?

———— done or commanded servile work for a considerable space of time without necessity upon those days?

SINS AGAINST OUR NEIGHBOUR.

SINS IN THOUGHT.—Have you judged rashly of your neighbour?

Have you wilfully harboured any thoughts of rancour or of revenge against him?

———— from hatred avoided any one, or refused to show him ordinary civility?

———— maliciously envied any one for his merit, reputation, talent, fortune, or employment?

Have you harboured any desire of revenge?

SINS IN WORDS.—Have you spoken very harshly to your neighbour, or used abusive language towards him?

———— grievously deceived your neighbour?

———— wilfully misconstrued his actions?

———— said what was false of your neighbour?

———— detracted him by revealing, to his injury, without just cause, what was true but secret?

———— encouraged calumny or detraction by listening with pleasure to reports of that kind?

———— been a scandal to any one by giving bad advice or bad example, by instilling bad principles, or by using bad language in the presence of any one?

SINS OF DEED.—Have you cheated your neighbour in buying or selling?

———— injured any one by stealing, helping to steal, or usury, extortion, or by any unlawful contract?

———— knowingly bought or received stolen goods?

———— refused or neglected to pay your just debts?

———— neglected the work or business for which you were hired, and were obliged by contract to perform?

———— neglected to restore ill-gotten goods, or to make compensation for wrong done to your neighbour when it was in your power to do so?

———— shared in the sin of another by counsel, by command, by consent, by flattery, or by silence?

———— neglected to restore the character which you may have injured by calumny or detraction?

SINS OF OMISSION.—Have you neglected your duties as a Christian? as a parent? as a husband? as a wife? as master? or as servant? In short, any duty belonging to your state of life or calling?

Have you been wanting in your duty as son or daughter? ———— been guilty of grave disrespect or of grave disobedience to your Parents? ———— despised or insulted them? ———— provoked them to great anger, to curse or to swear? ———— treated them in a haughty and insulting manner? ———— spoken evil of them?

———— omitted to assist your neighbour in his great necessity when you could have helped him?

SINS AGAINST OURSELVES.

BY PRIDE.—Had you too great an esteem of yourself, or boasted unduly, and haughtily despised others?

Did you feel a secret pleasure in hearing others seriously disparaged?

BY COVETOUSNESS.—Have you through covetousness been unjust to your wife and family?

Have you been seriously wanting in charity and compassion towards the poor? Did you use towards them unmerited, imperious, ill-natured, or insulting language?

———— received exorbitant interest for money lent?

Have you charged exorbitant prices ?

—— knowingly kept that surplus of change which was given to you by mistake ?

—— desired to steal, defraud, or commit any other kind of injustice ?

BY IMPURITY.—Have you sinned against chastity, by wilfully dwelling upon and taking pleasure in unchaste thoughts ?

By desiring to commit immodest actions ?

By going into bad company ?

Talking immodestly ? Listening with pleasure to impure language ? Singing any unchaste songs ?

Reading any immodest books, or lending any such book to others ? Looking unchastely at immodest objects ?

Doing any immodest action either alone or with others ? Permitting any indecent liberty to be taken with you ?

BY ANGER.—Have you harboured great dislike towards any one ?

Have you given way to great angry passion ?

—— of set purpose taken part in serious quarrels or duels ?

—— provoked others to quarrel or fight ?

—— struck your wife or husband ? struck your children unduly ?

—— struck any one else in anger ?

Have you been guilty of wanton cruelty to any animal ?

Have you refused to forgive any injury ? or refused to be reconciled ? or refused to give signs of reconciliation or forgiveness ?

Have you been guilty of great impatience ? too severely correcting those under your charge ? of cruel and abusive treatment ?

BY GLUTTONY.—Have you exceeded the bounds prescribed by temperance, by eating or by drinking to excess ?* Have you induced others to do so ?

Have you through drunkenness been a scandal to your neighbour, a source of unhappiness and quarrel and injustice to your family ?

---

* See Appendix, No. 33. Extract from the Writings of His Eminence Cardinal Manning on Total Abstinence.

By Envy—Have you felt sorry at the prosperity of others? or did you rejoice at their misfortune?

By Sloth—Have you for a long time neglected prayer or other religious duty?

Did you perform these duties carelessly?

Did you lead a life of idleness?

Did you neglect to admonish those whom it was your duty to admonish?

Did you neglect to pray when assailed by great temptation or in great danger of sin?

Did you remain voluntarily in proximate (that is, near) occasions of sin?

Examine yourself whether any of the sins committed have been the cause of bad example or scandal to others?

Secondly, Be Heartily Sorry.

Having tried to bring to your memory the different sins of which you have been guilty, together with their number, and such circumstances as may have considerably increased their malice or changed their nature, you should pass to the next thing to be done in preparation for Confession—namely, you should endeavour to excite in your heart a great sorrow for having committed them, and a sincere detestation of them. For this purpose you should—

First, Beg of Almighty God to give you grace to feel this abhorrence of your sins.

Secondly, Consider those things which may help you to detest your sins; as, for example, that by your sins you have lost heaven, merited hell, rebelled against your Creator, grieved and offended a God of infinite goodness, been very ungrateful to your greatest Benefactor, your Heavenly Father, and your Redeemer who suffered so much, and died on the Cross for you; that you have deprived yourself of the grace of God, and become an object hateful to Him.

Thirdly, By saying with great fervour, and more than once, the following or similar act of contrition:—

ACT OF CONTRITION.

O Lord Jesus, behold at Thy feet a great sinner. I am ashamed and confused on account of the many sins which I have committed.

I reproach myself bitterly for having been so ungrateful and wicked. I have abused Thy goodness, O Lord, my Redeemer, my best Benefactor.

I have offended Thee, O God of infinite goodness! Every time I committed a grievous sin, I have deserved and called down upon myself that dreadful sentence: "*Depart from me, ye cursed, into everlasting fire, which was prepared for the Devil and his Angels.*" (S. Matt. xxv. 41.) I cannot complain of this sentence, for of my own accord I have departed from Thee, and lived wilfully away from Thee, and in a state of rebellion against Thee.

How often did Thy sweet voice invite me to repentance!

How often have Thy corrections warned me to return! and I was deaf to Thy call, and hardened my heart against Thee.

Often hast Thou stretched out Thy hand to me, O Lord, and I turned my back upon Thee: but, O Lord, I now repent: I am sorry indeed. Who shall give "*a fountain of tears to my eyes,*" that day and night I may weep for my ingratitude to Thee, O Lord? My transgressions are a heavy burden to me. The thought of being astray from Thee alarms me; I am wretched, buried as I am in the depth of sin and misery.

Shall I despair? No, I will not despair; if my sins are many and great, Thy mercy, O Lord, is still greater. Thou hast waited for me until now to give me time to repent. A humbled and contrite heart Thou wilt not despise; why shall I not trust in Thee? Yes, I do trust in Thy infinite mercy, O Lord, in Thy Precious Blood shed for me, in Thy Divine promise of receiving the repentant sinner, like the prodigal son, as soon as ever he returns to Thee.

Full of confidence, therefore, and out of the depth of my poor heart, I cry out to Thee: "*O God, be merciful to me a sinner* ". (S. Luke xviii. 13.) I detest all my sins; I heartily wish that I had never committed them. They are hateful now in my sight; but as my repentance can never be sufficient, I beg to offer Thee, O Lord, the sighs, the tears, the fainting and the sweat of blood, the horror and the grief for sin, with which, in the Garden of Gethsemane, Thou didst supply the poorness of my repentance.

Touch my stony heart, O Lord, with Thy powerful grace, that with tears of sorrow I may bewail my ingratitude and all my past sins in the bitterness of my heart.

Root out of my soul whatever is displeasing to Thee, and lay in me the foundation of a new life. I love Thee, O Lord Jesus, with all my heart and soul, and wish to love Thee more and more. With the help of Thy grace, I will never offend Thee again; no, never more. Strengthen Thou my resolution.

THIRDLY, MAKE A FIRM RESOLUTION NEVER TO SIN AGAIN.

A true sorrow for having offended God must contain a firm purpose of amendment. Without this, the sorrow would not be true nor sufficient for making a good confession.

It is clear that if a person, though displeased for having offended God, yet were wavering whether he should or should not commit sin again, whether he should be true to his duty or not, faithful to God or not, he would not be truly sorry nor be in a fit state to obtain pardon of his sins.

Would a father show readiness to forgive a son who had grievously offended him, if that son should remain sullen, or showed himself disposed to repeat the same fault?

When a person is truly sorry for having offended God, he is also determined, with the help of God's grace, not to offend Him ever again, and is resolved also to avoid proximate occasions of sin.

It might happen that, notwithstanding this resolution

to quit all sin, you might after some time yield to temptation, change your mind for the worse, and fall again into sin; because neither this resolution nor the absolution you receive will render you impeccable. Yet it is no less true that when you are sincerely determined to avoid sin, you are then in a fit state to receive pardon, and if you are not so resolved, you would not be in a fit state for receiving absolution.

It would be foolish to hesitate to make such a resolution, on the ground that it is a promise, and to say: If I make a promise, and then fail to keep my word, it would be still worse.

But it is not so, because, strictly speaking, it is not a promise which is demanded of you, but only a *resolution*— that is, a determination—that you will do what you are bound to do—namely, observe the commandments and avoid sin.

Now, to resolve over and over again, "*I will not offend God, I will do my duty,*" does not create a new obligation, but it encourages one to do what he is simply bound to do. If a sentry at his post, with a view to drive away timidity and encourage himself to do his duty, were to repeat to himself: "*I will be brave, I will not desert my post,*" that would not surely be contracting a new obligation.

Whether you make such resolutions or not, you are *equally bound* not to offend God; but the making of fresh resolutions serves to strengthen your will, and confirm you in your duty and fidelity to God; and you do not thereby impose upon yourself a fresh obligation.

It is clear, therefore, that to make such resolutions is a real gain, and that it can only be profitable to your soul. It would therefore be your interest to repeat often and fervently such purpose of amendment as the following:—

O my God! with the help of Thy grace, I will never offend Thee again.

Rather would I die than offend Thee, O my God!

I will no longer be unfaithful and ungrateful to Thee. I will no more add to the number of my sins, but put a stop to them, dear Lord. Henceforth I will be altogether

Thine. By myself I can do nothing, but with the help of Thy grace I can resist all temptations and keep Thy commandments. Help me, O Lord, with Thy powerful grace, that I may never more offend Thee. Oh, what a happiness could I live without offending Thee any more!

The Psalm 118 (119), beginning, "*Blessed are the undefiled in the way,*" or part of it, might be recited with great spiritual profit, as it is full of beautiful resolutions to observe God's commandments.

FOURTHLY, MAKE A CANDID AND HUMBLE CONFESSION.

After having prepared yourself in this manner, you should go to Confession with modesty and humility, determined to be sincere, and willing to suffer some shame in penance for your sins, and thus avert the greater shame and confusion which you will otherwise certainly have to endure at the Day of Judgment. Then kneel down at the side of the Confessional where the Priest is for hearing confessions.

Before your confession, turning towards the Priest, say—

"*Bless me, Father, for I have sinned.*"

Immediately after these words recite the first part of the "Confiteor," consisting of the following words (in English or other language):—

"*I confess to Almighty God, to Blessed Mary, ever Virgin, to Blessed Michael the Archangel, to Blessed John the Baptist, to the Holy Apostles Peter and Paul, to all the Saints, and to you my spiritual father, that I have sinned exceedingly in thought, word, and deed; through my fault, through my fault, through my most grievous fault.*"

You then begin to confess your sins to the Confessor, that is, to the Priest who hears your confession. If needed, he will readily help you in the matter, if you ask him. Tell him, if he does not know it, that it is your first confession.

If it is your first confession, you have to confess all the grievous sins committed during your life; or, if you have been to Confession before, the sins you have committed since your last confession, and at which time you received absolution.

The Priest will give you some advice, and in the end, if he finds you properly disposed, give you, in God's name, absolution of your sins, whilst you make an act of sincere contrition,* and which absolution will be made good by God in Heaven, according to His promise to His Apostles: "*Amen, I say to you, whatsoever you shall bind upon earth, shall be bound also in Heaven; and whatsoever you shall loose upon earth, shall be loosed also in Heaven.*" (S. Matt. xviii. 18.) And according to what we read in St. John: "*He said therefore to them again: Peace be with you. As the Father has sent Me, I also send you. When He had said this, He breathed on them; and He said to them: Receive ye the Holy Ghost: whose sins you shall forgive, they are forgiven them; and whose sins you shall retain, they are retained*" (xx. 21).

You will now leave the Confessional, and, kneeling in the church, offer a hearty thanksgiving to God for the great helps and wonderful blessings received. And, if time allows, you will then perform the penance, usually some prayers, enjoined on you by the Priest.

A true penitent, who wishes to repair by well-doing the evil done, has a choice in the following Virtues, Works, and Beatitudes.

The Seven Deadly Sins, and the opposite Virtues.

Sins		Contrary Virtues
Pride.	}	Humility.
Covetousness.		Liberality.
Lust.		Chastity.
Anger.		Meekness.
Gluttony.		Temperance.
Envy.		Brotherly love.
Sloth.		Diligence.

* *Act of Contrition (from the Catechism approved for England and Wales.)* —O my God, Who art infinitely good, and always hatest sin, I beg pardon from my heart for all my offences against Thee; I detest them all, and am heartily sorry for them, because they offend Thy infinite goodness; and I firmly resolve, by the help of Thy grace, never more to offend Thee, and carefully to avoid the occasions of sin.

The Seven Spiritual Works of Mercy.

To reclaim sinners.
To instruct the ignorant.
To counsel the doubtful.
To comfort the sorrowful.

To bear wrongs patiently.
To forgive offences.
To pray for the living and the dead.

The Seven Corporal Works of Mercy.

To feed the hungry.
To give drink to the thirsty.
To clothe the naked.
To harbour the harbourless.

To visit the sick.
To visit the imprisoned, and
To bury the dead.

The Seven Gifts of the Holy Spirit (Isaias xi. 2).

1. Wisdom. 2. Understanding. 3. Counsel. 4. Fortitude. 5. Knowledge. 6. Piety. 7. Fear of the Lord.

The Eight Beatitudes.—In St. Matt. v. JESUS said—

1. Blessed are the poor in spirit; for theirs is the kingdom of heaven.
2. Blessed are the meek; for they shall possess the land.
3. Blessed are they that mourn; for they shall be comforted.
4. Blessed are they that hunger and thirst after justice; for they shall have their fill.
5. Blessed are the merciful; for they shall obtain mercy.
6. Blessed are the clean of heart; for they shall see God.
7. Blessed are the peacemakers; for they shall be called the children of God.
8. Blessed are they that suffer persecution for justice' sake; for theirs is the kingdom of heaven.

No. 16.—LIST OF THE FATHERS OF THE CHURCH AND OTHER NOTED ECCLESIASTICAL WRITERS.

B. signifies Bishop, fl. flourished, c. (circa) about, d. died.

The Fathers of the Church are writers, for the most part Bishops, who flourished in the Church within the first twelve centuries, who have always been highly esteemed for their great learning in matters of Christian

Religion, and almost all of them for their exalted holiness of life.

They are considered as trustworthy witnesses of what was generally taught in the time in which they lived, and of the Apostolic Tradition.

As such, they have been venerated by all antiquity and by the later ages; and their teaching about faith and morals has always been considered of great weight, especially when they all agree in what they state.

It is, therefore, important to know something about them, especially in what part of Christendom they lived, and in what time they flourished. The nearer they are to Apostolic times, the weightier is their authority.

The following list will be useful to many:—

Fathers of the First Century.

S. Barnabas, who died about A.D. 76.
Hermas, who flourished about the year 90.
S. Clement, Roman Pontiff, d. 100.

Fathers of the First and Second Cent.

S. Ignatius, *B.* of Antioch, Martyr, d. 114.
S. Polycarp, *B.* of Smyrna, Martyr, d. 155.
S. Papias, *B.* of Hierapolis, *fl.* about 120.
S. Quadratus, *B.* of Athens, *fl.* about 123.

Fathers of the Second Cent.

S. Justin of Palestine, Martyr, d. 163.
Tatianus, Disciple of S. Justin, Martyr, d. c. 170.
S. Hegesippus, d. about 180.
S. Apollinaris, *B.* of Hierapolis, *fl.* about 176.
Melito of Sardis, *fl.* about 176.
Athenagoras, *fl.* about 176.
S. Theophanes of Antioch, d. about 186.
S. Dionysius, *B.* of Corinth, *fl.* between 161-192.

Fathers of the Second and Third Cent.

S. Irenaeus, *B.* of Lyons, d. 202.
Apollonius of Rome (Senator), *fl.* 180-210.

LIST OF FATHERS OF THE CHURCH. 291

Clement of Alexandria, *d.* about 217.
S. Hippolytus, Bishop and Martyr, *d.* 235.
Tertullian of Carthage, *fl.* between 195-230.

Fathers of the Third Cent.

Caius of Rome, *fl.* between 211-217.
Minutius Felix of Rome, *fl.* about 220.
Julius of Africa, *fl.* about 221.
Origen of Alexandria, *d.* 253.
S. Cyprian, *B.* of Carthage, Martyr, *d.* 258.
S. Dionysius of Alexandria, *d.* 265.
S. Gregory, Thaumaturgus, *d.* 265-270.
S. Archelaus of Cascari, Bishop, *fl.* 276-282.
S. Anatolius of Laodicea, *fl.* between 270-283.

Fathers of the Third and Fourth Cent.

S. Victorinus Petavionensis, *B.*, Martyr, *d. c.* 302.
S. Methodius, *B.* of Patara, Martyr, *d. c.* 303.
S. Pamphilus of Caesarea, Martyr, *d.* 309.
S. Peter of Alexandria, *d.* 311.

Fathers of the Fourth Cent.

Arnobius of Africa, *fl.* about 310.
Lactantius of Fermo, *d.* about 325.
Eusebius, *B.* of Caesarea, *d.* 340.
S. James of Nisibi, *d.* between 338-350.
Firminius, Martyr, *fl.* about 340.
S. Hilarius of Poitiers, *d.* 367-368.
S. Eustachius, *B.* of Antioch, *d.* 360-361.
S. Athanasius, *B.* of Alexandria, *d.* 371-373.
Lanferus of Cagliari (Sardinia), *d.* 371.
S. Basil of Caesarea, *d.* 373.
Titus, *B.* of Bostra, *d.* about 378.
S. Ephrem of Mesopotamia, *d.* 379.
S. Zeno of Verona, *d.* about 380.
S. Damasus from Spain, Roman Pontiff, *d.* 384.
S. Cyril of Jerusalem, *d.* in the year 386.
S. Gregory of Nazianzum, Asia Minor, *d.* 389.
S. Macarius, Senior (or the Elder), *d.* 390-391.
S. Anphilochius, *B.* of Iconium, *d.* after 394.

S. Gregory of Nyssa, *d.* after 394.
S. Philostratus of Brescia, *d.* between 387-397.
S. Pacianus of Barcelona, *d.* 392.
Didymus of Alexandria, *d.* about 395.
S. Ambrose, Bishop of Milan, *d.* 397.
S. Optatus of Milevi, *fl.* about 370.

Fathers of the Fourth and Fifth Cent.

S. Jerome of Stridon (Dalmatia), *fl.* 370, *d.* 420.
S. Epiphanius of Salamina, *d.* 403.
S. John Chrysostom of Antioch, *d.* 407.
S. Gaudentius of Brescia, *d.* about 410.
Prudentius from Spain, *fl.* about 405.
Rufinus of Aquileia, *d.* 410.
Sulpicius Severus of Agen, *fl.* about 415.
S. Augustine, Bishop of Hippo, *fl.* 386, *d.* 430.
S. Paulinus of Nola, *d.* about 431.

Fathers of the Fifth Cent.

Sinesius, *B.* of Ptolemais, *d.* about 429.
S. Nilus of Mont Sinai, *d.* about 430.
S. Isidorus of Pelusium, Africa, *fl.* 400-434.
Cassian John of Marseilles, *fl.* between 416-433.
S. Cyril, *B.* of Alexandria, *fl.* between 412-444
S. Proclus, *B.* of Constantinople, *d.* 446.
S. Hilarius of Arles, *d.* 449.
Marius Mercator, *fl.* between 418-450.
S. Peter Chrysologus, *B.* of Ravenna, *fl.* 433-450.
S. Eucherius of Lyons, *d.* about 450.
Theodoret, *B.* of Cyrus, *fl.* 423, *d.* 458.
S. Vincent of Lerins, *fl.* between 434-450.
S. Basil of Seleucia, *d.* about 459.
S. Leo the Great, Roman Pontiff, *d.* 461.
S. Prosper of Aquitania (Gascogne), *fl.* 428-463.
S. Maximus of Turin, *d.* about 465.
Salvian of Marseilles, *fl. c.* 430, *d. c.* 485.
S. Apollinaris of Sydon, *d.* 484-490.
Faustus of Riez, *d.* after 490.
Gennadius, *B.* of Marseilles, *fl. c.* 494.

LIST OF FATHERS OF THE CHURCH.

Fathers of the Fifth and Sixth Cent.

Vigilius, B. of Tapsa, fl. about 485.
S. Ennodius of Pavia, d. 521.
S. Avitus of Vienne (France), d. 523.

Fathers of the Sixth Cent.

Boëthius of Pavia, d. 524.
S. Fulgentius of Ruspa (Africa), d. 533.
S. Caesarius, B. of Arles, d. 542.
Facundus, B. of Hermiana, fl. about 545.
Cassiodorus of Squillace (Calabria), d. c. 562.
S. Gregory of Tours, d. 595.
S. John Climacus of Palestine, d. 598.

Fathers of the Sixth and Seventh Cent.

Venantius Fortunatus of Italy, fl. c. 565.
S. Gregory the Great, Roman Pontiff, d. 604.

Fathers of the Seventh Cent.

S. Isidore of Seville (Spain), d. 637.
S. Maximus, Abbot of Constantinople, d. 662.
S. Ildephonsus of Toledo, 667.

Father of the Seventh and Eighth Cent.

Venerable Bede of Jarrow, Northumberland, England, d. between 732-735.

Fathers of the Eighth Cent.

S. Boniface of England, Bishop of Maintz, Germany, and Martyr, d. 755.
S. John of Damascus, d. about 730.
S. Paulinus, B. of Aquileia, fl. about 780.

Father of the Eighth and Ninth Cent.

Alcuin of York, d. 804.

Fathers of the Ninth Cent.

Paschasius Rathbertus of Soissons, d. 865.

Hincmar of Reims, *d*. 882.
Anastasius, Keeper of the Vatican Library (Rome), *d*. 886.

Fathers of the Tenth Cent.

Alto of Vercelli, *d*. about 945.
Hodoardus of Epernay, *d*. 966.
Ratherius of Verona, *d*. 974.

Fathers of the Eleventh Cent.

Burchard of Worms, *fl*. 1020.
Theophylact of Constantinople, *d*. about 1071.
S. Peter Damianus of Ravenna, *d*. 1072.

Fathers of the Eleventh and Twelfth Cent.

S. Bruno Carthusian, Cologne, *d*. 1101.
S. Anselm of Aosta, Piedmont, Archbp. of Canterbury, *d*. in 1109.
Hugo of S. Victor, *fl*. 1120.

Fathers of the Twelfth Cent.

Rupertus, Abbot of Deutch, *d*. 1135.
Peter Lombard, *B*. of Paris, *fl*. 1145.
S. Bernard, Abbot of Clairvaux (Champagne) *d*. 1153.

No. 17.—CANONISED FOUNDERS OF ORDERS AND CONGREGATIONS IN THE CHURCH.

Month of Feast.		Names, Orders, and Congregations.	Died. A.D.
Jan.	15.	S. Paul, first Hermit	342
,,	16.	S. Anthony, Patriarch of Monks	356
,,	29.	S. Francis of Sales, Doctor, Visitation Nuns.	1622
,,	31.	S. Peter Nolasco, Order of Our Blessed Lady of Mercy	1258
Feb.	7.	S. Romuald, The Camaldoli	1027
,,	8.	S. John of Matha, Trinitarians	1213

LIST OF CANONISED FOUNDERS.

Month of Feast.		Names, Orders, and Congregations.	Died. A.D.
Mar.	11.	S. John of God, Order of Charity, for the sick	1550
,,	21.	S. Benedict, Abbot, Patriarch of Monks of the West, Order of Benedictines	543
April	2.	S. Francis of Paula, Order of Minims	1507
,,	8.	S. Albert, Compiler of Carmelite Rules	1214
,,	28.	S. Paul of the Cross, Passionists	1775
May	19.	S. Peter Celestine, Founder of Celestines	1296
,,	26.	S. Philip Neri, Oratorians	1595
,,	31.	S. Angela of Brescia, Ursulines	1134
June	6.	S. Norbert, Premonstratensians	1134
,,	9.	S. Columb, Ab., Founder of Monasteries	597
,,	19.	S. Juliana Falconieri, The Mantellate	1340
,,	25.	S. William, Monte Vergine near Naples	1142
July	12.	S. John Gualbert, Valombrosa	1078
,,	18.	S. Camillus de Lellis, for Visiting the Sick	1648
,,	19.	S. Vincent de Paul, Lazarists and Sisters of St. Vincent of Paul	1660
,,	20.	S. Jerome Emilianus, The Somasky	1537
,,	31.	S. Ignatius of Loyola, Founder of the Society of Jesus	1556
Aug.	2.	S. Alphonsus Liguori, Doctor, Redemptorists	1787
,,	4.	S. Dominic, Friars Preachers	1221
,,	7.	S. Cajetan, Theatines	1547
,,	12.	S. Clare of Assisi, Poor Clares	1253
,,	21.	S. Jane Frances de Chantal, Foundress, with St. Frances de Sales, of many Convents of the Visitation	1641
,,	21.	S. Bernard Ptolemy, Olivetans	1348
,,	23.	S. Philip Benizi, Promoter of the Order of the Servites of Mary	1285
Aug.	27.	S. Joseph Calasanctius, Founder of the Order of the Pious Schools, called also Piarists	1648
,,	28.	S. Augustine, Bp. Doc., Augustinians	430
Oct.	4.	S. Francis of Assisi, Franciscans	1226
,,	6.	S. Bruno, Carthusian Monks	1101
,,	15.	S. Teresa, Barefooted Carmelites	1582
,,	21.	S. Ursula, Patroness of Ursulines	650
Nov.	4.	S. Charles Borromeo, Oblates of St. Charles	1584
,,	20.	S. Felix of Valois, Trinitarians	1221

No. 18.—Census of Religions in the World.

Dr. Hurst's "Outline History of the Church" (1875) gives the following populations to the creeds of the world :—

Christianity, 407 \
Judaism, 7 \
Buddhism, 340 \
Mohammedanism, 200 } Millions. \
Brahmanism, 175 \
Confucianism, 80

All other forms of Religious belief, 174 millions.

Of the Christian populations of the world, 131,007,449 are assigned to Protestantism; 200,339,390 to Roman Catholicism, and 76,390,040 to the Oriental Churches. In the New World, comprising North and South America, the Roman Catholics are in the majority, having about sixty millions, and the Protestants about thirty-seven millions.

According to Hübner, in his *Statistical Tables of all the Countries of the Earth*, there are in the German Empire 25,600,000 Evangelical Christians, 14,900,000 (Roman) Catholics, 38,000 Orthodox Greek Christians, 512,000 Jews, 6,000 of all other denominations or of none. In Austria-Hungary there are 23,900,000 (Roman) Catholics, 3,600,000 Evangelical Christians, 7,220,000 Greek and other Christians, 1,375,000 Jews, 5,000 Mahomedans and others. In France there are 35,390,000 (Roman) Catholics, 600,000 Evangelical Christians, 118,000 Jews, 24,000 Mahomedans and others. In Great Britain and Ireland there are 26,000,000 Protestants of various denominations 5,600,000 (Roman) Catholics, 26,000 Greeks, &c., 46,000 Jews, 6,000 Mahomedans, and others. In Italy there are 26,660,000 (Roman) Catholics, 96,000 Evangelical Christians, 100,000 Greeks, &c., 36,000 Jews, 25 Mahomedans, and others. In Spain there are 16,500,000 (Roman) Catholics, and 180,000 adherents of other denominations (details not given). In European Russia there are 56,100,000 'Orthodox' Greek Christians, &c.,

2,680,000 Evangelical Christians, 7,500,000 (Roman) Catholics, 2,700,000 Jews, and 2,600,000 Mahomedans and others. In Belgium there are 4,920,000 (Roman) Catholics, 13,000 Reformed Church, 2,000 Jews, and 3,000 belonging to other denominations. In the Netherlands there are 2,001,000 members of the Reformed Church, 1,235,000 (Roman) Catholics, 64,000 Jews, and 4,000 of other denominations. In Sweden and Norway there are 4,162,000 members of the Evangelical Church, 4,000 Greeks and other Christians, and 2,000 Jews; the number of (Roman) Catholics is not officially given—it is estimated at less than 1,000.

No. 19. CENSUS OF CATHOLICS IN THE WORLD.—The *Deutsche Reicheszeitung* estimates the number of Catholics in the world as follows :—Number of Catholics in France, 36,405,000; Austro-Hungary, 25,357,000; Italy, 27,942,000; Spain, 16,912,000; German Fatherland, 15,950,000 Russia (including Poland), 18,300,000; England, Ireland, Scotland, and Malta, 6,140,000; Belgium, 5,450,000; Portugal, 4,433,000; Holland, 1,652,000; Switzerland, 1,127,000; Turkey, 500,000; Roumania, 114,000; Montenegro, 25,000; Greece, 10,000; Eichtensein, 9,000; Monaco, 7,000; Servia, 4,000; Denmark, 2,000; and Norway, 1,000—total in Europe, 153,344,000.

Brazil, 10,000,800; Mexico, 9,389,460.

United States, 8,000,000; Columbia, 2,950,017; Peru, 2,699,945; Bolivia, 2,325,000; Chili, 2,116,718; Argentine, 1,812,490; Venezuela, 1,784,197; Guatemala, 1,190,754; Ecuador, 946,053; Hayti, 550,000; Uraguay, 440,000; Salvador, 434,520; Honduras (census of 1858), 357,700; Nicaragua, 300,000; Paraguay, 293,844; San Domingo, 250,000; Costa Rica, 185,000; British America, 2,100,000; Spanish West Indies, 2,080,652; French, 340,000; Dutch, 34,000; Danish, 26,000; total in America, 51,400,391.

Philippine Islands, 5,700,000; British India, 1,600,600; Portug, Timor, and Macao, 70,000; China, 423,887;

Cochin China and Tonkin, 510,581; Japan, 20,000; Corea, 20,000; Mongolia, 5,000; Mantchooria, 9,000; Thibet, 9,300; Siam, 11,150; Cambodia, 11,000; Burmah, 11,950; Malaya, 6,000; Dutch possessions, 31,324; Maronites, 530,000; United Jacobites, 35,000; Armenians in Syria and Asia Minor, 10,000; Chaldeans, 20,000; Melchites, 20,000; Levant (Latin rite), 60,000; Siberia and Caucasus, 52,000—total in Asia, 9,166,192.

Algeria, 270,000; Reunion, 150,000; Noyotte and Nossi-be, 20,000; Tetuan, 15,000; Canary Islands, 283,000; Fernando Po, 500; Madeira, 121,753; St. Thomas, 21,441; Cape Verde, 90,604; Continent, 500,000; Cape and Natal, 30,000; Mauritius, 90,000; Madagascar, 30,000; Tunis, 26,000; and Egypt, 35,000—total in Africa, 1,686,998.

New Holland, Tasmania, New Zealand, 590,000; Sandwich Islands; 25,000; Wallis, 4,000; Futuna, 1,000; Tonga, 2,000; Figi, 5,000; Samoan Islands, 5,000; on French territory, 20,000—total in Australia, 652,000. Grand total, 219,249,531.

CENSUS OF CATHOLICS AND PROTESTANTS IN EUROPE.

The *Evangelical Messenger* of April 1875 invites attention to what it calls the "ominous figures" in the statistics of religion in Europe.

Austria, in the year 1869.—Protestants, 3,509,013; Catholics, 23,964,233.
Belgium (1870).—Prot., 15,120; Cath., 5,069,105.
Denmark (1870).—Prot., 1,774,239; Cath., 1857.
France (1872).—Prot., 511,621; Cath., 35,497,235.
Germany (1871).—Prot., 25,581,709; Cath., 14,867,091.
Great Britain and Ireland.—Prot., 26,100,000; Cath., 5,520,000.
Greece (1870).—Prot., 6522; Cath., 6013.
Italy (1871).—Prot., 39,480; Cath., 26,624,600.
Netherlands (1869).—Prot., 2,193,281; Cath., 1,313,084.
Portugal.—Prot., 500; Cath., 3,994,600.
Russia in Europe (1867).—Prot., 2,565,345; Cath., 7,209,464.

Spain.—Prot., 20,000; Cath., 16,710,050.
Sweden and Norway (1871).—Prot., 5,903,587; Cath., 887.
Switzerland (1870).—Prot., 1,566,347; Cath., 1,084,369.
Turkey in Europe.—Prot., 25,000; Cath., 640,000.

No. 20.—"Sects Battling within One Church."

The following analysis abridged from the Anglican *Church Times* of February 1875 of the state of the parties in the Church of England is worthy of note. It is in itself a final comment on the assumption that Anglicanism can be Divine:—

The (Anglican) clergy are, in round numbers, about twenty-three thousand. Of these, fully one half belong to the High Church school in all its shades and degrees. Twelve of the bishops may be similarly classed.

The 'Evangelical' (or Low Church) clergy, on their own computation, are about five thousand, and have six bishops definitely on their side, besides two more on whose alliance they can usually count.

The 'Broad Church' clergy have, perhaps, a thousand members, with the Primate and four (or five) other bishops to support them.

The unclassifiable and colourless, inclusive of the mere Establishmentarians, mainly absorb the remaining five thousand, and can boast of the Archbishop of York and the remaining prelates as partaking their moral weight and influence.

If we put this statement of the *Church Times* into figures, it runs thus:—Anglican Bishops.—High Church, "all shades," 12;—Evangelicals, 6;—Broad Church, 5 and the primate;—Unclassified and colourless, 3 and "York"; total, 28.

Again, High Church, "all shades," Anglican Clergy, 12,000;—Evangelicals, 5,000;—Broad Church, 1,000;—Unclassified and colourless, 5,000;—total, 23,000.

No. 21.—List of One Hundred and Fifty-one Religious Denominations in England and Wales in 1878.

Extracted from a List of more than one hundred and sixty Religious Sects, having Registered Places of Worship in England and Wales, inserted in "Whitaker's Almanack" of 1879. This List is stated to have been certified by the Registrar-General, A.D. 1878.

Advent Christians.
Advents, The.
Apostolics.
Arminian New Society.
Baptists.
Baptized Believers.
Believers in Christ.
Believers in the Divine Visitation of Joanna Southcote, (prophetess) of Exeter.
Believers meeting in the name of our Lord Jesus Christ.
Bible Christians.
Bible Defence Association.
Brethren.
Calvinists and Welsh Calvins.
Calvinistic Baptists.
Cath. (not Roman) Apostolic Ch.
Chapels of other Wesleyans than those enumerated.
Christians owning no name but the Lord Jesus.
Christians who object to be otherwise designated.
Christian Believers.
Christian Brethren.
Christian Disciples.
Christian Eliasites.
Christian Israelites.
Christian Mission.
Christian Teetotalers.
Christian Temperance Men.
Christian Unionists.
Christadelphians.
Church of England.
Church of Scotland.
Church of Christ.
Church of the People.
Church of Progress.
Congregational Temperance Free Church.

Countess of Huntingdon's Congregations.
Covenanters.
Coventry Mission Band.
Disciples in Christ.
Disciples of Jesus Christ.
Eclectics.
Episcopalian Dissenters.
Evangelical Free Church.
Evangelical Mission.
Evangelical Unionists.
Followers of the Lord J. Christ.
Free Catholic Christian Church.
Free Christians.
Free Christian Association.
Free Church.
Free Church (Episcopal).
Free Church of England.
Free Evangelical Christians.
Free Grace Gospel Christians.
Free Gospel and Christian Brethren.
Free Gospel Church.
Free Gospellers.
Free Methodists.
Free Union Church.
General Baptist.
General Baptist New Connection.
German Evangelical Community.
German Lutheran.
Glassites.
Glory Band.
Greek (Schismatic).
Halifax Psychological Society.
Hallelujah Band.
Hope Mission.
Humanitarian.
Independents.
Independent Methodists.
Indep. Religious Reformers.
Independent Unionists.
Inghamites.

Latter-Day Saints.
Lutherans.
Methodist Reform Union.
Missionaries.
Modern Methodists.
Moravians, or United Brethren.
Mormons.
Newcastle Sailors' Society.
New Connection Wesleyans.
New Jerusalem Church. ..
New Church.
New Methodist.
Old Baptists.
Open Baptists.
Particular Baptists.
Peculiar People.
Plymouth Brethren.
Polish Society.
Presbyterian Church in England.
Presbyterian Church of England.
Presbyterian Baptists.
Primitive Congregation.
Primitive Free Church.
Primitive Methodists,
Progressionists.
Protestant Members of the Church of England.
Protestants adhering to Articles 1-18, but rejecting Ritual.
Protestant Trinitarians.
Protestant Union.
Providence.
Quakers (Society of Friends).
Ranters.
Reformers.
Reformed Church of England.
Reformed Episcopal Church.
Reformed Presbyterians or Covenanters.
Recreative Religionists.
Refuge Methodists.

Reform Free Ch. Wesl. Methd.
Reformed Presbyters.
Revivalists.
Revival Band.
Salem Society.
Sandemanians. = Glassites
Scotch Baptists.
Second Advent Brethren.
Secularists.
Separatists.
Seventh Day Baptists.
Society of the New Church.
Spiritual Church.
Spiritualists.
Strict Baptists.
Swedenborgians. 1688-1772.
Temperance Methodists.
Testimony Congregational Church.
Trinitarians.
Union Baptists.
Unionists.
Union Churchmen.
Union Congregationalists.
Unitarians.
Unitarian Baptists.
Unitarian Christians.
United Christian Church.
United Free Methodist Church.
United Presbyterians.
Universal Christians.
Unsectarian.
Welsh Calvinistic Methodists.
Welsh Free Presbyterians.
Welsh Wesleyan Methodists.
Wesleyans.
Wesleyan-Methodist Association.
Wesleyan Reformers.
Wesleyan Reform Glory Band.
Working Man's Evangelistic Mission Chapels.

No. 22.—RELIGIOUS STATISTICS IN IRELAND, EXTRACTED FROM "*The Tablet*," AUGUST 21, 1875.

"The Irish Census extended to religion, and the result is a list of nearly 150 forms of faith. Nine-tenths of the people range themselves in five classes: 4,150,867 Roman Catholics; 667,998 Protestant Episcopalians; 497,648, Presbyterians; 43,441 Methodists; 52,423 belong to 'other denominations.' Among them are 1,538 Covenanters; 2,600 Brethren and Christian Brethren, the majority of them women; 6 Exclusive Brethren, 3 of them women; 40 Non-Sectarians; 4 Orthodox; 5 Christadelphians; 5 Humanitarians; 44 Christian Israelites; 33 Mormons and 10 Latter-Day Saints, 17 of them women. A few call themselves followers of some man more or less known; there are registered 10 Darbyites, 9 Puseyites, 6 Walkerites, 5 Morisonians, and 1 Kellyite; 60 Free-Thinkers, 49 persons of 'no denomination,' 16 Deists, 6 Theists, 1 Atheist, 8 Secularists, 1 Materialist."

No. 23.—List of Protestant Denominations in the United States.

The total number of Protestants in the United States of America in the year 1868 was 6,396,110, divided between 51 sects, and in the proportion and rate of increase as here stated.*

	Church Members in 1867.	Average Annual Increase in 25 years.
1. Lutheran	332,155	7,182
2. German Reformed	110,408	3,431
3. United Brethren	97,983	1.319
4. Moravians	6,655	26
5. Dutch Reformed	57,846	1,261
6. Mennonites	59,110	380
7. Reformed Mennonites	11,000	200
8. Evangelical Association	58,002	1,791
9. Christian Connection	500,000	7,954
10. Church of God	32,000	960
11. Old School Presbyterians	246,350	6,958
12. New School Presbyterians	161,538	2,167
13. Reformed Presbyts. (Genl. Synod)	8,324	153
14. Synod of Reformed Presbyts.	6,000	—
15. Associate and United Presbyts.	63,489	1,000

* This list is taken from an article in No. 74, May, 1871, of the "Catholic World," a monthly magazine printed in New York, declaring it to have been taken entirely from Protestant sources, and chiefly from official documents published by the respective Denominations before the year 1868.

LIST OF PROTESTANT DENOMINATIONS. 303

		Church Members in 1867.	Average Annual Increase in 25 years.
16.	Associate Reformed Presbyts.	3,909	80
17.	Free Presbyterians	1,000	—
18.	Cumberland Presbyterians	100,000	1,819
19.	Baptists	1,094,806	13,796
20.	Free-Will Baptists	59,111	204
21.	Seventh-day Baptists	7,038	41
22.	Dunkers	20,000	500
23.	German Seventh-day Baptists	1,800	30
24.	Free Communion Baptists	104	—
25.	Anti-Mission Baptists	105,000	6,143
26.	Six-principle Baptists	3,000	—
27.	River Brethren	7,000	80
28.	Disciples (Campbellites)	300,000	4,762
29.	Congregationalists	278,362	4,734
30.	Unitarians	30,000	300
31.	Universalists	80,000	1,000
32.	Protestant Episcopal	194,692	6,536
33.	Methodist Episcopal	1,146,081	30,377
34.	Methodist Protestant	50,000	—
35.	Methodist Church	50,000	2,000
36.	True Wesleyan	25,000	200
37.	African Methodist	200,000	7,500
38.	Zion African Methodist	60,000	2,008
39.	Methodist Epis. (South)	535,040	4,087
40.	Free Methodist	4,889	617
41.	Western Primitive Methodist	2,000	40
42.	Independent Methodist	800	—
43.	Friends, or Quakers	100,000	1,000
44.	Hicksites	40,000	400
45.	Shakers	4,713	60
46.	Adventists, or Second Adventists	30,000	1,500
47.	Swedenborgians	5,000	186
48.	Spiritualism	165,000	8,000
49.	Mormon Church	60,000	2,000
50.	Christian Perfectionists	255	10
51.	Catholic Apostolic Ch. (not Roman)	250	10
	Total,	6,396,110	134,802

The following statistics, extracted from the "Weekly Register," London, August 28, 1875, will show the numerical strength of some of the Religious Bodies in America for the year 1874:—

"The Protestant Episcopalians have 3040 ministers, 2750 parishes, and 273,555 communicants. The Roman Catholic Church has 4873 priests, 4731 churches, 1902 chapels and stations, and 8,761,242 Catholic population. It has now one Cardinal, His Eminence John MacClosky, Archbishop of New York. The Baptists have 943 associations, 21,510 churches, 13,354 appointed ministers, and 1,761,171 members. The United Brethren have 2950 churches, 1886 ministers, and 131,895 members. The Universalists have 624 churches, 674 ministers, and 300,391 members. The returns of the Annual Conference of the Methodist Episcopalians in the United States show that there are now in that Body, 10,854 travelling preachers, 1581 local preachers, 18,628 Sunday Schools, with 200,484 teachers, and 1,363,876 scholars. The number of members is 1,563,522."

No. 24. DAWN OF A REMARKABLE CONVERSION IN ROME.

The following truthful account of the dawn of a remarkable conversion of modern time, is taken from the "*Unità Cattolica*," an excellent Catholic journal of Turin, of August 10, 1875.

Many a time have we adverted to the conversion of His Eminence Cardinal Manning. How did it come to pass? Not long ago His Eminence himself told it thus, in private conversation:—

I was in Rome; I visited the museums, the ruins, the churches; I witnessed the ceremonies like the rest of my fellow-countrymen, making a study of the city from every point of view. I had no doubt at all about the truth of Protestantism, of which I was a minister; I had no thought, I never even dreamt of changing my religious belief. Upon this subject, nothing of all that I had seen made any impression to affect me; in fact, I was as far from Catholicism as when I left England.

One morning I went into the French Church of Saint Louis (S. Luígi dei Francési); there, on the Altar, was exposed the Most Blessed Sacrament, for the purpose of giving Benediction, a service I had never seen before.

Nothing more simple. Some incense and some candles burning; the priests in their plain choir-dress. At the foot of the Altar knelt a handful of the faithful in prayer. What a contrast between this and those solemn Pontifical functions in Saint Peter's; but it was the moment in which God called me to Himself.

I felt my soul stirred within me in a mysterious way. I saw a little gleam of light. For the first time in my life it came into my mind that there might be truth in Catholicism; my conversion no longer seemed to me an impossibility. I found myself, however, a long way from being made a convert; but God had called me, and I did not remain deaf to His voice. I prayed, I searched, I studied with all sincerity; every day the light shone clearer, and the grace of God did the rest.

No. 25.—The Conversion of Mr. Alfred Newdigate, M.A., 1875.

The Rev. Alfred Newdigate, late Vicar of Kirkhallam, Derbyshire, who lately joined the Church, has addressed a farewell letter to his late parishioners and friends, stating at some length the reasons which induced him to leave the Church of England.

He refers to several passages and incidents of Scripture which, as he says, "suffice to show how thoroughly scriptural the Roman Catholic doctrine appears when candidly examined; and how inconsistent is every other system with the plain sense of the Bible.

"This conviction," he continues, "was confirmed in me by history, which taught that from the earliest ages of Christianity the Bishop of Rome has been recognised as its earthly head, and union with the Church of Rome and agreement with its doctrines as a test of orthodoxy.

"All our old churches and ruined abbeys at Dale and elsewhere attest the fact that they who built them and our English forefathers for a thousand years were united in this one religion: and thus they continued until the notoriously wicked King Henry VIII., quarrelling with the Pope, usurped the headship of the Church, which we believe to have been committed by Christ to St. Peter and his successors.

"In this Henry followed the example of '*Jeroboam, the son of Nebat, who made Israel to sin.*' Hence that great rending of the State religion of England from the rest of Christendom, which has been so fruitful a source of schisms and such a hindrance to missionary success, by enabling the heathen to point to our divisions as an argument against the truth of Christianity, whereas it was the exhibition of Catholic unity that Christ appointed to be the means of persuading the world to believe in Christianity itself, when he prayed, '*that they all may be one, that the world may believe that Thou hast sent Me*'."

No. 26.—AN ANGLICAN SECESSION TO ROME.

Mr. Gordon Thompson, M.A., Anglican Curate of Christ Church, Albany Street, has given the following explanation to the Bishop of London of his reasons for resigning the Curacy and joining the Catholic Church:—

"March 18, 1875.

"My Lord,

"It is my duty, though owing to your great kindness a duty I shrink from, to inform you that I have resigned the Curacy of Christ Church, Albany Street. The reasons that compel me to take this step are chiefly the three following:—

"1. Upon more mature reflection I can in no way satisfy either my conscience or my reason that the Anglican Church is one and the same with that which our

Lord built upon St. Peter, with the promise that nothing should prevail against it.

"2. In the Nicene Creed the following words are to be found: 'I believe *one* Catholic and Apostolic Church.' I cannot therefore any longer act as though there were two or six. There may be many sects; but the Church, that is, our Lord's Body, can be but one.

"3. That, under the existing relations between the Anglican Church and the State, I believe it to be impossible for her to be faithful to primitive doctrine, even if she were not guilty of schism. Under these circumstances I have sought reception into the Catholic Church.

"My residence abroad for two years as a Consular Chaplain enabled me to view the English Church at a distance and in comparison with the Catholic Church. I became gradually convinced that the spirit of comprehension which animated the Reformers resulted in a compromise of the great truths of Christianity. The way, moreover, in which the Anglican Church has accepted the recent judgments and legislative acts convinces me the more strongly that her watchwords are 'Establishment and Expediency.'

"I have only to thank your Lordship for the great kindness I have ever received from you from my first introduction until now; but I know that it is impossible to soften the judgment of others in a step of this character, and that no course is open to your Lordship but to condemn it. I have the honour to be your Lordship's humble servant,

"GORDON THOMPSON."

No. 27.—MR. SHIPLEY'S CONVERSION THROUGH NOTICING THE NECESSITY OF BELIEVING ON THE GROUND OF AUTHORITY.

Mr. Orby Shipley has written to the *Times* of November, 1878, the following letter. (The italics are not in the original):—

"SIR,—Two years and a half ago you allowed me to state that the report which had appeared in your columns—viz., that I had submitted to the Catholic Church was incorrect.

"Will you now permit me to say that the report which has lately appeared in some of your contemporaries is true? After much thought and consideration I have felt it my duty to leave the Church of England, and I ask you to allow me to occupy a small space in your paper in order to give some reasons for this momentous change in my religious life. I cannot otherwise reach many with whom I formerly worked, or to whom I once ministered, and I shall be grateful, sir, for this exercise of your kind liberality.

"The cause of my taking this important step was, so far as I can perceive, a simple following of Catholic instinct to its legitimate, and, in my case, logical conclusion—of course at the call of God. It certainly was not due to personal influence; for though I have never willingly lost a friend, yet, practically, I have not been enabled to remain on intimate terms with any who have preceded me whither eventually I have been led. Nor has it been caused by controversy, which I have studiously avoided. Nor has it been, save indirectly, from any outward reason.

"The result has arisen mainly from a silent, gradual, and steady inner growth of many years in religion. I have long held, I have long taught, nearly every Catholic doctrine not actually denied by the Anglican formularies, and have accepted and helped to revive nearly every Catholic practice not positively forbidden. In short, intellectually and in externals, so far as I could as a loyal English clergyman, I have believed and acted as a Catholic.

All this I have held and done, as I now perceive, *on a wrong principle*—viz., *on private judgment*. When I became convinced that the *right principle of faith and practice in religion was authority;* when I saw clearly that it is of less moment what one believes and does than *why* one accepts and practises, then I had no choice as to my course. The only spiritual body which I could realize that actually claimed to teach truth upon authority, and that visibly exercised the authority which she claimed, was the Church of Rome. For the last time I exercised my private judgment, as every person must exercise that gift of God in some way and to some extent, and I humbly sought admission into the communion of the Catholic Church.

"I venture to ask you, Sir, to publish this simple statement, not because it contains anything which is new, but because I have reason to know that there are a large number of persons of High Church principles in the Church of England who still occupy a similar position to the one which I lately occupied. There are many, both clergy and laity, who believe what I believed, and who act as I acted, but who do not yet feel able, or feel called, to make the momentous change which I have had power given me to make. And these I know to be thoroughly honest, as I was; to be absolutely convinced of their position, as I was: to be determined never to leave it, as I was—until God's grace calls them as it called me.

"I do not expect that those I worked with and ministered to will renounce the obedience of a lifetime at the same moment, in the like manner or on similar grounds, as myself. On the contrary, they will think me, at the first, inconsistent, changeful, weak, and wrong. But I have not made my great change in youth, nor precipitately, nor in any particular crisis or panic, nor without due and anxious deliberation. I have never vacillated in my loyalty till I could be loyal no longer. I have never had anything to unlearn, but rather have ever advanced in Divine knowledge. I gave myself to be led not whither I would, but where I was constrained to go. And at last, and after a painful period of conflict, I have gone from whence God had placed me to whither He has been pleased to lead me.

"That some, that many of my old friends—as I wish still to be allowed to call them—eventually will be led to accept all truth *upon the true principle*, I do not doubt. It is inevitable if only they will persevere in using the grace which they possess, and in following the light with which they are blessed. None can know better than myself what leads men onwards—what keeps men in their position from being led to mine. There are numberless souls in the Church of England, both men and women, who have only to accept the true principle for all that they already believe rightly, and rightly practice —on a false principle—in order to be guided, as I was guided, into all truth. They have only to exchange— though the change indeed is great, and is not made without cost—the *principle of private judgment* for the *revealed basis of faith, which is authority.*"

No. 28.—CONVERTS TO CATHOLICITY NOT UNHAPPY.

Two Letters written to the Author of the Book entitled "Recollections of Cardinal Wiseman."

"St. Mary's, Bayswater,
"My Dear Sir, "April 16, 1859.

"I am much obliged by your telling me of my expected return to Protestantism. It is not the first time I have heard of it, and I always hear of it with a kind of consolation, for nobody would take so much trouble about so unimportant a person, if in some way I were not bearing witness to the truth ; and also it gives me the joy of saying, that from the hour that I submitted to the Divine voice, which speaks through the one only Catholic and Roman Church, I have never known so much as a momentary shadow of doubt pass over my reason or my conscience. I could as soon believe that two and two make five as that the Catholic Faith is false or Anglicanism true. I enclose a little paper which may explain what I have not time to write.

"If the clergyman who made this statement will be so kind as to communicate to me the grounds on which he made it, I shall be happy to see him. I cannot suppose that he said so grave a thing lightly, as it would be a serious act.

"Believe me, with sincere hope and prayer that all

dear to you may be brought into this only way of life; always your faithfully,

"HENRY EDWARD MANNING."

"The Oratory, Birmingham,
"My Dear Sir, "April 18, 1859.

"I suppose Dr. Manning's account of the matter is the right one. It irritates the judgment, feelings, and imagination of Protestants to know that religious men have deliberately, and at a great sacrifice, acted on the conviction that Protestantism is not a safe religion to live in or to die in. It is a great difficulty in their way, and the fact of this deliberate sacrifice on the part of men now alive is urged against them by others, and unsettles those whom they wish to keep contented in Protestantism. The consequence is that they are always hoping that Dr. Manning and I may come back; and from wishing and hoping they proceed to mention that it is likely; and those who hear them say that it is likely, misinterpret them on account of their own similar hopes and wishes, and say that it is to be expected; and then the next hearer says that it is a fact which is soon to be, for he has heard of the expectation on the best authority; and then the next hearer says that he has the first authority for saying that Dr. Manning or Dr. Newman is coming back in the course of the next few months. And then, lastly, some one perhaps puts into the newspapers that he knows a person who was told by Dr. Newman himself that he had discovered the unreality or hollowness of Romanism, and meant to return in the course of April, May, or June, to the bosom of the Establishment. Thus can I account for the most absurd and utterly unfounded reports which, ever since I have been a Catholic, have been spread abroad about the prospect of my return from the Mother of Saints to the city of confusion.

"Very faithfully yours,
"JOHN HENRY NEWMAN.*

"You may make what use you will of this letter."

* See "Annals of the Tractarian Movement from 1842 to 1867," by Kirwan Brown, Esq., Washbourne. 2s. 6d.

After giving these two letters, the author of the book just mentioned adds:

"I sent these letters to the clergyman, and they were returned, accompanied by a polite note of thanks for allowing them to be read, in which note, however, was the following sentence:—'I am sorry for these gentlemen's own sakes that the reports have not proved to be correct.' Not long since, however, thanks be to God, this Protestant clergyman has himself submitted to the Catholic Church."

No. 29.—LETTER FROM THE VERY REV. DR. (NOW HIS EM. CARDINAL) NEWMAN, RESPECTING A REMARK OF THE RIGHT HON. W. E. GLADSTONE.

Dr. Newman has appended a postscript to the fourth edition of his "Letter to the Duke of Norfolk," issued in April, 1875, on Mr. Gladstone's pamphlet entitled "Vaticanism". In answer to a remark by Mr Gladstone, Dr Newman writes: "From the day I became a Catholic to this day, now close upon thirty years, I have never had a moment's misgiving that the Communion of Rome is that Church which the Apostles set up at Pentecost, which alone has 'the adoption of sons, and the glory, and the covenants, and the revealed law, and the service of God, and the promises,' and in which the Anglican Communion, whatever its merits and demerits, whatever the great excellence of individuals in it, has, as such, no part. Nor have I ever for a moment hesitated in my conviction, since 1845, that it was my clear duty to join that Catholic Church, as I did then join it, which in my own conscience I felt to be Divine.

Persons and places, incidents and circumstances of life which belong to my first forty-four years, are deeply lodged in my memory and my affections; moreover, I have had more to try and afflict me in various ways as a Catholic than as an Anglican; but never for a moment have I wished myself back; never have I ceased to thank my Maker for His mercy in enabling me to make the great change, and never has He let me feel forsaken by Him, or in distress, or any kind of religious trouble."

No. 30.—CONVERTS WITHIN THE LAST THIRTY YEARS.

I should have been glad, had it been possible, to insert a list of the principal English converts received of late years into the Catholic Church, but I find that, were I to do justice to the undertaking, it would fill many pages. Therefore I shall content myself with stating that I have before me a list of English converts within the last thirty years, kindly lent to me by the respected late Major Chisholm, the sum of which is as follows:—

Clerical gentlemen, 355; gentlemen, including 64 of the aristocracy, 523; ladies, including 90 ladies of title, 428. The number of converts from the humbler classes are much more numerous.*

In a recent Protestant publication, entitled "*Rome's Recruits*," about 3000 names are given of distinguished converts to the Catholic Church in England within the last fifty years, including 450 of the Anglican Clergy (from Oxford 290, from Cambridge 160), and 340 of Peers, Peeresses, and members of titled families. And in a Catholic work, entitled "*The Roll of Honour*" (Burns and Oates, 1879, price 2s. 6d.), appear classified alphabetical lists of about the same number of recent converts to the Church, besides many interesting letters of Catholic converts.

No. 31.—ENGLAND NEVER REJECTED OF HER OWN ACCORD THE CATHOLIC FAITH.

His Eminence Cardinal Manning, preaching in the Church of St. Augustine, Manchester, as reported by the *Weekly Register* of September 11, 1875, said:—

* Since the year 1875, when this calculation was made, the number of converts in each class has largely increased.

"The English people are a baptized people—a Christian people; they love the Christian name. I believe they would give up their lives if brought to the test (for God would give them grace to do so), rather than forsake their Christianity. What may not, therefore, come hereafter?

Most assuredly there is a jealousy for the Word of God among us. Men love their Bible. They give an immensity every year to print and scatter the written Word of God throughout the nations of the world. They believe the Word of God to be the Bible, and the Bible to be the Word of God. They believe it to be inspired, and in this they do right. But the Word of God is wider than that which was written. There was a living Word of God filling the world, of which the written Word of God is only part. Nevertheless, Englishmen are jealous of that written Word of God, and honour it.

Nay, more, they are jealous for the Spirit of God. They believe in God the Holy Ghost. They do not believe that God is to be worshipped by formulated, empty ceremonies; they feel that mere postures and forms of prayer, unless they come from the heart, are unmeaning things. They would say of them, as was said of Jerusalem: "*I hate your sacrifices and your feasts*," if they did not spring from a spirit of faith. The English people have a keen sense of this—they feel that they must worship God in spirit and in truth. So it was; and if they understood the Holy Mass as a Catholic child understood it, they would see through the transparent ritual, and see that it was the worship of Almighty God in spirit and in truth.

Their jealousy of the Spirit of God made them jealous also of the liberty of conscience. They said—"My soul is my own; I must answer for it. God made it, and Jesus redeemed it; and I must answer to the Spirit of God for the fidelity of my conscience." There was, indeed, a Divine liberty into which we were redeemed by the Precious Blood of Jesus Christ. Where the Spirit of the Lord is, there is liberty. This was true; and in this Englishmen were right.

And they were right, lastly, in one more point, in which his whole soul went with them, and the soul of every Catholic on the face of the earth. They refuse to be bound by *human* teachers. They refuse to be taught by human authority what they must believe, and what they must do to be saved.

Nay, more, they are jealous of human teachers. They have an instinct that no man has a right to get up and say: "I am your teacher; I am right and you are wrong." They say: "We are all on the same level; every man has his own opinion, and no man has a right to say to us, 'We are your teachers.'" And why? Because they believe that all men are but human, and they feel that there is something in their very faith itself binding them to reject all human teaching, and leading them to place their reliance upon a *Divine* teacher who cannot err. "*If the blind lead the blind, shall not both fall into the ditch?*"

They said, justly: "Who are you? How can you call upon me to believe what you say or do what you command? Produce your authority." This was what a Catholic child would say. They knew of no other who could bind their conscience but one, who could say: "*It seemed good to the Holy Ghost and to us.*" They submit to no teacher who has not a *Divine* warrant. He hoped he had given evidence to show that the authority of the Catholic Church was an authority guided by Divine assistance. . . . The Church of God had in it the Spirit of Truth inseparably united with it, and dwelling there perpetually; and when they submitted themselves to its teaching and to its decrees, they did so because it was not a human authority, but a Divine one. Let them pray the Holy Spirit to lead them, and let them remember that the test of the guidance of the Spirit of Truth was this, that it taught them that which it taught throughout the whole world. God's Spirit taught the same thing in every place; and the man who believed that the Spirit of God had led him to any doctrine which was not taught by the Universal Church, fell into error. The words of St. John to those who believed in the doctrine of the

Apostles, who said: "*It seemed good to the Holy Ghost and to us,*" were: "*You have the unction from the Holy One, and know all things. You need not that any man teach you; but as His unction teacheth you of all things, and is truth, and is no lie. And as it hath taught you, abide in him.*" (1 S. John ii. 20, 27.)

England was once an evidence of the luminous universality of the Kingdom of JESUS CHRIST; but England is not so any longer. There was a time when there was but one faith over the whole face of this land. There was a time when in every church the holy sacrifice was offered, when there was the same priesthood everywhere, the same ritual, the same worship. There was a time when every man and every little child not only repeated the same symbol of faith, but knew and understood it, every letter, to possess exactly the same meaning. There were no divisions, no desolations then. Divided in all other things, at least they were united in those things which are divine. There was the divine unity of the Body of *Jesus Christ*, and the Spirit and the Word of Christ, in the midst of all the rudeness and the roughness of early civilisation and conflicting temporal interests. Alas! dear brethren, is it so now? The English people have a consciousness that England is not now what it once was, and desire to restore unity among themselves, and to reunite their country to that great Christian world, from which it has so long been parted.

And how was it thus parted? Not through your sins, brethren. If any are listening to me this morning who are not of our flock, I say boldly that the English people never rejected the Catholic faith. A thousand times I have said it, for in my soul I believe it, that Englishmen never rejected the Catholic faith—they were robbed of it. They were robbed of it by force. They rose up to defend it in arms, but they were beaten down. They were beaten down by foreign persons, and their children were born disinherited. But generation after generation was removed further and further from that great offence. The present generation had no part in the great religious uproar and confusion of the sixteenth century. They reject, it may be, that which is put before them as the Catholic faith. But what is it that had been put before them? A gospel which had not the true lineaments of the Catholic faith had been put before them by Protestant controversialists and historians. Let them reject that as much as they would, *for they were not rejecting the truth of God in rejecting a monstrous and miscalled representation.* I hold that multitudes in this land are innocent of any participation in the religious divisions and the heresies which have rent the veil asunder, and if they knew how they could be healed they would make any sacrifices to heal them.

The English people of this time have been born into the midst of religious contention and division, uncertainty and doubt; and so far as the present state of things is concerned, they are not responsible for its creation, but they may be for its continuance. They who 300 years ago were cast out of the unity of the truth, even they did not reject the Catholic faith, except in the case of individuals — a Sovereign, a Court, hungry men, who desired the land and gold of the Church of God, false teachers, high-minded men, inflated with false science, and puffed up with a notion that they were destined to be the teachers of mankind. Men of this sort broke down the unity of the faith, but the people of England did not do it; on the contrary, they rose up to try and preserve their faith, even at the peril of their lives, but they were trampled down.

But once more the light of God's countenance has been lifted up on His Church, and I feel confident that the jangling contentions which have been distracting the minds of Englishmen will die out, and that when they feel that no merely human teachers can guide them into the way of salvation, they will ask themselves, "Are we then left without a teacher? Are the promises of God come to nought? His promise: '*I will send you another Paraclete, who shall abide with you for ever*'—is not that for us? '*Even the Spirit of Truth; He shall lead you into all truth,*'—shall I never hear a voice saying: '*This is the way, walk ye in it?*' As God is true, His promises shall not fail. There is a *Divine teacher* somewhere, and that teacher I will find ; and having found Him, I will be His disciple, I will believe what He teaches me, and I will follow that which He commands me. Never has the world been left without the presence of a Divine teacher from the hour that the Son of God came into it, and I know it never will be left until He comes again with glory."

His Eminence concluded with the prayer that God, in His infinite mercy, would pour out the light of faith, of charity, and of unity upon the whole of this people and land, that religious contentions might cease, and that the full brightness of His truth might be revealed.

No. 32.—THE POSITION OF THE CATHOLIC CHURCH IN ENGLAND.

In October, 1875, His Eminence the Cardinal Archbishop was presented with an address by the Catholic Association of Bolton, in Yorkshire, congratulating him on his elevation to the Cardinalate.

In reply, His Eminence, as reported by the *Catholic Times*, said :—" I believe that the people of England at this moment have ceased to regard the Catholic Church as an antagonist, or enemy, or invader, or conspirator. I believe that Ultramontane conspiracies they class with nursery fables. We have had the 'Arabian Nights,' a thousand and one, and I have no doubt we shall have many more ; but I hope my friends who have indulged in them will pardon me if I go to sleep. I cannot but believe that the English people of all classes are coming to be persuaded that the mission of the Catholic Church in England is one of faith, one of piety, one of charity, one of well-doing, and one of peace ; that we are men of peace, and makers of peace. There is one thing I will add—Englishmen profess that a fair field and no favour is all they desire for themselves—and that is all I ask. I ask for no Act of Parliament to restore the Catholic religion; I won't even ask for an Order in Council; no, nor for a Minute of the Privy Council to be laid on the table of the House of Commons. I won't invoke either the influence of the great unpaid in the country districts. I ask nothing in this world to help me in preaching the Catholic faith. Fair play, then, and no favour; and if the Catholic Church expands in England by its own native force, if, by the power of intellectual conviction, and the power of charitable persuasion, and the grace of Almighty God, it shall spread its supernatural unity, and gather into one fold the multitude which have the true mark—for they have been baptized—I hope they will lay aside all animosity against the poor pastors who, labouring in poverty, have achieved that success."

No. 33.—CARDINAL MANNING ON TOTAL ABSTINENCE. *Extract from the Introductory Letter by His Eminence Cardinal Manning to Father Bridgett's interesting book entitled* "*The Discipline of Drink*". (Burns & Oates. 1876. 3s. 6d.)

"When I see around me every day the wreck of men, women, and children, from the highest to the lowest class, the utter desolation of homes once happy and innocent, the destruction of the domestic life of the millions of our great working class, upon whom the whole fabric of our commonwealth must rest, I feel that temperance and total abstinence ought to be familiar thoughts in the mind even of those who have never in all their life been tempted to excess. If they would all conscientiously unite by example, by word, and by influence to save those who are perishing in the dangers from which they themselves are happily safe, many a soul and many a home now fearfully wrecked, would, I believe, be saved.

"When St. Paul told the Christians in Rome that it '*is good not to eat flesh, and not to drink wine, nor anything whereby thy brother is offended, or scandalised, or made weak*' (Romans xiv. 21), he certainly did not intend to limit the wide reach of this principle of Christian charity to meats offered to idols. . . . If any self-denial on our part, in things that are lawful and to us altogether safe, shall help, or encourage, or support, or give even a shadow of strength, to those to whom such lawful things are not only dangerous but often deadly, then assuredly the love of souls will prompt us to place ourselves at their side, and, in sharing their acts of self-denial, to give them a hand and a heart of sympathy.

"Now I say this not as a precept, but as a counsel. If it be good, as St. Paul says it is, freely to forego lawful things for the sake of others, it is certainly good for us, of our own free will, to offer any little mortification we can in reparation, and expiation, and intercession for others. It is on this ground, as it seems to me, that total abstinence may be affirmed to be a wise and charitable use of our Christian liberty.

"And if, by laying on ourselves so slight a privation, we can in any way help those who are perishing, and those who are tempted, I do not think we shall ever have cause to regret that we freely chose that slight self-denial.

"I thank you for your excellent book, and trust that it may powerfully help the work of saving souls from the pestilence of drink.

"Believe me always, my dear Father Bridgett, yours affectionately in Jesus Christ,

"HENRY EDWARD,
"*Cardinal Archbishop of Westminster.*"

FIVE GOOD REASONS FOR TOTAL ABSTINENCE.*

The late Dr. Guthrie of Edinburgh, said: "I have four good reasons for being an abstainer—My head is clearer, my health is better, my heart is lighter, and my purse is heavier." And we would add, "My ear is readier at the cry of the poor." "*Now we that are stronger ought to bear the infirmities of the weak, and not to please ourselves.*" (Romans xv. i.)

* See Temperance Lesson Book. Tweedie & Co. 1s. 6d.

No. 34.—The Truth about Cusa, Copérnicus, Galileo, and Kepler.[*]

The astronomical system which had prevailed in the world down to the seventeenth century is what is called the *geocentric* or *Ptolemaic* system, by which it was supposed that the earth was motionless, and that the sun went daily round it, causing the days and the nights; and that the sun in the course of twelve months moved gradually forward and backward outside the equatorial zone in such a way as to cause the different seasons.

This was the system received by the Arabians, the Chinese, the Persians, and the Europeans. "For," says an eminent French philosopher, "all the researches which have been prosecuted with the most scrupulous exactness have failed to bring to light any other astronomy than that of Ptolemy." In accordance with this theory, which is so strongly and constantly suggested by our senses, is of course the language of Revelation addressed to man.

Such being the state of Astronomy from the remotest antiquity, to have departed from a system rendered so venerable by age, required an intellect of the boldest originality. With such an intellect was gifted a priest of humble origin, Nicholas Cusa, son of a fisherman.

This celebrated man was born in a small hamlet called Cusa on the banks of the Moselle. Having studied in the most famous Universities of Germany and in Italy, he became Archdeacon of Liège, and in that capacity he assisted at the Council of Basil in 1431. He had previously written several works, and among them was a treatise on Astronomy, in which, well-nigh two centuries before Galileo, he boldly laid it down as his conviction that the earth and not the sun is in motion, and that the true system of Astronomy should be called not *geocentric*, but *heliocentric*. This opinion he maintained side by side with his friend

---

[*] What is said here about Cusa, Copernicus, and Galileo, is for the most part taken from a lecture recently delivered before the Catholic Union of Dublin by Canon Murphy, an abridgement of which appeared in the *Weekly Register*, Feb. 1, 1879.

Cardinal Cesarini before the assembled Fathers of the Council. What was the consequence? Was he summoned to Rome to answer for his bold speculations? Yes, he was summoned before the reigning Pontiff, Nicholas V., but it was to receive the highest dignity the Pope could confer on him: to receive the Cardinal's hat, and with it the Bishopric of Brixen in the Tyrol.

But the glory of Cusa is cast into the shade by the transcendant lustre of the immortal COPERNICUS. This great man left early his native town of Thorn, òn the banks of the Vistula, and journeyed to Rome under the conviction that in no other place on earth could he display his talents more advantageously. Nor did he err. Already in the year 1500, he is professor in the Pope's University, and is engaged in giving lectures on his new astronomical theory to more than 2,000 pupils.

During his long sojourn in Rome, Copernicus enjoyed the friendship and confidence of the highest dignitaries of the Church, and when he was about to return to Germany, a pension for life was given him. Nor did the liberality of his ecclesiastical friends stop here. When afterwards he was unable, out of his slender income as Canon of Frouenburgh, to give to the world the great work on which he had devoted the labour of his life, Cardinal Schomberg, with princely munificence, came forward and undertook the entire expense of the publication. No wonder, then, when the great work appeared it should have on its title page a tender and grateful dedication to the reigning Pontiff, Paul III.

If the Roman authorities have showed themselves so favourable to the cultivation of science in the instances of Cusa and Copernicus, how is it that the fate of GALILEO was so different?

It may be said that all the troubles which befell Galileo arose from his wilful and obstinate departure from the prudent course which had been pursued both by Cusa and Copernicus.

Neither of these philosophers had ever claimed for his scientific opinion more than the arguments advanced to support it warranted him to claim—that is to say, a strong and very strong *probability* in its favour.

Again, Cusa and Copernicus had kept the question of Religion altogether aloof from their philosophical speculations. Now, these are precisely the two points on which Galileo committed his capital errors.

The discoveries which Galileo had made by the use of the telescope, especially the discovery that the planet Venus has changing phases, so convinced him of the truth of the Copernican system that he not only asserted it as a *demonstrated fact*, but *treated with scornful disdain all who called it into question*.

Now, was Galileo justified in doing so? Had he really proved the truth of his scientific views? All modern philosophers affirm that he had done no such thing. The celebrated Delambre, who, under the direction of the French Constituent Assembly, measured the arc of the meridian between Dunkerque and Barcelona, says that till the velocity of light was ascertained by Reaumur, and the aberration of light was calculated by Bradly, and till the laws of gravitation were established by Newton, all the Copernicans were reduced to mere probabilities. Hence we are told by Lord Macaulay that the Founder in England of the inductive school of philosophy, Lord Bacon, rejected the theory of Galileo with scorn; and so did Descartes. No wonder, then, that when he went to Rome for the first time to defend himself from his assailants, though gardens and palaces were thrown open to him, and the highest dignitaries lavished on him every mark of respect; though a commission of the ablest astronomers in Rome, appointed by Cardinal Bellarmine, declared that the discoveries made by Galileo were undeniable, yet did not regard his proofs as demonstrative of the truth of the Copernican system. Thus, after obtaining the blessing of Paul V. and bidding farewell to troops of friends, the philosopher returned to Florence.

The second capital error committed by Galileo was to pretend to prove his theory from Holy Scripture, asserting that portions of the Scripture could not be satisfactorily explained unless his theory was admitted. A denunciation was drawn up against him; he was formally accused of interpreting the Scriptures in a sense at variance with the teaching of the Fathers. This denunciation was quashed in the very first stage of the proceedings, in hopes that Galileo would desist from his imprudent attempts. But, on the contrary, he became more and more persisting. Letter after letter came to him from his numerous friends in Rome entreating him not to interfere with the Scriptures, and to confine himself to scientific argumentation. Monsignor Ciampoli wrote, "I have been emphatically assured by Cardinal Barberini (afterwards Pope Urban VIII.) that you will be put to no trouble provided you do not travel out of the limits of physics and mathematics."

But Galileo would not be content either to hold his opinion as a philosophical probability, or to uphold it on merely scientific grounds. He would have it acknowledged as an unquestionable truth, and would have it declared by the Inquisition as conformable to Scripture. For this purpose he set out for Rome a second time, and was again well and warmly received. With great ability and vehemence he defended on every occasion the Copernican system; but his keen satire and sarcasm excited and inflamed many opponents. The Tuscan ambassador writing to his Court, says of him, "He is so heated that he seems not to know how to govern himself." At a most inopportune moment, Galileo forced the Pope to send his affair before the Inquisition. In a few days a Papal Decree, founded on a decision of the Inquisition, was issued compelling him to promise that he would no more teach that the earth moved around the sun, as such opinion appeared contrary to Scripture. To this Decree he humbly submitted, returned to the fair city on the banks of the Arno, in his pleasing villa called Segni, situated in the lovely suburbs of Bellosguardo.

Seven years after, that is in 1632, Galileo was cited before the Inquisition for having broken his promise and taught in a printed sarcastic dialogue the forbidden system. After a trial of ten months, Galileo was condemned in

June, 1633, and was forbidden two different times. During these ten months, with the exception perhaps of three days (others say one night, when for his own convenience he slept near the Court), he resided in the palace of the Tuscan Ambassador. He was compelled to abjure as false the teaching that the earth was in motion, as it appeared against the express words of Scripture. He was, moreover, sentenced to remain a prisoner at the good will of the Court, and to recite the seven Penitential Psalms once a week for three years. To this sentence Galileo submissively bowed; and without ever uttering "*eppur si muove*" *still it (the earth) moves*, words constantly attributed to him, he left the presence of his judges.

It was at the pleasing villa of Ascetri, about a mile from Florence, that Galileo was located, at a short distance from the church of St. Matthew, where his two daughters were cloistered nuns. To this convent the father used often to go in order to enjoy their sweet conversation, and to be comforted by the many proofs of tender affection which his children gave him. Thus the theory of the rotation of the earth, which Cusa and Copernicus had been by Roman Catholic dignitaries allowed and encouraged to teach, and even rewarded for teaching, Galileo was forbidden to teach on account of his pretension of teaching it, not as a mere theory, but as a demonstrated truth, and moreover as a truth proved from Scripture.

To us who live in times when the system of Copernicus is no more regarded as a theory but as a demonstrated truth, it seems very easy to reconcile it with Holy Scripture by saying that Scripture never intended to teach any astronomical system, but that it spoke of the earth, sun, moon, and stars as they appear to the human eye (as all men, including astronomers, still commonly speak of sun-rise and sun-set), accommodating herself to the popular way of speaking; but it was not an easy thing when the Copernican system was only a theory supported by mere probabilities.

No wonder then that Protestants of that age fell into

the same sad mistake of denouncing as warmly as Catholics the rotary system of the earth as clashing with Holy Scripture.

As a proof of this I here subjoin a part of a correspondence written in the year 1853, about KEPLER, to the Editor of the London *Catholic Standard*.

DEAR SIR. On perusing in a German newspaper a few days ago, a very full report of an eloquent discourse delivered at Leeds by the Cardinal Archbishop of Westminster (Wiseman) on the encouragement given to science by the Catholic Church, it occurred to me, *apropos* of Galileo and the Roman Inquisition, that we Catholics would do well to bring more prominently forward than we are accustomed to do, another contemporaneous event of a similar kind—one which entitles us to reply to every taunt cast at us on account of Galileo, that, even granting his ecclesiastical judges condemned him in the manner popularly supposed, they at least did not do so without first having the example set them by a Protestant tribunal not unlike their own, and under circumstances just the same.

I allude here to the condemnation of the celebrated astronomer Kepler by the Theological Faculty of Tubingen, in 1596, for affirming the identical scientific truth, which 37 years later got Galileo into trouble. The great majority of English Protestants are, without doubt, ignorant of this interesting case, which I venture to think a very fair set-off to their favourite story about Galileo. It may very likely have escaped the attention of many Catholics also; and therefore with your permission, Mr. Editor, I will just give the heads of it as briefly as possible.

John Kepler, born in Wurtemberg in 1571, I need scarcely remark, reflected no less lustre on Protestant Germany in the seventeenth century than Galileo on Catholic Italy. Kepler it was who, by his great discovery of the elliptical form of the planetary orbits, was led to establish those laws in astronomy known by his name, which first settled the truth of the Copernican system on an immovable basis, purifying it as he did from the erroneous hypothesis of the circular orbits, which its great author had still left adhering to it. For doing this, Bailli, in his *Histoire de l'Astronomie Moderne*, calls Kepler "one of the greatest men that ever appeared on the earth," and "the true founder of Modern Astronomy."

When he wrote his celebrated work, whose lengthy title begins with the words, "*Prodromus Dissertationum Cosmographicarum*", &c., in which he undertook by argument to demonstrate the truth of the Copernican system, not less reprobated at that time by the Protestants of Germany and England than by the Catholics of Italy, he had to lay it before the Academical Senate of Tubingen for their approbation, without which, in the regular course of things, it could not be printed. The unanimous decision of the divines comprising this senate was that Kepler's book contained a deadly heresy, because it contradicted the teaching of the Bible in that passage where Joshua commands the sun to stand still. To this Kepler replied, "that, as the Bible addressed itself to mankind in general, it spoke of things in the life of men as men in general are accustomed to speak of them; that the Bible was in no respect a Manual of Optics or Astronomy, but had much higher objects in view; that it was a blamable abuse to seek in it for answers to worldly things; that Joshua had wished to have the day prolonged, and God had responded to his wish; how this had happened was not a subject for enquiry." Such an answer as this might at least have been expected to make an impression on a body of Theologians, the very pillar and foundation of whose religious creed was the right of every man to explain the Bible for himself. So far from this, they repeated their condemnation with more acerbity than before, and had not the Duke of Wurtemberg, who was personally attached to Kepler, interposed in his behalf, he would inevitably have been subjected to a persecution far more rigorous than anything Galileo had to undergo. As it was, the vexations with which his clerical opponents contrived to embitter his existence on account of his opinions, in spite of the Duke's protection, were such as occasioned him to write in despair to his friend Mästlin, "that he held it for the best to imitate the disciples of Pythagoras, and keep silence on the discoveries he had made, lest, like Apian, he should lose his situation, and be doomed to die of hunger." The upshot was that he quitted Wurtemberg, and fled for refuge— whither?—to the Jesuits of Gratz and Ingoldstadt! who, staunch Protestant as he was to the last, honoured his great talents, and received him with open arms because of the services he had rendered to science. Eventually, on the death of Tycho Brahe, he received the appointment of Court Astronomer to the Emperor Rudolph II., at Prague. . . . .

I am very truly yours,

R. RABY.

Munich, Saturday in Holy Week, 1853.

No. 35.—THE DUKE OF WELLINGTON ON CATHOLIC LOYALTY.

The following extract from the speech of the great Duke of Wellington, in the House of Lords, delivered on the question of Catholic Emancipation may be read with advantage. The calm and manly testimony of one who had so many opportunities of witnessing the loyalty of Catholics and their unwavering devotion upon many a blood-stained field, ought surely to carry more weight than the heated words of party politicians.

"It is already well known to your lordships that of the troops which our gracious Sovereign did me the honour to intrust to my command at various periods during the war—a war undertaken expressly for the purpose of securing the happy institutions and independence of the country—that at least one-half were Roman Catholics.

My lords, when I call your recollection to this fact, I am sure all further eulogy is unnecessary. Your lordships are well aware for what length of period and under what difficult circumstances they maintained the Empire buoyant upon the flood which overwhelmed the houses and wrecked the institutions of every other people ; how they kept alive the only spark of freedom which was left unextinguished in Europe ; and how, by unprecedented efforts, they at length placed us, not only far above danger, but at an elevation of prosperity for which we had hardly dared to hope. These, my lords, are sacred and imperative titles to a nation's gratitude.

My lords, it is become quite needless for me to assure you that I have invariably found my Roman Catholic soldiers as patient under privations, as eager for the combat, and as brave and determined in the field as any other portion of his Majesty's troops ; and in point of loyalty and devotion to their king and country, I am quite certain they have never been surpassed. I claim no merit in admitting that others might have guided the storm of battle as skilfully as myself. We have only to recur to the annals of our military achievements to be convinced that few indeed of our commanders have not known how to direct the unconquerable spirit of their troops, and to wreathe fresh glories round the British name. But, my lords, while we are free to acknowledge this, we must also confess that, without Catholic blood or Catholic valour, no victory could ever have been obtained, and the first military talents in Europe might have been exerted in vain at the head of an army.

My lords, if on the eve of any of those hard-fought days, on which I had the honour to command them, I had thus addressed my Roman Catholic troops :—' You well know that your country either so suspects your loyalty, or so dislikes your religion, that she has not thought proper to admit you amongst the ranks of her citizens ; if on that account you deem it an act of injustice on her part to require you to shed your blood in her defence, you are at liberty to withdraw '—I am quite sure, my lords, that, however bitter the recollections which it awakened, they would have spurned the alternative with indignation: for the hour of danger and glory is the hour in which the gallant, the generous-hearted Irishman best knows his duty, and is most determined to perform it. But if, my lords, it had been otherwise; if they had chosen to desert the cause in which they were embarked, though the remainder of the troops would undoubtedly have maintained the honour of the British arms, yet, as I have said, no efforts of theirs could ever have crowned us with victory.

Yes, my lords, it is mainly to the Irish Catholics that we all owe our proud pre-eminence in our military career; and that I, personally, am indebted for the laurels with which you have been pleased to decorate my brow, for the honours which you have so bountifully lavished on me, and for the fair fame (I prize it above all other rewards) which my country, in its generous kindness, has bestowed upon me. I cannot but feel, my lords, that you yourselves have been chiefly instrumental in placing this heavy debt of gratitude upon me, greater, perhaps, than has ever fallen to the lot of any individual, and, however flattering the circumstance, it often places me in a very painful position. Whenever I meet, and it is almost an everyday occurrence, with any of those brave men, who, in common with others, are the object of this Bill,* and who have so often borne me on the tide of victory; when I see them still branded with the imputation of a divided allegiance, still degraded beneath the honest mind, and still proclaimed unfit to enter within the pale of the Constitution, I feel almost ashamed of the honours which have been lavished upon me—I feel that, though the merit was theirs, what was so freely given to me was unjustly denied to them; that I had reaped though they had sown; that they had borne the heat and burden of the day, but that the wages and repose were mine alone.

My lords, it is a great additional gratification to me

---

* The Catholic Emancipation Act became Law, April 13, A.D. 1829. See the "*Jubilee of the Catholic Emancipation*" by the Very Rev. Dr. Norbert Sweeney, O.S.B., Burns & Oates, 1879, &c.

to advocate these principles in conjunction with a distinguished member of my family, so lately at the head of the Government of his native country—a country ever dear to me from the recollections of my infancy, the memory of her wrongs, and the bravery of her people. I glory, my lords, in the name of Ireland; and it is the highest pleasure of my ambition to be thus united with the rest of my kindred in the grateful task of closing the wounds which seven centuries of misgovernment have inflicted upon that unfortunate land."

No. 36.—St. Peter in Rome.

In the face of millions of Catholics recognizing generation after generation, the Bishops of Rome as the Successors of St. Peter in that See—in the face of the most ancient and most illustrious of all dynasties, the unbroken line of 257 Roman Pontiffs (A.D. 1879), who have at all times claimed to succeed to the chair of Peter—and in the face of a large number of historians and other ancient writers who have asserted the same thing, without one single ancient writer asserting the contrary, some modern writers have boldly denied that S. Peter ever was in Rome.

As it has happened in other instances that the bitter attacks of our adversaries only served to bring out the Catholic truth in greater relief, so it is in this case. The comparatively modern denial that S. Peter was ever in Rome only gave an opportunity to Catholics to bring forth a host of historical documents in proof of this point of established general belief.

To prove that S. Peter was in Rome as the founder and first Bishop of that Church, it would almost suffice to see the great embarrassment into which they have thrown themselves who deny it.

They feel unable to tell us, if this is not the fact, how it happens that the whole Catholic Church, in all nations and through all ages, believed that S. Peter was the first Bishop of Rome.

They cannot explain how it is that this fact was never doubted or gainsaid, even by schismatics, heretics, and other bitter enemies of the Roman See, for upwards of fourteen centuries, though they were deeply interested in raising doubts about it.

Holy Scripture informs us that before S. Paul went to Rome, in the tenth year of the Emperor Claudius, there was already in Rome a large number of Christians, to whom S. Paul wrote, and of whom he could say that *their faith was spoken of in the whole world.* (Romans i. 8.) Now, if S. Peter did not convert the Roman people, and was not their Pastor, how is it that our opponents cannot tell us who first converted the Romans and who was their Bishop?

They cannot explain how so important a belief, if untrue, could be imposed upon all Christianity, even at the time when S. John the Evangelist was still living, without any one protesting against it, or even noticing the imposture, but rather all taking it for granted.

As it cannot be supposed that S. Peter had no See during the last twenty-five years of his life, if S. Peter was not Bishop of Rome during that period, they ought to tell us of what other place he was Bishop, and where he died, and how and when his mortal remains have been transferred to Rome. But of these things they tell us nothing.

If S. Peter was not the first Pontiff of Rome, they ought to be able to explain how since S. Linus the supremacy over the whole Church was ever claimed, and is still claimed, by the Roman See, and not by any other, not even by the See of Antioch, which S. Peter occupied for a time. But this also they are unable to explain.

Besides this grave embarrassment, also their not being able to bring forth in support of their assertion any positive argument, but only *negative* ones, serves to betray the weakness of their cause. These are their objections.

Chronologists, they say, vary in fixing the time that S. Peter went to Rome. It is difficult to reconcile that assertion with certain passages of Scripture. We cannot account why S. Paul in his letter to the Romans did not send his salutations to S. Peter if S. Peter had then been the Bishop of Rome. Holy Scripture, they say, does not state that S. Peter went to Rome, or lived or died there.

In answer to this I would reply, that the disagreement of writers regarding the *time* in which a fact occurred renders, at most, doubtful only the thing upon which those writers differ, namely, *time*, not the *fact* upon which they agree. Indeed, if the disagreeing about some point regarding a fact renders that point doubtful, their agreeing about the fact itself which they relate is a very great sign of truth.

Therefore, even supposing that the historians disagree in fixing the exact date in which S. Peter went to Rome or died in Rome, this is not a reason for denying that S. Peter lived and died there. Thus no one thinks of denying the birth, the baptism, and the death of our Lord, merely because chronologists are divided in fixing the exact years when these facts occurred.

Thus, likewise, because ignorant of certain particulars, we are unable to reconcile one fact with another, or to explain some expressions, or account for certain omissions, this is not a reason for denying what is otherwise satisfactorily proved from trustworthy documents.

Thus, suppose we were unable to account why mention is not made in Holy Writ of S. Peter going to Rome, and of his dwelling and teaching there; suppose we could not explain why S. Paul, writing to the Romans, did not send his salutations to S. Peter—this is not a reason why we should deny what is otherwise testified about S. Peter by positive and solid authority; otherwise we might deny that S. John was Bishop of Ephesus, and S. James Bishop of Jerusalem, on the ground that S. Paul, writing to the Ephesians, did not send his salutations to their Bishop, S. John, and writing to the Hebrews, did not salute S. James their Bishop in Jerusalem.

We attach more value to the testimony of a few trustworthy witnesses asserting a thing than the silence of a hundred persons saying nothing about it, provided these do not deny what the others affirm.

Sometimes the very notoriety of a fact universally ad—

mitted is the very reason why no pains are taken to establish it. Thus, for example, the historian Eusebius, Bishop of Caesarea, who lived in the fourth century, after having stated that S. Paul was beheaded and S. Peter crucified under Nero, adds, "I think it superfluous to look for other testimonies in proof of these facts, for that these things have taken place, is testified by remarkable and most splendid monuments." (Book ii., chap. 25.)

These seeming discrepancies can, I think, be reconciled and these difficulties surmounted. I will here give a short sketch of the movements of S. Peter in his Apostolic labours, which, I trust, will enable the reader to solve, at least most of those difficulties.

St. Peter began his Apostolic labours ten days after the Ascension of our Lord into Heaven, that is, on the Day of Pentecost, 15th of May of the year 34 from the birth of Christ. In fact, on the very Day of Pentecost, S. Peter, full of the Holy Ghost, preached before a large crowd of people and converted three thousand persons. (Acts ii. 41.) Some days after, being freed from prison by an angel (Acts v. 19), he preached in the Temple and converted five thousand more. During the four years that he stayed in Jerusalem he visited and preached the Gospel in many parts of the Samaritans (Acts viii. 25), and visited especially the City of Samaria itself, where he administered the Sacrament of Confirmation to the baptised Christians of that city, and sharply rebuked Simon Magus. (Acts viii.)

In the beginning of the fourth year of his dwelling in Jerusalem S. Peter was visited by S. Paul. (Acts ix. 27, 28.) During the same year S. Peter "*passed through, visiting all, and went to the saints who dwelt at Lydda*" (Acts ix. 32), where he miraculously cured Eneas from his eight years' infirmity; then he went to Joppe (now called Jaffa), and there he raised to life Tabitha (Dorcas), who had died shortly before. It was in that same town of Joppe that S. Peter had the vision of the great linen sheet descending from Heaven. (Acts x. 11, 12.) After a few days he went, by God's direction, to Caesarea, and there he instructed the Centurion Cornelius, and his household, all of whom he baptised and received into the Church. (Acts x. 23.)

From Caesarea he returned to Jerusalem (Acts xi. 18), but did not tarry there long.

Having heard that in Syria, in the city of Antioch, the Gospel had made wonderful progress, Barnabas and several of the disciples hastened there, and S. Peter also; which thing, though not mentioned by S. Luke, because the principal subject of his history was not S. Peter but S. Paul, is, however, attested by Anacletus (Epistola iii.), by Marcellus (Epistola iii.), by S. Innocent I. (Epistola xiv.), by S. Damasus in the Pontifical Book, by S. Jerome (De Viris Illustribus), by Eusebius (in Chronicon), by S. Leo (Sermone i., De SS. Petro et Paulo), and by others.

During his episcopacy in Antioch, which lasted seven years, S. Peter made excursions to the near Provinces of Pontus, Asia Minor, Galatia, Cappadocia, and Bithynia, as S. Leo testifies (Sermon on Saints Peter and Paul).

In the eleventh year after the Ascension of our Lord, which was the second year of the reign of the Roman Emperor Claudius, S. Peter left the Bishopric of Antioch, which he intrusted to Evodius, and chose for himself Rome. Before, however, going to Rome, he first went to Jerusalem. Then it was that Herod cast him into prison, as related in the Acts of the Apostles, chap. xii. But being miraculously delivered from prison a second time by an angel, he made his way to Rome.

St. Peter was the first to preach the Gospel in Rome, and owing to his sanctity, zeal, prudence, and power, it was not long before he made many converts. The number of Christians increasing steadily every year, he chose the most distinguished among them and sent them to different parts of the world, as recorded in the Roman Martyrology. To Sicily he sent Pancras, Marcian and Berillus; to Capua, Priscon; to Naples, Aspren; to Terracina, Epaphroditus; to Nepe, Ptolomeus; to Fiesole, Romulus; to Lucca, Paulinus; to Ravenna, Apolinaris; to Verona, Exuperius; to Padua, Prosdorimus; to Ticinus, Syrus; to Acquileia, Hermogora. To

Gaul (France), likewise, S. Peter sent to Toulouse, Martial; to Cologne, Maternus; to Rheims, Sixtus; to Arles, Trophimus; to Vienne, Crescent. To Germany he sent Eucharius, Egistus, and Marcian. To Spain he sent Torquatus, Ctesiphons, Secundus, Indalesius, Cecilius, and Esikius; and others to other places.

In the seventh year of S. Peter's Pontificate in Rome the Emperor Claudius expelled from that city all the Jews. With the Jews the Christians, who were considered by the Pagans a Jewish sect, had also to go.

St. Peter leaving Rome, directed his journey, according to some, first to Britain; according to Metaphrastes, first to Carthage, where he placed Crescent as Bishop of the Christians who were in that city, then to Alexandria, where he raised that See to a Patriarchate, and placed in it S. Mark, with jurisdiction over all the surrounding regions.* He also made Rufus Bishop of Thebes, after which he continued his journey to Jerusalem.

About that time there rose a great dispute at Antioch, some holding that the Christians were bound to observe circumcision and other legalities of the law of Moses, others maintaining the contrary; and as they could not come to any conclusion, hearing that S. Peter had returned to Jerusalem, they sent there S. Paul and S. Barnabas to consult him and the other Apostles and Priests who were there on the matter. A Council was held, and after sufficient time had been given to debate, S. Peter, who was then Bishop of Rome, stood up, and, referring to a special revelation made to him by God, declared that certain Jewish legalities were not binding on Christians; which decision was immediately confirmed by S. James, Bishop of Jerusalem, and by all the rest. (Acts xv. 8.)

That that Council took place in the tenth year of Claudius, S. Jerome gathers from the Epistle to the Galatians; for S. Paul, who was converted the year next after our Lord's Ascension, went to Jerusalem to visit S. Peter the third year of his conversion (Galat. i. 18),

---

* St. Mark died a martyr in Alexandria in the 8th year of Nero.

and fourteen years after that visit he went again to Jerusalem (Galat. ii. 1) and attended the Council. (Acts xv.) So that altogether there elapsed eighteen years between our Lord's crucifixion and the Council of Jerusalem; and the eighteenth year from the death of Christ was the tenth of the reign of the Emperor Claudius.

Claudius died after a reign of thirteen years, and his edict of expulsion against the Jews, which he enacted four years before, ended with his life.

To Claudius succeeded Nero (at the age of eighteen), who, in the beginning of his reign, was of a peaceable disposition. This encouraged many of the Jews and Christians to return to Rome, as Aquila and Priscilla did. S. Peter hastened also to Rome in the very first year of Nero. Two years after this (2d of Nero), S. Peter was joined in Rome by S. Paul, who, some years before, when Peter was absent, had written his Epistle to the Romans, and now came there a prisoner. A difficulty is advanced here from the Acts of the Apostles that S. Paul found in Rome that the Jews knew of the Christian religion only by report. How could this be if S. Peter had preached to them? We must bear in mind that S. Peter's first entrance into Rome was before the expulsion of the Jews by Claudius. S. Paul was conducted to Rome in the reign of Nero, after the Jews had been permitted again to reside in the city. Those who had heard S. Peter had been banished, and probably had not returned. Two years afterwards (4th of Nero), being set free, S. Paul passed some time in that capital, and then left for Spain and other parts.

In the tenth year of the reign of Nero, (the twenty-second of S. Peter's Roman Pontificate), Rome was set on fire. Nero, to exculpate himself from being the author of that conflagration, and turn elsewhere the menacing rage of the people, threw the blame on the Christians, and under that pretext many of them were made to suffer imprisonment and death.

The following year Nero enacted the first sanguinary persecution against the Christians, which was kept in full vigour for the remainder of his life.

In the twelfth of Nero, (the twenty-fourth of S. Peter's Roman Pontificate), S. Peter, who had absented himself for a time, came back to Rome, and S. Paul also, to revive the Church, which through Nero's persecution was being cruelly wasted. During this year it was that S. Peter wrote his second Epistle, in which he foretells his approaching death: "*Being assured that the laying away of this my tabernacle is at hand*" (Chapter i. 14).

At that time Simon Magus so captivated the Romans, and Nero especially, by his magical arts, that they decreed to him divine honours.

On the day that Simon Magus was to delight the Romans by an ascent in the air, and they were in most anxious expectation to see such a prodigy, S. Peter and S. Paul went to the spot where this was to take place, full of confidence in God, that He would confound that impostor and undeceive the poor deluded people. And so it was: as Simon Magus, before an immense crowd of people, was already carried by the wicked spirits on high in what appeared to be a carriage drawn by fiery horses, S. Peter made a fervent prayer to God that He would abase that man, and, behold, in an instant, the fiery horses and chariot vanished away, and Simon Magus fell headlong to the ground and died.

This defeat of Simon Magus, wrought by S. Peter, enlivened the spirits of the Christians, and was the cause of a great many conversions. But Nero, exasperated at seeing himself and the Romans deprived henceforward of the magical amusements of Simon Magus, ordered S. Peter and S. Paul to be cast into the Mamertine prison, and there they were kept in strict confinement for nine months. From that prison S. Paul wrote his second letter to S. Timothy requesting him to come to Rome to be witness of his martyrdom, which then was near.

While prisoners they converted to the faith Process and Martinian, the keepers of the prison, and forty-seven other prisoners, who were baptised with the water which S. Peter miraculously caused to spring forth in the rock-floor of the prison itself, which prison and fountain of pure water still exist in wonderful preservation under the Church of S. Joseph at the foot of the Capitol.

In the year 74 of the common era, that is, in the year 80 since the birth of Christ, in the year 35 after the Ascension of our Lord, in the 34th year of S. Paul's conversion, in the 25th year since S. Peter took possession of the See of Rome, in the 13th year of Nero, July 29, S. Peter and S. Paul were sentenced, S. Peter to be crucified, S. Paul to be beheaded, on account of their being Disciples of Jesus Christ. They were in consequence taken out of prison, and S. Peter was crucified on Mount Janiculum, not far from the Vatican Hill,* with his head towards the earth, as he wished, because, in his humility, he thought himself unworthy to die in the same manner as his Lord and Saviour did; and S. Paul was taken to the Salvia Waters, about four miles southward from Rome, on the left of the road to Ostia, and there beheaded. When his head fell under the sword, it made three bounds, and a fountain sprung forth at each place where the head touched the ground. The three fountains, known as—*le tre fontane*—are still to be seen on that spot, about two miles beyond the noble Basilica of S. Paul, which stands outside the walls *(fuori le mura)* of Rome, by the left bank of the Tiber on the Ostian Way.

This simple sketch of S. Peter's life from the Day of Pentecost to his death will enable any one to explain several of the difficulties which have been raised through not knowing how to reconcile certain facts with others ; how, for example, S. Peter could have been seven years at Antioch and twenty-five years Bishop of Rome, and yet be in Jerusalem in the 4th, 11th, and 18th years after our Lord's Ascension, as inferred from the Epistle to the Galatians and from the Acts of the Holy Apostles.

S. Peter having fixed his See in Rome to the end of his life, and having died there a martyr, it follows as a matter of course, that his heirs and successors in that See should enjoy the prerogatives of that Episcopate, that is, the Primacy which St. Peter received, not for his

---

* The very spot is venerated at *St. Pietro in Montorio*, Rome.

own private advantage, but for the good of the Church; for if any Bishop can say with S. Augustine "That we are Christians is for our own sake, that we are Bishops is for your sake"—"*Quod christiani sumus propter nos est, quod præpositi sumus propter vos est*" (Libro de Pastoribus, c. i.), how much more pointedly S. Peter and his successors can say: that we are Pontiffs is not for our sake but for the good of the Church, which at all times needs a Primacy to set in order many things which would otherwise remain unsettled, and keep all the flock of Christ together. And as the need ever is greater as the flock of Christ increases, so the Primacy is to be enjoyed in perpetuity by all the successors of S. Peter.*

To give more satisfaction to those who may have been prejudiced in this matter, or who wish to enter more fully into this subject, I will here subjoin some other proofs to confirm this fact.

I must premise that amongst the first Christians pagan Rome was often designated under the name of Babylon, and naturally so, especially among the converted Jews, who saw the great similarity between the two capitals on account of their vastness, pagan immorality, superstition, and common antagonism to the people of God.

For this reason no one mistook what S. John in the Apocalypse designated under the figure of Babylon.

In the end of the first general Epistle of S. Peter we have these words: "*The Church that is in Babylon, elected together with you, saluteth you: and so doth my son Mark*"; in which passage the word Babylon must be taken figuratively to mean Rome; in fact, it is not recorded either in Holy Scripture or elsewhere that S. Peter or S. Mark had ever been to ancient Babylon in Asia; and no ancient writer has ever said that this letter was dated really from ancient Babylon, or that it was so understood by any one; on the contrary, it is recorded positively in the history of Eusebius (Book II., chap. 15) as having been stated by Papias, the disciple of S. John the Evangelist and friend of S. Polycarp, that S. Peter, in his first

---

* See Supremacy of the Bishop of Rome, Chap. XXVII.

Epistle which he wrote from Rome, called Rome figuratively Babylon. The same thing is asserted by S. Jerome in his Book of *Illustrious Men* when he speaks of S. Mark.

That S. Peter was in Rome is also proved from those ancient writers who relate as a notorious fact that S. Mark wrote his Gospel in Rome as he heard it there preached by S. Peter. This is stated by Eusebius (History, Book II., chap. 15)—by Irenaeus (Book II., chap. 1)—by S. Jerome in his book of *Illustrious Men* just quoted, when speaking of S. Mark—by S. Damasus in his *Pontificate* in the Life of S. Peter—by Isidorus in the Life of S. Mark—by Ado of Vienne in France in his Chronicon, year 45—by Tertullian (Book IV. against Marcion), who also adds that the Gospel of S. Mark is attributed to S. Peter, because S. Mark was the interpreter and disciple of S. Peter.

I might dispense with quoting testimonies of ancient writers to the fact that S. Peter was the first Bishop of Rome as it is a thing recognised by a good number of Protestant writers, as, for instance, by Cave, who in his *Literary History of Ecclesiastical Writers* writes thus: "That S. Peter was the first Bishop of Rome we affirm boldly with the whole multitude of the ancients. We give testimonies above all exceptions, taken from the remotest antiquity, Ignatius, Bishop of Antioch, disciple of S. Peter, and certainly his successor in the See of Antioch (Epistle to the Romans); Papias of Hierapolis, hearer of S. John the Evangelist, at least in his old age (see Eusebius II. 15); Irenaeus of Lyons, a man belonging to the Apostolic times, disciple of S. Polycarp (Against Heresies III. 1); Dionysius of Corinth (see Eusebius II. 25); Tertullian (in the Book of Prescriptions xxxvi.—of Baptism iv.—Scorpiate, last chapter), the Roman Priest Cajus, an ecclesiastic of great repute (see Eusebius II. 25); Origenes (see Eusebius III. 1—VI. 14). After names so venerable, and after monuments of antiquity so illustrious, who will call in doubt a thing so clearly and constantly attested?"

To Cave I might add the learned Ernestus Bunsen, who in a letter to the *Times*, June 5, 1871, admits the coming of S. Peter to Rome in the year 42. He grounds his belief especially on a passage of the History of Eusebius (Armenian version), in which Eusebius says that in the second year of the reign of Claudius, that is in the year 42 of the Christian era, Philo had familiar intercourse with S. Peter whilst in Rome preaching the Gospel.

Also Dollinger, who cannot be accused of partiality to the Holy See, writes thus: " All the Fathers understood the word Babylon used in S. Peter's Epistle to signify Rome. It has been asserted, especially by those who maintain the monstrous opinion that S. Peter never was at Rome, that we must take the word literally for Babylon on the Euphrates. These authors do not remember that the Jews had been driven from Babylon and Seleucia a short time previous to the writing of this epistle, and we cannot suppose that S. Peter, the Apostle of the circumcision, would travel to so distant a city in which he could find none of his nation. In the Epistle S. Peter says that S. Mark was with him; we know from the writings of S. Paul that S. Mark was at Rome about this time. It has been said that in an epistle in which there exists no allegory, nor allegorical form of speech, S. Peter could not, without some qualification, call Rome by the name of Babylon. Now be it observed that S. Peter wrote to those Jewish converts who were familiar with the writings of the Prophets, by whom Rome, the centre of Paganism, is frequently designated by that appellation. I might cite the example of Luther, who, without previous allusion to the Apocalypse, dates his letter, written at Wortburg, from the Island of Patmos."
—(*History of the Church.*)

Calvin himself writes: " I cannot withstand the consent of those writers who prove that Peter died at Rome."
—(*Institutions,* Book IV.)

Wishing, however, to give as much satisfaction as I can to my readers in this important point, I will here name some illustrious ancient authors, who plainly assert that S. Peter went to Rome; others, that he was the first to teach there; others, that he there held the Pontitical Roman See for twenty-five years; others, that he died there a martyr, being suspended on the cross, and that his successors, the Bishops of Rome, were sitting on the chair of Peter.

S. Peter went to Rome and first taught Christianity there.

Thus S. Leo says: "The most blessed Peter, the Prince of the Apostolic Order, is destined to be the bulwark of the Roman Empire." (First Sermon on the Birthday of the Apostles.)

Theodorétus says plainly that S. Peter was the first to dispense the Evangelical doctrine to the Romans. (Chap. i. in his comments on the Epistle to the Romans.) The same thing is said by Eusebius. (*History*, Book II., chap. 14.)

Paul Orosius in the seventh book of his *History* (chap. vi.) confirms the same thing in these words: "In the beginning of the reign of Claudius, Peter, the Apostle of our Lord Jesus Christ, came to Rome, taught with faithful word the saving faith, and confirmed it with very powerful signs; from thence Christians began to be there".

S. Peter was Bishop of Rome 25 years.

Eusebius says that S. Peter having preached the Gospel in Rome, persevered twenty-five years Bishop of Rome. (Chronicon, 74.)

The same is asserted by Isidorus in the Life of S. Peter, and by Sulpicius. (*History*, Book II.)

The same thing is implied by those Fathers or ancient writers who call the Roman See "the chair of Peter"; as

S. Jerome. (First Letter to Pope Damasus.)
Sozomenus. (Book IV., chap. 14.)
S. Augustine. (Book II., chap. 51, against the Letters of Petilian.)
Prudentius. (Hymn of S. Laurence.)
S. Cyprian, very frequently in his works. (See an instance in Book I., Letter 3, to Cornelius.)

S. Prosper, with his noted expression, "Rome, the See of Peter, on account of that pastoral honour is made the head of the world".

> "Sedes Roma Petri
> Quae pastoralis honoris
> Facta caput mundo."—(Book de Ingratis.)

To these should be added those Fathers who, in their list of the Roman Pontiffs, place S. Peter at the head of it; as

S. Irenaeus. (Book III., chap. 3.)*
Dorotheus. (In Synopsis.)
S. Augustine. (Epistola 53 and Generosum, tit. 2, and contra Epistolam Fundamenti, chap. iv. tit. 8.)

St. Peter died in Rome.

That S. Peter ended his life in Rome is stated by—
S. Augustine. (Book I., de Consensu Evangelistarum.)
Eusebius. (Chronicon 71, a Christo nato.)
Paul Orosius. (History, Book VIII.)
S. Maximus. (Sermon v. on the Birthday of the Apostles.)
Origen. (Book III. on Genesis, as stated by Eusebius, *History*, Book III., chap. 2.)
S. Jerome, who writes thus: "*Simon Peter goes to Rome to combat Simon Magus; he retains there the sacerdotal chair twenty-five years, up to the last, that is, up to the year 13 of Nero, by whom being nailed to the cross, died a martyr, with his head downward*". (Book of Illustrious Men.)

Tertullian adds that S. Peter was crucified in Rome, after having ordained S. Clement for his successor. (Book of Prescriptions, chap. 32.) S. Clement, in fact, succeeded S. Peter, though after Linus and Anacletus, who were previously the Bishop-coadjutors of S. Peter,

---

* For one who is not a Catholic it should be remarked here that if he throws aside the testimony of S. Irenaeus in this instance, he will find himself in a difficulty with respect to the authenticity of the Gospels, for except Papias, who mentions S. Matthew and S. Mark, no earlier Father than Irenaeus mentions the four Gospels.

and therefore St. Clement, in his humility and discretion, wished they should succeed before himself. The same Tertullian, alluding to the death of S. Peter and S. Paul in Rome, addresses that city thus: "*Happy Church, over which the Apostles have poured forth the whole of their doctrine together with their blood.*" (Book of Prescriptions, chap. 36.)

I abstain from giving the quotations of Pope S. Clement I., S. Anacletus, S. Marcellus I., S. Damasus I., S. Innocent I., S. Leo, S. Gelasius I., John III., S. Gregory I., S. Agatho, Adrianus, S. Nicholas I., who all have asserted that they were succeeding to Peter, and sitting in the chair of Peter.

Some might take the exception that they were speaking in their own cause. Yet no one will deny that their testimony is of great weight if he considers that they were all holy, truthful men, who would not claim as a right that which they were not lawfully entitled to, and that they did so without any one protesting or doubting, or showing surprise, or finding fault with what these holy Pontiffs asserted.

I close this short essay by quoting two General Councils in support of this assertion—that of Ephesus in the year 431, and that of Chalcedon in 451.

In the Council of Ephesus the Roman Pontiff Celestinus I. is called "The ordinary successor and Vicar of Blessed Peter, the Prince of the Apostles"—"*Ordinarius successor et Vicarius Beati Petri Apostolorum Principis*". (Chap. 16.)

In the Council of Chalcedon, as the letter of Pope S. Leo the Great, the Roman Pontiff of that time, was read, all the 630 Fathers that were sitting in that Council exclaimed, "Peter has spoken through Leo".—"*Petrus per Leonem locutus est.*" (Art. II)

In the quoted expressions used by these two General Councils, their belief that S. Peter was the first Bishop of Rome is evidently implied.

No. 37.—COMMUNION IN ONE KIND.

The Church has always believed that there is no command from our Lord Jesus Christ for the laity to receive the Holy Communion under two kinds, that is, under the species both of bread and of wine. She holds that this two-fold reception was not demanded by the nature or by the institution of this holy Sacrament.

The Church therefore either left the faithful free to receive under both kinds or under one kind, or she regulated this point of discipline as she thought proper under existing circumstances.

When the Church left the lay people free to receive either under one or under both kinds, the custom sometimes inclined more to one side, sometimes more to the other.

If at any time it became an obligation for the laity to receive under both kinds or to receive only under one, it was when the Church, for good reasons, thought proper to issue an express command on the matter, or when some general custom prevailed that had the force of law.

Up to the fifth century the Church left the people free to receive Holy Communion either under one or under both kinds.

The Manichean heretics considered wine as the "gall of the devil," and held that Christ had no real blood. Owing to the permission which existed at that time of receiving Communion under one kind alone, these heretics could approach to the altar with Catholics and receive the Most Holy Eucharist under the form of bread alone, without causing surprise; and by so doing they would not manifest their heretical principles, or be known as members of that heretical sect.

On this account Pope Leo I. in the year 443, and Pope Gelasius in 490, commanded that all should communicate under both species—not for the sake of correcting any abuse that had crept into the Church, but because they considered that such a command would deter these heretics from profaning this holy Sacrament, and would serve to detect them and expose their heresy.

When the Manichean heresy died away, the law which was made on their account was relaxed. The faithful were again left free to receive Holy Communion either under both kinds or under one, just as they felt piously inclined; and by degrees the custom of taking Holy Communion under the species of bread alone prevailed, especially in the twelfth and thirteenth centuries, when it became universal, without any positive law binding to this effect.

It was only in the fifteenth century, when some turbulent men began to accuse the Church of error for permitting Holy Communion under one kind, that the Church in the Councils of Constance and of Trent, sanctioned with a positive law the then prevailing custom among the laity of taking Holy Communion under the species of bread only, lest, by introducing and permitting Communion under both kinds, she might appear to connive at the errors of those innovators, and to admit, contrary to truth, that for fifteen centuries she had not known the nature of this Sacrament; that she had allowed this Sacrament to be mutilated and profaned; that she had gone directly against Christ's command of receiving the Sacrament under both kinds; that consequently she was no longer the true Church of Christ. The necessity of counteracting all these errors and their destructive consequences was considered a sufficient reason for enacting a general law that the people of the Latin rite should receive Holy Communion under the species of bread only.

It has always been believed that in those things which are not immediately connected with the essence of a Sacrament, the Church has a right to change her discipline and the mode of administering the Sacraments according to the needs of time and circumstances. Hence we find different changes introduced in the Roman ritual, according as it was considered advisable at different times and places, in reference to things that are not of the essence of the Sacraments.

At this very day the Roman Catholic Church sanctions different rites, languages, and ceremonies in the administration of the Sacraments and in the celebration of the Holy Sacrifice of the Mass; namely, the Latin, United Greek, Armenian, Chaldaic, Syro-Chaldaic, Maronite, and Coptic rites, each in their respective language; all of which, while they agree in points of faith defined by the Church, differ in many usages of less importance. Amongst other things they differ in the manner of administering the Holy Communion; some being permitted to give it under both kinds, some having to administer it under one kind alone.

It might be contended, that even admitting that the administration of this Sacrament under the species of wine is non-essential with regard to a Christian who receives under the species of bread, yet that it would seem more profitable and consoling to receive under both, and that therefore it does not seem right that a command should have been given enjoining what is less profitable and less consoling.

To this it may be answered, that the privation of this additional comfort and advantage is abundantly compensated, with regard to the receiver himself in particular, by affording him the opportunity of an act of obedience, and with regard to the Church at large, by rendering the administration of the Sacrament more easy and less subject to irreverence. For if the Holy Eucharist had always to be given under both kinds, those unable to bear the taste of wine, the sick, and those who live in remote and almost inaccessible countries, or in very hot or very cold climates, where the wine can with very great difficulty be procured or preserved, these people would, in many instances at least, have to go without Communion. The same may be said of those poor localities where they cannot afford to buy the wine, especially for a large number of Communicants.

Also the administration of the Holy Eucharist under the species of bread alone is less subject to irreverence, for experience has proved that in the administration of the chalice there is occasionally danger of spilling the sacred Blood, especially when great crowds are approaching to

Communion, besides other difficulties and irreverences easy to happen.

But there are two other very important reasons which have induced the Church to confirm by a positive law the custom, which had already generally prevailed, of giving Communion under the species of bread only. One was that the Church herself might not seem to countenance the error of those who denied the real presence of the Body and Blood of Christ under each species; the other, to oppose the error of those who, in the fifteenth century, as we have already remarked, taught that the Holy Eucharist is no Sacrament unless given under the two species; which error, if admitted, would have sapped the very foundation of the Church, inasmuch as it would have been equivalent to saying that the Church had been teaching what was false for fifteen centuries.

No one, therefore, should blame the Church for having enacted such a law, based on a constant belief of the Church that Communion under one kind was a complete Sacrament of the Body and Blood of Christ, and resting also on the custom then prevailing, and on the greater facility thus afforded of promoting the well-being of the Church at large.

On the other side, it is not to be wondered at that people who had already formed a party in opposition to the Catholic Church, who denied Christ's presence under either kind or under both kinds, and regarded the Sacraments as mere empty symbols, and who were moreover guided by the novel principle of private interpretation, should have also opposed this law of the Church. Alas! what dogma or law is there that cannot be attacked under the destructive principle of private interpretation? How easy it is, even with the best intention, to make Holy Scripture speak according to one's inclination or fancy, when all authority to decide is rejected except one's own.

From the fact that S. Paul frequently mentions Communion in both kinds, some conclude that therefore there must have been a Divine precept obliging the faithful to receive under both.

Such a consequence does not follow, as it might have been a mere privilege, of which the fervent primitive Christians gladly availed themselves.

That it was neither universal as a custom nor a Divine precept to receive under both kinds appears from what our Lord Himself did on the day of His Resurrection, when He made Himself known to the two disciples at Emmaus, as we read, *"in the breaking of bread"* (S. Luke xxiv. 30, 31), which passage S. Jerome. S. Augustine, and S. Chrysostom understand as signifying a real Communion; as seems also clear from the context itself, and from the spiritual effect produced by the breaking of the bread; for their eyes were then opened to recognise our blessed Lord.

That the primitive Christians were in the habit of receiving Communion under one kind alone is seen from the Acts of the Apostles (ii. 42), by which we learn that the first baptised converts of Jerusalem *" were persevering in the doctrine of the Apostles and in the communication of the breaking of bread, and in prayers,"* and also from Acts xx. (verse 7), where the inspired writer says: *" And on the first day of the week, when we were assembled to break bread, Paul discoursed with them"*. In these passages no mention is made of the species of wine.

Besides, we know from genuine historical documents that the early Christians were permitted to carry home the holy Sacrament with them under the species of bread only, in order to receive Holy Communion privately.

These texts of Holy Scripture and this custom of early Christians prove that the Apostles and their immediate successors gave Communion, at least sometimes, under one kind alone, and that, therefore, the giving Communion under both kinds was not considered to be required either by the nature of the Sacrament or by the command of Christ, but that it was left to the judgment of the Church.

Some Protestants refer us to the fifty-fourth verse of the sixth chapter of the Gospel of S. John: *" Except you eat the flesh of the Son of Man and drink His blood, you shall not have life in you,*" in order to prove the necessity of receiving Communion under both kinds.

When Catholics quote the latter part of this chapter of S. John in proof of the real presence of Christ in the blessed Sacrament, many Protestants take upon themselves to declare that the whole chapter refers only to faith and not to Holy Communion.

It is remarkable, therefore, that when they wish to prove the necessity of receiving Communion under both kinds, Protestants should quote from this sixth chapter of S. John.

It is again somewhat strange that they who hold that in this chapter the eating and the drinking mean one and the same thing (namely, partaking of Christ's Body and Blood *by faith*), should oppose Catholics who hold that to receive our Lord either by eating or by drinking is the same thing; that by taking Holy Communion under the species of bread they do eat and drink in reality the Body and Blood of Christ; and that therefore they fulfil the precept contained in this passage.

Yet as an objection is drawn from this passage, I will not leave it unnoticed.

It appears that the scope of our Lord in this passage of S. John was not to reveal the *mode* of partaking of His Body and Blood; and thus His hearers understood His words. They did not strive about the manner or medium of reception of His Body and Blood whether under the species of oil, or of milk, or of wine, or of bread, or of fruit, or other chosen thing. This point our Lord did not touch at all, and therefore His hearers could not have anything to say on the matter, but they strove only about the *possibility* of His giving His real Flesh as food. "*How can this man,*" said they, "*give us His flesh to eat?*" (verse 53). Therefore the answer of our Lord should be taken to mean merely a precept to partake of His Flesh and Blood *in reality*, and not as referring to the mode of reception of His Body and Blood under the particular species of bread and wine. The elements of bread and wine are not even once mentioned in the whole chapter.

Some may think that, though wine was not mentioned, natural bread at least was mentioned in the latter part of the chapter, which relates to the Holy Eucharist. But on examination it will be found that not once in the whole chapter can the word "bread" be taken in the sense of natural bread.

Every time that the word *bread* occurs there, it is so qualified that it signifies not natural bread, but a peculiar bread, that is, JESUS CHRIST Himself, and relates to what Christ had said before at verse 51: "*I am the living bread.*" Thus in verses 52 and 59, He says: "*This* bread,"—in verse 52: "The bread *that I will give*,"—in verse 59: "The bread *that came down from heaven.*" Therefore from the above-quoted text (chap. vi. 54) the necessity of receiving Christ's Body and Blood is indeed clearly made known, but whether His Body and His Blood is to be received under the species of bread and of wine, or of some other elements, whether under one species alone, or under two different species or more, is not pointed out.

It is necessary here to remark, that according to the Catholic belief, Jesus Christ in the blessed Sacrament is not partly contained under one species and partly under another—that is to say, Christ is not with His Body but without His Blood under the species of bread; and with His Blood but without His Body under the species of wine separately:—but He is in the blessed Sacrament whole and entire, with His Divinity, Soul, Body, and Blood, under the species of bread, and likewise Christ is whole and entire, with His Divinity, Soul, Body, and Blood, under the species of wine; and this by the exigency of the case, that is, by virtue of what is called *concomitance*, which means that the Body and Blood of Christ, with His human Soul and His Divine nature, must always be together. This might be called inseparableness, that is, the impossibility of the Body and Blood, Soul and Divinity of Christ ever being separated.

It is part of the doctrine of the Incarnation that the *inseparability* arising from the *union*, known as "*hypostatic*" of the two natures, Divine and human, in Christ is such that His Divinity can never be separated from His humanity, nor from any part of it, even when those parts were separated from each other, as occurred at Christ's death; and that after Christ's Resurrection that inseparability became still more stringent, not even admitting the possibility of any part of His manhood being ever for an instant separated from each other. S. Paul assures us when he says: "*Christ rising again from the dead, dieth no more.*" (Romans vi. 9.) His soul cannot any more be separated from His Body or Blood, as it was at His death on Calvary. His glorified human nature does not admit of mutilation or separation of its parts, so that the Body, and Blood, and Soul, and Divinity of Christ must always remain united.

The words of consecration, therefore, which realise the presence of the Body under the species of bread, and of the Blood under the species of wine, involve the belief that under either kind alone Christ Himself is present in the perfection of His human and divine natures.

Hence, under the species of bread is received not only Christ's Body, but also His Blood, Soul and Divinity; and under the species of wine not only Christ's Blood, but also His Body, Soul and Divinity.

Therefore the Communicant who receives under the species of bread alone, receives the same precious gift, the Body and the Blood, the divine and the human nature of our Lord, and all those graces which He brings with Him, as truly and entirely as the one who receives Holy Communion under both the species of bread and of wine.

It might be urged that there must be some reason why our Lord Jesus Christ in this passage (S. John vi. 54) used the figure of *eating* and *drinking*.

The reason seems clear. In verse 52 Christ had promised to give His Flesh to be eaten. As some of His hearers disbelieved the possibility of this, Christ confirmed His teaching by adding that they had not only to partake of His Flesh, but of His blood also. Now, having previously used the word "*eat*" with regard to His Flesh, He could not with propriety of language use the same word "eat" with regard to the Blood and say: "Unless you eat my Flesh and Blood," but was compelled to use the word *drink* respecting the Blood, that He might speak with propriety of language. Thus, for example, a man after having said: "Eat this orange," and wishing for some reason to advert to its juice, could not with propriety say: "Eat this juice," but he would be obliged to say: "Drink this juice."

Some think that the commemoration of our Lord's Passion, which we should make in receiving the Holy Eucharist, requires the presence of both species; but no necessity exists, for it is evident that a person can, if he wishes, call to mind Christ's bitter Passion when he receives the Holy Eucharist under one kind alone as perfectly as the one who receives Communion under the two species.

The commemoration of Christ is commanded (1 Corinth. xi. 24, 25) after each of the species, and by S. Luke (xxii. 19) after the species of bread; therefore the commemoration of Christ and His Passion and Death can be well made on taking Communion under one kind only. To commemorate depends upon our free-will, and we can commemorate or call to mind the death of Christ perfectly on taking Communion under one kind only.

Let us see now whether the nature of this Sacrament requires both species, as some imagine, or in other words, whether Communion under one kind only is, or is not, a true Sacrament, conferring on the receiver the same essential grace as is conferred by this Sacrament when given under the two species.

Here should be recalled to mind the Catholic doctrine just stated of the real presence of Christ's Body and Blood, Soul, and Divinity, under each kind in this Sacrament, from which doctrine it clearly follows that he who receives Communion under the species of bread only, thereby receives Christ as entirely as the one who receives Him under both kinds.

Communion under one kind only is an outward sign conferring the inward grace which it signifies; and therefore it is a true Sacrament. Between a member of the Latin Church who receives communion under the species of unleavened bread, and a member of the Greek Schismatic who receives it under the species of a small piece of leavened bread and a few drops of wine in a spoon, there is no essential difference.

The Greek Schismatic Church, in fact, in some instances gives Communion also under one kind only, and never insisted upon this difference as a cause of separation from the Church of Rome.

It is true that receiving Communion under both kinds separately might help the receiver to call to mind more vividly the death of Christ, but between a remembrance and a more lively remembrance there is no difference in essence but only in degree; and this seeming disadvantage cannot render the Sacrament invalid. Baptism by immersion, as practised in some parts of Christendom, signifies more vividly the Burial and Resurrection of Christ, yet Baptism by infusion, that is, by pouring water on the head, is equally valid, and is generally used in the Western Church.

In this way may be fairly answered those accusations so freely made against Catholics of mutilating and profaning this Sacrament, of defrauding the laity of their inheritance, or of giving them only, as some strangely maintain, half a Sacrament, half the inheritance. All these accusations fall to the ground of themselves, for whether under one kind or under both, the Communicant receives the entire Sacrament, that is, the Body and Blood, the Soul and Divinity, of Jesus Christ.

Catholics might with justice reply to the accusations of their opponents by saying that Protestants, instead of an inheritance more precious than any *jewels*, only give to the receiver, so to speak, an empty coffer. Instead of realities, they give natural elements, more empty, poor, and weak than those that were formerly in use under the Old Testament; instead of a Sacrament that signifies what it contains, and gives what it signifies, they dispense empty signs signifying what they do not contain, and not giving what they signify; instead of a Sacrament in which Christ is really present, they give that from which the Body and Blood of Christ are truly absent; careful to declare it at the same time that what they dispense is but bread and wine; that Christ's Body is nowhere but in heaven, as far distant from their Sacrament as heaven is from earth.

It is hardly the part of those who give the cup without the Precious Blood to accuse Catholics of giving the Divine Blood without the cup, for we have already remarked that Catholics receiving the Body of Christ under one kind necessarily receive His Blood also.

Nor can they accuse us of giving to the laity a mutilated Sacrament. To suppose that Communion in one kind is a mutilated Sacrament would involve consequences both awful and absurd.

A mutilated Sacrament is a sacrilege both in the giver and in the receiver, as it would then be a profanation of a holy thing instituted by Christ. Can we think that the early Christians in the East and West were habitually sacrilegious? Did an Ambrose, a Jerome, a Basil, a Serapion, and so many other Saints who at their death partook of this Sacrament under one kind only, receive a mutilated Sacrament? Did they make a sacrilegious Communion before appearing in the presence of their Lord? Shall the Catholic Church be accused of having throughout all ages profaned the most august of Sacraments, or of having all along been ignorant of its nature?

Protestants may refer us to Holy Scripture and say: If it cannot be shown from the nature of this Sacrament that both kinds are required in the Communion, it can at least be proved from the fact that our Saviour in giving the chalice said: "*Drink ye all of this*" (S. Matth. xxvi. 27), implying thereby that *all*, priests and laymen, were bound to receive the chalice besides the consecrated bread.

It is remarkable, they say, that Jesus Christ did not use this expression when He gave the consecrated bread. It seems, they add, that Christ foresaw that people would in course of time be tempted to neglect this sacred rite, and that therefore He used this expression to caution His followers and put them on their guard.

We reply, that there is no reason why we should take those words: "*Drink ye all of this*"—as addressed to the laity; for, first, it is clear that our Saviour addressed these words only to the Apostles, "*the twelve*" then present, and the Apostles were priests, not laymen. If everything that was said to the Apostles (that is, to priests) must be understood as addressed to laics, it would follow that also the words delivered by our Saviour to the Apostles: "*Going, therefore, teach all nations, baptizing them*" (S. Matth. xxviii. 19), "*Whose sins ye forgive they are forgiven, and whose sins ye retain they are retained*" (S. John xx. 23), should be taken as addressed to every layman, woman, and child, as well as to priests. (See S. Matth. xxvi. 29).

That the word *all* in the alleged text refers only to the Apostles present, and not to any one absent, is shown clearly by the words that occur in S. Mark (xiv. 23): "*And they all drank of it;*" for if all who had to drink actually drank, there remained no one else to whom the word *all* could be applied.

Again, the expression: "*Drink ye all,*" clearly refers to the same persons to whom He said "*Do this,*" therefore it means: Do in after time what you have seen Me do now; that is, give thanks, bless, consecrate, and take. If the words "*drink ye all*" were to be taken as addressed to laymen as well as to consecrating priests, it would follow that the laity, men, women, and children, have the right and the power, and are bound to consecrate; as it would be arbitrary indeed to say that the words "*do this*" mean *thank, bless, consecrate, and take* when applied to priests, but when applied to laymen only mean "*receive this*".

The natural interpretation, acknowledged also as such by some Protestants, of the words: "*Drink ye all of this*," is, Hand the chalice from one to another, and drink each and all of you a portion out of it.

Christ had no need to say the like words respecting the bread, as He had broken it, (probably into as many pieces as there were Apostles), and given one portion to each; but with regard to the chalice, which was only one, and of which all the Apostles had to partake, it was natural that Christ should say: "*Drink ye all of this*".

This interpretation, which appears so genuine from the context, seems evidently more so by the corresponding expression used by S. Luke: "*Take and divide it among you*" (xxii. 17), which expression is clearly used as equivalent to the other: "*Drink ye all of this.*"

Some will perhaps say: Why then did our Saviour, at the very time that He instituted the Holy Eucharist, distribute it under the species of bread and of wine, if there were no more necessity for receiving under both kinds?

We answer: Christ instituted the Holy Eucharist under both species, and the consecrating Priest is bound to partake of it under both species, because the Holy Eucharist, besides being a Sacrament, is also a Sacrifice. It is requisite for a Sacrifice that the victim should be really present and immolated or destroyed, at least mystically, in order that it may represent the death of the victim. This was done at the Last Supper, and is still done in the Mass, by the symbolical disunion through the separate consecration of the Body and Blood of Christ.

It is also requisite for the completion of the *Sacrifice* that the Priest who has immolated the great Victim, by mystically separating, by a distinct consecration, the Body and the Blood of that Victim, should consume it in both these kinds as often as he celebrates Mass, in order to show forth in a still more striking manner "*the death of the Lord until He come*" (1 Corinth. xi. 26); whereas, at other times, when they do not act as sacrificers, neither Priests nor Bishops, nor the Pope himself, even upon their death-bed, receive Communion in the Western parts of Christendom otherwise than the rest of the faithful, namely, only under the species of bread which has been previously consecrated by a Priest during Mass.

We do not read that our Lord at the Last Supper said anything about the distribution of the Sacrament to the laity, as we have already noticed, much less whether it should be given to them under both kinds or under one alone. Christ having said nothing on this point, nothing can be deduced from the words of the institution of the Holy Eucharist for or against, but must be learnt from other sources.

The Apostles as we have already remarked, used to give Communion also under one kind. It is said in the Acts of the Apostles that the first Christians "*were persevering in the doctrine of the Apostles, and in the communication of the breaking of bread and in prayers*" (ii. 42), "*breaking bread from house to house*" (ii. 46), "*on the first day of the week, when we were assembled to break bread*" (xx. 7).

The Apostle Paul is far from insisting on the necessity of receiving under both kinds, for in the following passage of his first Epistle to the Corinthians his words imply that under either kind alone we receive a full Sacrament, namely, the Blood and Body of Christ. He writes: "*Therefore, whosoever shall eat this bread,* OR *drink the chalice of the Lord unworthily, shall be guilty of the Body and Blood of the Lord*" (1 Corinth. xi. 27). If by taking Communion unworthily under one kind alone a person becomes guilty both of the Body and Blood of the Lord, it follows that by receiving worthily under *one kind* a person receives the entire Sacrament, and the whole essential fruit of the Sacrament, namely, the whole Jesus Christ.

The mistranslation of this passage which occurs in the authorised Protestant English Version must have materially served to fix more deeply into the minds of the readers the Protestant view of the Communion of the laity under both kinds; for the Protestant version puts the conjunction "AND" in place of the disjunctive "OR," contrary to the original Greek from which the Protestant version is presumed to be made, as well as contrary to the Latin Vulgate, and even contrary to the translation of Beza, and the German translation of Luther, which has the word "*oder*" "OR."

Many Protestant scholars have acknowledged the corruption of this text in the English Protestant authorised version. Amongst others, the present Dean of Westminster, Doctor Stanley, who wrote these remarkable words: "Probably from the wish to accommodate the text to the change of custom, or from hostility to the Roman Catholic practice of administering the bread without the cup, the English translators have unwarrantably rendered ἤ 'and' (that is 'and' for 'or'): καὶ for ἤ occurs only in the Alexandrian, and in three cursive manuscripts." (Comments on 1 Epistle to Corinthians xi. 27, note p. 211.)

The ancient Sinaitic Codex discovered by Tischendorf in 1844 has "OR" not AND.

What took place in the time of the Apostles was done in all after ages, so that there never was a time in which the Communion under one kind, and especially under that of bread, was not practised. Even when by universally prevailing custom, or by positive law of the Church, Communion was given under both kinds, there were yet exceptional cases in which Communion under one kind was allowed.

Both ways of giving Communion run side by side throughout all ages, not only in the Latin Church, but also in the Greek and other Eastern Churches, both before and after these latter had detached themselves from the communion with the Roman Catholic Church.

That in Holy Scripture no Divine command is given nor any other kind of necessity can be discovered compelling the priests to give, and the laity to receive, Communion under both kinds, is a thing which seems also admitted by a great number of Protestants.

The Protestant Confession of Augsburg, alluding to the Catholic custom of giving Communion under one kind, excuses the Catholic Church from any blame in this matter. (See Augsburg Confession, page 235.)

When the Protestant religion was established in England, the King Edward and Parliament in 1548 by separate Acts, under the title of "Communion under both kinds," provided that this Sacrament should only be *commonly so delivered and ministered*, yet an exception was made in case *necessity should otherwise require.* (Burnet's History of the Reformation, part. ii., p. 41.)

The Calvinists of France, in their Synod of Poitiers 1560, decreed thus: "The bread of our Lord's Supper ought to be administered *to those who cannot drink wine,* on their making a protestation that they do not refrain from it through contempt." (On the Lord's Supper, chap. iii., p. 7.)

All this tends to confirm what we have tried to prove with a fair number of arguments, that though we are commanded by Christ to receive the Holy Communion, yet, that Communion under *both kinds* does not fall under a Divine precept, and that it is not a thing demanded by the institution of this Sacrament, nor by the nature of it; but that Christ left this point as a matter of discipline, to be regulated by the Church, according to time and other circumstances.

Yet it is sad to think, that, notwithstanding all this, some who may read these pages will perhaps persist in maintaining (such, alas! is the force of education, habit, and prejudice) that this Sacrament, if taken under one kind alone, is no Sacrament at all, or that it is only a mutilated Sacrament, that is, one that gives only the Body, and not the Blood of Christ.

In this case the manner of reasoning adopted by such persons seems to be as follows:—" In spite of the foregoing observations I hold to my private opinion that the words of the institution of this Sacrament, imply a necessity and a command to the laity of communicating under both kinds. The passages which you bring to prove that Communion was given by the Apostles under the species of bread alone do not satisfy me; nor is the expression you quote from S. Paul enough to convince me that the Body and the Blood of Christ is received under each kind. I am not moved by the historical fact that even in those centuries when Communion in both kinds was in use, yet in a vast number of cases, as of sick, of infants, of prisoners, of persons living in remote places, or keeping themselves concealed through raging persecutions and other cases, the Church sanctioned Communion under one kind. I am not willing to admit that the word ALL is clearly confined to those 'of whom it is said; '*They all drank*,'—nor am I concerned about the consequences of my opinion, which implies that the Church, during fifteen centuries before the Reformation, was ignorant of a most important Divine precept, and of the nature of the most holy of Sacraments, and that she was a constant profaner of the same. I do not even pay regard to the view of those Protestants, or bodies of Protestants, who, by admitting exceptional cases, seem to agree with Catholics in this matter. Their way of thinking is not an authority for me; my opinion is as good as theirs; my opinion is my own; I will not recede from it."

It is to be hoped, however, that many candid Protestants will argue differently; perhaps in this manner:—

"From the observations made in this essay it appears that no proof can be drawn from the words of the institution of a Divine precept binding upon *all persons* to receive Communion under both kinds. One thing, however, is clear from Holy Scripture, that Christ intrusted the dispensation of this and the other Sacraments to the Apostles and their successors, who must therefore have been well informed and competent to regulate this point. It belonged to them to determine whether this Sacrament ought to be distributed under two kinds, or under one alone. I cannot suppose that the Apostles and their successors were uninformed of this most vital point of religion. It is known that in the time of the Apostles, and in all after centuries, Communion under one kind alone was, to say the least, occasionally given, and this is enough to prove that the Church always held that no divine percept existed commanding all the faithful to receive Communion under both kinds, or forbidding to receive Communion under one kind alone. I cannot suppose for a moment that the Saints on their death-bed consented to receive, and the Church dared to give, Communion under one kind, as undoubted historical testimonies prove was done, if to give it under one kind were to mutilate a Sacrament; to suppose that this did really take place would reflect on our Lord Himself, as having been unable to foresee or provide properly for His Church in this most important point.

"Therefore I think I cannot do better in this matter than distrust myself, my prejudices, and my private interpretation, or the interpretation of those who claim no higher authority than their own private opinion in deciding the sense of Holy Scripture, and put my confidence in the Holy Catholic Church to guide me in this point—that Church which shows every mark that her pastors are the lawful successors of the Apostles to whom Christ said:—"*Teach ye all nations . . . teaching them to observe all things whatsoever I have commanded you: and behold I am with you all days, even to the consummation of the world*" (S. Matth. xxviii. 19, 20).

From this passage a candid Protestant might fairly conclude and say: "It seems to me evident that the Apostles were made the interpreters, promulgators, teachers, and the natural guardians, together with their successors, of the commands of Christ. It was therefore their business, and not that of laymen, or other unauthorised persons, to declare which commandments are Divine and which are not, and how far the obligation of such commandments extends. To the Apostles was promised the Holy Ghost, to abide personally with them and their successors for ever. (S. John xiv. 16.) Therefore I cannot do better than accept, what is held on the subject by the Catholic Church.

No. 38.—The transmission of the Sin of Adam to his Children Considered.

The transmission of original sin is a mystery which Catholics believe on the authority of God Who reveals it. It is in harmony with reason, and to some extent admits of explanation.

God decreed to raise human nature to a supernatural order of love and friendship with Himself, with a right and duty of aspiring to Him as our supernatural end, and without dying, of finally possessing Him in the "beatific" vision of Him in Heaven.

No sooner did God create Adam than He bestowed upon him, as head of the whole human family, all the supernatural gifts called *holiness* and *original justice*, to be transmitted, together with human nature itself, to all his children.

Unhappily, Adam by his sin of disobedience, which was also a sin of pride, disbelief and ambition, forfeited, or, more properly speaking, rejected that original justice; and we, as members of the human family, of which he was the head, are also implicated in that guilt of self-spoliation, or rejection and deprivation of those supernatural gifts; not indeed on account of our having willed it with our personal will, but by having willed it with the will of our first parent, to whom we are linked by nature as members to their head.

Hence it appears that not the whole sin of Adam is imputed to us, not his ambition, his pride, his disbelief, not even his disobedience, regarded only as such; in short not his sin so far as it was only personal to Adam; but we are implicated in that special guilt of his sin in which he could and did act as head of the human family; for only in that capacity could the guilt of his act be attributed to his posterity, and be transmitted with nature itself to every human being descended from him.

Now what was this special and transmissible guilt of the sin of Adam?

Inasmuch as Adam received certain supernatural gifts to be transmitted by him to his descendants, the special guilt of the sin of Adam consists in this, that he sinfully rejected those gratuitous supernatural gifts; and, on account of our union with him as his offspring and members of the human family of which he is the head, we also have shared with Adam in that his self-spoliation and voluntary deprivation of original grace.

Therefore, original sin does not consist in the *privation*

of original justice considered as a mere *privation*, as a mere *misfortune*, or even as a *punishment*, because *mere privation, mere misfortune,* and *mere punishment* are not sin. But when we speak of original sin, we speak of sin properly so called in the sphere of morality; and therefore, although the essence of original sin consists in the privation of original justice, yet it consists in this privation or more properly *deprivation* or *self-spoliation,* inasmuch as this deprivation is offensive to God and ruinous to us, having been (and being) *willed* by our human nature in Adam, with the will of Adam.

Hence *original sin* is also called sin of nature; sin in which our *personal* will has no part, but with which only our nature has to do, as being one with that of Adam.

According to this explanation, there is no need to suppose that our will was included in the will of Adam like as in law the will of the infant is said to be included in that of a guardian.

Nor is there any need to suppose an express or an implied bond between God and Adam, to the effect that, if Adam had remained faithful to God, he and his offspring should enjoy those supernatural gifts, but if not faithful, he should lose them for himself and for his posterity.

Nor can we suitably employ as an illustration the example of a man who, having by his own fault lost his estates, his children are also deprived of them; for with regard to the children this would be a *mere misfortune,* unaccompanied by any fault or stain of sin.

It is not by an arbitrary act on the part of God that we inherit original sin, nor is it on His part an imputing to us a guilt which we really have not. On the contrary, original sin is a necessary consequence of the sinful breaking by Adam of the supernatural order established by God; in which sin we share, inasmuch as we form one moral body, that is one family, with him.

In this mystery of original sin we have great reason to humble ourselves, and to adore God's judgments; but we have no ground to complain, as if our contracting the guilt of original sin were unjust.

It was a great favour that the supernatural gifts of

sanctity and original justice should have been gratuitously conferred upon Adam. It was also a great favour that such gifts should have been intended not only for Adam but for the whole human race, so that each of the children of Adam should receive it on receiving human nature, and that they should receive it without any merit, or even without any predisposition on their part.

But from this order of things it followed, that if the first man should sin, human nature, which was all included in him, should lose those gifts.

Therefore, on account of the sin of the first man, all men are indeed born deprived of certain gifts, but gratuitous gifts. They are born averse to God, but averse to God as a supernatural end which is not demanded by nature. If God is said to hate them, the meaning of this hating is only that God, who loves them as His intelligent creatures, does not love them with a love of gratuitous friendship, with a love ready to confer on them a supernatural blessedness. They are truly sons of wrath, but only inasmuch as the supernatural beatitude is denied to them, and in which privation their condemnation consists. They are called sinners, but not because any *actual personal guilt* of Adam is imputed to them, but inasmuch as the *deprivation of grace* brought upon himself by Adam as a necessary consequence of his sin is justly considered voluntary in them by the will of the head of the human race. Therefore they are sinners, not by any personal sin of their own, but by a sin, so to speak, of nature, because brought upon nature by the actual refusal of those gifts by Adam in the name of the whole human nature, and as head of the whole human family.

Nor can it be said that God does thereby impute to us the personal sin of another. He imputes a sin which is ours, though, at the same time, also of another; because it is not the sin of Adam (inasmuch as that was personal) which God imputes, but the necessary effect of his sin, that is, the deprivation, the rejection, as it were, of *original justice*, which Adam wilfully incurred as head of the whole human race, and which therefore we also, as united to Adam, have incurred.

In this no vestige of injustice appears. Men do not thereby lose anything which their nature requires. God cannot be charged with being the cause of the sin of nature; but the cause of it is the free-will of Adam, the head-parent of all men. This sin, therefore, is justly attributed to all his descendants.

All complaint that could possibly be raised might be reduced to this: Why did God give these supernatural gifts to human nature to be passed on to all men through Adam only, and not given them successively to each individual? But such a complaint comes to this: Why did not God create another order of Providence rather than this, in which as many as derive their nature from the first parent, if this should have happened to become sinful, they would have to be born in sin?

It is evident that there is no just ground for this complaint; for God being Master of His gifts and of His creatures, has a right to choose the mode whereby to commmunicate those gifts to them.

Were we to grant, for *argument's sake*, that the other mode would have been in some respect better, yet as God is not bound to do what is in itself absolutely best, but only what is good or relatively best, it follows that not only God's justice, but not even His goodness can be justly found fault with for having acted thus.

The supernatural gifts destined by God for all human nature could not be lost by human nature through the sin of any one else but that of Adam. For only the will of the head of the human family could be considered in this point the will of the whole human family. As those gifts were given to human nature, they could only be lost by the will of one whose will, in respect to those gifts, was the will of the whole human nature; and such the will of Adam was.

If Eve alone had sinned, we should not have incurred original sin, because Adam alone and not Eve, was the head of the human race. Hence both Tradition and Scripture attribute the fallen state to one alone, namely, Adam; and to this one they contrast the only one second

Adam, our Lord Jesus Christ. Eve therefore was the first to give occasion to our ruin, but not to effect it.

From this teaching it is easy to understand that only the first sin of Adam could transmit its guilt to posterity, because only at the committing of the first sin of our first parent was there annexed the implied rejection of original justice granted to nature, and should a second or a third sin have been committed by Adam, there was no more original grace to reject, and therefore nature could no more be affected thereby.

The grace also which Adam might have recovered through the merits of Jesus Christ being applied to him, was not transmissible, because received for himself alone as an individual, through faith and other personal dispositions, and not for human nature.

So also the justice, and sanctity which any parent except Adam, might have obtained through being regenerated in Christ does not pass to his children. The reason is this, because that recovery of grace is granted by God to the individual, and not simply to nature, and could not therefore pass to another by generation; for generation, which is an act not of the superior, but of the inferior part of the man, is only capable of transmitting nature, and the gifts, if any, attached to nature and not the gifts granted and attached to an individual person.

The generation by which human nature and original sin are propagated is done in virtue of the old Adam, and not in virtue of the second Adam, or of the newness of Life in Christ. They who generate do not generate as being Children of Christ, but inasmuch as they are children of Adam.

No. 39.—PREDESTINATION.

I begin by premising that God on account of His goodness, mercy, and holiness, desires the salvation of all men. S. Paul says: That God "*will have* ALL MEN *to be saved, and to come to the knowledge of the Truth. For there is one Mediator of God and men, the man Christ* JESUS, *who gave*

Himself a Redemption FOR ALL, *a testimony in due times."* (1 S. Timothy ii. 4-6.) And in another passage which follows close upon the mention of predestination to life the same Apostle says: *" He that spared not even His own Son, but delivered Him up* FOR US ALL." (Romans viii. 32.) S. Peter declares that God is "*Not willing that* ANY *should perish, but that* ALL *should return to penance.*" (2 S. Peter iii. 9.)

If any one is lost notwithstanding the means of salvation that God affords to every one, such a one cannot justly blame God, but only himself and his sins. Sin is the only cause of exclusion from heaven. No one is a reprobate but by his own fault.

Grace is a gift of God entirely gratuitous in itself, and so excellent, that no creature, independently of Christ, is able to merit it by his own works; but our Divine Saviour has merited it for us by His Precious Blood; and, on account of Christ's infinite Merits, Divine Mercy gives to *every man* a measure of grace at *least sufficient* for his salvation. (See 1 S. Timothy ii. 4.) Even the greatest sinner is moved from time to time by grace, to return to God, and God gives him sufficient grace to correspond.

It is nevertheless true that God distributes this precious gift in an unequal manner, giving more to some and less to others, according to the inscrutable designs of His mercy and of His wisdom; but to no one does He give less grace than what is sufficient for salvation.

The goodness of God goes before and meets the soul, and gives to every soul gratuitously a *first grace*, (an *actual*, not *justifying* grace), by the aid of which the soul can perform good works (not however deserving heaven), and obtain further grace. The holy Patriarchs Job and Abraham, the Syro-Phœnician woman, Nicodemus, and the Centurion, are examples. Most frequently one of the first graces is the grace to pray in order to obtain more abundant help. This first grace may be compared to a sum of money given to a poor person, which if turned to a good account may make his fortune, but, if abused or not accepted will be of no benefit to him. Every one can, by prayer, obtain more grace from God, prepare himself to obtain the free gift of justification, and, by co-operating or working with it, arrive at everlasting life.

Almighty God, because He is *Eternal* and *All-knowing*, knows beforehand the co-operation of the good with His grace, their good works, preseverance, and final salvation. As the salvation of the good is owing to God's grace, given to them in the measure that He foreknew they would make use of, and not resist, though they *could* have resisted it, it follows that those that are saved must be considered to have been *predestined*, because their salvation was not only foreseen but effected by God, through His grace, which sanctified them and helped them in the good use of their free-will left in them unconstrained.

Thus there is predestination of the good who are saved, but it cannot be said, strictly speaking, that there is predestination of the wicked who are lost; because, although God knows beforehand their resistance to His grace, their obstinacy in sin, and their final condemnation, yet it cannot be said that because He knows beforehand He therefore *wills* beforehand, and by *willing* causes the works of the wicked; nay, His having poured upon them His grace to enable them to do good proves the very contrary. If God by His grace, which He refuses to none, stirs and enables us to avoid sin, He cannot be said to lead us into sin should we resist His grace.

The second Council of Orange, (near Avignon, in France), A.D. 529, pronounced thus: "That any persons are by the Divine power predestined to evil, we not only do not believe, but if there be any persons minded to believe so great an evil, with utter detestation thereof we say anathema to them." (Canon 25). S. Fulgentius says: "Never could God have predestined man to that which He had Himself intended to forbid by His precept, and to blot out by His mercy, and to punish by his justice."

Catholics do not believe that any soul is predestined by God to be lost, or that God causes any man to fall into sin and thus be lost. This the Catholic Church condemns as an impious and monstrous doctrine.* She teaches that as God foresees everything, so it must ever have been known to Him that many of the children of Adam, would not attain everlasting life in Heaven, notwithstanding the plenteous Redemption through the blood of Jesus Christ, because His Precious Blood has not been, through their own fault, applied to them to free them from the stain of original sin; or that, though freed from original sin and justified, they would of their own free-will resist His grace, *which is given in a sufficient measure to all*, would plunge into sin, forfeit justification, die without repenting, and consequently be justly condemned.

Now, this *foreknowledge* cannot properly be called predestination in the strict sense; and in fact the word "predestination" is never applied in Holy Scripture to those who are lost. It may properly be called *prescience, prevision*, or *reprobation*, which expressions do not imply that God had an active part in their having deserved that doom. The doctrine of predestination to life and prevision to everlasting misery, as taught in the Catholic Church, is reconcilable with God's goodness, justice, holiness, and wisdom; with the just man's merits, and the wicked man's demerits; it is reconcilable with God's commands and threats; with His rewarding the good, and punishing the wicked, and agrees with that saying of S. James (i. 13), that God "*tempteth no man*."

If any should ask, why God, Who can predestinate some to eternal life, cannot predestinate others to everlasting condemnation, the answer is plain. Salvation is an act of mercy, and can be granted even to one who has no merit; condemnation is an act of justice and a punishment, and can only be inflicted on a guilty person; and therefore God can predestinate only in the former case and not in the other, because God cannot be unjust.

To this purpose S. Augustine of Hippo eloquently says: "God renders evil (physical) for evil (moral) because He is just; good for evil because He is good; good for good

---

* See Council of Trent, Session vi. Canon 6.

because He is good and just; only He does not render evil for good because he is not unjust." (On Grace and Freewill, chap. 23).

On the other hand, the prevision of God about the perdition of some men has not the least influence over their actions; and no one will be lost in consequence of God's necessary foreknowledge, but only because that one has himself deserved such condemnation.

That no one is condemned without some great fault of his own is clear from these declarations in Holy Scripture: that God "*will render to every man according to his works.*" (Romans ii. 6.) "*Depart from Me, all ye workers of iniquity.*" (S. Luke xiii. 27.) "*Depart from me, you cursed, into everlasting fire, which was prepared for the devil and his angels. For I was hungry, and you gave me not to eat, I was thirsty, and you gave Me not to drink.*" (S. Matt. xxv. 41.)* "*The wicked shall be turned into hell, all the nations that* FORGET *God.*" (Psalm ix. 18.) All which, and other similar passages, show that those who are lost are lost on account of their being guilty of grievous sin.

It may be objected that some texts represent God as the author of sin; that He "*loved Jacob*" and "*hated Esau*" (Malachias i. 2, and Romans, ix. 13); † that He darkened the mind of some so that they might not see; hardened the heart of others that they might not be moved to repentance; that there is no evil of which He is not the cause—and such-like expressions.

The answer to this difficulty is, that when there is a truth plainly stated in the Holy Scripture, which truth other texts seem to contradict, the universally admitted rule of interpretation, demands that these passages should be explained in a sense consistent with that plain doctrine, as there cannot be any contradiction in the Word of God. Therefore all the expressions just quoted and similar ones must be understood to mean that God darkens the mind, hardens the heart, and offers temptation, *not directly* but *indirectly*, that is, by permitting or not stopping these

* See Job xxxiv. 9—11.
† See Note in Douay Version.

evils as He might, but which He is not in His justice bound to do.

Most ungrounded and unwise it would be to say, that since only those who are predestined to life will be saved, therefore that it is of no use to pray, or to try to do good, as though, if predestined to life, no matter what amount of evil we commit, we should be saved.

Nor is it true to say that he who is not predestined to life, whatever he may do, will be lost, and that the predestined one, whatever he may do, will be saved; for none will be lost but the wicked, and none will be saved but the good: and the more good works the just man by God's grace shall do on earth, the higher shall be his blissful mansion in heaven, "*for star differeth from star in glory*" (1 Corinth. xv. 41); and the more works of darkness the wicked man shall do in this world, the greater shall be his punishment hereafter. There is being "*beaten with many stripes*" and "*beaten with few stripes.*" (S. Luke xii. 47, 48.)

The doctrine of predestination, understood in the Catholic sense, far from discouraging prayer, diligence, faithfulness, hope and all good works, is an incentive to the same, because God has so predestined men that they should attain their salvation through those very means by which we strive to imitate our Saviour Jesus Christ, and become, as S. Paul says, "*conformable*" to his image. (Romans viii. 29).[*]

As long as we live, though the testimony of the Holy Spirit [†] and of a good conscience can give us a holy confidence, and even a great confidence, yet unless (as declared by the Council of Trent, Session vi. chap. 9) a person has received from God a special revelation, our salvation cannot be certainly known to us with certainty of faith, and therefore no one should presume upon his security or be cast down by despair. We must love God and rely on His justice and mercy, and follow the advice of S. Paul, "*with fear and trembling work out your salvation*"

---

[*] See footnote in Douay Bible on this passage.
[†] See footnote in Douay Bible at Romans viii. 16.

(Philippians ii. 12), who also writes: "*I chastise my body, and bring it into subjection, lest perhaps, when I have preached to others, I myself should become a cast-away*" (1 Corinth. ix. 27); and remember the admonition of S. Peter: "*Wherefore, brethren, labour the more, that by good works you may make sure your calling and election.*" (2 S. Peter i. 10).

No. 40.—"Justification by Faith Alone" Considered.

1. As in revolutions the leaders try to gain the people over by the bait of promised independence so at the time of the Reformation—which was a revolution against Church authority and order in religion—it seems that it was the aim of the Reformers to decoy the people under the pretext of making them independent of the priests, in whose hands our Saviour has placed the administering of the seven Sacraments of pardon and of grace.

They began, therefore, by discarding five of these Sacraments, including the Sacrament of Order, in which Priests are ordained, and the Sacrament of Penance, in which the forgiveness of sins is granted to the penitent, by virtue of those words of Christ: "*Whose sins you shall forgive, they are forgiven them; and whose sins you shall retain, they are retained.*" (S. John xx. 23).

They then reduced, as it appears, to a mere matter of form the two Sacraments they professed to retain, namely, Holy Baptism and the Holy Eucharist, called by Protestants the Lord's Supper. To make up for this rejection, and enable each individual to prescribe for himself, and procure by himself the pardon of sins and Divine grace, independently of the Priests and of the Sacraments, they invented an *exclusive means*, never known in the Church of God, and still rejected by all the Eastern Churches and by the Roman Catholics throughout the world, by which the followers of Luther ventured to declare that each individual can secure pardon and justification for himself independently of Priests and Sacraments. They have framed a new *Dogma*, not to be found in any of the Creeds, or in the Canons of any General Council; I mean, the new dogma of *Justification by Faith alone, or by Faith only.*

2. This new doctrine has gone through many changes in course of time. It exists even now under many shades of variety in its details. Still, it may be asserted, that the vast majority of Protestants think that the only means appointed by our Saviour for our being pardoned, justified, and adopted by God, that is, for our passing from a state of condemnation, to a state of acceptance, with God, with the consequent blessings of grace, and state of salvation (or as Catholics would say, from a state of sin to a state of grace), is *faith alone.*

By adding the word *alone*, Protestants profess to exclude all exterior, ceremonial, pious, or charitable works, works of obedience or of penance, and good moral acts whatever, as *means of apprehending* justification, or as conditions to obtain it. All Protestants by that word *alone* mean also to exclude the Sacraments of Baptism and Penance as *means of apprehending* or possessing themselves of justification, which they maintain is only apprehended by faith.

By the word *alone*, Wesleyans (who as a body seem, next to the Anglican Establishment, to retain more of Catholic doctrine than other Dissenters), and some others, do not shut out *hope, repentance, belief in Gospel truths, fear of God, and a purpose of amendment.* They teach that although it is not the part of these moral acts, to secure justification, yet the faith which alone takes hold upon Christ has necessarily these results. Other Protestants, on the contrary, by the word *alone* seem to exclude (with the exception of belief in the plan of redemption and repentance) belief in all other revealed truths, and all other interior good moral acts whatsoever, love of God and neighbour, resolution to avoid sin, fear of God, obedience, readiness to do works of penance and the desire to receive the Sacraments of Baptism and Penance; either because they hold it impossible to make these works properly, or because they consider them sinful in themselves, or dispositions unnecessary and useless for justification.

Indeed, some of them go so far as to consider these interior good acts as well as other exterior good deeds, rather hindrances than dispositions to justification.

To do these acts with the view of being justified, they say, is like giving a penny to the Queen to obtain from her a royal gift. Come as you are, they add; you cannot be too bad for Jesus. Through *faith alone* in His promise, they assert, you can and should accept Christ's merits, seize Christ's Redemption and His justice; appropriate Christ to yourself, believe that Jesus is with you, is yours, that He pardons your sins, and all this without any preparation and without any doing on your part; in fact, that however deficient you may be in all other dispositions which Catholics require, and however loaded with sins, if you only trust in Jesus that He will forgive your sins and save you, you are by that *trust alone* forgiven, personally redeemed, justified, and placed in a state of salvation.

3. Nothing certainly can be better for us poor sinners than to be converted, pardoned, actually redeemed, saved and united with Christ. Catholics, indeed, cannot aim at anything more needful and desirable than this. The question, however, is not about that. The question is—Is justification, according to Scripture, to be had *only* by this *trusting* or *faith in Christ for personal salvation*, or is it not?

We know that Christ died for all, and yet that all are not saved, but only such are saved as fulfil certain conditions and become just; so that the promise of salvation is not absolute but conditional. Hence S. Paul says: "*He became to all that obey Him, the cause of eternal salvation*".*

Now these conditions, these dispositions demanded by Christ before making us share His merits, His grace, and the fruit of His Redemption, before pardoning and justifying us, are they many, or is there only one? And

---

* See Hebrews v. 9: also S. Matthew xxv. 46.

if only one, is it the *reliance* or *faith in Christ for personal salvation* taught by Protestants, or is it another kind of faith, or some other means?

If I have Jesus Christ with me I cannot wish for more, provided by this *kind of faith* I can really have Him; but if this *kind of faith* is not the *right* means, and if *faith* is not the *only* means appointed by Him for that purpose, I may imagine that I possess Christ, whilst in reality I do not.

To people who are brought up in the belief of justification by faith alone, and who are constantly told that the word *faith* in Holy Scripture mostly means simple *acceptance* or *reliance on Christ for personal salvation*, this theory of justification by *faith alone* must naturally appear very Scriptural indeed; for they imagine it to be confirmed every time that mention is made in Scripture of being saved by faith. But on examining, with unprejudiced mind, all the texts generally adduced in proof of that doctrine, it is found that *not one* of them tells *clearly* in favour of it.

The word "faith," in Scripture, sometimes means *confidence* in God's omnipotence and goodness, that He can and is willing to cure or benefit us by some miraculous interposition. Mostly it refers to revealed truths, and signifies *belief* in them as such. No one has a right to give to the word faith a new meaning, and take it, for instance, to signify reliance on Jesus for being personally saved through this very reliance alone, unless Jesus Christ or the Apostles had, in some instance, *clearly* attributed such a meaning to the word faith, and had taught in some place the doctrine of *trust in Christ for personal salvation* as the only requisite for justification. No one should attach a particular meaning to the word *faith*, without having a good warrant in Scripture or in Tradition.

4. Now, in many passages of Holy Scripture in which *saving* faith is plainly spoken of, by *faith* is not meant *a trust in Christ for personal salvation*, but evidently a firm belief that Jesus is the Messias, the Christ, the Son of God; that what is related of Him in the Gospel is true,

and that what He taught is true. This faith, however, does not exclude, but leads to trusting in Christ.

The following are instances. In S. John we read— "*These are written that you may believe that* JESUS *is the Christ the Son of God; and that believing you may have life in His name*" (xx. 31.) It is evident that the saving belief here mentioned is not *a trust in Christ for personal salvation*, but the believing what is asserted of Christ in the Gospel.

Thus, likewise, the whole eleventh chapter of S. Paul's Epistle to the Hebrews (which, as is admitted on every side, treats of saving faith), evidently shows that the object of this *saving faith* is not to make a person confident of actually obtaining mercy through trusting in Christ, but it is to make him certain of the existence of truths not to be discovered by simple reason, but revealed by God.

The saving faith of the Chamberlain of Queen Candace required by S. Philip was not directly a confidence in Christ for mercy, but a belief in His Divinity. (Acts viii. 37.) The faith of the man sick of the palsy, that gained for him the pardon of his sins, was not a reliance on Christ for the forgiveness of his sins, but a belief in the Divine omnipotence and goodness of Christ, that He could and would heal him. (S. Luke v. 20.) When Jesus Christ said to Martha: "*Every one that liveth and believeth in Me shall not die for ever. Believest thou this?*" Martha answered: "*Yea, Lord, I have believed that Thou art* CHRIST *the Son of the living God, Who art come into this world.*" (S. John xi. 26, 27.) This was not a trust in Christ for pardon, but a belief that JESUS was the Son of God, the Messias.

Again, Jesus Christ declared that saving faith was to know and believe that His Father was the only true God, and that He Himself was His Divine Son, sent by Him to redeem the world. "*Now this is eternal life; That they may know Thee, the only true God, and* JESUS CHRIST *whom Thou hast sent.*" (S. John xvii. 3.)

S. Paul, explaining the nature of justifying faith, says: "*For if thou confess with thy mouth the Lord* JESUS, *and believe in thy heart that God hath raised Him up from the dead, thou shalt be saved."* (Romans x. 9.)* It is clear that to believe in Jesus Christ, and consequently to believe what He teaches and what He promises, is not the same as a mere confidence in Christ for pardon. When our Saviour said: *"Going therefore, teach ye all nations, . . . teaching them to observe all things whatsoever I have commanded you."* *"He that believeth and is baptized shall be saved; but he that believeth not shall be condemned"* (S. Matth. xxviii. 19, 20, and S. Mark xvi. 16), our LORD evidently spoke of saving faith, and this faith was simply to believe the revealed truths taught by Christ and preached by the Apostles, with the intention of practising them, as a necessary condition of justification.

These texts, which all refer to saving faith, prove to evidence that not *trust* in Christ for *personal salvation*, but the *faith of the Creed, the faith in revealed truths, the faith of the Gospel,* as S. Paul calls it (Philippians i. 27), *is the faith availing for justification*, though this saving faith, as we have said, does not exclude *trusting* in Christ, but leads to it.

S. Paul confirms all this plainly in his second Epistle to the Thessalonians, where he says that *the love of the truth* is necessary for salvation (chap. ii. 10)—that not to believe the truth is to wish not to be justified, but to be *judged* (verse 11)—that we are chosen to salvation and sanctification *through belief of the truth* (verses 12, 13.) That by faith of the truth S. Paul meant, believing everything revealed by God, and taught by the true Messengers of God, he makes sufficiently clear in verses 14, 15, where he tells them to stand fast and hold everything they had been taught by him.

5. Now surely it must be admitted, that whenever in other parts of Holy Scripture saving faith is spoken of without any clear indication of its meaning (the word *faith* being left unexplained by the context), such a meaning should be attached to this word *faith* as is

* See also Philippians iii. 9, 10.

clearly set forth in other texts; according to the universally accepted rule of interpretation, that we must interpret the obscure or less clear texts of Scripture by those that are more clear. To interpret passages of Scripture which are not clear as though clear, and some even in contradiction to other clear texts, is against reason, and violates the first rule of interpretation.

In no text of Holy Scripture in which *saving* faith is clearly mentioned, are we compelled by the context to take the word *faith* to mean *primarily trust*, and not *belief in Gospel-truths* as the *first* and *direct* meaning. Therefore to take certain texts of Scripture in which faith, or belief, or approaching to Christ is mentioned, and take them to mean *reliance in Christ* for pardon as a primary meaning, and that reliance as the sole means of justification, is a mere assumption, and contrary to the rule of interpretation just mentioned.

6. To trust in God for mercy and pardon has certainly its place along with the other *dispositions* in the plan of justification. But nowhere in Holy Scripture is justification clearly attributed to *that trust as the sole apprehending instrument of justification.*

Thus we see that if the penitent Publican *trusted* in the mercy of God, it was not at the same time without some *love of God, fear, repentance, prayer, confession of his guilt, and humility*, shown by his standing at the far end of the Temple, striking his breast, and calling himself a sinner; and there is no allusion made to his having been forgiven in view of his trust as *the sole apprehending instrument of justification*, but rather having regard to all the aforesaid dispositions, *trust* included, and especially his humility, which our Saviour contrasted with the pride of the Pharisee, who boldly felt assured that he was justified. And of the penitent Publican our Saviour declared: "*I say to you this man went down into his house justified rather than the other.*" (S. Luke xviii. 14.) Thus S. Peter, speaking to Simon the sorcerer, though he raised somewhat his hope for pardon, yet he said to him: "*Do penance therefore from this thy wickedness:* and pray to

God if perhaps this thought of thy heart may be forgiven thee." (Acts viii. 22.)

Thus it is also clearly said that we are "*saved by hope*" (Romans viii. 24); but it is not said that this *hope* or *trust* is the only *apprehending instrument of justification; and faith or belief in Gospel-truths* is not excluded, but implied in it, as Protestants also teach; and this faith in Gospel-truths demands in its turn, and leads to all the other dispositions which the revealed Word of God requires, not for apprehending justification, but for being rendered fit to receive it. If you pretend that by trusting in Christ you apprehend Christ and become justified, then it is through your efforts and through your work you get justification—then the getting of justification depends on you, not as merely disposing yourself, as Catholics teach, but as on an active agent; then would justification not be *gratis*, but partly a fruit of your work.

This novel *apprehending*, besides being *unscriptural*, is also *uncalled for*. God bestows His justification on us when He finds us disposed to receive it. No *apprehending instrument* is required. We simply receive His justifying grace when it is given to us, just as we receive any other grace. Trusting is not in itself apprehending; it is quietly expecting and waiting the gift of God to be given by Him when He shall be pleased to bestow it on us, even without our perceiving it. Thus a man on the point of drowning, without his grappling at anything, is caught and rescued by another, moved to compassion by his miserable condition, by his cries, by his humble prayer, and by the confidence he places in him who comes to his rescue.

Luther admitted that justification and salvation by faith alone was a new doctrine, for in his comments on 1 Corinthians, v., he was vain enough to speak of himself as one "to whom the mystery of genuine faith, *hidden from former ages in God*, had been revealed." But having determined to introduce his newly-invented doctrine of justification by a mere reliance in Christ for pardon, which he called faith, and despairing to find another text that could serve his purpose better than the text of S. Paul, Romans iii. 28, *"For we account a man to be justified by faith without the works of the law,"* thought of making this text the great bulwark of his new doctrine; and being at the same time fully convinced that even this text was insufficient to establish his new principle, he betook himself to the mad expedient of corrupting this passage, adding the word *only* ("*allein,*" which word still remains in the Protestant German version of the Bible) to the word *faith*, in order to make it appear that saving faith was not only in contrast to the works of the Old Law, called by S. Paul the *law of works*, but also to the deeds of the New Law, called by the same holy Apostle the *law of faith;* that thus it might help him to start a new method of justification by faith alone.

People remonstrated with him on every side on this account; even his fellow-reformer Zuinglius accused him in these sharp words: "Luther, thou corruptest the Word of God. Thou art seen to be a manifest and common corrupter and perverter of Holy Scripture;" but it was of no avail. Despairing to find one text in the whole Scripture to prop efficiently his device, and seeing the necessity of introducing this word "*only*" in order to give this passage some appearance of favouring his novel principle of justification by faith *alone*, he declared unblushingly that this word should remain in spite of everything and of everbody; and this on no other but his own authority, and for no other reason than his own will.

The new doctrine started by Luther was adopted by the State Church of England, and embodied in the eleventh of the "*Thirty nine Articles of Religion*" of 1562, *still in force*, in these words: "Wherefore that we are justified by faith only is a most wholesome doctrine, and very full of comfort."

During fifteen centuries, both in the Western and Eastern Churches, the *saving faith* mentioned in Holy Scripture was always understood to signify belief in God and God's revelation, as such belief naturally leads to the adoption of all prescribed dispositions and means for being justified; and the kind of apprehending saving faith which means *confidence to get pardon*, without the Sacraments, by the sole means of that confidence, as taught in these later times by Protestants, was then unknown.

Luther invented this doctrine, and was the first to affix such meaning to the word *faith*. His new interpretation of the word was adopted in course of time by a vast number of Lutherans, Calvinists, and other Protestants; and from that period only there existed men who saw in the word *faith*, occurring so frequently in Holy Scripture, that which had never been seen by the Fathers, by the Doctors, by the Saints, and by the whole Church of God.

To show the unfairness of taking the word *faith* occurring in Holy Scripture in this new Protestant sense *of trust in Christ for pardon, to the exclusion of any other dispotion or means*, and not in the Catholic sense of belief in revealed truths, which belief virtually implies the use of all dispositions, *trust included*, and of all proper means, allow me to use the following illustration.

Suppose that a man afflicted with a grave disease sends for a physician of repute. The physician comes and prescribes, and to inspire the patient with more confidence, tells him, "Only believe, and you will be cured." Can we suppose that the poor sufferer, on the departure of the physician, would say: "I shall take no medicine, for the physician said: *only believe and you will be cured?*"

Such way of reasoning and acting seems impossible to occur with regard to the cure of the body, but respecting the cure of the soul it is an unhappy matter of fact that thousands of persons are daily falling into this sad mistake.

7. We seem to hear JESUS, our Heavenly Physician, say: I died for all, and thereby prepared in my Blood a remedy for all. If you would have the merits of My Passion and Death applied to you, and free your souls from sin, you must come to Me, you must believe that I am what I represent Myself to be, and you must

believe all that I teach. (S. Mark xvi. 15, 16.) Moreover, assisted by My grace, you must fear and serve Me. (S. Luke i. 50; Proverbs i. 7, xiv. 27, and xix. 23; Psalm lxxxiv. 10 (or Prot. version lxxxv. 9); Psalm cii. (or ciii. 11-13.) You must hope and trust in My goodness, omnipotence, and mercy. (1 S. John iii. 3; Romans viii. 21; Psalm xxxii. (or xxxiii. 18.) You must love Me. (Galatians v. 6; 1 S. John iv. 19; S. Luke x. 27.) You must love your neighbour (1 S. John iii. 14, and iv. 7-16; 1 S. Peter iv. 8; S. James ii. 25; Daniel iv. 24); and forgive your enemies. S. Matth. vi. 14, 15; S. Mark xi. 25, 26; 1 S. John iii. 15) You must humble yourselves, and be sorry for the sins you have committed, hate the evil you have done, and repent. (Psalm l. (or li.) 19; Psalm cxlvi. (or cxlvii.) 3; S. James iv. 6; 1 S. Peter v. 5; Isaias lvii. 15; S. Luke i. 51, 52.) You must turn to Me, amend your lives, have a good intention of avoiding sin for the future, of keeping My commandments, and of doing works of penance. (Zacharias i. 3, 4; S. Luke x. 13, and xiii. 5; Ezekiel xviii. 21, 30, 31; S. Matth. iii. 7, 8; Acts ii. 38.) If, assisted by My grace, you come to Me with these dispositions, then I am ready to apply to you the Atonement of My Passion and Death, not as though this mercy were *due to any merit of yours*, but *freely without any price* to grant you forgiveness of your sins, to unite you to Myself by justifying grace, and place you in a state of salvation through the Sacrament of Baptism (Acts ii. 38; S. John iii. 5; S. Titus iii. 5; Ephesians v. 26), or through the Sacrament of Penance. (S. John xx. 23.) In one word, I say to you, Believe; and you are saved.

The natural import of these last words would be, believe that I am what I declare Myself to be, and believe what I teach. Do also what I have told you to do, and then you shall have the merits of My Passion and Death applied to you, and you shall be justified.

It would be unwarrantable to detach the last words, *believe and you are saved*, to disconnect them from what preceded, and then cry out: "The Lord declares that faith alone is necessary, faith alone is sufficient for our justification; we have *only to trust in Christ for pardon*, and we are justified."

The Catholic Church, therefore, teaches the necessity of faith or belief in revelation, of hope or trust, fear and love of God, humility, repentance, purpose to observe the Commandments and to apply for the Sacraments to obtain justification. Her teaching accords with Holy Scripture, whilst the Protestant theory of justification by *faith alone* is not according to Scripture rightly interpreted, but is opposed to it.

8. Even by the light of reason and common sense, one can see that it is right on the part of God that He should require these dispositions in a sinner before granting him the free gift of justification. What more reasonable than that our Saviour should say: If you wish that I should grant you pardon of your sins and apply to you the merits of My Passion and Death and justify you freely, do not contradict Me and disbelieve what I have revealed, but believe Me and have faith; do not despise Me, but fear and revere Me; do not despair, and do not distrust me as if I were unmerciful, but trust and hope in Me; do not reject Me, but love Me; be not unconcerned about having offended Me, or about offending Me again, but detest your sins, be sorry for them, and be determined with the help of My grace to avoid all sin in future, and to keep My Commandments; for if you be wanting in these dispositions, you set yourself in opposition to Me, you offend Me, and reject Me; and, so long as you are in this deplorable state of opposition to Me, you are unfit to receive My mercy, My pardon, and My grace.

9. The common pretext put forward by many Protestants for looking upon *reliance on Christ for pardon* as the only thing required for justification, and for rejecting all other, seems to be, that they regard this *kind of faith* as *simple acceptance* of a gift freely offered, and do not consider it a work; whilst the other dispositions, they think, not being simple acceptance, but something else, are *works*, and, if such, they cannot be admitted as requirements for justification, for S. Paul, they

say, expressly declares that we are not justified by works.

This, however, should not create a difficulty, for S. Paul, as we have already pointed out, when he said that we are justified by faith without the works of the law, clearly meant that Christian justification was totally different from the kind of justification which the Jewish converts imagined it to be. They thought it was nothing else but the result of their own exterior good works, independent of grace; whilst Christian justification, or justification by faith, is a free gift of God; he therefore insisted that the Jewish rites and ceremonies, now done away with, never could of themselves effect justification: and that, though the moral precepts are still in force, and therefore good and necessary to be kept, yet that justification was not a natural fruit of, nor due to, the keeping of them as a strict debt; but justification was granted freely as a free gift, *undeserved as a claim or merit* by good works done without grace, or even by works done with the help of Divine grace.* But S. Paul never meant to discountenance Gospel works, that is, internal or external moral acts or good works, done by God's grace before being justified, and done, not as deserving, but as a preparation to justification; for if he had meant to assert such a thing, he would have set faith against faith, grace against grace, God against God, just as if God were discountenancing what He Himself had inspired and helped them to do. S. Paul could never have meant that.

Protestants admit that these works are *good* and *necessary* to be done after being justified, as fruits and signs of justification. How can it be wrong or useless to do them before? How can they be supposed to have been discountenanced by S. Paul, merely because he said that justification is not the natural result of ceremonial, or even of good moral works? Although justification is not the result of good works, yet good works

---

* The Council of Trent declares: "None of those things which precede justification, whether faith or good works, can merit this grace" (of justification). (Session vi,. chapter 9.)

are congenial to and in harmony with justification, and an indisposition to moral works is an indisposition to justification; and therefore a willingness to do those moral works is a good disposition to justification. S. Paul cannot be supposed by the expression just quoted to have discountenanced good works before being justified, in view of being justified, so long as we regard them as dispositions or preparations to justification, and not as producing justification, since justification is *purely a gracious, free gift of God*.

To be convinced that S. Paul, in that passage and in other similar passages, did not mean to depreciate good moral works, done with the help of Divine grace as dispositions for justification, but only meant to set aside *certain kind of works*—as the Jewish rites and ceremonies, or works merely done in the order of nature without faith and grace—let us observe that, if we had to understand S. Paul in these passages to exclude all sort of good moral works, faith itself would have to be excluded, as faith is evidently the work of the mind and of the will, as much as fear, love, and repentance. Even that kind of faith which resolves itself into a mere *confidence for personal salvation* is also an *act* of the mind and of the will, and therefore a *work;* and pre-supposes two acts, of the mind and of the will, namely, belief in revelation, and consent of the will and affection to this plan for obtaining justification.

In fact, faith is clearly called work in the Gospel itself in which we find these words:—" *What shall we do that we may work the works of God?* Jesus *answered, and said to them: This is the work of God, that you believe in Him whom He hath sent.*" (S. John vi. 28, 29.)* Now *faith*, though a *work*, is not excluded but required by S. Paul, because a *work of faith*, and not a *work of the law;* for the same reason the *fear* of God, *hope, charity, repentance, humility, willingness to obey*, and other dispositions, though acts of the mind and of the will, are works, and

---

* Also S. Paul calls faith a work. "*Being mindful of the work of your faith.*" (1 Thess. i. 3, and 2 Thess. i. 11.)

not excluded by S. Paul. Even supposing that these inward acts of virtue have been carried out into outward acts, yet because they are *works of faith*, done through, and as fruits, of faith and grace, and are not *works of the Jewish law* nor mere efforts of natural strength, they should not be regarded as excluded by S. Paul as dispositions to justification.

In that and other instances S. Paul makes mention only of faith, because faith (that is, belief in revealed truths) is the root and foundation of all other supernatural virtues, and because a true lively faith cannot remain inactive, but makes a man ready to carry at once into practice all that faith requires to the intent for which faith is given; therefore it was not necessary that S. Paul should mention the works of faith. It was enough to mention *faith*, since *faith* (that is, belief in revealed truths) leads to all other dispositions which faith requires to effect its purpose, being itself, so to speak, a spring of work. And this is still more apparent if we consider the people whom he was addressing. They certainly would not even have dreamt of an inactive principle of religion, or of an idle faith, and, therefore, it was quite enough, for his purpose, to discard the works of the Old Law and mention only *faith*. To do so answered better the object he had most at heart in his Epistle of winning them. He took care not to excite their susceptibility or opposition by putting flatly before them a New Law superseding the Old, but insinuated it in an inoffensive manner by the word *faith*, meaning *belief in the New Law of Grace*. As the word LAW in common speech amongst the Jews meant the *whole system* of the ancient Dispensation, so the word FAITH was introduced as a contradistinction to mean the *whole system* of the new Christian Dispensation.

10. That S. Paul in these passages, by the expression *without the works of the law*, did not exclude other dispositions except faith, but implied them in the word *faith*, is made still more clear by other passages of his, in which he also attributes justification to hope, charity, fear of God, penance, willingness to keep the law, and Holy Baptism.

Thus with regard to hope he says: "*We are saved by hope*". (Romans viii. 24.)

As to charity, he says: "*If I should have ALL faith (therefore also what Protestants call saving faith), so that I could remove mountains, and have not charity, I am nothing*". (1 Corinth. xiii. 2.) Again, The faith that availeth is a "*faith that worketh by charity.*" (Galat. v. 6.)

As to penance, he says: "*For the sorrow that is according to God worketh* PENANCE *steadfast* UNTO SALVATION." (2 Corinth. vii. 10.)

As to willingness to keep the Commandments, he says: "*The doers of the law* (of faith) *shall be* JUSTIFIED." (Romans ii. 13 and 1 Corinth. xiii. 2.) Again: "*Know you not that to whom you yield yourselves servants to obey, his servants you are whom you obey, whether it be of sin, unto death, or of* OBEDIENCE, UNTO JUSTICE." (Rom. vi. 16).

As to the Sacrament of Baptism, he says clearly that by it we partake of Christ's Death and Redemption and are justified from sin. "*He* SAVED *us, by the* LAVER OF REGENERATION, *and renovation of the Holy Ghost.*" (S. Titus iii. 5.) "*Know ye not that all we, who are baptised in Christ Jesus, are baptised in His death? For we are buried together with Him by Baptism into death.*" (Rom. vi. 3, 4.)

Now, unless we were to accuse S. Paul of contradicting himself, we must conclude from these passages that by the expression "*without the works of the law*" he did not exclude the *works of faith;* on the contrary, we are compelled to admit that in the word *faith* he included them. And as it would be unreasonable to pick out one of these passages, and say, for example—We are clearly told by S. Paul that we are "*saved by penance,*" therefore neither faith, nor hope, nor humility, nor prayer, nor anything else is necessary for salvation, but penance alone is required and is sufficient, or at least penance is the only thing that apprehends justification; so equally unreasonable would it be to look upon *faith* in the sense of *trust* as the only disposition or condition necessary, or the only means to attain justification. By this Catholic interpretation, not only is S. Paul made to agree with himself, but also with other parts of Holy Scripture, as, for instance, with those already quoted.

11. The necessity of these various dispositions to fit us for the reception of the free gift of justification is in such harmony with Scripture, reason, and common sense, that although Protestant ministers preach very warmly and frequently upon this cherished theory of *justification by faith alone*, yet in practice, as can be seen in their tracts, books, sermons, and hymns, they not unfrequently, by way of preparation for the reception of justification by faith, excite people to repentance, to the love of God and of our neighbour, to a fear of wrath to come, to confidence in the mercy of God and to prayer.* They even pray with them on their knees, and often repeat with them those words of the penitent Publican: "*Lord, be merciful to me a sinner*". In fact, practically, they excite the people to all those dispositions which Catholics teach should always accompany faith, confession itself included. Thus, during the American Revivalism of Messrs. Moody and Sankey in London in the year 1875, all could witness that each of those, who, being moved by Mr. Moody's earnest appeals to seek conversion, had resorted to the "Inquiry Room," was handed over to a Protestant minister or other person, to whom the distressed one opened his or her conscience, making acts of contrition, and expressing determination to lead a good life; in fact, the penitent may be said to have made to the other a candid confession.

All this evidently shows that a great many Protestants, whatever be their theory, encourage in practice those other good dispositions which Catholics believe to be requisite for justification, feeling that to do so is con-

---

* Thus, for instance, in the "*Justified Believer*" of Mr. W. Mackenzie, M.A., the person to be justified is encouraged to prepare himself to it by feeling alarmed and terrified, by believing the Gospel record, by intense anguish and sorrow, by conflict of spirit, and by feeling the trouble, the wounds, and the burden of the soul, by readiness to obey, by feeling unworthy, sorrowful, and ashamed like Ezra by making a strict examination of conscience (p. 65), by weeping like S. Peter and Mary Magdalene. The same thoughts occur in the "*Pilgrim's Progress*," and other Protestant works on Justification.

sistent with Holy Scripture, with reason and good sense, with the honour due to Jesus Christ, and with His free gift of justification.

Wesleyan Ministers, in fact, professedly teach that faith is not saving faith unless it includes repentance, fear of God, belief in Gospel truths, and obedience. If the requirement of these four acts, or moral works, does not prevent the Wesleyans and other Protestants from considering a believer to be justified "*gratis by God's free grace through the redemption that is in Christ Jesus,*" the same should be said of Catholics, though, besides the four moral acts mentioned, and admitted by Protestants, they require a few more, namely, consent to the suggestions of preventive grace, incipient love of God, and desire to receive the Sacraments. Catholics can thus truly speak of having "*their hearts purified by faith*" (Acts xv. 9), because actuated by a *lively faith in Gospel truths*, as it embraces, or rather holds forth not only some, but *all* the requirements for justification.

Another proof that very many Protestants in their hearts look upon the Catholic system of justification as Scriptural and reasonable is, that when they undertake to oppose it, they do not give as their reason of opposition that Catholics require belief in God's revelation, fear of God, repentance, humility, a willingness to do penance, and to keep the Commandments (which indeed is all that the Catholic Church teaches to be needful for receiving pardon and justification in the Sacrament of Penance); but the reason they assign is, that Catholics, as they imagine, exact a long series of penitential or other works in order to be justified.

The fact, however, is, that there is not one Catholic theologian who teaches that these penitential works should be done *before* justification in order to be justified. Nor does the Council of Trent teach it. The only conditions for justification which that General Council requires (Session vi., chapter 6), are *faith* in God and in our Saviour JESUS CHRIST, *consent to* the suggestions of preventive grace inciting us to conversion, *dread* of the effects of Divine justice, excited by motives derived from the teaching of faith, united at the same time with *hope*. In this hope, *love's dawn*, or the *initial love of God*, may already be traced, called forth by the consideration of Divine mercy and Christ's merits. Finally, sincere *hatred* of sin, and a firm *resolution* of amendment of life.

A sinner may receive justification in the Sacrament of Penance without having previously performed any penitential work. To be willing to perform them afterwards suffices.

The necessity of performing penitential works before justification is not even mentioned by the Council of Trent. Hence the constant ordinary practice of the Church is to grant absolution to the penitent in the tribunal of penance, before he has performed any exterior act of penance. No doubt it is better if a person by way of preparation does any penitential actions,* but this is not absolutely necessary.

About the works of penance Catholic theologians say that a man who wishes to be justified *must be willing* to bring forth worthy fruits of penance, because Christ says: "*Except you do penance you shall all likewise perish*". (S. Luke xiii. 5.) That the word *penance* includes also exterior works of penance, appears clearly from the 21st verse of the eleventh chapter of S. Matthew. Surely Protestants cannot find fault with us because we teach that in order to be justified, at least a *willingness* should be required of the sinner to observe this commandment as well as all other commandments. Are they prepared to say that a man can be justified whilst determined to break the Commandments? I think not; for this would amount to saying that a man is in a fit disposition to make peace with his enemy while offering him a new insult, or in a fit condition for receiving a gift while striking the giver, or that the giver cannot show his readiness and freedom in giving, unless He should give to a person who is in open revolt against him.

Our Protestant brethren, therefore, cannot do better than adopt openly the teaching of the Catholic

---

* See Isaias i. 16, 17, 18.

Church, so clearly set forth in the General Council of Trent, which requires the above enumerated dispositions for the reception of the grace of justification in the Sacraments of Baptism or of Penance, and at the same time professes to believe, and solemnly teaches that justification is *not merited* by those dispositions, but that a man is, notwithstanding those dispositions, justified *freely* and *gratis*, purely through the *gracious goodwill* of God. Here are the precise words of the Council:—
"*Gratis autem justificari ideo dicamur, quia nihil eorum quæ justificationem præcedunt, sive fides sive opera, ipsam justificationis gratiam promerentur; si enim gratia est, jam non ex operibus, alioquin ut idem Apostolus inquit, gratia jam non est gratia.*" (Session vi., chap. 8.) "But that therefore we are said to be justified freely (gratis), because none of those things which precede justification, either faith or works, deserve that same grace of justification; *for if it be grace, then it is not from works; otherwise,* as the same Apostle says, *grace is no more grace.*"

As the Catholic Church is always guided in her teaching by the Holy Spirit (Acts xv. 28), if we set ourselves against the Church we set ourselves against the Word of God and against the Holy Spirit; but if we allow ourselves to be guided by the Church, we cannot go wrong, and we feel sure that we are guided by the Holy Spirit; "*the Spirit Himself giveth testimony to our spirit that we are the sons of God*". (Romans viii. 16.) "*For whosoever are led by the Spirit of God, they are the sons of God.*" (Romans viii. 14.)

I wish that our Protestant friends would see that their theory of justification is built upon a *mystification*, by attributing to the word *faith*, occurring in Holy Scripture, the sense of trust as primary meaning, under the specious reason that *trust* supposes *faith in Gospel truths*, and *faith in Gospel truths* leads to *trust in Christ for pardon;* not perceiving that the same thing could be said of the fear and love of God, of repentance and of obedience, all of which, in germ, are implied in *faith in Gospel-truths,* and *faith in Gospel-truths* leads to them; and that therefore *trust* is no more apprehending justification than is *faith in Gospel-truths* itself, and the other above-mentioned acts of virtue, but *all* must be placed only in the rank of dispositions or conditions towards being justified.

In a sermon on "*Justification by Faith*," preached in 1812, in Albion Street Chapel, Leeds, by Mr. Jabez Bunting, and published at the request of the Methodist Conference, then assembled in that town, the Preacher devotes a full page of his pamphlet to prove that justification is nothing else in itself than the pardon of our sins. But regeneration, and therefore justification and pardon of sins, are clearly attached by our Lord to the Sacrament of Baptism (S. John iii. 5), which is emphatically styled by S. Paul "the laver of regeneration" (S. Titus iii. 5); and again when we see that our Lord Jesus Christ has so plainly and so peremptorily attached the pardoning of sins to the sacramental absolution of the priest in S. John xx. 21-23, and not to mere *trusting;* though *hope* or *trust in God* is in itself a necessary disposition, never to be omitted on coming to the Sacrament of Penance, as the Catholic Church teaches.

Let our Protestant friends not forget that there is such a thing as a perverted trust, called presumption, when a man will trust and at the same time neglect the necessary conditions, and the use of the necessary means appointed by God to obtain salvation. In that case it is not *trusting in Christ*, but rather *against Christ*. This is not doing a thing *pleasing to God*, but rather *tempting God*. It is not then *to hope against human hope* as Abraham laudably did, but rather to *trust against godly trust*.

Prayer.—O GOD, GIVE LIGHT TO SEE, AND STRENGTH TO EMBRACE THE TRUTH, TO THY HONOUR AND GLORY, AND FOR THE SALVATION OF OUR SOUL, THROUGH JESUS CHRIST OUR LORD.—*Amen.*

No. 41.—Lines by the American Poet Longfellow (yet a Protestant).

PRINCE HENRY (*on gaining a view of Italy after passing the Alps*).

Oh, had I faith, as in the days gone by,
That knew no doubt, and feared no mystery!
. . . .
This is indeed the blessed Mary's land,
Virgin and Mother of our dear Redeemer!
All hearts are touched and softened at her name;
Alike the bandit with the blood-stained hand,
The priest, the prince, the scholar, and the peasant,
The man of deeds, the visionary dreamer,
Pay homage to her as one ever present!
And even as children, who have much offended
A too indulgent Father, in great shame,
Penitent, and yet not daring unattended
To go into his presence, at the gate
Speak with their sister, and confiding wait
'Till she goes in before and intercedes;
So men, repenting of their evil deeds,
And yet not venturing rashly to draw near
With their requests an angry Father's ear,
Offer to her their prayers and their confession,
And she for them in Heaven makes intercession.
And, if our faith had given us nothing more
Than this example of all womanhood,
So mild, so merciful, so strong, so good,
So patient, peaceful, loyal, loving, pure,
This were enough to prove it higher and truer
Than all the creeds the world had known before.

No. 42.—OBSERVATIONS ON RANKE'S "LIVES OF THE POPES" AND ROMAN CATHOLIC CHURCH. EXTRACTED FROM THE ESSAYS OF THE PROTESTANT HISTORIAN, LORD MACAULAY.

"There is not, and there never was on earth, a work of human policy so well deserving of examination as the Roman Catholic Church. The history of that Church joins together the two great ages of human civilisation. No other institution is left standing which carries the mind back to the times when the smoke of sacrifice rose from the Pantheon, and when camelopards and tigers bounded in the Flavian amphitheatre. The proudest royal houses are but of yesterday when compared with the line of the supreme Pontiffs. That line we trace back in an unbroken series from the Pope who crowned Napoleon in the nineteenth century, to the Pope who crowned Pepin in the eighth; and far beyond the time of Pepin the august dynasty extends till it is lost in the twilight of fable. The Republic of Venice came next in antiquity. But the Republic of Venice was modern when compared to the Papacy; and the Republic of Venice is gone, and the Papacy remains. The Papacy remains, not in decay, not a mere antique, but full of life and youthful vigour. The Catholic Church is still sending forth to the farthest ends of the world missionaries as zealous as those who landed in Kent with Augustine, and still confronting hostile kings with the same spirit with which she confronted Attila. The number of her children is greater than in any former age.

"Her acquisitions in the New World have more than compensated for what she has lost in the Old. Her spiritual ascendancy extends over the vast countries which lie between the plains of the Missouri and Cape Horn, countries which, a century hence, may not improbably contain a population as large as that which now inhabits Europe. The members of her communion are certainly not fewer than a hundred and fifty millions; and it will be difficult to show that all other Christian sects united amounted to a hundred and twenty millions.

Nor do we see any sign which indicates that the term of her long dominion is approaching. She saw the commencement of all the governments and of all the ecclesiastical establishments that now exist in the world; and we feel no assurance that she is not destined to see the end of them all. She was great and respected before the Saxon had set foot on Britain, before the Frank had passed the Rhine, when Grecian eloquence still flourished at Antioch, when idols were still worshipped in the temple of Mecca. And she may still exist in undiminished vigour when some traveller from New Zealand shall, in the midst of a vast solitude, take his stand on a broken arch of London Bridge to sketch the ruins of St. Paul's."

Again he says:
"Four times since the authority of the Church of Rome was established on Western Christendom has the human intellect risen up against her yoke. Twice that Church remained completely victorious. Twice she came forth from the conflict bearing the marks of cruel wounds, but with the principle of life still strong within her. When we reflect on the tremendous assaults she has survived, we find it difficult to conceive in what way she is to perish."

No. 43.—Parting Words to a Protestant who feels Convinced of the Truth of the Roman Catholic Religion, and who does not Join the Church.

To you, my dear friend, who feel convinced that you ought to become a Roman Catholic and have not the courage to do so, I cannot say in the words of our Saviour: "*If thou also hadst known, and that in this thy day, the things that are to thy peace.*" (S. Luke xix. 42.)

No, I cannot say that. But I must say in tears:—A thousand pities it is, my dear friend, that, *knowing* as you do in this your day the things that are to your peace, you behave, alas! as if you knew them not.

And what is it that thus keeps you back? Can it be

that grace fails you? Grace will not fail you, especially if you pray for it. It cannot be that God who has brought you to the gate of His Holy City, and made you admire the immovable rock upon which it is built, the massive turrets, the impregnable walls that surround it, will abandon you now in the most important and decisive step that remains to be taken, that is, entering within the Gate of His City.

Therefore what keeps you back must be either neglect of prayer, or human respect, or worldly considerations, want of humility, want of the spirit of self-sacrifice, of confidence in God, or of noble courage.

These things, therefore, you must endeavour to remedy, that you may not be unfaithful to the grace of God.

If what hinders you were a fear lurking within your breast that perhaps one day you may have to regret the step taken, and have to retrace it, you should treat this as a temptation, calculated, if listened to, to prevent all conversions. The way to get rid of this temptation is very simple. Say to yourself: "I cannot do wrong in following, after mature consideration, the dictates of my *conscience*, which urges me to join the Roman Catholic Church".

I hope you are not ensnared by that fanciful saying—"No question will be asked in the day of Judgment as to what sort of Religion or Denomination we have belonged to." We shall surely have to give an account whether we belonged to the true Church of Christ or not; to the mystical Body of Christ or not. Suppose that in a war a regiment should detach itself from the rest of the army, and from the General-in-Chief, under the plea that the General was incapable of command, and that this regiment knew better how to manage and carry on the war independently of the rest of the army, would not that regiment be answerable and be punished for defection, though it should continue in its own way to do service to the king?

Being convinced as you are now of the truth of the Roman Catholic Religion, you cannot remain as you are without great inconsistency, believing one Religion and acting as if you believed another. To remain as you are is a practical denial of the Catholic truths, which you now believe. It is choosing for yourself a false, unsafe position. It is trifling with your eternal salvation. It is obstinately wishing to remain where conscience, illuminated by grace, does not allow you any longer to remain, and refusing to be what God wants you to be.

The boat on which, up to the present, you have been sailing, you have by God's mercy discovered to be unsafe; and in the meantime a strong and safe ship is before you. You are invited on board. Can you hesitate for a moment what to do?

Now that you have discovered that the Roman Catholic Church is the true Church of God, you will never find rest elsewhere. May God grant that, as the dove of Noah when in her weary wandering she found no fitting place whereon to rest her foot, directed her happy flight to the Ark, so you may resolve to seek for rest in the Roman Catholic Church, called by the holy Fathers *the Ark of Salvation*.

The Good Shepherd wants you to be a sheep of His within His one Fold; why do you linger perishing without? Why do you want to be a sheep of His, but outside His Fold? Is it Christ's wish that the wandering sheep, or the sheep that is not within the Fold, should be left where it is?

The true Church is the mystical Body of Christ. (Colossians i. 24.) Then I shall address you in the words of S. Augustine: "You must belong to the Body of Christ if you wish to live by the Spirit of Christ. Only the Body of Christ lives by the Spirit of Christ. You as a man are composed of soul and body; now tell me, is it your soul that lives by your body, or your body that lives by your soul? You say, of course it is my body that lives by my spirit. Well, then, if you wish to live by the spirit of Christ, delay not to be incorporated into the mystical Body of Christ." (26 Treatise on S. John.)

I feel as though I could never part from you, but we must part, and this is the last thought I would leave with you.

What you did not know before, by the grace of God you know now—namely, that the Roman Catholic Church being the true Church of Christ is the Bride of Christ (Apocalypse xx. 2, 9), and that consequently she " is our mother". (Galatians iv. 26.) Do not hesitate for a moment to run to the embraces of your tender Mother, the more quickly for having once disowned her. FAREWELL.

BLESSED BE JESUS FOR EVER!

No. 44.—LIST OF SOME CATHOLIC BOOKS.

The earnest inquirer who would examine the claims which the Catholic Church, the Church of *Jesus Christ*, has to his love and obedience, will be glad to know the title and price of some useful popular works of Catholic instruction.

Protestants, in general, believe in the Divine inspiration of the *Holy Scriptures*, and therefore accept their Divine authority. Many of them, in their search after truth, will naturally desire to possess a copy of the Catholic Version of the entire *Holy Bible*, in English, as published, with explanatory notes, throughout the United Kingdom. It can be had of any Catholic bookseller, price 2s. 6d., pocket edition, or the octavo size, 6s.

The New Testament only, also with notes, can be had or 1s., or large print, 2s.

Among the most necessary and simple of little books of Catholic instruction are:—

The Catechism of Christian Doctrine. New edition, 1879. Approved for all England and Wales. 1d.
Explanatory Catechism. 2d. Burns & Oates.
Children's Companion to Christian Doctrine. 2d. Do.
The Abstract of the Douay Catechism. 1½d.
The Poor Man's or People's Catechism. By Rev. Anselm Mannock (O.S.B.). 1s., very useful.

LIST OF SOME CATHOLIC BOOKS. 401

Catholic Christian instructed. By Bp. Challoner. 9d.
The Catholic Doctrine on the use of the Bible. By His Em. Card. Wiseman. 3d.
The Garden of the Soul. Catholic Prayer-Book, or Manual of Spiritual Exercises and Instructions for Christians, who, living in the world, aspire to devotion. By Bishop Challoner. Cheap edition, 6d ; or, with the Epistles and Gospels for Sundays, 1s. Most useful.
Ordinary of the Mass. Latin and English. 1d. Burns & Oates.
Missal for the Laity. Abridged edition. 1s. Do.
Parochial Vespers Book. 1s. Do.
Rosary Book. Fifteen good engravings. 2d. Burns & Oates.
The Path to Paradise. A Prayer-Book useful for schools, and the aged (large print, cheap and good, with pictures of Holy Mass and of the 14 Stations of the Cross). 4d. R. Washbourne. M. Gill, Dublin.
The Stranger's Guide at High Mass. Very useful. 2d. and 4d.
Grounds of Faith. By His Eminence Card. Manning. 1s.
Love of Jesus to Penitents. By the same. 1s. 6d.
The Rule of Faith. By Bishop Milner. 6d.
The End of Religious Controversy. By the same. 1s.
Reasons of my Conversion. By late Rev. John Gordon, of the Oratory. 1s. Burns & Oates.
Twelve Reasons for becoming a Catholic. By the same. 1s. Do.
Oremus. A Book of Catholic Devotion. Washbourne. 1s. 6d. and 2s.
Meditations for every day in the year. By Bishop Challoner. 2 vols. 2s.

In addition to these useful little works, there are some others earnestly recommended to the notice of those inquirers who cannot afford to buy more costly books, or who may not have much time for reading; namely—

Controversial Catechism. By Rev. Stephen Keenan (good, though somewhat harsh at times in his expressions). 1s. 6d. New edition. Booker.
Grounds of Catholic Doctrine. By Bishop Challoner. 4d.
Think Well On't. Meditations. By the same. 4d. Homely and good.
The Poor Man's Controversy. By Rev. A. Mannock (O.S.B.). 4d.
Conversion of Andrew Dunn. 2d. and 4d.
Papist Represented and Misrepresented. 2d. and 4d.

Sure Way to find out the True Religion. 2d. and 4d.
Glover on the Mass. Very useful. 4d.
What do Catholics Really Believe? By Rev. Fr. Anderdon (S.J.). 2d.
H. Wilberforce's Letters to his Parishioners. 3d.
Reasons for my Submission. By H. Sconce, M.A. 2d.
Cottage Conversations. 3s. Burns & Oates.
Reply to the Protestant Bishop of Ripon's Attack on the Catholic Church. By a Layman. 6d. 1874.
Religion of Common Sense. By H. Pye, M.A., 1s.
Auricular Confession. By the late Rev. Dr. Raphael Melia (P.S.M.). Very useful. 1s. 2d. Duffy.
Pittar's Conversion by her Bible and Prayer-Book. 1s.
A Manual of the Catholic Religion. By Rev. F. Weninger (SJ.). 5s.
Sincere Christian. Instructed from the Written Word. By Bishop Hay. 2s. Very useful.
Manual of Instructions in Cath. Doctrine. 3s. Burns & Oates.
Lectures on the Catholic Church. By His Em. the late Card. Wiseman. 3s. 6d. Very plain and very useful.
On the Holy Eucharist. By the same. 1s. 8d.
The Life of Our Lord commemorated in the Mass. By the Bp. of Nottingham. 1s.
Catechism (textually) *Illustrated from Holy Scripture.* By Rev. John Bagshawe, Missionary Rector of Richmond, Surrey. 2s. 6d.
Threshold of the Catholic Church, being a Course of Plain Instructions for those entering her Communion. Clear and practical. By the same. 4s.
Credentials of the Catholic Church. By the same, 4s.
Catechism of the Council of Trent. In English. 6s.
The Church of the Bible. By Canon Oakeley. 3s. 6d. Clear.
Ceremonies of the Mass. By the same. 1s.
Catholic Worship. By the same. 1s.
The Sacramentals of the Holy Catholic Church. By Rev. W. Barry. Richardson. 1s. 6d.
Protestant Principles Examined by the Written Word. 1s. Clear and concise. Washbourne.
The Following of Christ. With Prayers by Bishop Challoner. 1s. Richardson. 6d. Duffy.
Popular Delusions and Objections. By W. Dodsworth, M.A. 1s.
Lectures on the Grounds, Nature, and Home of Faith. By Very Rev. Norbert Sweeney (O.S.B.), D.D., Bath. 3s. 6d

LIST OF SOME CATHOLIC BOOKS. 403

Lectures on Cath. Faith and Practice. By same. 3 vols. 9s.
Claims of the Catholic Church. By H. Pye, M.A. 2s. 6d.
The Invitation Heeded. By J. Kent Stone, late President of Hobart College, New York. 5s. 6d.
Questions of the Soul. By Rev. Fr. Hecker. N. York. 2s.
Catholic Truth Tracts. 1s. 6d. the packet. Burns & Oates.
The Clifton Tracts. Separately or in 4 vols. 10s.
Narratives of Conversions. 1s. Burns & Oates.
Use and Abuse of the Bible. By Rev. W. Maclachlan. 2s. 6d.
The Spirit of Faith; or, What Must I do to Believe? By Bishop Cuthbert Hedley (O.S.B.). 1s. 6d.
S. Anselm's (O.S.B.) *Meditations.* With Preface. 5s.
All for Jesus; or, the Easy Ways of Divine Love. With copious Index. By Very Rev. Dr. Faber. 5s.
The Precious Blood; or, The Price of our Salvation. By the same. 5s.
The Blessed Sacrament; or, the Works and Ways of God. By the same. 7s. 6d.
The Bible and the Rule of Faith. By Abbé Louis Bégin, D.D., From the French. By G. M. Ward. 3s. 6d.
The Written Word; or, Considerations on the Sacred Scriptures. By Rev. Fr. Wm. Humphrey (S.J.). 5s.
The Sacrifice of the Eucharist, and other Doctrines of the Catholic Church explained and vindicated. By late Rev. Ch. Garside, M.A. Very good. 5s. 6d.
The Eternal Truths (Preparation for Death). By St. Alphonsus Liguori. 2s.

And among the most popular works of special interest to our Anglican friends are—

Principles of Church Authority. By Isaac Wilberforce, M.A. 5s.
Anglican Prejudices against the Catholic Church. 1s.
Catechetical Instructions. By John Lingard, D.D. 1s.
Difficulties of Anglicans. By Very Rev. John Henry Newman, D.D., of the Oratory. 5s. 6d.
History of my Religious Opinions. By the same. 6s.
Catholicism in England. By the same. 4th edition. 7s.
Loss and Gain. By the same. 5s. 6d. Very interesting.
Introduction to the Study of Holy Scripture. By Dr. Dixon, Archbishop of Armagh. 10s.
See of St. Peter. By T. W. Allies, Esq., M.A. 4s. 6d.
Cathedra Petri. The titles and prerogatives of *S. Peter, his See, and Successors.* By C. F. Allnatt. 4s.

Which is the true Church? By the same. 1s.
The True Church of the Bible. Rev. W. Fleming. Burns. 1s.
The Divine Teacher. By Rev. F. Humphrey (S.J.). 2s. 6d.
Lectures on the Œcumenical Council. By Dr. J. N. Sweeney (O.S.B.). 5s.
Trials of a Mind. By Dr. Ives, LL.D,, New York. 4s.
Annals of the Tractarian Movement from 1842 to 1867. By Kirwan Brown, Esq. 2s. 6d. Very interesting. Washbourne.
The Love and Passion of Jesus. By the Right Rev. Herbert Vaughan, Bishop of Salford. 2d.
The Holy Sacrifice of the Mass. By the same. 2d.
The Liturgical Year. By Dom Prosper Guéranger (O.S.B.) Translated by Dom Laurence Shepherd (O.S.B.) 12 vols. About 5s each. Very good and solid. Duffy.
Spiritual Exercises of S. Iynatius. Mauresa. 3s.
Remarks on the Syllabus and Encyclical of the 8th Dec., 1864. By Mgr. Dupanloup, Bp. of Orleans. Authorised Translation, by W. Hutchison, Esq. Second edition. 1s. Burns & Oates.
Catholic Directory and Ordo. Yearly. 1s. 6d. Burns & Oates.
Lives of the Saints. By Rev. Alban Butler. Pocket edition. 12 vols. 1s. each. Octavo size, 4 vols. 30s.
Miniature Lives of the Saints. For every day in the year. Edited by Rev. H. Bowden, of the Oratory. Second Edition. In 2 vols., 4s.; or in Monthly Packets, 4d. each.

All to be obtained, postage included, at the price here stated, of Messrs. Burns & Oates, 17 Portman Street, W., and 63 Paternoster Row, London, E.C.; Messrs. M. H. Gill & Son, Upper Sackville Street, Dublin; R. Washbourne, 18 Paternoster Row; T. Richardson, 26 Paternoster Row, & Derby; J. Duffy, 15 Wellington Quay, Dublin, and 1 Paternoster Row; Williams & Butland, 13 Duke Sreet, Smithfield, E.C.; Ed. Dillon, Brompton Road, S.W., near the Oratory, or by order of any bookseller.

"MAY GOD BE GLORIFIED IN ALL."

ALPHABETICAL GENERAL INDEX.

	PAGE
Absolution, Sacramental	61, 288
Abstinence, Total—Extract from an Introductory Letter by His Eminence, Cardinal Manning	319
Good Reasons for, by Dr. Guthrie	320
Acts of Faith, Hope, Charity, and Contrition	270
Act of Contrition	284
Addresses of some Clergy-Houses in and near London, and abroad	245-247
"*Adeste fideles*"	264
"*Adore in Spirit*"—how it is to be understood	82, 83
The Most Holy Sacrament is to be adored	85
Angelus	250
Answer to some difficulties and questions of earnest enquirers seeking the true Religion	209-222
Appeal, Earnest, to Protestants	235
Apocrypha	11
Apostles' Creed	228
Apostolicity, Fourth Mark	149
The Catholic Church only is Apostolic	150
The Greek Schismatic Church has ceased to be Apostolic, *Footnote*	150
Baptism, Its effects	51
Necessity of it	52
When a lay person can administer it	52
Baptism of blood, and Baptism of desire	52
Of infants	53
Dispositions required in grown-up people	58
Baptism under condition in most instances is administered to Protestants on their being received into the Church	218
Beatitudes, The eight	289
Benediction of the Blessed Sacrament	86-88
Hymns sung at Benediction, and prayers	88
BIBLE, The Holy	7
Of which Books composed	7, 8
Apocrypha (hidden)	11
The Canon or list of inspired Books sanctioned by the Church agrees with that of the Council of Hippo in the year 393	8
Catholics are encouraged to read it	30
Its interpretation	21
"Private interpretation" considered	24-29
"To stand by the Bible alone" considered	22, 23
"Search the Scriptures" considered	25
Catholic teaching wonderfully agrees with Scripture	30, 31
Books—List of some useful Catholic books	400
Calendar of the Church of England—Roman Catholic Saints are inserted in it	128, 129
Candles, Lighted, why used at Mass	79
And at Benediction	86
Canon, or list of the inspired Books issued by the Council of Hippo in the year 393	9
The Apocrypha	11
To fix the Canon of Scripture belongs to the Church	11
Catholicity, Third Mark of the true Church	141
Catholics are truly Catholics in *fact* and in *name*	142
Protestants attempt to weaken the force of this Mark by distinguishing between *Roman* and *non-Roman* Catholics	142-145

	PAGE
By saying that the Church is invisible	145
And that she is composed of the Roman and Schismatic Churches	146-148
Census of principal Religions in the World	295
Of Christian Religions in the World, by Hübner	296
Of Catholics in the World	297
Of Protestants in Europe	298
Of Protestant Sects in England and North America	300-303
Ceremonies do not form an essential part of Religion	74
It is proper that Divine Service be accompanied by Ceremonies	75
The real presence of Christ in the Holy Sacrament demands them	75, 76
Ceremonies do not lead to formalism	76, 78
Holy water and lighted candles	79
Rich vestments, why used	79, 80
Music, singing, sign of the Cross, incense	80-82
Church, What it is	99
There is only one true Church	99, 100
Communion, In it we receive the Body and Blood of Christ	352, 353
An Act of Spiritual Communion	90
Of spiritual goods	101
Communion of Saints extends to the souls in Purgatory	117
Communion in one kind, Essay	346-363
Conception, The Immaculate	186
Dogmatical definition of it	188
In accordance with Scripture	190
Witnessed by the Fathers	191, 192
Conclusion	206
Concomitance, What it is	352
Confession, Its definition	61
Its necessity	62
Not so difficult as some imagine	219, 222
When to be made by a convert	216
Is a part of the Sacrament of penance	60
How it is to be made	287
Confirmation, Sacrament of	91
"*Confiteor*," The	222
Contents, Index of, i.e., of chapters	xiv.
Contrition, Act of	284
Other Act of Contrition	288
Conversion, Dawn of a remarkable conversion in Rome	304
Of A. Newdigate, M.A.	305
Of Mr. Gordon Thompson, M.A.	306
Of Mr. Orby Shipley, M.A.	307
Of Victorinus, a great Rhetorician of Rome	239
A prayer for another's conversion	258
Converts, List of some distinguished converts	237, 238
Distinguished American converts	243
Converts within the last thirty years	313
Converts to Catholicity not unhappy	310
Within the last fifty years	313
Letters of converts	289, 304
Copernicus	322
Councils, List of General	114
Creed, Apostles' Creed	223
Known as the Creed of Pope Pius IV	224
Cross, sign of the	159

ALPHABETICAL GENERAL INDEX.

	PAGE
How it is made. *Footnote*	277
Crucifix, Indulgenced prayer recited before a	253
Cusa, Copernicus, Galileo, and Kepler	321-327
Definition, A new dogmatical definition, not a new doctrine	204
One dogmatical definition can never clash with another	44
Of the Immaculate Conception, by Pope Pius IX	168
Of the Pope's infallibility, by the Vatican Council	40-41
"*De profundis*," Psalm	257
Difficulties of private interpretation of Scripture	230-234
Divine praises	252
Divisions arising from private interpretation	29, 300-308
Edition, Notice on the third edition	ix.
England never of her own accord rejected the Catholic Faith	313
Ejaculations	208
Era, Vulgar, *Footnote*	151
Eucharist, The Sacrament of Holy, contains Christ's Body and Blood	63
Examination of conscience	279
Extreme Unction, The Sacrament of	92
Faith cometh by *hearing*	15
Observations on Faith by Cardinal Newman	206
Act of Faith	270
Good faith; In which instances Protestants in good faith can be saved?	204-206
"Justification by Faith alone" considered, Essay	374
Fathers, List of the Fathers of the Church	289
Founders, Canonised, of Orders	294
Galileo	323
Gifts, The seven gifts of the Holy Ghost	289
"*Gloria Patri*"	248
God and His Perfections	1
Good Faith, Protestants in good faith can in some instances be saved	204
Grace of justification	44
Actual	47
Leaves freewill intact	47
We stand in continual need of actual grace	47
Good works done through grace by one who is not in grace are not, strictly speaking, meritorious	47
Greek, The, Schismatic Church *not Apostolic*, *Footnote*	150
"Hail Mary" The	248
Heresies cannot be condemned if the principle of private interpretation is maintained	29
Heretics, Not all Christians who are outside the true Church are heretics. *Footnote*	20
Holiness, Second Mark of the true Church	122
Some faulty and unholy principles held by some Protestants	123, 124
The Catholic principles of faith and morality are holy	125, 127
Protestants acknowledge that many Saints flourished in the Catholic Church	128, 129
Holy Water	79
Hymn to Jesus	166
On the Precious Blood	262
To the Holy Ghost	263
"*Adeste fideles*"	264
On the love of Jesus	264
On the Passion of Jesus	265

ALPHABETICAL GENERAL INDEX.

	PAGE
"Stabat Mater"	266
"Te Deum laudamus"	268
Of repentant sorrow	272
Images, Reverence to holy	193
The use of Holy Images not against God's Commandments	193-196
Immaculate Conception	186
Definition of it in Latin and English	188
Proved from third chapter of Genesis	190
By the Holy Fathers	191, 192
Revolting consequences arising from disbelieving this Dogma	192
Incarnation of the Son of God	5
Incense, Why used at Mass	81, 82
Index of Chapters	xiv.
General Alphabetical, of matters	405
Of subjects found in the Appendix	xvii.
Indulgence, What it is	169
Power of granting indulgences left by Christ to the Church	170
Indulgenced prayer recited before a crucifix	253
Infallibility of teaching necessary in the Church	81
Of the Church	33
Depends on the aid of the Holy Ghost	34
Of the Pope proved from Scripture	35
From the Holy Fathers	38-40
Defined as Dogma by the Vatican Council	40
Limitations of it	41, 42
Differs from *impeccability*	42
Interpretation of Holy Scripture	21
Private	27
Difficulties of private interpretation of Holy Scripture by Rev. Father Bampfield	230-234
Introduction	page xi.
Invocation of Saints laudable	178
The Saints know our petitions	179
Does not interfere with Christ's Mediation	181
Ireland, Religious Statistics of	323
St. Jerome's opinion about the *Apocrypha* before and after the Council of Hippo	11
Jesus, our only Mediator of Redemption	6
Joan, or Johanna, a pretended female Pope	155
Justice, Original, lost by Adam for himself and his posterity	4
Justification, What it is	44
Not merely covers but blots out sin	45
Dispositions to justification required	45, 46
We are justified gratuitously	46
May be lost	46
The works done by a justified man are meritorious	48
"Justification by faith alone" considered	374-394
Kepler	326
Latin language, Why used in the Catholic Liturgy?	197-200
Not against St. Paul's direction	199
List of the Canonical Books of Holy Scripture	9
Of General Councils	114-122
Of Saints who flourished in the Roman Cath. Church	130-141
Of Sovereign Pontiffs	151-159
Of the Fathers of the Church	289
Of canonised Founders of Religious Orders	294
Of distinguished converts	237, 243

ALPHABETICAL GENERAL INDEX. 409

	PAGE
Of Christian Sects in England	300
In Ireland	301
In the United States	302
Of classes of mortal sins	279
Of some Catholic Books	400
Longfellow, Protestant American Poet, Lines on the B. Virgin Mary	395
LORD'S PRAYER, THE	247
Loyalty, Catholic, Noble Speech of the Duke of Wellington	325
Macaulay, Lord, on the Popes and on the Roman Catholic Church	396
Manning, Cardinal, Dawn of his conversion	304
Letter on his peace of mind	310
A speech to prove that England never rejected of her own accord the Catholic Faith	313
On the position of the Catholic Church in England	318
On total abstinence	319
MARKS of the true Church, which the Cath. Church alone possesses	100
First, ONENESS of faith, worship, and Sacraments	100
Second, HOLINESS	122
Third, CATHOLICITY	141
"We are Catholics, not Roman Catholics," considered	142-145
The Ritualistic notion of Catholicity inadmissible	146-148
Fourth, APOSTOLICITY	149
Mary, The Blessed Virgin, rightly called "Mother of God"	181
Difficulties explained	182, 183
Devotion and honour paid to her right and just	184-186
Her Immaculate Conception	186, 187
Immaculateness defined	188, 189
Proved from 3rd Chapter of Genesis	190
From the Fathers	191
From Theological reasons	192
Lines from the American Poet Longfellow (yet a Protestant)	395
Being a creature is infinitely below God	201, 202
Strong, loving expressions addressed to the B. Virgin by Catholics are to be taken in a limited sense	202
Mass, The Holy Sacrifice of the—	
Prefigured and foretold in the Old Law	67
A commemorative Sacrifice	68
In what *mystical death* consists	69
Same Sacrifice in essence as that on *Calvary*	70, 71
Serves to apply Christ's Redemption to men	71
Does not detract from the Sacrifice on Calvary	73, 74
Short Method of hearing Mass	272-277
Ceremonies of the Mass	75
Matrimony, Sacrament of Holy	94
Marriage-tie indissoluble	95, 97
Divorce in the strict sense of a legitimate Christian marriage is never allowed	98
Indissolubility of marriage beneficial to society	98
Mediator, JESUS our only Mediator of Redemption	201
Mercy, Corporal and Spiritual works of	289
Merits, Man's, always dependant on CHRIST'S MERITS	203
Method of hearing Mass	272, 277
Of Confession	278
"*Miserere*," Psalm	255
Music and singing, why used at Divine Service	80
Mysteries of the Rosary	249

410 ALPHABETICAL GENERAL INDEX.

	PAGE
Newdigate, A., M.A.	305
Newman, Cardinal, Letter on his happiness of mind	311
Other remarks on the same subject	312
Observations on faith	269
Notice on the third edition	ix.
On the quotations of Holy Scripture	vii.
Order, Sacrament of Holy	94
Original sin	2
Its difference from actual sin	2
In what it consists	3
Is not concupiscence	3
Its direful effects	4
How the sin of Adam is transmitted to his posterity	363-368
Parting words of the author to a Protestant who feels convinced of the truth of the Roman Catholic Religion and does not join it	397
Penance, Sacrament of	60
Requisites on the side of the penitent	60, 61
Power to absolve left by Christ to the Church	61
An act of the virtue of penance, or an Act of Contrition	270, 284
Works of penance or penitential works necessary	167, 168
Peter, Saint, was in Rome	331-345
Pope, The Pope is infallible	81
List of Popes	151
Many of them Saints and Martyrs	129
Position of the Catholic Church in England	318
"Praises, The Divine"	252
Prayer, Nature and necessity of	162, 163
A sweet duty	163
Rightly made, always obtains favours	164
The Conditions of a good prayer are *devotion, attention, confidence, humility, perseverance*	165
We should pray for others	166
The Lord's prayer	247
Hail Mary / *Gloria Patri* / Daily Prayer / Rosary	248
Angelus	250
"*Regina Cœli*"	251
In behalf of the dying	251
The divine praises	252
To our Crucified Lord	253
For our Holy Father the Pope	253
In sickness or affliction	254
For another's conversion / For a friend in distress / For the sick	258
For a Bishop or Priest	259
For the dead	259
For light to find out the true Church of Christ	207
Ejaculations, or little Prayers	208
Predestination	368-373
Preface	v.
Profession of faith to be made by a Protestant on being received into the Roman Catholic Church	224
Short Profession of faith	229

ALPHABETICAL GENERAL INDEX. 411

	PAGE
Outward Profession of faith necessary for salvation	229
Protestant Churches or Denominations not *Apostolic*	151
What has a Protestant to do who believes nearly all the Catholic Doctrines	215
What is to be done by a Protestant who is quite decided to embrace the Catholic Religion	215
Words to a Protestant who feels convinced that he ought to become a Catholic and does not	397
Some Protestants, according to the Roman Catholic teaching, may, in certain cases, be saved	204
Psalm "*Miserere mei Deus*"	255
De profundis	257
Purgatory	171
Its existence proved from the Fathers	172
And from Scripture interpreted by the Fathers	173, 174
Some objections met	175, 176
We may pray for souls in Purgatory	177, 178
Questions: Answers to several questions which Protestants are apt to make against or about joining the Catholic Church	209-222
Received formally, Is it necessary to be formally received into the Catholic Church in order to belong to it?	213, 214
Reception, What must a person do who wishes to be received into the Catholic Church?	215, 216
Reception of a Protestant into the Catholic Church. In what it consists	216, 219
Redemption of Christ needs to be applied to men—	
It is applied especially through the Sacraments	49
And through the Holy Mass	71
"*Regina Coeli*"	251
Relics, Reverence to	96
Religions, Great number of ; see census,	
Not all Christian Religions are good	209
When is one obliged to give up the Religion of his fathers	210-213
Repentance, or sorrow for sin, An act of	288
Resolution not to sin again	285
Reverence to images	193
To Relics	96
Rosary	249
Sacrament is a sign conferring grace	50
Serves to apply Christ's Redemption to men	50
There are seven Sacraments	50
Holy Sacrament, *i.e.*, Holy *Eucharist*	63
Saints, We may invoke them	179
Know our petitions	179, 180
Praying for us, not thereby Mediators as Christ is	181
Salvation only for those, who in *some sense*, are within the pale of the Roman Catholic Church	205, 209, 213
Satisfaction, Sacramental, what it is	61, 288
Scriptures, Holy, of which Books composed	7
Interpretation of Scripture necessary	21
Private interpretation not safe	22, 23
Who is the legitimate interpreter of Scripture	26
Catholics are encouraged reverently to read Holy *Scriptures*.	30
The reading of Scripture with pure and unprejudiced mind leads to Catholicity	30, 31
"Search the Scriptures," Its true meaning	24, 25
Sects battling within one Church	299

	PAGE
List of Sects	300
Shipley, Mr. Orby, Letter on his conversion	307
Sign of the Cross	159
The banner of Christians	160
Is an excellent act of Faith	160
Was used in primitive ages of Christianity	161
Why used by the Priest at Mass ?	81
Sin of Adam, how transmitted to his children	363-368
Original	2-4
Actual	54
Difference between mortal and venial sin	54, 55
Awful malice of mortal sin	56-60
Seven deadly sins	288
Some things that Catholics do *not* believe	201-205
"*Stabat Mater*,"	266
Statistics of Religions in the world	296
Of Catholics in the World	297
Of Catholics and Protestants in Europe	297
Of Religious Denominations in England and Wales	300
Of Protestants in Ireland	301
Of Protestants in the United States of America	302
Supremacy of the Church necessary	102
Of the Bishop of Rome	101
Exercised by the Pope from the time of St. Peter	103
Maintained by St. Gregory the Great	104
Acknowledged by General Councils	106, 107
Also by the Holy Fathers	108
Appealed to by Bishops in all ages	108
From all parts ; from places most distant	109
Texts of Holy Scriptures support it	109
"*Te Deum laudamus*,"	268
Temperance and Total Abstinence, A few thoughts of Cardinal Manning	319
Thompson, Gordon, M.A.	306
Total Abstinence, Five good reasons for	320
Tradition, its meaning	13
Divine Tradition is Word of God	13-16
Divine Tradition, or unwritten Word of God is, safer and more useful than the written Word of God	17-21
Transubstantiation	64-66
Trinity, The Most Holy	1
Unction, The Sacrament of Extreme	92
"*Veni Creator Spiritus*"	268
Vestments, Rich, Why used at the Holy Mass, and other Divine Services	80
Victorinus, Conversion of	237
Wellington, The Duke of, speech	328
Word of God, unwritten	12
We are bound to believe it	14
Its authority proved from Scripture and from the Holy Fathers	16
Safer and more useful than the written Word	17-21
Works, Spiritual, of mercy	289
Corporal, of mercy	289
Works of penance	166-168
Good works done by the *Penitent thief*	168
Water, Holy, Its use is ancient	79